READING for COLLEGE

CORINNE FENNESSY

READING for COLLEGE

PEARSON

Boston Columbus Indianapolis New York San Francisco Upper Saddle River
Amsterdam Cape Town Dubai London Madrid Milan Munich Paris Montréal Toronto
Delhi Mexico City São Paulo Sydney Hong Kong Seoul Singapore Taipei Tokyo

PEARSON

Editor in Chief: Eric Stano
Editorial Assistant: Jamie Fortner
Senior Development Editor: David Kear
Director of Marketing: Roxanne McCarley
Senior Supplements Editor: Donna Campion
Executive Digital Producer: Stefanie A. Snajder
Digital Editor: Sara Gordus
Digital Content Specialist: Julia Pomann
Production Manager: Ellen MacElree
Project Coordination and Electronic Page Makeup: Integra
Cover Designer/Manager: Wendy Ann Fredericks
Cover Photo: © Nugene Chiang/AsiaPix/Corbis
Senior Manufacturing Buyer: Roy L. Pickering, Jr.
Printer/Binder: Courier/Kendallville
Cover Printer: Lehigh-Phoenix Color/Hagerstown

DK

Design Development and Art Direction: Anthony Limerick
Design Director: Stuart Jackman
Publisher: Sophie Mitchell

Credits and acknowledgments borrowed from other sources, and reproduced, with permission, in this textbook appear on pages 377–379.

Library of Congress Control Number: 2013956403

10 9 8 7 6 5 4 3 2 1—CRK—16 15 14 13

PEARSON www.pearsonhighered.com

Student ISBN-13: 978-0-321-85315-8
Student ISBN-10: 0-321-85315-6
A la Carte ISBN-13: 978-0-321-96053-5
A la Carte ISBN-10: 0-321-96053-X

CHAPTER 1

THE FOUR-STEP READING PROCESS

CHAPTER
2 BUILDING VOCABULARY SKILLS

CHAPTER 3

TOPICS, STATED MAIN IDEAS & SUPPORTING DETAILS

CHAPTER 4 DRAWING CONCLUSIONS, IMPLIED MAIN IDEAS AND CENTRAL POINT

CHAPTER 5

PATTERNS OF ORGANIZATION

CHAPTER 6

CRITICAL THINKING

CHAPTER 7 STUDY SKILLS

APPENDIX

PREFACE

More than fifteen years ago, when I started teaching college preparatory reading, the textbooks available at that time required students to struggle through the reading selections and extensive multiple-choice practice exercises. My students did not understand how either their textbook or their college preparatory reading course related to their lives or future goals. I saw the need for a textbook that would relate what they learned in the classroom to real-life applications, including academic reading and real documents they will encounter outside of school. My goal is to bring the developmental readers using this book to higher levels of reading comprehension using higher thinking skills, and to prepare them for academic reading in their coursework for all disciplines.

Research has shown that students who are engaged in the learning process are more successful than passive learners. When students are motivated, they are more likely to participate in the learning process. To accomplish this, they need materials and activities that are related to their academic and personal needs. They also need interesting articles that will inspire them to succeed and opportunities to discuss and engage in critical thinking. *Reading for College* engages students in reading through an activities-based learning approach to help them master key reading skills and strategies.

Learning Principles Incorporated into *Reading for College*

Reading for College is shaped by several pedagogical principles backed by research. First, students are most successful when they are active learners. Students learn best by participating, not by just listening or reading extensively about how to do something. Furthermore, this text teaches reading as a thinking process by taking students through the steps of reading actively. As you go through each chapter, you will find a multitude of instructive features that support the active learning approach. Furthermore, in order to support instructors, the Instructor's Manual includes complete instructions to enable instructors to easily incorporate active learning, collaborative learning, and closure activities.

Second, student motivation increases when the material students are reading is related to their lives and their goals. Each chapter is focused on a thematic topic that reflects the maturing interests of first-year college students. As the book progresses, the scope of the topics widens, beginning with topics relating to understanding one's self, then others, then society, and lastly, global issues. These selections lead students through the process of reading actively to help them master key reading skills and strategies. The selections also provide critical thinking questions for discussion or writing.

Third, research has shown that collaborative learning is one of the most effective ways that students learn. In response to this, many of the activities and assignments in *Reading for College* are done in pairs or teams. This book provides ample opportunities for students to talk through their thinking processes and to learn from each other. This also benefits students who have an auditory learning style, who learn best by listening and speaking. In addition, it reinforces active learning by engaging more students in the learning process.

Chapter Features in *Reading for College*

The multitude of features within every chapter of *Reading for College* supports the book's goal to engage students in preparatory college reading through active learning and real-life connections.

HOW *Reading for College* MAKES READING REAL

STEP **1**
Preview Before You Read

Learning Objectives **PREVIEW** the key concepts and skills of the chapter, and visual aids like the outline highlight the headings and sections of each chapter.

STEP **2**
Read Actively

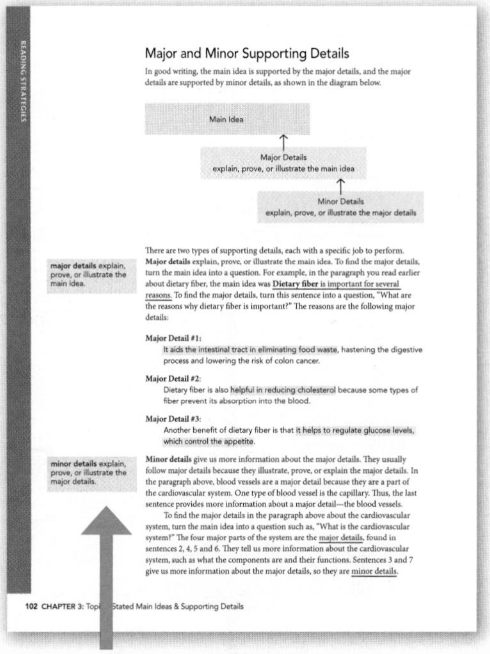

Clear headings, marginal glossaries and questions, underlining, highlighting, and visual aids help students **READ ACTIVELY**.

STEP **3**
Highlight and Annotate

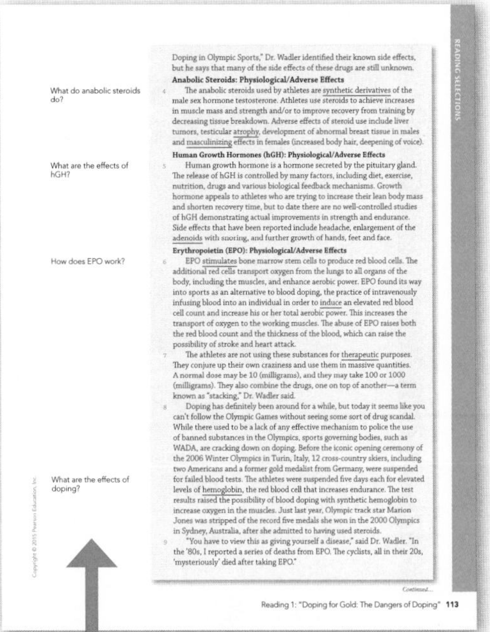

Practices and Reading activities develop **HIGHLIGHTING AND ANNOTATING** skills, and reading questions keep the reading process active.

STEP **4**
Review

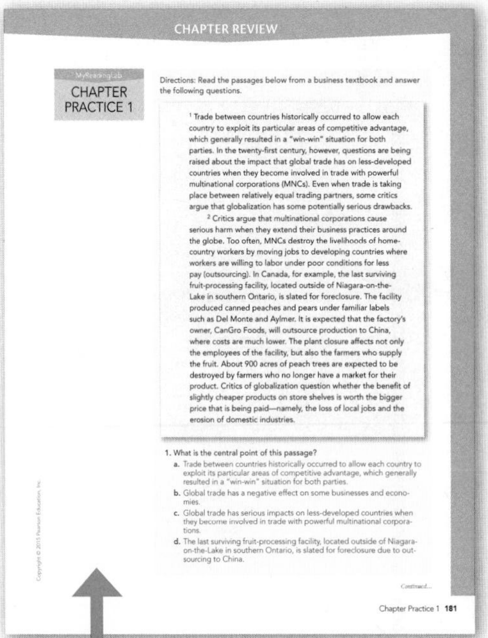

The **CHAPTER REVIEW** section reviews key concepts using a variety of study skills such as note cards, diagrams, charts, concept maps, and chapter practices.

HOW *Reading for College* ENGAGES STUDENTS THROUGH ACTIVITIES

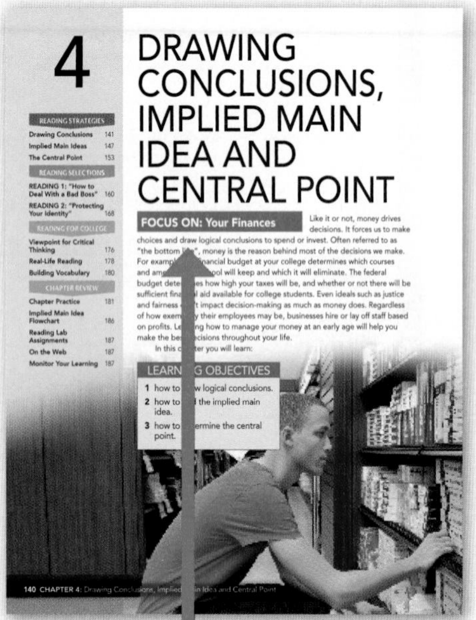

Each chapter is organized around a **THEME** related to the maturing interests of first-year college students.

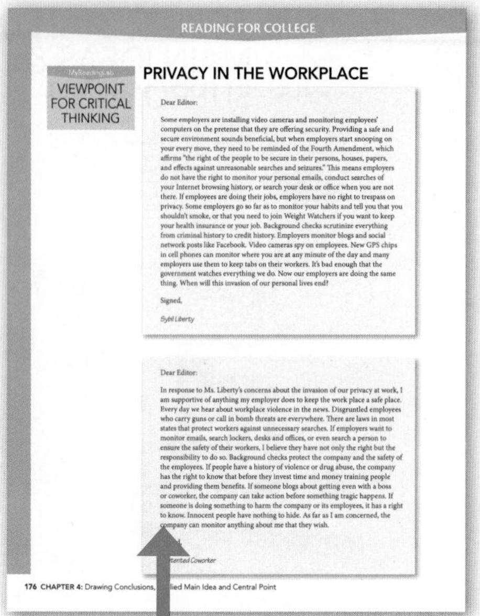

The **VIEWPOINT** feature includes "letters to the editor" that offer opposing arguments related to a real-life issue. This section is designed to help students develop their critical-thinking skills.

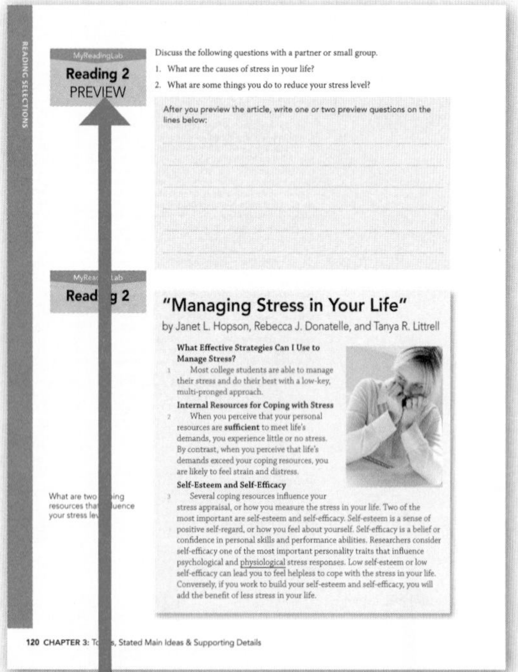

READING SELECTIONS
Reading 2 PREVIEW
Discuss the following questions with a partner or small group.
1. What are the causes of stress in your life?
2. What are some things you do to reduce your stress level?
After you preview the article, write one or two preview questions on the lines below:
Reading 2
"Managing Stress in Your Life"
by Janet L. Hopson, Rebecca J. Donatelle, and Tanya R. Littrell
120 CHAPTER 3: Topics, Stated Main Ideas & Supporting Details

PREVIEW questions begin each reading selection so that students can connect their prior knowledge with the reading topic.

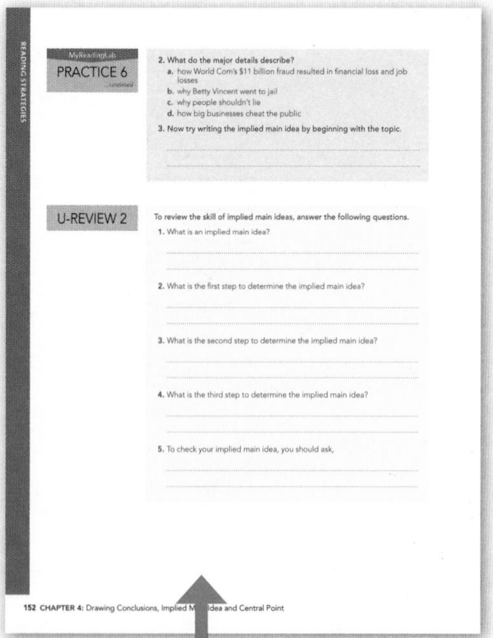

U-REVIEW sections appear immediately after students practice key reading skills to bring closure to the reading skills.

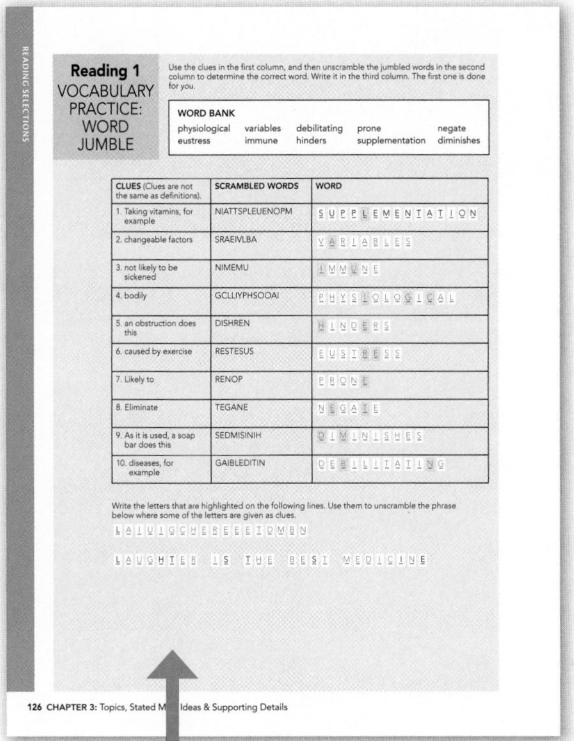

READING SELECTIONS

Reading 1
VOCABULARY PRACTICE: WORD JUMBLE

Use the clues in the first column, and then unscramble the jumbled words in the second column to determine the correct word. Write it in the third column. The first one is done for you.

WORD BANK
physiological variables debilitating prone negate
eustress immune hinders supplementation diminishes

CLUES (Clues are not the same as definitions).	SCRAMBLED WORDS	WORD
1. Taking vitamins, for example	NIATTSPLEUENOPM	S U P P L E M E N T A T I O N
2. changeable factors	SRAEIVLBA	V A R I A B L E S
3. not likely to be sickened	NIMEMU	I M M U N E
4. bodily	GCLLIYPHSOOAI	P H Y S I O L O G I C A L
5. an obstruction does this	DISHREN	H I N D E R S
6. caused by exercise	RESTESUS	E U S T R E S S
7. Likely to	RENOP	P R O N E
8. Eliminate	TEGANE	N E G A T E
9. As it is used, a soap bar does this	SEDMISINIH	D I M I N I S H E S
10. diseases, for example	GAIBLEDITIN	D E B I L I T A T I N G

Write the letters that are highlighted on the following lines. Use them to unscramble the phrase below where some of the letters are given as clues.

L A I U I G C H E R E E E T D M B N

L A U G H T E R I S T H E B E S T M E D I C I N E

126 CHAPTER 3: Topics, Stated M[...] Ideas & Supporting Details

A variety of **GAMES AND ACTIVITIES** is included to further engage students in active and collaborative learning.

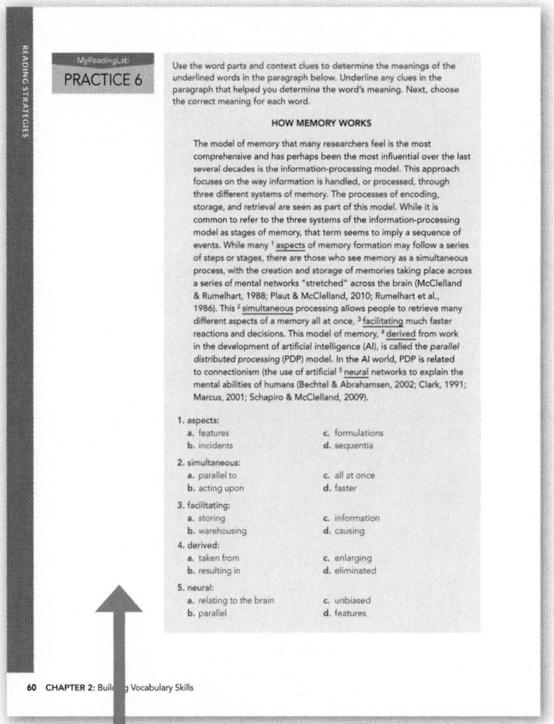

READING STRATEGIES

MyReadingLab
PRACTICE 6

Use the word parts and context clues to determine the meanings of the underlined words in the paragraph below. Underline any clues in the paragraph that helped you determine the word's meaning. Next, choose the correct meaning for each word.

HOW MEMORY WORKS

The model of memory that many researchers feel is the most comprehensive and has perhaps been the most influential over the last several decades is the information-processing model. This approach focuses on the way information is handled, or processed, through three different systems of memory. The processes of encoding, storage, and retrieval are seen as part of this model. While it is common to refer to the three systems of the information-processing model as stages of memory, that term seems to imply a sequence of events. While many [1] aspects of memory formation may follow a series of steps or stages, there are those who see memory as a simultaneous process, with the creation and storage of memories taking place across a series of mental networks "stretched" across the brain (McClelland & Rumelhart, 1988; Plaut & McClelland, 2010; Rumelhart et al., 1986). This [2] simultaneous processing allows people to retrieve many different aspects of a memory all at once, [3] facilitating much faster reactions and decisions. This model of memory, [4] derived from work in the development of artificial intelligence (AI), is called the *parallel distributed processing* (PDP) model. In the AI world, PDP is related to connectionism (the use of artificial [5] neural networks to explain the mental abilities of humans (Bechtel & Abrahamsen, 2002; Clark, 1991; Marcus, 2001; Schapiro & McClelland, 2009).

1. aspects:
   a. features **c.** formulations
   b. incidents **d.** sequentia
2. simultaneous:
   a. parallel to **c.** all at once
   b. acting upon **d.** faster
3. facilitating:
   a. storing **c.** information
   b. warehousing **d.** causing
4. derived:
   a. taken from **c.** enlarging
   b. resulting in **d.** eliminated
5. neural:
   a. relating to the brain **c.** unbiased
   b. parallel **d.** features

60 CHAPTER 2: Buil[...]g Vocabulary Skills

Abundant **PRACTICES** and **SKILL-BUILDING EXERCISES** are included so students can apply the key reading and study skills.

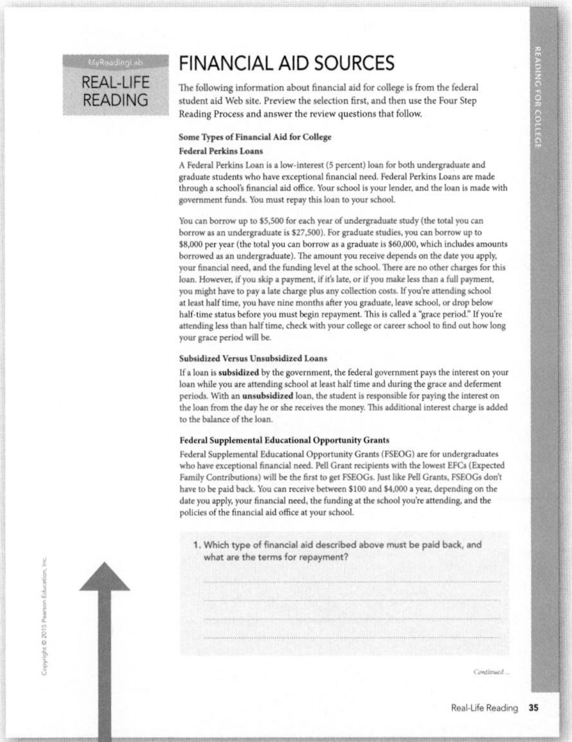

MyReadingLab
REAL-LIFE READING

FINANCIAL AID SOURCES

The following information about financial aid for college is from the federal student aid Web site. Preview the selection first, and then use the Four Step Reading Process and answer the review questions that follow.

Some Types of Financial Aid for College

Federal Perkins Loans

A Federal Perkins Loan is a low-interest (5 percent) loan for both undergraduate and graduate students who have exceptional financial need. Federal Perkins Loans are made through a school's financial aid office. Your school is your lender, and the loan is made with government funds. You must repay this loan to your school.

You can borrow up to $5,500 for each year of undergraduate study (the total you can borrow as an undergraduate is $27,500). For graduate studies, you can borrow up to $8,000 per year (the total you can borrow as a graduate is $60,000, which includes amounts borrowed as an undergraduate). The amount you receive depends on the date you apply, your financial need, and the funding level at the school. There are no other charges for this loan. However, if you skip a payment, if it's late, or if you make less than a full payment, you might have to pay a late charge plus any collection costs. If you're attending school at least half time, you have nine months after you graduate, leave school, or drop below half-time status before you must begin repayment. This is called a "grace period." If you're attending less than half time, check with your college or career school to find out how long your grace period will be.

Subsidized Versus Unsubsidized Loans

If a loan is **subsidized** by the government, the federal government pays the interest on your loan while you are attending school at least half time and during the grace and deferment periods. With an **unsubsidized** loan, the student is responsible for paying the interest on the loan from the day he or she receives the money. This additional interest charge is added to the balance of the loan.

Federal Supplemental Educational Opportunity Grants

Federal Supplemental Educational Opportunity Grants (FSEOG) are for undergraduates who have exceptional financial need. Pell Grant recipients with the lowest EFCs (Expected Family Contributions) will be the first to get FSEOGs. Just like Pell Grants, FSEOGs don't have to be paid back. You can receive between $100 and $4,000 a year, depending on the date you apply, your financial need, the funding at the school you're attending, and the policies of the financial aid office at your school.

1. Which type of financial aid described above must be paid back, and what are the terms for repayment?

Continued...

READING FOR COLLEGE

Copyright © 2015 Pearson Education, Inc.

Real-Life Reading 35

REAL-LIFE READING selections show students the value of reading skills to situations in everyday life.

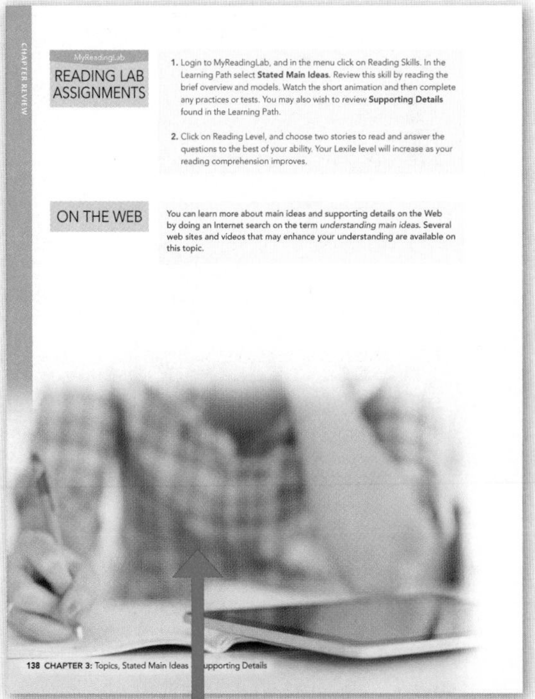

CHAPTER REVIEW

MyReadingLab
READING LAB ASSIGNMENTS

1. Login to MyReadingLab, and in the menu click on Reading Skills. In the Learning Path select **Stated Main Ideas.** Review this skill by reading the brief overview and models. Watch the short animation and then complete any practices or tests. You may also wish to review **Supporting Details** found in the Learning Path.
2. Click on Reading Level, and choose two stories to read and answer the questions to the best of your ability. Your Lexile level will increase as your reading comprehension improves.

ON THE WEB

You can learn more about main ideas and supporting details on the Web by doing an Internet search on the term *understanding main ideas.* Several web sites and videos that may enhance your understanding are available on this topic.

138 CHAPTER 3: Topics, Stated Main Ideas [...]upporting Details

READING LAB ASSIGNMENTS direct students to MyReadingLab for additional practice of skills, reading comprehension, and research opportunities.

ACKNOWLEDGMENTS

I would like to thank David Kear, my Senior Development Editor, for his guidance and support in writing *Reading for College*. He has been my rudder and the wind in my sail. I would also like to acknowledge my editor, Eric Stano, for providing me the opportunity to publish this book with Pearson. My sincere gratitude goes to Anthony Limerick at DK in London, and Amanda Zagnoli at Integra for their conscientious attention to every detail in the beautiful design of this text. I wish to thank Karen Cowden, a colleague and friend, for writing the Instructor's Manual and Test Bank. There are also many other people who worked behind the scenes to publish this book, and I am indebted to all of them. It may take a village to raise a child, but it takes an international coalition to publish a book!

I have been blessed to work with many dedicated colleagues at Valencia College in Orlando, FL, who have supported and encouraged me throughout this process. Their feedback has been a tremendous help in shaping the first edition of *Reading for College* and in refining the second edition of *Reading for Life*.

Last, but never least, I would like to acknowledge my husband, Craig, for his patience and his support of my career as a writer and instructor. Writing demands long hours at the computer, and he has understood my passion for expressing my ideas with the hope that others may benefit from them.

I would also like to gratefully recognize the invaluable insights provided by the following colleagues and reviewers:

Karin Alderfer
Miami-Dade College Kendal
Carla Bell
Henry Ford Community College
Teresa Carrillo
Joliet Junior College
Gail Charrier
Delaware Technical Community College
Lincoln Davis
Imperial Valley College
Allison DeVaney
El Camino College
Maureen Gibson
Kentucky Community and Technical College System
Aileen Gum
San Diego City College
Forrest Helvie
Norwalk College
Judy Hubble
Austin Community College
Suzanne Hughes
Florida State College at Jacksonville
Janice Johnson
Missouri State University West Plains
Leslie Johnson
North Central Texas College
Patty Kunkel
Santa Fe College
James May
Valencia College
Laura Meyers
Hawkeye Community College
Susan Monroe
Housatonic Community College
Lance Morita
Leeward Community College
Mary Nielson
Dalton State College
Linda Remark
Stark State College
James Rogge
Broward College
Nancy Schafer
Yavapai College
Rhonda Sharman
Delaware Technical Community College

READING for COLLEGE

1 THE FOUR-STEP READING PROCESS

FOCUS ON: Your College Experience

New place, new people, new experiences—for many of you, it is your first year in college. You have hopes and dreams of building an exciting and rewarding future. To succeed, you need a clear vision of what kind of future you want and a plan to accomplish it. This chapter will help you to begin making a plan and provide you with helpful tips to succeed in college. This chapter focuses on the skills, information, and advice needed to make your first year the most positive and memorable experience of your life.

By the end of this chapter, you will be able to:

LEARNING OBJECTIVES

1 read using an active thinking process.

2 read to learn by previewing, reading actively, highlighting and annotating, and reviewing.

In college, you will be expected to do a great deal of reading and studying outside of class—much more than you did in high school. Simply reading through a textbook chapter once is not enough to learn the material; by doing this, you'll be wasting valuable time. You must learn to read and study at the same time, which means that you need to adopt a study system that will help you to understand *and* learn the material.

Have you ever found yourself reading the same sentence or paragraph over more than once because you missed the message? Have you read an entire page or even an entire chapter and couldn't remember what you read? Perhaps distracting thoughts or events pulled your attention away from what you were reading and as a result you forgot what you read. One way to remedy this is to practice active reading.

OBJECTIVE 1

Read using an active thinking process.

ACTIVE READING

Reading is an active thinking process. When you read, your brain should be fully and actively engaged, constantly thinking about and questioning the reading material. Reading without thinking is *passive reading*, which results in not being able to remember most of what you read. This and other principles of learning in this book are based on scientific research into how the human brain learns best. Research shows that the process you should use for effective, active reading has three phases: before reading, during reading, and after reading. Within these phases are four separate steps.

STEP 1 Preview Before You Read

STEP 2 Read Actively

STEP 3 Highlight and Annotate

STEP 4 Review

STEP 1
Preview Before You Read

OBJECTIVE 2

Read to learn by previewing, reading actively, highlighting and annotating, and reviewing.

(reading) **comprehension**: understanding the meaning of a written selection.

Previewing before you read means getting your brain activated by thinking through what you already know about the topic at hand. Previewing takes less than one minute, and it can have a powerful impact on learning because it brings to mind what you already know about a subject and provides a context, or framework, for understanding what you are about to read. Students who preview before they read have better **comprehension** because they can see the whole picture and how each part is related to the whole. This process helps you organize the information so you can understand it and remember it much more easily.

Think of a time when you had to look at a map to find a location. You may have used an online map to locate an unfamiliar place. At first glance, the street names and street grids resemble a complex maze of unrelated, unfamiliar material. As you zoom out, you begin to recognize places such as the names of cities, states, lakes, rivers, and other places of interest. With a wider frame of reference, the new unfamiliar place now has a context for meaning because you see it in relation to something with which you are familiar. Now you're able to see where you're going and how to get there.

Using the same approach to reading new material in your college courses can similarly help you see the wider, bigger picture. Previewing a chapter gives your brain a context so you can begin to put the new pieces of the puzzle into a recognizable form. You form new relationships between ideas and understand the relevance of what you are reading.

How Do I Preview?

To preview, you look through the selection and read the most attention-grabbing material, which includes:

- titles, headings, and subheadings
- the learning objectives (if they are listed)
- the author's introduction to the chapter, telling you what you are going to learn
- the first sentence in each section
- words in bold print
- notes in margins
- photos, diagrams, tables, charts
- any questions at the end of the selection
- summaries at the end of the chapter

Developing Preview Questions

While you are previewing, you should develop some questions that you think will be answered in the reading selection, for two important reasons. First, it gets you thinking about the topic so you can recall what you already know about it. Second, having questions will establish a purpose for reading that will help you stay focused and remember what you read.

Turn Headings into Questions

Use the headings and turn them into questions. When you create questions, include words like *why* and *how*. Writing good questions that require more thought and detail will give you a deeper understanding of what you are reading. Take a moment to preview Chapter 1 of this textbook, reading all of the headings, and then develop preview questions as described in the next section.

PRACTICE PREVIEWING

On the lines below, use the headings in the selection "Having the Right Attitude" to write questions. The first one is done for you.

1. Having the Right Attitude

   What is the right attitude and how will it help me in college?

   ....

2. The Hard Work Habit

   ....

   ....

3. You're Not in High School Anymore

   ....

   ....

PRACTICE PREVIEWING
...continued

4. Higher Education Means Higher Income

....

....

5. Greater Satisfaction

....

....

The article below has a model of what you should preview before reading. The text to read during the preview is highlighted in tan.

Having the Right Attitude

As a professor of reading, I have seen thousands of students over the past thirty years, and usually within the first 3 weeks of school, I can spot the ones who are going to make it through college. They are not the students who are the "smartest," nor are they the ones who correctly answer the most questions in class. They're not even the ones who have the highest test scores. The ones who succeed in college, and in life, are the ones with the right attitude.

Having the right attitude means taking your education seriously. Students who have the right attitude are not in class to just show up or to waste time. They want to learn and master new skills to get the best grades possible. They are organized and pay attention to the instruction and not to their phones. They take notes, do all of the assigned work to the best of their ability—both in and outside of class—and study for tests well in advance so they can pass them. Even though they may not have an A in every subject, these are the students who succeed in college and in life. If you are one of these students, you have learned the importance of having the right attitude and this will help you succeed throughout college and beyond.

The Hard Work Habit

The habit of working hard doesn't come from avoiding work. Hard workers see results, which motivates them to continue working. Putting forth a half-hearted effort will not help your understanding of subject matter, nor will it result in good grades in college. Students who always take the easy shortcuts—like cheating, copying answers, skipping homework, or skipping classes—never succeed for very long. They may make it through one or two courses this way, but eventually they realize it doesn't work because the only way to learn new material is by studying. Students who continue taking shortcuts eventually give up and drop out.

You're Not in High School Anymore

The habit of working hard, both in and outside of class, is expected of every student in college. Your professor's job is to help you understand concepts and skills in class. It is your job to learn them using every resource available to you on your own time, including meeting outside of class with professors and tutors. As a wise college graduate once

initiative: the ability to take action without being told to do something.

said, "Everything I learned in college I learned on my own." Unlike your teachers in high school, your college instructors expect you to take the **initiative** to learn what you must, any way you can, *on your own time*. This means you must look at how much time you are allocating to your education.

A college degree is an investment in your future, just like buying stocks, bonds, or certificates of deposit at a bank. You invest your time now so you will reap the benefits later. Putting the time in to learn and study will result in earning a college degree so you can have a better lifestyle.

Higher Education Means Higher Income

Employed college graduates earn significantly more money over their lifetime than people with high school diplomas. This means a completely different lifestyle. You will have money to live in a better place, to own a better car, to have better health care, to provide more for your family, and to have a much better retirement than those without college degrees or special training. It's a small sacrifice to invest your time and money now for the payoff that will be compounded over the remainder of your lifetime. Decide to make the time investment now. Cut back on the hours at your job if you must. Sacrifice some of your relaxation time during the semester so that you can study more and get better grades. Going to college is a commitment, like getting married: you've got to put in the time to make it work.

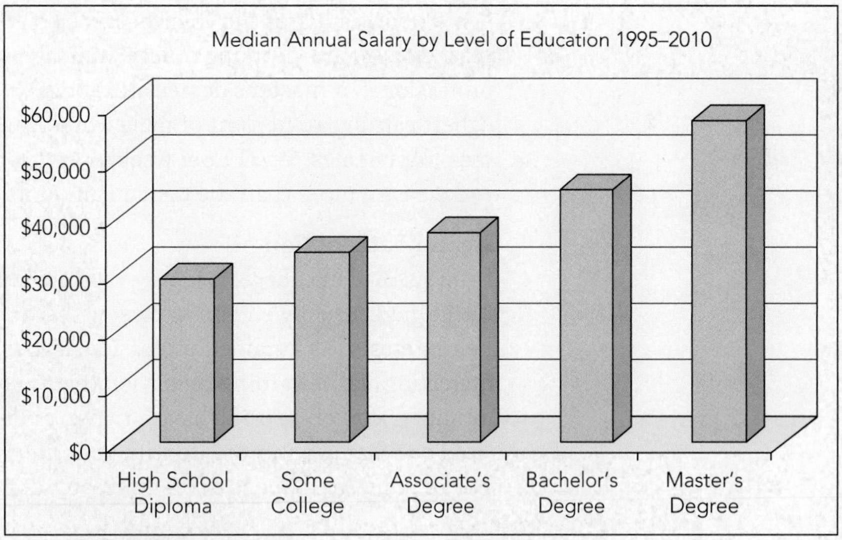

Median annual earnings of full-time, full-year wage and salary workers ages 25–34, by educational attainment: 1995–2010.

The graph above shows the median annual salary of workers age 25-34 over a ten-year period, so the salary levels shown are significantly less than the actual salaries earned today. (A median number is the "middle number" in a collection of data.)

Continued...

PRACTICE PREVIEWING

...continued

The graph below shows the median weekly earnings of workers by their level of education. Because these are median numbers, remember that half of these workers make more than the amounts shown.

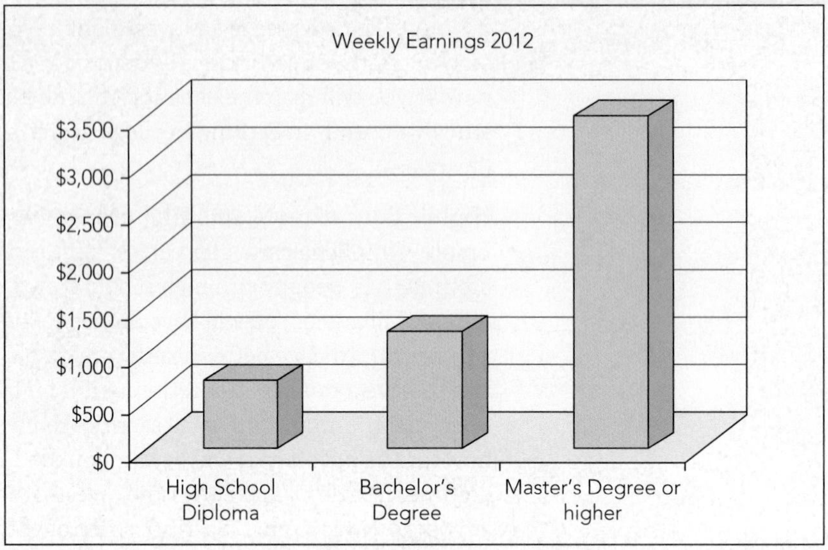

Average Weekly Earnings by Educational Attainment. Source: Bureau of Labor Statistics U.S. Department of Labor, October 18, 2012.

In 2012, full-time workers age 25 and over without a high school diploma had median **weekly** earnings of $464, compared with $648 for high school graduates (no college) and $1,170 for those holding at least a bachelor's degree. Among college graduates with advanced degrees (professional or master's degree and above), the median income of the highest earning 10 percent of male workers was $3,448 or more per week (for females, $2,311 per week). Keep in mind that half of these workers earn more than the median amounts shown.

Greater Satisfaction

If you succeed in college, not only will you have higher earnings, but college grads usually end up in careers that they have chosen based on their interests. As a trained professional, your job will be much more interesting and rewarding than a job that is given to an unskilled, untrained worker. You will have a richer, more satisfying career if it is based on what *you* want to do with your life. Education gives you more choices in life, and opens doors to greater opportunities.

STEP 2
Read Actively

Reading actively means thinking about what you are reading, looking for answers to your preview questions, asking new questions, and making predictions about what the author will say next. This helps you to stay focused and to think about the ideas in the text so you will understand and remember the information better. Ask questions such as

- What is the subject of this selection?
- What is the author's most important point?
- What key ideas help to explain the most important point?
- How does this new information relate to the last concept I read about?
- How will this information help me?

As you read, try to see connections between ideas to understand how concepts are related to each other. In particular, try to connect the new ideas from the text to your own **prior knowledge** about the topic by recalling what you already know and trying to figure out how the new information fits into it.

prior knowledge: everything that you have learned in the past up to now

Visualizing

One practice that good readers do automatically is visualization. It involves a creative process whereby readers form images of what they are reading. This is a very powerful learning tool; creating an image of something will help you to understand and remember it better. It also makes reading more interesting and keeps you focused on the information in the text as, guided by the words on the page, you paint a mental picture. Despite the fact that everyone reads the same words, each person's image will look different. For example, read the following definition of water and try to visualize the water molecule:

> Water is composed of one atom of oxygen and two atoms of hydrogen that are bonded together by sharing electrons. Electrons are negatively charged particles found outside of the atom's nucleus in an electron cloud.

Can you picture three objects bonded together surrounded by a cloud? What colors were your atoms? What shapes were they? Were they suspended in midair or attached to something? Did the electrons move? Did they orbit the atoms quickly or slowly?

Visualizing is especially interesting when reading about people. You can be a casting director and create your own cast of characters for the roles of the people in the reading. Because of media like television, movies, and the Internet, people have become less reliant on their imaginations. Since visualizing uses your imagination, it may take some practice to become proficient. Improvement will follow with practice.

Make Predictions

To improve your comprehension, it is also important to make predictions as you read. For example, what word would you expect to complete the following sentence?

> To create hydrogen fuel, water molecules are broken down into two separate atoms. The two atoms are oxygen and ________________.

Because you had the prior knowledge that water is made up of oxygen and hydrogen from a previous paragraph, you were able to predict that the sentence ended with *hydrogen*. Predicting while you read helps you to connect what you know to new learning and to draw logical conclusions based on the facts at hand. It will also keep you focused on what you're doing. You'll be able to remember what you have read and not drift off thinking about something else.

STEP 3
Highlight and Annotate

Highlighting

After you've previewed the material in a section and read through it while visualizing and asking questions, go back through the section to highlight it. Highlighting is an important part of the learning process that will help you remember what you have read because as you go back through the reading, you will be asking questions such as, "What information is important to remember?" and, "What should I highlight, and why?" This kind of thinking forces you to analyze and review what you have just read. Remember to highlight (or underline) only the most important ideas and skip the minor details. To practice this, when you finish reading the first section between the subheadings, go back through the section and underline or highlight the most important information.

Don't highlight as you read through the first time; this will result in too much highlighting. Only highlight information that you would include if you were writing a short summary or taking notes. Focus on the big ideas. Think, for instance, of the preview questions that you developed for the reading selection. Underline or highlight answers to those questions. Also, try to think like a professor: What would you expect your students to learn from this reading selection? By highlighting and annotating after your initial reading, you will be reviewing the information a second and third time, and will be less likely to forget what you read.

As you work through this textbook, you will become more proficient at highlighting. You will notice key transitions such as *first, second*, and *third*. You will learn to discriminate between major details and minor ones. These skills will help you to find the most important ideas quickly.

Annotating

annotate: to make brief notes in the margins of a text

Next, **annotate** by making brief notes in the margins (or in your notebook) about the information you highlighted. This gives you another review of the important data that you need to remember because you will be thinking about how to summarize the information in your own words. Keep your annotations concise, and try to summarize the most important ideas in a short phrase. Study the model below from the first section of this chapter. Notice how the important points have been highlighted and how the notes in the right margin summarize the key points.

Example of highlighting and annotating:

In college, you will be expected to do a great deal of reading and studying outside of class—much more than you did in high school. Simply reading through a textbook chapter once is not enough to learn the material; by doing this, you'll be wasting valuable time. You must learn to read and study at the same time, which means that you need to adopt a study system that will help you to understand *and* learn the material.	*Reading once through -waste of time* *Adopt a study system*
Reading is an active thinking process. When you read, your brain should be fully and actively engaged, constantly thinking about and questioning the reading material. Reading without thinking is ***passive reading***, which results in not being able to remember most of what you read. This and other principles of learning in this book are based on scientific research into how the human brain learns best. Research shows that the process you should use for effective, active reading has three phases: before reading, during reading, and after reading.	*Reading: active thinking process* *Passive reading: reading w/out thinking* *Effective reading process phases: before, during & after reading*

Using E-Texts

Highlighting and annotating can also be accomplished with an e-text. Most e-text readers come with highlighting and note-taking tools that allow students to complete this process in the same way that you would in a printed textbook. You can practice the Four Step Reading process with the e-text of this book by going online to MyReadingLab and clicking *e-text* in the menu.

PRACTICE HIGHLIGHTING AND ANNOTATING

Go back to the section titled "Having the Right Attitude" and highlight key points. Complete one section, then go back and annotate in the margins to summarize important points. Use as few words as possible, mostly listing the subject of the paragraph. Think of them as "idea bytes" to keep notes concise. When you are finished, compare your highlighting and annotations with a classmate's. Discuss which points were important enough to mark. After checking with your partner, continue previewing, actively reading, highlighting, and annotating the rest of the article, one section at a time.

STEP 4
Review

When you review what you have just read, it's like putting the lid tightly on a jar so the contents won't leak out. You are moving information from your short-term memory, the temporary storage area in your brain, to a permanent location in your long-term memory. Information in your short-term memory fades quickly; this is why students often say, "I understand the concepts when I'm in class, but when I try to do the homework later on, I struggle with it." This happens because the concepts you learned in class are not in your long-term memory yet. You can help your brain move the information into your long-term memory by taking a few minutes to review what you just learned. To review, you should:

- Summarize what you just read in your own words.
- Read the highlighted sections and your annotations in the margins.
- Answer the questions you developed before reading.
- Turn the headings into questions and say the complete answers.
- Use questions at the end of the chapter to review.
- Say major points out loud, counting them off on your fingers.
- Make concept maps or drawings.
- Review with a partner by telling each other what you just read.
- Review, in short 15–20 minute sessions, ***every day.***

Whenever possible, do your review right after your learning session. If you were just in math class, for instance, and have time before your next class, spend whatever time you can reviewing what was taught while it is still fresh in your mind. Go over your class notes and add details to them. Do not trust your memory to recall those details from class later that evening or the next day. Instead, write them down as soon as possible after class. Review your notes from each class 15–20 minutes **every day**, and by the end of a week, you will recall the information without much difficulty because the brain learns best with *short, frequent* practice. In Chapter 7 you will learn more techniques on how to study using various learning styles.

MyReadingLab

PRACTICE 1

Follow the Four Step Reading Process for the paragraph below.

1. After previewing the title and first sentence, write one or two preview questions below.
2. Read the selection and then highlight a few main points.
3. Answer the questions in the margins. These answers would be your margin notes if you were annotating the reading selection.

PREVIEW QUESTIONS:

....

....

....

SETTING GOALS

Why is it important to set goals?

....

....

....

What should you know about your goals before you make them?

....

....

....

How can you make goals achievable?

....

....

....

To get anywhere in life, you need a plan that begins with setting goals. Setting goals is the first step to success for any endeavor you choose in life, whether it is finding a place to live, landing a job, choosing a mate, or earning a college degree. Make your goals as specific as possible. Instead of saying, "I want to get a college degree so I can have a better life," be specific about the life you want, the type of college degree or training that life would require, and when and where you intend to get it.

Also, consider the amount of time, effort and money required to achieve your goals. Wanting to be a doctor and having the perseverance to study and work long hours for 8 years while paying tens of thousands of dollars in tuition to become one are two different things. In addition, think about how you will have to manage your time and lifestyle to achieve your goals. If you have commitments, such as working full-time to support a family, it may take longer to reach your goal, so set a realistic time frame.

Prioritize your goals by listing the most important ones first. Take a good look at your abilities, time, and resources and decide what is most important to focus upon first. Ask yourself which goals you are willing to put off until later so that you can focus on reaching a more important one. Doing this will help you to keep your goals more realistic and achievable.

Sometimes breaking goals down into smaller, achievable steps will facilitate success and help to avoid disappointment. Set short-term goals for 3 to 6 months, mid-term goals to achieve in one year, and long-term goals for 3 to 5 years. Briefly describe a plan for how you will achieve each goal and when you will achieve it. If your situation changes, you can always change your plans and rewrite your goals. Record these goals in a journal and modify them as time goes on. Taking the time to write your goals is the first step in your journey to success.

Continued...

MyReadingLab
PRACTICE 1
...continued

REVIEW

Review the most important points in the article by answering the following questions:

1. Why should you set goals?

2. What are some important points to keep in mind when writing goals?

MyReadingLab
PRACTICE 2

Follow the Four Step Reading Process for the paragraph below.

1. After previewing the title and first sentence, write one or two preview questions below.
2. Read the selection and then highlight a few main points.
3. Answer the questions in the margins. These answers would be your margin notes if you were annotating the reading selection.

PREVIEW QUESTIONS:

GETTING MOTIVATED AND STAYING MOTIVATED

What can you do to help motivate yourself to do your work?

Most college students will honestly admit that one of the most difficult things to do in college is to get motivated to do their work. We all want to be like those students who seem driven to perform, but for most students, studying and doing homework is a chore. This is where having a good imagination and visualizing can help. Visualize yourself getting a good grade on the assignment. Imagine how good you'll feel when you accomplish your goal and get a good grade. Now imagine how you'll feel when you get the zero for not doing it, or an F for doing it poorly. Which way would you rather feel? Imagining that feeling may help you get motivated to work.

Many students get caught up in the excuse syndrome. It's easy to excuse your failure by telling yourself you don't have time because you have to work, or take care of your family, or don't have the resources you need. It's easy to find excuses for *not* doing something. Many students are masters at it, and feel that they have valid excuses for their failure. But the truth is, very few students face circumstances that prevent them from doing their work. They often put off doing work by procrastinating until it's too late to do the work effectively. They end up cheating, cutting corners, or doing a poor job because they didn't start working soon enough. Success is within your own control. Making excuses to avoid work, or waiting until you "feel" like doing it will not get it done. Even good students have assignments they don't want to do, but they do them. College takes a lot of self-discipline—making yourself do things you would rather not do. But the long-term benefits of a college degree or special training will make it all worthwhile.

REVIEW

Review the most important points in the article by answering the following questions.

1. What are some reasons why students don't do their work in college?

....

....

2. What are some ways to get motivated to do your work?

....

....

....

....

MyReadingLab

PRACTICE 3

Follow the Four Step Reading Process for the paragraph below.

1. After previewing the title and first sentence, write one or two preview questions below.
2. Read the selection and then highlight a few main points.
3. Answer the questions in the margins. These answers would be your margin notes if you were annotating the reading selection.

PREVIEW QUESTIONS:

....

....

....

WHAT IS A SYLLABUS?

On the first day your college classes meet, you will probably receive a syllabus for each course. Think of a syllabus as a user's manual, because it contains all of the objectives, expectations, and regulations for the course. Read through it carefully, marking the important information, such as the course objectives, which describe what you will learn by taking the course. The syllabus also includes the contact information for the instructor, including his or her office location, office hours, phone number, e-mail address, and faculty Web site. A syllabus will explain how your grades are weighted, meaning how much the tests, assignments, and other work count in the total grade. For instance, your tests may count 25%, assignments 25%, participation 25%, and the final exam 25% of the total grade. Often professors will consider your class participation as part of your grade. If so, be alert to the expectations for class preparation, class attendance, conduct, and group participation. Know how many absences you are allowed so you won't be withdrawn—yes, that means *dropped from the course* for excessive absences with no refund. Each professor has different standards; just because your friend's instructor allows unlimited absences doesn't mean your professor will.

What kinds of information are in the course syllabus?

....

....

....

....

....

Find out if there are any requirements, such as a minimum grade to pass. What are the policies for missing a test or a major assignment? Your professor may not allow make-ups for late tests or assignments, so know this ahead of time to avoid disappointment.

Seasoned professors will often include a course calendar that lists the dates of tests, quizzes, and assignment due dates. Don't expect your professors to remind you about these events. The course calendar is provided so they won't have to, so record all important dates (such as the dates of your exams) ahead of time in your personal planner. Also, find out the date and location of the final exam. Most colleges post a final exam schedule on their Web sites. You should know that final exams may not be held in the same location or during the same

Why is it important to pay attention to the course calendar?

day or time slot as your regular class time. Most colleges hold these exams during finals week in locations all over the campus, and if you miss the final, you may fail the course.

The course syllabus is one of the most important documents you will read all semester, so read it carefully and don't be afraid to ask questions about anything in it. It's better to know the answers and avoid doing something that could result in failure.

REVIEW

Review the most important points in the article by answering the following questions.

1. Why is it important to read the syllabus carefully and ask questions about the course?

2. What could happen if you were unaware of the attendance policy or the date of an important exam?

U-REVIEW

To help you review what you just learned, answer the following questions and then share your answers with a partner. Discuss any information your partner left out and think of ways that you can apply what you have learned to your own studies.

1. Why do you need a study system in college?

2. What four steps are involved in the Four Step Reading process, and what do you do at each step?

3. Why will using the Four Step Reading Process improve your comprehension and recall for your college reading assignments?

READING RATE

At the conclusion of each reading selection in this book, there is a word count of the total words found in the selection. You can determine your speed, or reading rate, by dividing the total number of words by the number of minutes it took you to read the selection. For example, if you read 1200 words in 15 minutes, your reading rate would be 80 words per minute.

Having a fast reading speed can be helpful in college, but you should never try to read faster than you can comprehend. Comprehension of the material is the most important goal of reading. Consequently, you should expect the rate at which you read to vary according to the complexity of the material. Easy passages can be read quickly while more difficult ones must be read more slowly to give your brain time to process the information. Since everyone processes information at a different rate, we cannot expect everyone to read at the same rate, so read at the rate that is best for your own personal comprehension. Many students spend a great deal of time and effort trying to improve their reading rate, and there is little proof that these efforts pay off. Doing more reading and thinking about what you read will improve your comprehension *and* your speed over time.

MyReadingLab

Reading 1
VOCABULARY PREVIEW

"How to Succeed in College: New Advice and Insights" by Rahim Kanani

Match the words in the Word Bank to the correct meanings by finding and reading the words as they are used in the context of this textbook selection. Then, write the letter of the matching word next to the definition below The paragraph numbers in parentheses indicate the location of each word.

WORD BANK

a. entrepreneurial (3) b. dense (4) c. protocol (6)
d. rigor (6) e. tolerance (7) f. advocacy (10)
g. philanthropy (13) h. synthesizing (13) i. unfettered (14)
j. invaluable (15)

1. .... set of rules
2. .... unrestricted
3. .... complex
4. .... relating to starting a business venture
5. .... open-mindedness
6. .... creating something
7. .... promotion; support
8. .... charitable giving
9. .... strictness; challenge
10. .... having great worth

MyReadingLab

Reading 1
PREVIEW

Discuss the following questions with a partner or small group.

1. What are some of the reasons why you decided to attend college?
2. What do you hope to gain from your college experience?

After you preview the article, write one or two preview questions on the lines below:

....

....

....

....

....

MyReadingLab

Reading 1

"How to Succeed in College: New Advice and Insights" by Rahim Kanani

entrepreneur: one who creates a business

Rahim Kanani is a successful writer, advocate, strategist and **entrepreneur** for global social change. He offers his best advice for new college students based on his own experience and observations.

1 When I started high school in the mid-90s, the Internet was just beginning to boom. It was as amazingly exciting as it was amazingly mysterious. It was hard to describe, and even harder to ignore. This curiosity led me to learn **HTML** on my own and endlessly explore ways in which I could be a part of this new virtual playground.

HTML: A computer language used for Internet applications.

2 One day while browsing around, I came across Netflix, the world's first and largest online DVD rental store. It seemed like a great idea at the time, so I looked for a similar online DVD rental service in Canada. Nothing.

3 I figured that we Canadians like a lot of the same things Americans do, including food, fashion, music, and, of course, movies. Armed with my gut instinct and some seed money from my father, I launched Canada's first online DVD rental store from home in my junior year of high school. From managing the website's design and development, to identifying strategic partnerships online and offline, to individually responding to hundreds of customer service emails, I was truly in the thick of an entrepreneurial endeavor. The venture was indeed successful, and right before I started college, we sold the business — exactly 10 years ago. The lessons learned and insights gained from this experience were both timeless and priceless. Surely, a mastery of the digital world was my destiny, right? Not quite.

4 I switched majors twice in college, from computer science to business, and then from business to philosophy. Theories of software programming were extremely dense, and the difficulty I had with learning and understanding code led to my first moment of realization: perhaps the world of computer science was not for me. Switching to business because of my early entrepreneurial success, I thought I would enjoy learning the skills of accounting, marketing, strategy and operations. While interesting, I wasn't very interested. In other words, I felt my online DVD rental experience was much more connected to the reality of how enterprises start, operate and grow.

5 During this time, I took an elective course titled "Moral and Political Philosophy." It was a topic I wanted to explore further but not focus on. Soon after, this class changed my life.

6 It was an incredibly unique experience because in no other classroom setting had my own opinion been asked for or required. There was no reason to take an intellectual stand on software programming, or on the protocol and processes of accounting. In other words, philosophy forced me to think, and it forced me to formulate a position—a rigor of mind too often underdeveloped.

How did going to college help the author find his passion in life?

7 When our classroom discussion turned to the ethics of war and conflict and, in particular, the morality underpinning the conduct of soldiers on the

battlefield, Professor Julie Ponesse chalked this question on the board: "Is there a right way or a wrong way to kill someone?" The question sparked a never-ending series of mental gymnastics in the world of morality. Exploring issues of peace, justice, equality and tolerance followed — issues that have defined my personal and professional ambitions to date.

8 The lesson here is simple, especially for college-bound students: you never know where or in what setting your passions will be discovered, and so you must allow yourself the opportunity to explore and take the risk of learning something new. Your future may depend on it.

9 Most would advise our generation to find your passion. I would advise you to find your passions. It's likely that you have more than one, as I do, and it's important that you recognize when and in what setting you're at your best.

10 Currently, I work at the intersection of technological innovation, international development and strategic advocacy at the World Bank, a unique marriage of interests developed since high school. Alongside this position, I regularly blog on international affairs and social change for *The Huffington Post* and *Forbes*, and frequently interview global leaders, such as the White House's Valerie Jarrett on the advancement of women and girls, and Drew Faust, the President of Harvard, on higher education in the 21st century. And last but not least, along with a former colleague from Harvard's Kennedy School, we're moving at full speed to develop a global reality-TV show to highlight social entrepreneurs struggling to change the world.

What does the author do for a living?

11 The point is, do not be afraid to pursue multiple dreams and multiple passions.

12 Reflecting on the last five years since I graduated from the University of Western Ontario, I wanted to share a few secrets of my success to those of you heading off to college, or back to college, eager to begin anew.

13 ***Be curious.*** Read about the world in a way you are not accustomed to. For example, if you're majoring in humanities, read *Scientific American* from time to time to learn about the intersection of language and music or the science of sleep loss. If you're majoring in sciences, read *Stanford Social Innovation Review* to learn about philanthropy in the 21st century or social entrepreneurship in Brazil. The more curious you are in seeking new kinds of knowledge, the more creative you will be at synthesizing the complexities of our world.

14 ***Reach out***. Do not be afraid to e-mail people you've never met, whether professors, CEOs, scientists, technologists or otherwise — anywhere in the world — for advice. You will be amazed by how far a short note about yourself and a genuine interest in another person can take you. I cannot overstate this. Our generation is the first to have such unfettered and direct access to the hearts and minds of anyone on Earth. If you look hard enough, you will find their e-mail addresses.

coherently: logically, clearly

15 ***Write better***. The most valuable skill set I learned in college was to write clearly and **coherently**. Whether you pursue a career in business, science, technology or the arts, the ability to convey your ideas, as well as argue and persuade effectively, is simply invaluable. With this skill alone, you will be a treasured asset in any organization.

IT: Information Technology; using technology to gather and process information.

16 ***Seize opportunities for meaningful work***. While in college, I put my Web-development skill set to use as an **IT** consultant for the university,

Continued...

MyReadingLab
Reading 1
...continued

producing and managing course websites for dozens of faculty over the years. As a graduate student at Harvard Divinity School, I worked as a research associate in justice and human rights at the Center for Nonprofits at Harvard Kennedy School, a position I undertook full-time, and negotiated a part-time completion of my studies. Do not be afraid to bend the norms of regular course loads and timeframes, for I have found that such parallel work experiences have propelled my career, knowledge and networks far more effectively than living life in sequence.

17 Lastly, I urge you to embrace the study of philosophy, for it will help you define who and what you wish to become, and this is perhaps the most important of all.

1,133 words divided by .... minutes = ... words per minute

MyReadingLab
Reading 1
REVIEW

A good review strategy after reading is to summarize what you just read in your own words. Take a few minutes to think about the author's most important point and any key ideas that helped to support or explain it.

Write a two- or three-sentence summary on the lines below.

....

....

....

....

MyReadingLab
Reading 1
COMPREHENSION QUESTIONS

The following questions will help you to recall the main idea and the details of the article. Review any parts of the article that you need to review in order to find the correct answers.

1. Before reading the article, which of the following actions did you do to preview it? (Choose all that apply.)
   a. made notes in the margins
   b. read the title and subheadings
   c. made up questions that might be answered in the article
   d. underlined important ideas
2. As you read the article using active reading strategies you should have (Choose all that apply).
   a. predicted what would come next.
   b. skipped over large sections of text.
   c. visualized ideas using mental imagery.
   d. read the entire article without stopping.

3. When you finished reading a section of the article you should have (Choose all that apply.)

a. summarized what the section was about in your own words.

b. gone on to read the next section without stopping.

c. made notes in the margins to annotate.

d. underlined or highlighted key points.

MAIN IDEA

4. What is the topic, or subject, of this selection?

a. How to Succeed in College: New Advice and Insights

b. Rahim Kanani

c. college life

d. advice for college students

5. What was the author's most important point, or central idea, in this article?

a. You can learn many interesting things in college.

b. College wasn't what the author thought it would be.

c. Rahim Kanani offers helpful advice for college students.

d. College life

SUPPORTING DETAILS

6. What did the author do in high school that taught him about entrepreneurship?

a. He took courses in business and psychology.

b. He started his own online DVD rental business.

c. His parents gave him money to start his own business.

d. He learned how to create a web site using HTML.

7. Why didn't the author major in business while in college?

a. He couldn't learn the material because it was too dense.

b. He wanted to become a philosopher instead.

c. The business courses he took did not interest him.

d. He knew more about business than his professors.

8. According to the article, which of the following is false?

a. You should seek to learn new things that normally would not interest you.

b. You should reach out to others around the world and ask for advice.

c. You should learn to write well so you can express yourself coherently.

d. You should choose professors and courses based on their popularity.

9. According to the author, why should you explore different subjects in college?

a. so you will become a well-rounded educated person

b. because you never know what will ignite your passion in life

c. because it will help you communicate with other people better

d. so you won't appear ignorant before people who are better educated than you

VOCABULARY IN CONTEXT

10. Determine the meaning of the underlined word in this sentence from paragraph 7: When our classroom discussion turned to the ethics of war and conflict and, in particular, the morality underpinning the conduct of soldiers on the battlefield, Professor Julie Ponesse chalked this question on the board: "Is there a right way or a wrong way to kill someone?"

a. supporting

b. ignoring

c. discovering

d. conflicting

MyReadingLab

Reading 1 QUESTIONS FOR WRITING AND DISCUSSION

Review any parts of the article you need to answer the following questions.

1. In what ways did taking a philosophy course change the author's life?

2. What advice does the author give for discovering your passion?

3. Why do you think the author advises college students to be curious?

4. Why does the author believe that good writing skills are important?

5. What subjects are you curious about and would like to learn more about in college?

Reading 1 VOCABULARY PRACTICE: JUMBLED PHRASE

Complete the sentences with the correct word from the Word Bank. Use the highlighted letters as clues to solve the phrases below.

WORD BANK

entrepreneurial	protocol	tolerance	philanthropy	invaluable
dense	unfettered	rigor	advocacy	synthesizing

1. Because chemistry is such a _ _ _ _ _ subject, I have to spend twice as much time studying the material as I do the material for my other courses.
2. Johnson's _ _ _ _ _ _ _ _ _ _ _ _ _ _ _ experience made him a perfect candidate for the position of company manager.
3. The chemists were successful in _ _ _ _ _ _ _ _ _ _ _ _ a gasoline that is a combination of fossil fuel and synthetic fuel.
4. John likes being in the Army because he enjoys the _ _ _ _ _ of strict regulations, structured living, and serving his country.
5. If you ever meet Queen Elizabeth of England, you must follow the proper _ _ _ _ _ _ _ _ regarding how you should greet and speak to her.
6. Our sorority supports children's _ _ _ _ _ _ _ _ groups that help disadvantaged children in our community.
7. Professor Sellick doesn't have much _ _ _ _ _ _ _ _ _ for students who are late to his classes.
8. Many millionaires are noted for their _ _ _ _ _ _ _ _ _ _ _ _ and give generously to many charitable organizations.
9. This website is an _ _ _ _ _ _ _ _ _ _ resource for anyone who is doing historical research.
10. Most college students want to be free and _ _ _ _ _ _ _ _ _ _, away from family rules and parental restrictions.

Now arrange the highlighted letters to complete the phrase below.

_ O _ A Y ' _   _ E _ D _ R _   A _ E   T _ M _ R _ _ W 'S   L _ A _ _ _ S.

MyReadingLab

Reading 2
VOCABULARY PREVIEW

"Study Methods: Different Strokes for Different Folks" by Saundra K. Ciccarelli and J. Noland White

Match the list of words in the Word Bank to their correct meanings by finding and reading the words as they are used in the context of this textbook selection. Then write the letter of the matching word next to the definition below. The paragraph numbers in parentheses indicate the location of each word.

WORD BANK

a. accommodating (3)	b. supplement (3)	c. literature (4)
d. capabilities (4)	e. implication (5)	f. disservice (5)
g. modalities (5)	h. academia (5)	

1. .... wrongful act
2. .... ways of learning
3. .... adapting to
4. .... suggestion
5. .... relating to research studies
6. .... to add something
7. .... abilities or capacities
8. .... the academic world

MyReadingLab

Reading 2
PREVIEW

Discuss the following questions with a partner or small group.

1. What do you find to be the most difficult thing about studying?
2. What successful study methods have you used in the past? Describe them

After you preview the article, write one or two preview questions on the lines below:

....

....

....

....

....

MyReadingLab

Reading 2

"Study Methods: Different Strokes for Different Folks" by Saundra K. Ciccarelli and J. Noland White

1 Many students would probably say that their grades are not what they want them to be. They may make the effort, but they still don't seem to be able to achieve the higher grades that they wish they could earn. A big part of the problem is that despite many different educational experiences, students are rarely taught how to study. Many students entering college have developed a system of taking notes, reading the textbook, and reviewing for exams that may have worked pretty well in the past, but what worked in grade school and high school may not work in college, where the expectations from teachers are higher and the workload is far greater. Students should know five things in order to do their absolute best in any college course:

What five things should students know to do well in college?

- How to identify which study methods work best for them and for different kinds of materials
- How to read a textbook and take notes that are understandable and memorable the first time
- How to listen and take useful notes during lectures
- How to study efficiently for exams
- How to write good term papers

This introduction presents various techniques and information aimed at maximizing knowledge and skills in each of these five areas.

What are Some Different Methods of Studying?

2 Most college students, at one point or another in their educational experiences, have probably run into the concept of a learning style, but what exactly is it? In general, a **learning style** is the particular way in which a person takes in, or absorbs, information (Dunn et al., 1989, 2001; Felder & Spurlin, 2005). Educators and others who use this concept believe that people take in information in several ways: through the eyes, by reading text or looking at charts, diagrams, and maps; through the ears, by listening, talking things out, and discussing things with others; and through the sense of touch and the movement of the body, by touching things, writing things down, drawing pictures and diagrams, and learning by doing (Barsch, 1996).

What is a learning style and why is it important?

3 For quite some time now, many educators and psychologists have believed that accommodating their teaching methods to each student's learning style is a key element of good instruction: You find out what the learning style is and then adjust your method of teaching to that style. To adapt their teaching, educators began to supplement a straight lecture approach by adding visual elements such as slide presentations or videos, for example. This is not a bad thing, of course: The more varied the presentation, the more likely students are to pay attention. But trying to tailor one lecture to all of the various learning styles? Not so practical (Coffield et al.2004; Willingham, 2005). Research strongly suggests that a

Continued...

MyReadingLab
Reading 2
...continued

strong and varied teaching style will yield better student success regardless of any differences in students' learning styles (Geake, 2008; Zhang, 2006).

4 In a fascinating article in *Psychological Science in the Public Interest*, a journal published by the Association for Psychological Science (Pashler et al., 2009), researchers did an extensive literature review of learning-style studies and discovered several key points:

1. Students definitely have preferences about how information is presented to them.
2. Students do seem to have different capabilities when it comes to processing different kinds of information.
3. No real evidence exists that tailoring the presentation of information to different learning styles has any effect on a student's ability to learn the information (Pashler et al., 2009).

What has research proved about learning styles and studying?

5 What? What was that last bit? There was no real evidence that tailoring the instructional method to the student's learning style makes any difference in the student's ability to learn that material. While some learning-styles theorists are critical of the researchers' conclusions (Braio et al., 1997; Drysdale et al., 2001; Ford & Chen, 2001; Glenn, 2009), others go so far as to say that the implication that a student can have only one or two learning styles is a disservice to the student (Henry, 2007). Instead of trying to limit a student's study methods to just one or two modalities (which simply isn't going to happen very often in the world outside academia), wouldn't it be better to help students learn several different styles of studying? We learn many different kinds of things during our lives, and one method of learning probably isn't going to work for everyone. So instead of focusing on different learning styles, this (*Psychology in Action)* introduction will focus on different study methods—take the opportunity to try them out and find which methods work best for you. Table 1 lists just some of the ways in which you can study. All of the methods listed in this table are good for students who wish to improve both their understanding of a subject and their grades on tests. See if you can think of some other ways in which you might prefer to practice the various study methods.

6 No matter what the study method, students *must* read the textbook to be successful in the course. (While that might seem obvious to some, many students today seem to think that just taking notes on lectures or slide presentations will be enough.) The next section deals with how to read textbooks for understanding rather than just to "get through" the material.

Reading Textbooks: Textbooks Are Not Meatloaf

7 How should you go about reading a textbook so that you get the most out of your reading efforts? Students make two common mistakes in regard to reading textbooks. The first mistake is simple: Many students don't bother to read the textbook before going to the lecture that will cover that material. Trying to get anything out of a lecture without having read the material first is like trying to find a new, unfamiliar place without using a map or any kind of directions. It's easy to get lost. This is especially true because of the assumption that most instructors make when planning their lectures: They take for granted that the students have already read the assignment. The instructors then use the lecture to go into detail about the information the students supposedly got from the reading. If the students have not done the reading, the instructor's lecture isn't going to make a whole lot of sense.

What two mistakes do most students make regarding textbooks?

8 The second mistake that most students make when reading textbook material is to try to read it the same way they would read a novel: They start at the first page and read continuously. With a novel, it's easy to do this because the plot is usually interesting and people want to know what happens next, so they keep reading. It isn't necessary to remember every little detail—all they need to remember are the main plot points. One could say that a novel is like meatloaf—some meaty parts with lots of filler. Meatloaf can be eaten quickly, without even chewing for very long.

9 With a textbook, the material may be interesting but not in the same way that a novel is interesting. A textbook is a big, thick steak—all meat, no filler. Just as a steak has to be chewed to be enjoyed and to be useful to the body, textbook material has to be "chewed" with the mind. You have to read slowly, paying attention to every morsel of meaning.

SQ3R means survey (preview), question, read (actively), recite, and review. This is an alternative method to the Four Step Reading Process. To learn more about SQ3R, search the Internet.

10 So how do you do that? Probably one of the best-known reading methods is called **SQ3R**, first used by F.P. Robinson in a 1946 book called *Effective Study*. Read the various study methods in Table 1 to determine which methods would work best for you, and try using a few of them this semester.

Table 1: Multiple Study Methods

VERBAL METHODS	VISUAL METHODS	AUDITORY METHODS	ACTION METHODS
• Use flash cards to identify main points or key terms. • Write out or recite key information in whole sentences or phrases in your own words. • When looking at diagrams, write out a description. • Use "sticky" notes to remind yourself of key terms and information, and put them in the notebook or text or on a mirror that you use frequently. • Practice spelling words or repeating facts to be remembered. • Rewrite things from memory	Make flash cards with pictures or diagrams to aid recall of key concepts. Make charts and diagrams and sum up information in tables. Use different colors of highlighter for different sections of information in text or notes. Visualize charts, diagrams, and figures. Trace letters and words to remember key facts. Redraw things from memory.	Join or form a study group or find a study partner so that you can discuss concepts and ideas. While studying, speak out loud or into a digital recorder that you can play back later. Make speeches. Record the lectures (with permission). Take notes on the lecture sparingly, using the recording to fill in parts that you might have missed. Read notes or text material into a digital recorder or get study materials recorded and play back while driving or doing other chores. When learning something new, state or explain the information in your own words out loud or to a study partner. Use musical rhythms as memory aids, or put information to a rhyme or a tune.	Sit near the front of the classroom and take notes by jotting down key terms and making pictures or charts to help you remember what you are hearing. While studying, walk back and forth as you read out loud. Study with a friend. While exercising, listen to recordings you have made of important information. Write out key concepts on a large board or poster. Make flash cards, using different colors and diagrams, and lay them out on a large surface. Practice putting them in order. Make a three-dimensional model. Spend extra time in the lab. Go to outside areas such as a museum or historical site to gain information.

1,192 words divided by .... minutes = ... words per minute

MyReadingLab

Reading 2
REVIEW

A good review strategy to use after reading is to summarize what you just read in your own words. Take a few minutes to think about the author's most important point and any key ideas that helped to support or explain it.

After you preview the article, write one or two preview questions on the lines below:

....

....

....

....

....

MyReadingLab

Reading 2
COMPREHENSION QUESTIONS

The following questions will help you to recall the main idea and the details of the article. Review any parts of the article that you need to find the correct answers.

FOUR STEP READING

1. Before reading the article, which of the following actions did you do to preview it? (Choose all that apply.)

a. made notes in the margins
b. read the title and subheadings
c. made up questions that might be answered in the article
d. underlined important ideas

2. As you read the article using active reading strategies you should have (Choose all that apply.)

a. predicted what would come next.
b. read through the entire article without stopping.
c. visualized ideas using mental imagery.
d. related what you knew about the topic to new information.

3. When you finished reading a section of the article you should have (Choose all that apply.)

a. made notes in the margins to annotate.
b. gone on to read the next section without stopping.
c. summarized what the section was about in your own words.
d. underlined or highlighted key points.

TOPIC AND MAIN IDEA

4. What is the topic, or subject, of this selection?

a. Study Methods: Different Strokes for Different Folks
b. Learning styles
c. Study tips for college students
d. Keeping up with college work

5. Which of the following is the author's overall most important message, or central point?

a. Many college students have a hard time getting good grades.

b. To get good grades in college, students must study more.

c. College work is much more difficult than students expect it will be.

d. Students should know five things in order to do their absolute best in any college course.

6. What is the author's most important point, or main idea, of paragraph 7?

a. How should you go about reading a textbook so that you get the most out of your reading efforts?

b. Students make two common mistakes in regard to reading a textbook.

c. The first mistake is simple: many students don't bother to read the textbook before going to the lecture that will cover that material.

d. First-time college students have no idea how they should prepare for class.

7. Which of the following states the overall most important point, or main idea, of paragraph 8?

a. The second mistake that most students make when reading textbook material is to try to read it the same way they would read a novel: They start at the first page and read continuously.

b. With a novel, it's easy to do this because the plot is usually interesting and people want to know what happens next, so they keep reading.

c. It isn't necessary to remember every little detail—all they need to remember are the main plot points.

d. Meatloaf can be eaten quickly, without even chewing for very long.

SUPPORTING DETAILS

8. According to the article, a learning style is

a. the particular way in which a person takes in, or absorbs, information.

b. the method you should use to study if you prefer action methods of learning.

c. the method you use to study information.

d. the method an instructor uses when teaching.

DRAWING CONCLUSIONS

9. From reading this selection, you could conclude that

a. college is a challenge even for the most accomplished students.

b. reading college textbooks and preparing for classes requires preparation.

c. students who use the SQ3R method have higher grades than those who do not.

d. students can take notes on lectures or video presentations to learn without having to read their textbooks.

VOCABULARY IN CONTEXT

10. Determine the meaning of the underlined word in the following sentence: No real evidence exists that <u>tailoring</u> the presentation of information to different learning styles has any effect on a student's ability to learn the information.

a. suiting

b. developing

c. customizing

d. enlarging

MyReadingLab

Reading 2 QUESTIONS FOR WRITING AND DISCUSSION

Review any parts of the article you need to answer the following questions.

1. What is the reason why many students do not have the higher grades that they wish they could earn?

2. What are five "how to's" that students should know in order to do their best in college?

3. What is a learning style and how does knowing their learning styles help students?

4. What are four types of studying methods that students should learn to use?

5. Which of the four types of study methods do you prefer to use, and which specific study techniques have been most successful for you?

Reading 2
VOCABULARY PRACTICE: SENTENCE COMPLETION

Practice the vocabulary words from the article "Study Methods: Different Strokes for Different Folks" by writing the letters of the words from the word list in the blanks to complete each sentence correctly. (The numbers in parentheses indicate the paragraph number where the word can be found in the article.)

WORD BANK

a. accommodating (3)	b. supplement (3)	c. literature (4)
d. capabilities (4)	e. implication (5)	f. disservice (5)
g. modalities (5)	h. academia (5)	

1. If the storm continues to follow a straight path up the coast, the .... is that many more homes and businesses could lose power.

2. Studying by using several .... such as the visual method, auditory method, verbal method, and action method can improve your grades in college.

3. While doing research for my history paper, I read the .... from several different sources.

4. .... teaching methods to different learning styles requires a variety of approaches.

5. Telling students exactly what questions will be on a test is doing them a .... because they will only study what they need instead of the whole topic.

6. It is a good idea to .... your class instruction with some tutoring or a study group that meets regularly.

7. In .... you will find many professors who have devoted their entire lives to studying a specific subject.

8. Students are not always aware of their .... when they begin college, but they soon realize they are able to do more than they believed possible.

MyReadingLab

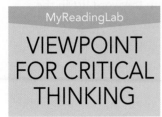

VIEWPOINT FOR CRITICAL THINKING

ONLINE DEGREE PROGRAMS

To help reduce the costs of higher education and accommodate the busy schedules of college students, most colleges and universities now offer online courses and some even offer entire online degree programs. Are online college degrees as valid as those earned by attending classes on campus? With a partner or team, list the positive points (pros) and negative points (cons) of online college degrees in the table below. After you complete this section, discuss the question in the box below to arrive at a conclusion and write in your answer.

Question: Do you think an online college degree is as good as one that has been earned on campus by attending classes (including hybrid classes)?

Pros of Online College Degrees	Cons of Online College Degrees

Conclusion: Are online college degree programs as good as college degrees earned on campus? Why or why not?

MyReadingLab

REAL-LIFE READING

FINANCIAL AID SOURCES

The following information about financial aid for college is from the federal student aid Web site. Preview the selection first, and then use the Four Step Reading Process and answer the review questions that follow.

Some Types of Financial Aid for College

Federal Perkins Loans

A Federal Perkins Loan is a low-interest (5 percent) loan for both undergraduate and graduate students who have exceptional financial need. Federal Perkins Loans are made through a school's financial aid office. Your school is your lender, and the loan is made with government funds. You must repay this loan to your school.

You can borrow up to $5,500 for each year of undergraduate study (the total you can borrow as an undergraduate is $27,500). For graduate studies, you can borrow up to $8,000 per year (the total you can borrow as a graduate is $60,000, which includes amounts borrowed as an undergraduate). The amount you receive depends on the date you apply, your financial need, and the funding level at the school. There are no other charges for this loan. However, if you skip a payment, if it's late, or if you make less than a full payment, you might have to pay a late charge plus any collection costs. If you're attending school at least half time, you have nine months after you graduate, leave school, or drop below half-time status before you must begin repayment. This is called a "grace period." If you're attending less than half time, check with your college or career school to find out how long your grace period will be.

Subsidized Versus Unsubsidized Loans

If a loan is **subsidized** by the government, the federal government pays the interest on your loan while you are attending school at least half time and during the grace and deferment periods. With an **unsubsidized** loan, the student is responsible for paying the interest on the loan from the day he or she receives the money. This additional interest charge is added to the balance of the loan.

Federal Supplemental Educational Opportunity Grants

Federal Supplemental Educational Opportunity Grants (FSEOG) are for undergraduates who have exceptional financial need. Pell Grant recipients with the lowest EFCs (Expected Family Contributions) will be the first to get FSEOGs. Just like Pell Grants, FSEOGs don't have to be paid back. You can receive between $100 and $4,000 a year, depending on the date you apply, your financial need, the funding at the school you're attending, and the policies of the financial aid office at your school.

1. Which type of financial aid described above must be paid back, and what are the terms for repayment?

....

....

....

....

Continued...

MyReadingLab

REAL-LIFE READING

...continued

2. Which type of financial aid described above will offer you the most money, and how much can you get?

3. What is the main difference between a subsidized loan and an unsubsidized loan?

4. What happens if you take a Perkins Loan and drop some classes so that you are less than half-time?

5. Have you applied for financial aid, and if so, what type of aid are you receiving?

MyReadingLab

BUILDING VOCABULARY

Knowing the meanings to many word parts will help you determine the meanings of unfamiliar words. Make a list of English words using only the word parts in the table below. If you are unsure about a word, consult a dictionary.

PREFIXES	ROOTS	SUFFIXES
re-: *again*	tract: *to draw, to drag*	-er, -or: *one who*
e-, ex-: *out*	port: *to carry*	-able, -ible: *being able to*
		-tion, -sion: *action, state of*

WORDS

Use one of the words in your word list in a sentence that reveals its meaning with a context clue. Read the sentence to a classmate and ask him or her to define the word.

MyReadingLab

CHAPTER PRACTICE 1

Follow the Four Step Reading Process for the passage below. Highlight and annotate key points in the margins. Use the lines below to write one or two preview questions.

1. Preview questions:

COLLEGE DO'S AND DON'TS

Punctual Payments
Be sure to read through your college catalog's sections on academic services and policies. Pay close attention to financial deadlines, such as when final payment is due for your tuition. If you're late with a payment, you may be withdrawn from all of your classes, and colleges sometimes send unpaid bills to a collection agency. Avoid this stress by planning how you will meet your financial obligations and making the payments early.

College Regulations
Abide by the college's rules regarding parking. Unpaid parking tickets may put a hold on your account, meaning you will not be able to receive your grades or register for courses until your parking fines are paid. Before classes begin, get your parking permit and know where you are allowed to park so you can avoid costly parking tickets. The same applies to library fees. If you are late returning materials and run up a fine, your account may be put on hold until all library fees are paid.

Getting Information
Read your emails! Your college and professors will send you important information through your college email account. Check it every day because you may have messages dealing with course payments, schedule changes, cancelled classes, special events, or scholarship information. If you change your address or phone number during the semester, be sure to let the admissions office know so they can contact you on matters of importance.

REVIEW

Review the information by answering the following questions.

2. What might happen if you don't pay your tuition and fees on time?

3. Why should you abide by the college's parking regulations?

....

....

4. Why is it important to read your college emails?

....

....

5. Make annotations in the margins.

MyReadingLab

CHAPTER PRACTICE 2

Follow the Four Step Reading Process for the passage below. Highlight and annotate key points in the margins. Use the lines below to write one or two preview questions.

1. Preview questions:

....

....

....

GETTING ALONG WITH PROFESSORS

Most college professors want to see their students succeed. They are willing to put in time and effort to help you learn, but they expect you to do your part. This is usually spelled out in detail on the course syllabus, but if it isn't, be sure to ask. In general, if you come to class on time, are not disruptive, keep your phone off and out of sight, and pay attention, you should have no problems getting along with professors. Most professors have high expectations for their students, meaning they expect you to attend class and do your work to the best of your ability.

Many professors do not accept late assignments or tests and if you miss one, you may receive a zero. However, if you encounter a real emergency and miss an important test or assignment, you should contact your instructor and explain your situation *before* it's due if possible, not after. Letting professors know that you are in a unique situation may sway them to allow you some extra time.

If you are failing a course, don't expect the professor to give you a passing grade based on your personality, contributions in class, or how much you enjoy the subject. In college, grades are based on your work and your ability to prove that you understand the material and can apply what you have learned. Your professor may like you

Continued...

immensely but if your grades are failing, you will not pass the course. If you need extra help, your professor is your best resource to help you through a difficult course. Establishing a good relationship with your professor can be very beneficial to your learning.

REVIEW

Review the information by answering the following questions.

2. What are some expectations that professors have for students?

....

....

3. What should you do if you have to miss a test or can't hand in an assignment that is due?

....

....

4. In college, what is the basis for your grade?

....

....

5. Make annotations in the margins.

MyReadingLab

CHAPTER PRACTICE 3

Follow the Four Step Reading Process for the passage below. Highlight and annotate key points in the margins. Use the lines below to write one or two preview questions.

1. Preview questions:

....

....

....

COLLEGE CATALOG EXCERPT: COURSE ATTEMPTS AND COURSE WITHDRAWAL

It is your responsibility to verify the effects of enrollment and/or withdrawal upon your financial assistance (financial aid, scholarships, grants, etc.). Agencies and organizations which provide financial assistance like scholarships (federal and state government, private organizations, etc.) may have requirements relative to withdrawal, course repeats and grade forgiveness that are more strict than state or college requirements. Requirements vary from state to state, so read your college catalog to find out the rules for course attempts and withdrawals.

According to some state rules you may attempt the same course only three times, including the original grade, repeat grades and withdrawals at any point in the term. Students in Bachelor's degree programs are limited to only two attempts. The "same course" means that the subject prefix and course number are the same when posted on your college transcript. Also, courses that have been deemed "equivalent" will all count as attempts, even if the current course number is different than the course in your previous attempt(s). Enrolling in a course for credit after the Drop/Refund Deadline counts as an attempt.

Before you withdraw from a course, you should be aware that course withdrawals:

- Will increase the cost of your education because you must pay for the course again each time you repeat it
- May affect your financial aid status because some scholarships have strict rules about withdrawals
- May affect your transfer grade point average
- May affect your anticipated graduation date if you have to repeat one or more courses
- May result in your being denied access to limited access programs
- May affect your eligibility for the Honors Program
- May affect your immigration status if you are attending college on a non-immigrant visa
- Will result in your required repayment of course fees paid by a state scholarship.

If you withdraw during a term, you are required to withdraw prior to the withdrawal deadline. The withdrawal deadlines for each term are published in the College Calendar in the official catalog. All requests for withdrawals must be submitted by 11:59 p.m. on the withdrawal deadline date. Before you withdraw:

- Talk with your professor to discuss your progress in the course, and whether withdrawal is the best course of action to take.
- Contact a student advisor to discuss how a withdrawal will affect your career and education plans and/or the status of your financial aid.

Continued...

2. Review: Write a short summary of the main points.

....

....

....

3. What are some of the implications of withdrawing from a course in college?

....

....

....

4. What should you do before withdrawing from a course?

....

....

....

5. Make annotations in the margins.

CHAPTER REVIEW: USING CORNELL NOTES TO REVIEW

To review the most important information in a textbook, it is often helpful to create notes either on paper or on the computer. One style of note-taking is the Cornell Notes method. To create Cornell Notes, you should:

1. Divide your paper into two columns.
2. Take notes on a lecture or reading in the right column.
3. Later, write questions or topics in the left side from the notes.
4. To study, cover the right column and read the questions in the left column, reciting the answers.
5. Check your answers using the right column to see if you are correct.

Directions: Complete the following Cornell Notes on the information in this chapter.

Question (Cue) Column	Notes Column
1. Why is reading an important skill for college?	
2. What does it mean to have "the right attitude" and how will it help you succeed?	
3. What are some ways you can help to improve your grades?	
4. What should students do before withdrawing from a class?	
5. Why should you read your syllabus carefully?	

ON THE WEB

To learn more about your learning styles, research online or visit the VARK Web site. Take a survey to find out your preferred learning styles. There are free surveys online at websites such as the learning-styles-online Web site.

MyReadingLab

MyReadingLab

MyReadingLab is a Web site published by Pearson Education. The lab assignments in this text coordinate with the skills that are taught in this course. Once you are registered to use MyReadingLab, your name and all of your scores will be recorded and saved, but only you and your instructor will be able to see the results. You will have a secure password to access your account.

What Is in MyReadingLab?

On this Web site, there are overviews and models of the reading skills, as well as animations to help illustrate them. Reading passages and questions provide independent skills practice and immediate feedback with explanations for incorrect answers. You can also answer the questions in this textbook online using the e-text.

Besides skill practices, MyReadingLab also contains study skill resources and Lexile readings. A Lexile is a type of score that measures your overall comprehension based on how many questions you answer correctly. You can choose your Lexile readings from a variety of interesting topics. As you improve in your reading comprehension, you will be given stories at higher Lexile reading levels. The more questions you answer correctly, the higher your Lexile score will go. By the end of the course, you will see an improvement in your reading comprehension if you read carefully and answer the questions to the best of your ability. Remember that the purpose of the lab is to help you to improve your reading comprehension. If you take short cuts and don't put in your best effort, you will not see much improvement. Plan enough time in your study schedule to complete the lab assignments without rushing through them. Do them to the best of your ability, and you will see improvement over the duration of the course.

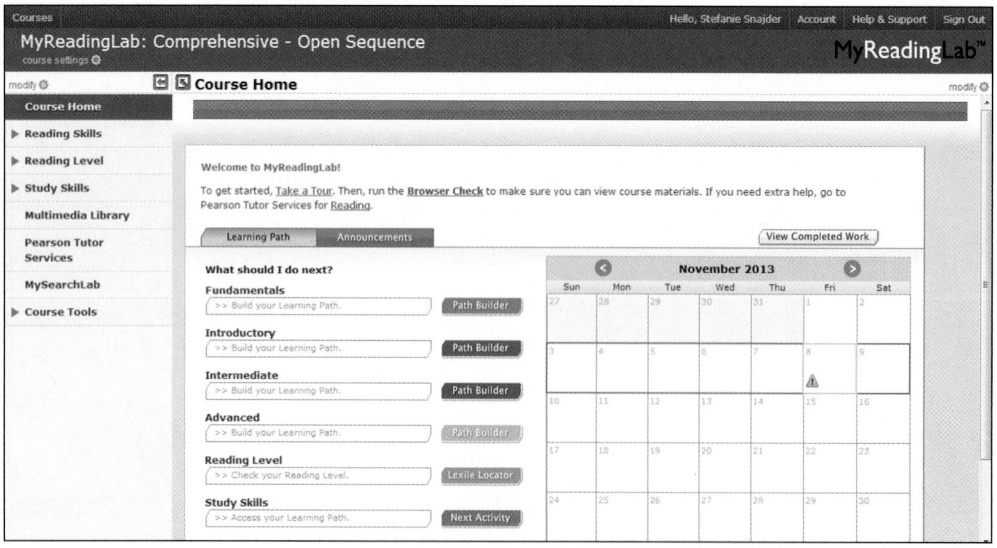

MyReadingLab

READING LAB ASSIGNMENTS

1. Login to MyReadingLab and in the menu click on **Reading Skills**. In the **Learning Path** on the main screen select *Active Reading*. Review this skill by reading the brief overview and models. Watch the short animation and then complete any practices or tests to check your understanding.

2. Click on **Reading Level** in the menu and take the reading diagnostic **Lexile Locator**. Once your initial Lexile reading level is measured, you will be able to choose interesting stories to read in future assignments. Your Lexile level will increase as your reading comprehension improves.

Metacognition

Metacognition is the concept of thinking about learning. By taking a few minutes to think about *how* you learned something, you can improve your learning significantly over the course of a semester. What methods did you use to learn? How did they work? What learning styles did you use? Which learning styles work best for you? As you answer the questions below, think about how you have learned the information in this chapter.

MyReadingLab

MONITOR YOUR LEARNING

In this chapter you learned about using context clues and word part clues to determine the meanings of unfamiliar words. Write a paragraph telling what you learned about these skills, how you learned them, and how you can use them to improve your learning and reading comprehension. When you have finished writing, read your paragraph as if you were reading someone else's paragraph for the first time. Check for missing words, spelling, punctuation, and sentence structure.

2 BUILDING VOCABULARY SKILLS

FOCUS ON: You

This chapter focuses on understanding and learning about you—your motives, your relationships, your personality and strengths. When you better understand your own motivations, ideals, and values, it unlocks doors in your relationships with other people, whether they are friends, coworkers, or romantic partners. Similarly, understanding the meanings of words in a written text unlocks the author's message. Knowledge is power, and the more you know about yourself, the better equipped you will be to face the challenges ahead.

In this chapter you will:

LEARNING OBJECTIVES

1. use context clues to determine the meanings of unfamiliar words.
2. learn how to monitor your comprehension as you read.
3. use word part clues to determine the meanings of unfamiliar words.

As you learn new words in this chapter, learn their standard pronunciations by using an online dictionary such as *Dictionary.com* to hear how they are most often pronounced.

Building Vocabulary Skills

The more words of which you know their meanings, the better your reading comprehension will be. For example, if you were told to *garez la voiture*, you wouldn't know what to do unless you understood the meanings of those words in French. Knowing the meanings of many words is the key to understanding any language, which is what reading comprehension is all about.

In college, you'll encounter many new terms for the first time. In some subjects you'll learn whole new languages of jargon, or terminology spoken only in particular fields. So you will be learning new vocabulary continually because you must know the meanings of the terms being used in order to comprehend the concepts. This chapter teaches you how to figure out the meanings of new words using two effective vocabulary strategies without having to look up every new word.

OBJECTIVE 1

Use context clues to determine the meanings of unfamiliar words.

WHAT ARE CONTEXT CLUES?

Context clues are words surrounding an unfamiliar word that help you to determine its meaning.

Context clues are words surrounding an unfamiliar word that help you to determine its meaning. Sometimes it is necessary to read the entire paragraph to figure out the meaning of a word, but in many cases you can find context clues within the sentence. For instance, what is the meaning of the word in bold print in the following sentence?

> When the defendant was brought to trial, he was **exculpated** and released by the judge.

What words in the sentence offer clues to the meaning of *exculpated*? What word or phrase would fit in place of the word *exculpated* in this sentence? Notice that the defendant "was released." What circumstances would allow this defendant to be released after the trial? Most likely he was found not guilty. And the word *exculpated* does mean *cleared of guilt.*

The key to finding meaning in context is to look for several different types of context clues. Generally, there are five types to look for; remembering the word "L.E.A.D.S." will help you remember them:

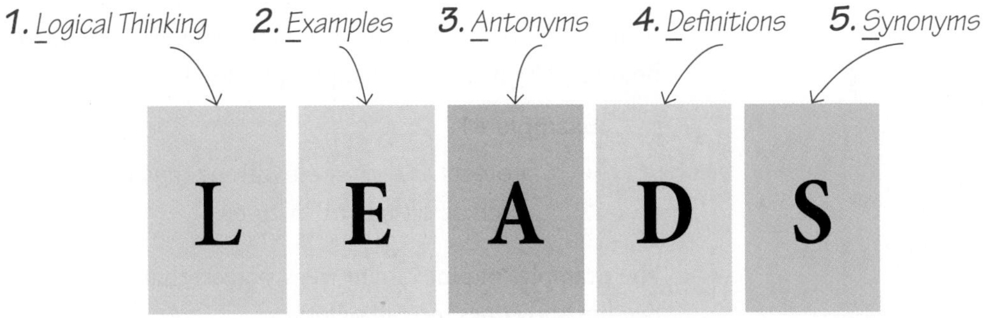

If you are trying to solve the mystery of a word's meaning, you must think like a detective and look for leads. Let's look at each type of clue in more detail.

CONTEXT CLUES: 1

Logical Thinking

When you come across an unfamiliar word or term, try reasoning, or logical thinking, to figure out the meaning. Substitute a blank for the unfamiliar word and use your prior knowledge (everything you know about a topic) to help you fill in the blank with a word or phrase familiar to you. Read the following examples and try to determine the meanings of the words in bold print by figuring out what word or phrase would make sense in place of the word in bold print. Look for clues in the sentences to help you.

Example #1:

> A person who administers emergency first aid must be **cognizant** of the patient's present condition. Factors such as pulse, respiration, and body temperature should all be taken into consideration.

Notice the second sentence that tells you all the factors that must be *known* before administering first aid. *Cognizant* means (being) *aware of,* or *knowledgeable about* something.

Example #2:

> Dr. Willard's work has been an **invaluable** part of our research in finding a cure for this disease. Without his contributions we wouldn't have discovered these new treatments and therapies.

In the second sentence we are told that the new treatments and therapies would not be possible without Dr. Willard's work. Therefore, *invaluable* means *of great value or importance.*

CONTEXT CLUES: 2

Example Clues

Sometimes you can determine the meaning of an unfamiliar word by studying the examples that are given in the sentence or paragraph. Look for transitional phrases that signal an example, such as:

such as   for example   to illustrate   for instance

Read the following sentences and try to determine the meanings of the words in bold print by using the examples provided.

Example #1:

> Forests at higher elevations may consist of **coniferous** trees such as pines and fir trees.

The examples of pine and fir trees suggest that *coniferous* trees are those with needles and cones instead of leaves.

Example #2:

> Our assignment was to collect samples of **zoophytes**, and I found some sponges and corals while I was snorkeling down on the reefs.

The examples of *sponges* and *corals* provide the clues that *zoophytes* are types of marine life.

CONTEXT CLUES: 3

Antonym Clues

antonym: a word that means the opposite of another word.

An **antonym** is a word that means the opposite of another word. Often an author will supply a word that means the opposite of the unfamiliar word, and will signal this with a transitional phrase such as:

however   on the other hand   although   but   yet   instead

Read the following examples and try to determine the meanings of the words in bold print by finding words with opposite meanings in the same sentence.

Example #1:

> *Although* Robert is not very **perspicacious**, his sister is very sharp mentally.

The word *although* indicates an opposite idea is being presented in the same sentence. Robert's sister is very sharp mentally but Robert is not; therefore, *perspicacious* means *mentally sharp*.

Example #2:

> The author was **prodigious** in his later years, but he did not produce many notable works in his early career.

The transition word *but* in the sentence indicates an opposite idea will be presented. The two opposite ideas are that the author produced *many* works in his later years but did *not* produce *many* works in his early career. Therefore, *prodigious* means *produced a great amount.*

CONTEXT CLUES: 4

Definition Clues

Authors often provide definitions of new terms, especially in textbooks. Often you will see a term in bold or italic print followed by a definition. A lengthy explanation may follow if the term is a difficult concept to understand, and may also include examples of the term. Definitions are often given in a sentence following punctuation such as commas, dashes, brackets, or parentheses. Also look for these transitional phrases whenever you encounter a new term in a sentence:

means   refers to   is defined as   is known as   is   are

Example #1:

> The applied field of psychology that seeks to assess, understand and treat psychological conditions in clinical practice *is known as* **clinical psychology**.

The definition precedes the term *clinical psychology* in bold print and is introduced by the transitional phrase *is known as.*

Example #2:

> **Psychiatry** *is* the study and treatment of mental disorders—which include various behavioral, cognitive, and perceptual disorders.

Notice the transitional word *is.* Terms are often defined after the transitional word *is* (or *are* for plural forms.)

Example #3:

> In recent years, the use of fluorescent light has become more popular than **incandescent** (an electric light bulb with a filament heated by an electric current) lamps.

The definition for *incandescent* is provided within the parentheses. Sometimes brackets, dashes, or commas are used to set off a definition.

CONTEXT CLUES: 5

synonym: a word that means the same as another word.

Synonyms

Synonyms are similar to definitions, but consist of one word that means the same as the unknown word. Transitional words may or may not be present with synonyms. Study the following sentences to find the words that mean the same as the words in bold print.

Example #1:

Chad's English teacher commented that his writing was **trite** due to his overuse of common phrases that became tiresome and stale.

The causes of Chad's *trite* writing were the *tiresome* and *stale* phrases he used; both *tiresome* and *stale* are synonyms for *trite.*

Example #2:

Her character in the film is so **malicious** that her mean and evil ways bring about her downfall.

In this sentence, the words *mean* and *evil* provide synonyms for the word *malicious.*

OBJECTIVE **2**

Learn how to monitor your comprehension as you read.

MONITOR YOUR COMPREHENSION —USE YOUR BRAIN'S GPS

Your car's GPS is programmed to tell you when you are going in the right direction and when you are off course while heading for your destination. It hastily announces "recalculating" in that annoying voice that tells you an error has been made. We all have our own mental GPS systems, but we often ignore them or don't turn them on. If we are reading something and it doesn't make sense, our **general practical sense—GPS** or *common sense*—should tell us to "recalculate," to go back and reread the sentence until it makes sense. Yet many students ignore this important warning system, or perhaps never turn it on. They look at the first few letters of a word and guess at it rather than looking at the entire word and all of its parts. This type of error results in poor comprehension for many readers. Their GPS, or common sense, fails to let them know that the sentence they read incorrectly is not making sense. Often the error is so great that it will completely destroy their comprehension of a paragraph or an entire chapter because they have misread so many words that nothing makes sense.

Always think and visualize as you read and if something doesn't make sense, go back and reread. Good readers monitor their comprehension as they read: They use their GPS!

Improve Accuracy by Reading Words Closely

One of the most common reading errors that destroys comprehension is misreading words. Many sight word readers do not differentiate between a word's parts, and misread words that look alike. Paying close attention to the syllables that make up words is important because even one letter can make a huge difference in a word's meaning. Read the following examples and the explanations that follow.

Example #1:

Daniella's (conscious, conscience) would not allow her to cheat on the exam.

The word *conscious* means awake, but the word *conscience* means one's sense of right or wrong, so the second word is the correct answer.

Example #2:

Psychologists believe that certain experiences will (elicit, illicit) specific memories and behaviors in most people.

Elicit means to bring forth, or evoke, whereas *illicit* means something prohibited by law or custom. Therefore, the first word is the correct one.

Parts of Speech

Knowing the structure of language can also provide clues to help you determine what type of word an unfamiliar word may be. **Parts of speech** identify types of words and can offer clues for the meaning for the unknown word. Some common parts of speech are:

nouns: persons, places, things, states, or qualities
adjectives: words that describe or modify nouns
verbs: action or state-of-being words
adverbs: words that describe or modify verbs

Using the list above, determine which parts of speech belong in the following sentences.

1. Whales are very .... animals that live in the oceans.

2. We were .... off the coast of Australia when the storm hit.

3. The child cried .... when her brother stole her candy.

4. A .... can be found within an animal cell.

Explanation:
The first sentence needs an adjective to describe the whales. Adjectives often precede nouns in sentences, so if the unfamiliar word comes before a noun, you will know that it is most likely an adjective. Intensifying adverbs like "very" also often modify adjectives, so adjective is the best choice here. In sentence two, the helping verb "were" indicates that a main verb will follow. In the third sentence, a word is needed to describe *how* the child is crying, so an adverb is needed. In sentence 4, the blank is preceded by an article, *a*. Nouns follow articles such as *a, an,* or *the*, so a noun is missing.

MyReadingLab

PRACTICE 1

Use context clues (L.E.A.D.S) and parts of speech to determine the meanings of the underlined words, write a brief definition, and identify the word's part of speech. Underline the part of the sentence that helped you determine the word's meaning.

1. Some children in itinerant families rarely stay in one place long enough for them to finish the school year at the same school.

   Brief definition: ....

   Part of speech: ....

2. Professor Callahan stood on the rostrum and welcomed the new graduates.

   Brief definition: ....

   Part of speech: ....

3. If you do not agree to the terms of this contract and do not sign your name, the contract will be nullified.

   Brief definition: ....

   Part of speech: ....

4. Every spring, the snake will exuviate its old skin after it has grown a new one.

   Brief definition: ....

   Part of speech: ....

5. Elsie was very thin, but her husband was quite corpulent.

   Brief definition: ....

   Part of speech: ....

MyReadingLab

PRACTICE 2

Use context clues (L.E.A.D.S) to determine the meanings of the underlined words, and write a brief definition. Underline the part of the sentence that helped you determine the word's meaning.

1. Instead of cooperating with the police, the accused was very renitent.

   Brief definition: ....

2. Many crustaceans, such as lobsters and crabs, are in danger of being over-fished.

   Brief definition: ....

3. The experience of receiving a reprimand can lower self-esteem, but receiving praise can raise it.

   Brief definition: ....

4. Viruses are not considered living things because they cannot replicate themselves without a host cell. However, bacteria are able to copy themselves and therefore are living things.

   Brief definition: ....

5. With the exception of smell, all incoming sensory information first comes into the thalamus and then is sent to other parts of the brain for processing.

   Brief definition: ....

MyReadingLab

PRACTICE 3

Use context clues (L.E.A.D.S) to determine the meanings of the underlined words, and choose the correct definition. Underline the part of the sentence that helped you determine the word's meaning.

Fritz Heider (1896–1988) outlined how expectations relate to internal and external forces of motivation. Heider (1958) [1] postulated that the outcome of your behavior (a poor grade, for example) can be [2] attributed to [3] dispositional forces, such as lack of effort or insufficient intelligence, or to situational forces, such as an unfair test or a biased teacher. These [4] attributions influence the way you will behave. You are likely to try harder next time if you see your poor grade as a result of your lack of effort, but you may give up if you see it as resulting from injustice or lack of ability (Dweck, 1975). Thus the identification of a source of motivation as internal or external may depend, in part, on your own [5] subjective interpretation of reality.

Directions: Match each underlined word to one of the definitions below. There will be one definition left over.

.... **1.** postulated	**a.** related to
.... **2.** attributed	**b.** causes
.... **3.** dispositional	**c.** personal
.... **4.** attributions	**d.** proposed
.... **5.** subjective	**e.** one's nature
	f. caused by

U-REVIEW 1

On the following chart, review the types of clues that help improve your vocabulary by filling in the missing details.

TYPE OF CLUE	DEFINITION	EXAMPLE OF CLUE
Logic of the Passage	Look for other words in the sentence or paragraph and your prior knowledge to provide clues.	....
....	Look for examples in the sentence or paragraph that illustrate the unfamiliar word.	Behaviors *such as* talking on the phone or texting while someone is speaking to you are ill-mannered.
Antonyms	....	*Instead of* trying to write about a specific episode in your book report, write a more *holistic* summary of the entire novel.
Definitions	....	Tree rings show how much *precipitation* (rain or snow) occurred during each year.
Synonyms	Look for a word that means the same as the unfamiliar word.	....
Parts of Speech	Nouns, verbs, adjectives, and adverbs	....

OBJECTIVE 3

Use word part clues to determine the meanings of unfamiliar words.

WORD PART SKILLS

The English language, though it has its roots in an ancient Germanic language, has vocabulary derived from many different languages. Most English words come from Latin and Greek, although many other languages are also represented and often found in the three main parts that make up words known as **prefixes, roots,** and **suffixes**. You are probably already familiar with many word parts and their meanings, such as *re-* (again) or *un-* (not). Knowing the meanings of more word parts will help you determine the meanings of many more words and improve your comprehension. To do this, you must break words down into smaller parts to figure out their meanings by looking for the following:

1. A **prefix** is found at the beginning of a word that changes a word's meaning

   Examples:

   different, **in**different   position, **re**position
   marital, **extra**marital

2. A **root** (or *base*) carries the meaning of a word.

   Examples:

   valid, in**valid**,   **believe**, dis**believe**,
   reasonable, un**reason**able

3. A **suffix** is found at the end of a word and changes the part of speech.

   Examples:

   vary **(verb)**   vari**able (noun or adjective)**   vari**ation (noun)**

Tips to Keep in Mind

1. Some words have no prefixes or suffixes, like the word *happy,* but prefixes and suffixes can be added to them (*unhappy, happiness*).
2. Sometimes the spelling of a word may change as prefixes and suffixes are added, but the root of the word still has the same meaning. For example, in the word *happiness*, the *y* changes to an *i* before the suffix is added.
3. Some word parts can have more than one meaning. For example: The root "mit" or "mis" means *to send.* In the word *transmit* the prefix "trans" means *across. Transmit* means *to send across.* In the word *misspell,* the prefix "mis" means wrongly or badly.
4. Because English uses words from many languages, there may be more than one prefix, root, or suffix that has a similar meaning. For example: *uni-* and *mono-* are both prefixes meaning *one.* For example: A *uni*cycle has one wheel and a *monorail* has one rail.

Using Word Parts

The following charts of prefixes, roots, and suffixes will help you determine the meanings of words. Learn the meanings to as many word parts as you can so you will figure out the meanings of unfamiliar words whenever you encounter them.

PREFIXES	ROOTS	SUFFIXES
anti-: against, opposite of	**cardia**, **cardium**: heart	**-able**, **-ible**: a condition of being able to
con-: together, with	**cap**: to hold	**-ate**: to cause to become
de-: to reverse	**circ**: around; circular	**-al**, **-ary**, **-ship**, **-hood**: pertaining to
dys-: ill or bad	**carcer**: prison	**-ance**, **-ence**: a condition or quality
ex-: out; former	**habit**: to hold or have	**-ant**, **-ent**, **-er**, **-or**, **-ist**: one who
il-, **im-**, **in-**: not	**humus**: earth; soil	-**ious**, **-ness**, **-ion**, **-ity**, **-ive**: a condition or quality
in-: to put into	**path:** feeling	**-less**: without
ir: not	**permit**: to allow	**-ment**: an action or product
neuro-, **neur**: nerve	**phob**: fear	**-ness**: having the quality of
over-: excessively	**sacra**: sacred	**-tude**: having the quality of
peri-: surrounding around, through	**scien:** to know	**-ward**: in the direction of
post-: after	**sens**, **sent**: to feel	
pro-: supporting	**tract**, **tric**: to pull	
pulmo-: lung	**worth**: value	
re-: again		

MyReadingLab

PRACTICE 4

Underline the words that correctly complete the following sentences by paying close attention to each word's spelling and word parts.

1. Jessica always did her homework and studied for every test. She was a very (contentious, conscientious) student.
2. The robber was arrested and charged with possession of (illicit, elicit) drugs and first degree larceny.
3. We have brought Dr. Kline, a very (notable, noticeable) speaker, to lecture about the latest applications of gene therapy in medicine.
4. My boss offered me a new job and made a very interesting (preposition, proposition) that I may seriously consider taking.
5. To succeed at math, I must use all of my (consecration, concentration) when studying it.

MyReadingLab

PRACTICE 5

Use the word parts and context clues to determine the meanings of the underlined words in the paragraph below. Underline any clues in the paragraph that helped you determine the word's meaning. Next, choose the correct meaning for each word.

1. The pathologist extracted the pulmonary tubes from the body to determine the cause of death.
   - **a.** pertaining to the heart
   - **b.** leading to the stomach
   - **c.** pertaining to the lungs
   - **d.** leading to the kidneys
2. The woman's antipathy toward her coworkers was obvious and they responded in like manner.
   - **a.** kindness
   - **b.** feelings against
   - **c.** disinterest
   - **d.** cooperation
3. The captain was awarded a medal posthumously for his bravery in battle.
   - **a.** before death
   - **b.** after the battle
   - **c.** during his lifetime
   - **d.** after death
4. Without our GPS we ended up taking a circuitous route to the county fairground.
   - **a.** direct
   - **b.** lost
   - **c.** long way around
   - **d.** short
5. The professor pointed to the pericardium on the anatomy illustration and asked students to give its name and function.
   - **a.** tissue surrounding the heart
   - **b.** tissue between the lungs
   - **c.** tissue around the brain
   - **d.** the lobe of an ear

MyReadingLab

PRACTICE 6

Use the word parts and context clues to determine the meanings of the underlined words in the paragraph below. Underline any clues in the paragraph that helped you determine the word's meaning. Next, choose the correct meaning for each word.

HOW MEMORY WORKS

The model of memory that many researchers feel is the most comprehensive and has perhaps been the most influential over the last several decades is the information-processing model. This approach focuses on the way information is handled, or processed, through three different systems of memory. The processes of encoding, storage, and retrieval are seen as part of this model. While it is common to refer to the three systems of the information-processing model as stages of memory, that term seems to imply a sequence of events. While many [1] aspects of memory formation may follow a series of steps or stages, there are those who see memory as a simultaneous process, with the creation and storage of memories taking place across a series of mental networks "stretched" across the brain (McClelland & Rumelhart, 1988; Plaut & McClelland, 2010; Rumelhart et al., 1986). This [2] simultaneous processing allows people to retrieve many different aspects of a memory all at once, [3] facilitating much faster reactions and decisions. This model of memory, [4] derived from work in the development of artificial intelligence (AI), is called the *parallel distributed processing* (PDP) model. In the AI world, PDP is related to connectionism (the use of artificial [5] neural networks to explain the mental abilities of humans (Bechtel & Abrahamsen, 2002; Clark, 1991; Marcus, 2001; Schapiro & McClelland, 2009).

1. aspects:
   - a. features
   - b. incidents
   - c. formulations
   - d. sequentia
2. simultaneous:
   - a. parallel to
   - b. acting upon
   - c. all at once
   - d. faster
3. facilitating:
   - a. storing
   - b. warehousing
   - c. information
   - d. causing
4. derived:
   - a. taken from
   - b. resulting in
   - c. enlarging
   - d. eliminated
5. neural:
   - a. relating to the brain
   - b. parallel
   - c. unbiased
   - d. features

U-REVIEW 2

For each of the following statements, write "T" if the statement is true or "F" if the statement is false. For each false statement, correct the statement to make it true.

1. .... Breaking words down into parts and looking at the meaning of each part can help you determine the meaning of an unknown word.

....

2. .... Suffixes come at the beginning of the word and change its meaning.

....

3. .... The prefix carries the meaning of the word.

....

4. .... The prefix comes at the beginning of a word and changes its meaning.

....

5. .... Some word parts can have more than one meaning.

....

MyReadingLab

Reading 1
VOCABULARY PREVIEW

"The Rules of Attraction" by Bjorn Carey

Match the list of words in the Word Bank to their correct meanings by writing the letter of the matching word next to the definition below. Use L.E.A.D.S. as you read the words in "The Rules of Attraction" to determine the correct meanings as they are used in context. The paragraph numbers in parentheses indicate the location of each word.

WORD BANK

a. infatuation (2)	b. symmetry (3)	c. encoded (7)
d. estrogen (9)	e. testosterone (9)	f. genes (15)
g. pheromones (16)	h. exude (16)	i. begets (20)
j. altruistic (23)	k. fidelity (29)	

1. .... to eject or emit
2. .... mirror image; both sides equal
3. .... female hormone
4. .... natural chemicals that influence behavior
5. .... causes
6. .... faithfulness
7. .... part of DNA; heredity
8. .... devoted to welfare of others
9. .... a foolish passion
10. .... male hormone
11. .... hidden in meaning

MyReadingLab

Reading 1 PREVIEW

Discuss the following questions with a partner or small group.

1. What biological factors do you think influence a person's attractiveness?
2. What traits or characteristics of another person's character do you find most attractive?

After you preview the article, write one or two preview questions on the lines below:

....

....

....

....

....

MyReadingLab

Reading 1

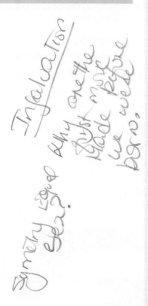

"The Rules of Attraction" by Bjorn Carey

What physical characteristics cause one person to be attracted to another? Scientists who have studied this phenomenon reveal their findings in this article about the scientific laws, or rules, of attraction. As you read the article, remember to use the Four Step Reading Process to monitor comprehension and study as you read.

1 To figure out how we pick mates, scientists have measured every shape and angle of the human face, studied the symmetry of dancers, crafted formulas from the measurements of Playboy models, and had both men and women rank attractiveness based on smelling armpit sweat. After all this and more, the rules of attraction for the human species are still not clearly understood. How it all factors into true love is even more mysterious.

2 But a short list of scientific rules for the game of love is emerging. Some are as clearly defined as the prominent, feminine eyes of a supermodel or the desirable hips of a well-built man. Other rules work at the subconscious level, motivating us to action for evolutionary reasons that are tucked inside clouds of infatuation. In the end, lasting love depends at least as much on behavior as biology. But the first moves are made before you're even born.

Symmetry equals sex

3 Starting at conception, the human body develops by neatly splitting cells. If every division were to go perfectly, the result would be a baby whose left and right sides are mirror images. But nature doesn't work that way. Genetic mutations and environmental pressures skew symmetry, and the

Continued...

MyReadingLab
Reading 1
...continued

What role does symmetry play in attraction?

Men & Women Rated symmetrical members of the opposite sex as more attractive and in better health than their less symmetrical counterparts.

results have lifelong implications. Good symmetry shows that an individual has the genetic goods to survive development, is healthy, and is a good and fertile choice for mating.

4 Randy Thornhill, an evolutionary biologist at the University of New Mexico has been studying symmetry for 15 years and scanned faces and bodies into computers to determine symmetry ratios. Both men and women rated symmetrical members of the opposite sex as more attractive and in better health than their less symmetrical counterparts. The differences can be just a few percent—perceivable though not necessarily noticeable. By questioning the study participants, Thornhill also found that men with higher degrees of symmetry enjoy more sexual partners than men of lower symmetry.

5 "Women's sex-partner numbers are dependent on things other than attractiveness," Thornhill told *LiveScience*. "Because of the way that the sexual system in humans works, women are choosey. They are being sexually competed *for*. They have to be wooed and all that."

Those hips

6 Body shape is of course important, too. And scientists have some numbers to prove it. Psychologist Devendra Singh of the University of Texas studied people's waist-to-hip ratio (WHR). Women with a WHR of 0.7—indicating a waist significantly narrower than the hips—are most desirable to men. And an analysis of hourglass figures of Playboy models and Miss America contestants showed that the majority of these women boast a WHR of 0.7* or lower.

(*This means that the waist measurement is approximately 70% of the hip measurement.)

Why is WHR important in selecting a mate?

It conveys information about health and fertility

7 In general, a range of 0.67 to 1.18 in females is attractive to men, Singh concluded in a 2004 study, while a 0.8 to 1.0 WHR in men is attractive to women; although having broad shoulders is more of a turn-on. What exactly is encoded in the hip ratio? A big fat clue to whether the person will have enough energy to care for offspring. People in the ideal hip-ratio range, regardless of weight, are less susceptible to disease such as cardiovascular disorders, cancer, and diabetes, studies have shown. Women in this range also have less difficulty conceiving.

8 "The idea is that beauty conveys information about health and fertility, and we admire that," Singh said in a telephone interview.

Face it

9 The structure of a person's face also gives insight to fertility. Estrogen caps bone growth in a woman's lower face and chin, making them relatively small and short, as well as the brow, allowing for her eyes to appear prominent, Thornhill explained. Men's faces are shaped by testosterone, which helps develop a larger lower face and jaw and a prominent brow.

How are estrogen and testosterone important in attraction?

10 Men and women possessing these traits are seen as attractive, Thornhill said, because they advertise reproductive health. Thornhill also points to the booming nip-'n'-tuck

business—which is very much about improving a person's symmetry—as evidence that people find the quality attractive.

Sniff this

11 Research reported last month found women both smell and look more attractive to men at certain times of the month. And symmetrical men smell better.

12 Borrowing sweaty undershirts from a variety of men, Thornhill offered the shirts to the noses of women, asking for their impressions of the scents. Hands down, the women found the scent of a symmetrical man to be more attractive and desirable.

13 By now you might be wondering how much of this we're consciously aware of. The rules of attraction, it turns out, seem sometimes to play out in our subconscious. In some cases, women in Thornhill's study reported not smelling anything on a shirt, yet still said they were attracted to it.

14 "We think the detection of these types of scent is way outside consciousness," Thornhill said.

What role does scent play in determining attraction?

15 A 2002 study found women prefer the scent of men with genes somewhat similar to their own over the scent of nearly genetically identical or totally dissimilar men.

Animal attraction

16 Pheromones clearly act as sexual attractants in the animal world. Older male elephants, for example, exude sexual prowess with a mix of chemicals the younger bulls can't muster. Milos Novotny of the Institute of Pheromone Research at Indiana University has shown that special molecules produced by male mice can simultaneously attract females and repel, and even anger, rival males. Other studies have found similar responses throughout the animal kingdom.

Sex goes visual

How do pheromones affect attraction?

17 Pheromones, like other scents, hitch a ride through the air on other particles, such as water droplets. They generally hover just 10 inches off the ground, however. So odds are slim they'll waft up to a human nose and fuel sudden passion at a nightclub.

18 Watch any construction worker whistling at a passing woman from half a block away, and you can see how visual cues can be more powerful.

Lasting relationships

19 The rules of attraction might drive our initial decisions, for better or worse. But lasting relationships are about much more than what we see and smell.

20 Behavior plays a key role, with biology an intriguing contributing factor. One of the oldest theories about attraction is that like begets like. It explains that eerie perception that married couples sometimes look awfully similar.

21 Last year, J. Philippe Rushton, a psychologist at the University of Western Ontario, looked into the relationships of people's genes. Based on a set of heritable personality traits, having similar genetics plays 34 percent of the role in friendship and mate selection, he found.

22 "The main theory is that some genes work well in combination with each other," Rushton told *LiveScience*. "If these genes evolved to work in combination, then you don't want to break that up too much for your offspring. Finding a mate with similar genes will help you ensure this."

Continued...

What other physical factors influence attraction?

23 If your spouse is genetically similar, you're more likely to have a happy marriage, for example. Child abuse rates are lower when similarity is high, and you'll also be more altruistic and willing to sacrifice more for someone who is more genetically like you, research shows.

24 It probably comes as little surprise people are drawn to individuals with similar attitudes and values, as psychologist Eva Klohnen at the University of Iowa found in a 2005 study of newlywed couples. These characteristics are highly visible and accessible to others and can play a role in initial attraction.

25 When it comes to sticking together for the long haul, researchers have shown that likeness of personality, which can take more time to realize, means more. Comedy can also help a relationship. But the importance of humor is different for men and women, says Eric Bressler of McMaster University. A woman is attracted to a man who makes her laugh, Bressler found in a 2005 study. A man likes a woman who laughs at his jokes.

True love

26 Somewhere amid attraction and sex, we all hope, are strong feelings of love. But which of all the motivations really drives us?

27 Interestingly, brain scans in people who'd recently fallen in love reveal more activity related to love than sex. "Romantic love is one of the most powerful of all human experiences," says Helen Fisher, an anthropologist at Rutgers University. "It is definitely more powerful than the sex drive."

28 The rules of attraction make up a pretty long list. No scientist knows the order of the list. But near the top is perhaps one of the toughest characteristics to gauge in advance in the search for the perfect partner.

What are the most important factors that influence attraction?

29 Despite all their differences, men and women place high value on one trait: fidelity. Cornell University's Stephen Emlen and colleagues asked nearly 1,000 people age 18 to 24 to rank several attributes, including physical attractiveness, health, social status, ambition, and faithfulness, on a desirability scale. People who rated themselves favorably as long-term partners were more particular about the attributes of potential mates. After fidelity, the most important attributes were physical appearance, family commitment, and wealth and status.

30 "Good parenting, devotion, and sexual fidelity—that's what people say they're looking for in a long-term relationship," Emlen says.

1,545 words divided by .... minutes = ... words per minute

MyReadingLab

Reading 1 REVIEW

A good review strategy to use after reading is to summarize what you just read in your own words. Take a few minutes to think about the author's most important point and any key ideas that helped to support or explain it.

Write a two- or three-sentence summary on the lines below.

Symetry plays a part in how attractive members of the opposite sex find each other.
The sent of a man is attractive to women with similar genes.
Overall men & women place high value on one trait which is fidelity.

MyReadingLab

Reading 1 COMPREHENSION QUESTIONS

The following questions will help you recall the main idea and details of "The Rules of Attraction." Read any parts of the article that you need to find the correct answers.

1. Which of the following Four Step Reading Process strategies did you employ while reading this article? (Choose all that apply).

a. made up preview questions before reading
b. highlighting and annotating after each section
c. checked comprehension with questions in margins
d. read the article quickly without stopping to determine reading rate

MAIN IDEAS

2. What is the topic, or subject, of this selection?

a. The rules of attraction
b. Men and women are attracted to each other for a variety of reasons.
c. Elements that cause attraction
d. Why are some people attracted to others?

3. What is the authors' overall central point (main point) of the entire selection?

a. Science reveals the physiological factors that cause people to be attracted to one another.
b. After all this and more, the rules of attraction for the human species are still not clearly understood.
c. The rules of attraction, it turns out, seem sometimes to play out in our subconscious.
d. There are many biological and psychological reasons why people are attracted to one another.

Continued...

MyReadingLab

Reading 1 COMPREHENSION QUESTIONS

...continued

4. What is the main idea, or most important point, of paragraph 4?

a. Thornhill has been studying symmetry for 15 years and scanned faces and bodies into computers to determine symmetry ratios.

b. Both men and women rated symmetrical members of the opposite sex as more attractive and in better health than their less symmetrical counterparts.

c. The differences can be just a few percent—perceivable though not necessarily noticeable.

d. By questioning the study participants, Thornhill also found that men with higher degrees of symmetry enjoy more sexual partners than men of lower symmetry.

SUPPORTING DETAILS

5. According to the article, why is waist-to-hip ratio important in selecting a mate?

a. Most people accept a standard of beauty that includes a smaller waist than hips.

b. People in the ideal hip-ratio range are less susceptible to disease, and women in this range also have less difficulty conceiving.

c. An hourglass figure is more attractive to most men.

d. Women with ideal hip-waist ratios are able to endure physical stress better than women with larger WHRs.

6. According to the article, which of the following was the most important characteristic in choosing a potential long-term partner?

a. fidelity

b. physical appearance

c. family commitment

d. wealth and status.

DRAWING CONCLUSIONS

7. Which of the following is true according to the information in this article?

a. It is easy to predict what will attract a mate based on scientific data.

b. Pheromones are the most powerful forces in attraction.

c. People are more attracted to others with genes similar to their own.

d. Men with less symmetry enjoy more sexual partners than men with more symmetry.

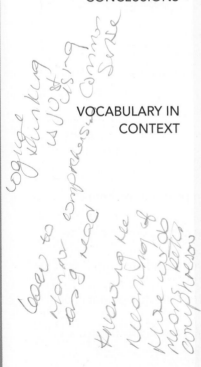

VOCABULARY IN CONTEXT

8. Using vocabulary skills, determine the meaning of the underlined word in this sentence from paragraph 3: Genetic mutations and environmental pressures <u>skew symmetry</u>, and the results have lifelong implications.

a. alter

b. destroy

c. similar

d. enable

9. Using vocabulary skills, determine the meaning of the underlined word in this sentence from paragraph 15: A 2002 study found women prefer the scent of men with genes somewhat similar to their own over the scent of nearly genetically identical or totally <u>dissimilar</u> men.

a. very much alike

b. somewhat alike

c. not alike

d. don't like

10. Using vocabulary skills, determine the meaning of the underlined word in this sentence from paragraph 22: "Finding a mate with similar genes will help you <u>ensure</u> this."

a. to make sure

b. unsure

c. avoid

d. initiate

Reading 1
VOCABULARY PRACTICE: WORD GAME

Object: Be the first player to get rid of all the word cards in your hand.

For 2 to 4 players

1. Tear one sheet of notebook paper in half vertically, and then fold and tear six small pieces from each half. Write one word from the Word Bank on each of the papers. Shuffle them and place them in a pile face down.

2. Each player takes two word cards from the pile to begin. (If there are 4 players, you may each take one word instead of two.)

3. The first player reads the first sentence from the questions below. The players will look at their words to see if one of them correctly completes the sentence. If not, taking turns, each player must draw another word until the correct word is found. You must keep the words you have drawn.

4. Once the correct answer is found, set it aside and read the next question. Continue play as described in step 3.

5. Once all the words in the pile are gone, players will take turns reading the sentences and putting down words from their hands that correctly complete the sentences. Once all the sentences have been completed, the player who runs out of cards first (or has the least number of cards left) wins.

WORD BANK

infatuation	symmetry	encoded	estrogen
testosterone	genes	pheromones	exude
begets	altruistic	fidelity	

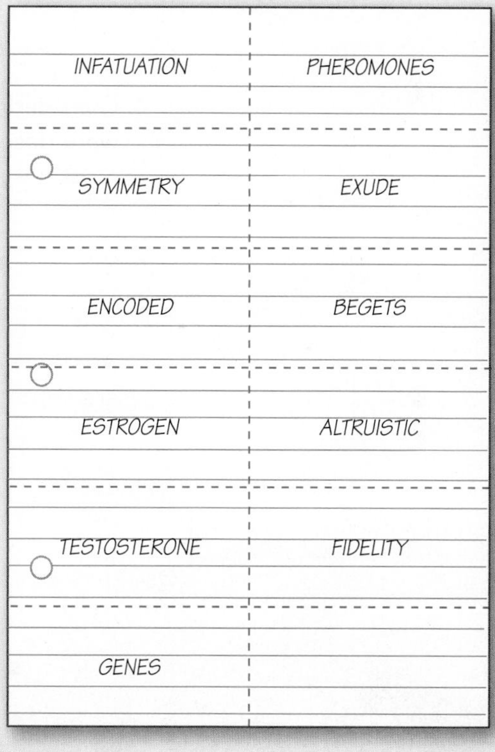

Sentences

1. Those flowers .... such a strong fragrance that it fills the entire room.
2. Mrs. Simms is very .... ; she served in the Peace Corps and volunteers for several charities in town.
3. Most couples consider .... the most important part of a marriage.
4. Many physical factors that we find attractive in the opposite sex are .... in our genes before we are even born.
5. I believe that kindness .... kindness—the more you are kind to others, the more they will be kind to you.
6. My older sister is always falling in love with a different guy almost every week. I told her it's not love, just ....
7. Some women take .... supplements when their hormone levels decrease with age.
8. Most people find the look of .... attractive in another person.
9. .... is a hormone that aids in creating the shape of a man's face.
10. Helen inherited her good looks from her mother, but her intelligence must come from her father's ....
11. Some perfume and cologne companies have used .... from animals to create fragrances to arouse the opposite sex.

MyReadingLab

Reading 1 QUESTIONS FOR WRITING AND DISCUSSION

Review any parts of the article you need to answer the following questions.

1. What are some of the physical factors that attract partners to each other?

2. What are some of the intangible, or non-physical, ways that people are attracted to each other?

3. Do you think the list of qualities that a person desires in a partner may change over time as the person ages? How might the list change?

4. Considering all the factors that attract two people to each other that were described in this article, which of these do you believe to be the most desirable traits in the opposite sex?

5. Are there any other qualities not discussed in the article that you feel are important in a potential partner?

MyReadingLab

Reading 2
VOCABULARY
PREVIEW

"Liking and Loving: Interpersonal Attraction" by Saundra K. Ciccarelli and J. Noland White

Match the words in the Word Bank by writing the letter of the word next to the matching definition. The paragraph numbers in parentheses indicate the location of each word in the reading selection. Read the words in "Liking and Loving: Interpersonal Attraction " to determine the correct meanings as they are used in the context of the selection.

WORD BANK

a. superficial (1)	b. proximity (3)	c. stimuli (3)
d. validation (4)	e. complementary (5)	f. reciprocity (6)
g. disclose (6)	h. intimacy (8)	i. companionate (9)
j. consummate (10)		

1. .... having both intimacy and commitment

2. .... one's needs fulfilled by another

3. .... things that bring about actions

4. .... visible physical characteristics; on the surface

5. .... confirmation

6. .... being physically near

7. .... mutual feelings

8. .... feelings of closeness to another person

9. .... ideal love

10. .... to share information

MyReadingLab

Reading 2 PREVIEW

Discuss the following questions with a partner or small group.

1. What factors do you think draw people together and keep them together?
2. When looking for a partner in a relationship, what do you think are the most essential qualities that person should have?

This article focuses on the psychological and emotional aspects of attraction. In this article, psychologists examine what makes two people fall in love and stay in love. As you read the article, remember to use the Four Step Reading Process to monitor comprehension and study as you read.

After you preview the article, write one or two preview questions on the lines below:

....

....

....

MyReadingLab

Reading 2

"Liking and Loving: Interpersonal Attraction"

by Saundra K. Ciccarelli and J. Noland White

In this article, psychologists look at the factors that cause the attraction of one person to another. As you read the article, remember to use the Four Step Reading Process to monitor comprehension and study as you read.

1 Several factors are involved in the attraction of one person to another, including both superficial physical characteristics, such as physical beauty and proximity, as well as elements of personality.

2 When people think about what attracts them to others, one of the topics that usually arises is the physical attractiveness of the other person. Some research suggests that physical beauty is one of the main factors that influence an individual's choice for selecting people they want to know better, although other factors may become more important in the later stages of relationships (Eagly et al., 1991; Feingold, 1992; White, 1980).

Proximity

3 The closer together people are physically, such as working in the same office building or living in the same dorm, the more likely they are to form a relationship. Proximity refers to being physically near someone else. People choose friends and lovers from the pool of people available to them, and availability depends heavily on proximity. One theory about why proximity

is so important involves the idea of repeated exposure to new stimuli. The more people experience something, whether it is a song, a picture, or a person, the more they tend to like it. The phrase "it grew on me" refers to this reaction. When people are in physical proximity to each other, repeated exposure may increase their attraction to each other.

Similarity

What are three factors involved in attraction?

4 Proximity does not guarantee attraction, just as physical attractiveness does not guarantee a long-term relationship. People tend to like being around others who are similar to them in some way. The more people find they have in common with others—such as attitudes, beliefs, and interests—the more they tend to be attracted to those others (Hartfield & Rapson, 1992; Moreland & Zajonc, 1982; Neimeyer & Mitchell, 1998). Similarity as a factor in relationships makes sense when seen in terms of validation of a person's beliefs and attitudes. When other people hold the same attitudes and beliefs and do the same kinds of actions, it makes a person's own concepts seem more correct or valid.

5 There is often a grain of truth in many old sayings, and "opposites attract" is no exception. Some people find that forming a relationship with another person who has complementary qualities (characteristics in the one person that fill a need in the other) can be very rewarding (Carson, 1969; Schmitt, 2002). Research does not support this view of attraction, however. It is similarity, not complementarity, that draws people together and helps them stay together (Berscheid & Reis, 1998; McPherson et al., 2001).

What draws and keeps people together?

Reciprocity

6 Finally, people have a very strong tendency to like people who like them, a simple but powerful concept referred to as reciprocity of liking. In one experiment, researchers paired college students with other students (Curtis & Miller, 1986). Neither student in any of the pairs knew the other member. One member of each pair was randomly chosen to receive some information from the experimenters about how the other student in the pair felt about the first member. In some cases, target students were led to believe that the other students liked them and, in other cases, that the targets disliked them. When the pairs of students were allowed to meet and talk with each other again, they were friendlier, disclosed more information about themselves, agreed with the other person more, and behaved in a warmer manner if they had been told that the other student liked them. The other students came to like these students better as well, so liking produced more liking. The only time that liking someone does not seem to make that person like the other in return is if a person suffers from feelings of low self-worth. In that case, finding out that someone likes you when you don't even like yourself makes you question his or her motives. This mistrust can cause you to act unfriendly to that person, which makes the person more likely to become unfriendly to you in a kind of self-fulfilling prophecy (Murray et al., 1998).

What role does self-esteem play in relationships?

Continued...

MyReadingLab

Reading 2

...continued

What was Sternberg's theory of love?

What is companionate love?

Types of Love

7 Psychologists generally agree that there are different kinds of love. One psychologist, Robert Sternberg, outlined a theory of what he determined were the three main components of love and the different types of love that combinations of these three components can produce (Sternberg, 1986, 1988b, 1997).

Three Components of Love

8 According to Sternberg, love consists of three basic components: intimacy, passion, and commitment. *Intimacy*, in Sternberg's view, refers to the feelings of closeness that one has for another person or the sense of having close emotional ties to another. Intimacy in this sense is not physical but psychological. Friends have an intimate relationship because they disclose things to each other that most people might not know, they feel strong emotional ties to each other, and they enjoy the presence of the other person. *Passion* is the physical aspect of love. Passion refers to the emotional and sexual arousal a person feels toward the other person. Passion is not simply sex. Holding hands, loving looks, and hugs can all be forms of passion. *Commitment* involves the decisions one makes about a relationship. A short-term decision might be, "I think I'm in love." An example of a more long-term decision is, "I want to be with this person for the rest of my life."

Love Triangles

9 A love relationship between two people can involve one, two, or all three of these components in various combinations. Two of the more familiar and more heavily researched forms of love from Sternberg's theory are romantic love and companionate love. When intimacy and passion are combined, the result is the more familiar romantic love, which is sometimes called passionate love by other researchers (Bartels & Zeki, 2000; Diamond, 2003; Hartfield, 1987). Romantic love is often the basis for a more lasting relationship. In many Western cultures, the ideal relationship begins with liking, then becomes romantic love as passion is added to the mix, and finally becomes a more enduring form of love as a commitment is made. When intimacy and commitment are the main components of a relationship, it is called companionate love. In companionate love, people who like each other, feel emotionally close to each other, and understand one another's motives have made a commitment to live together, usually in a marriage relationship. Companionate love is often the binding tie that holds a marriage together through the years of parenting, paying bills, and lessening physical passion (Gottman & Krokoff, 1989; Steinberg & Silverberg, 1987). In many non-Western cultures, companionate love is seen as more sensible. Choices for a mate on the basis of compatibility are often made by parents or match-makers rather than the couple themselves (Duben & Behar, 1991; Hortaçsu, 1999; Jones, 1997; Thornton & Hui-Sheng, 1994).

10 Finally, when all three components of love are present, the couple has achieved consummate love, the ideal form of love that many people see as the ultimate goal. This is also the kind of love that may evolve into companionate love when the passion lessens during the middle years of a relationship's commitment.

1,193 words divided by .... minutes = ... words per minute

MyReadingLab

Reading 2 REVIEW

A good review strategy to use after reading is to summarize what you just read in your own words. Take a few minutes to think about the author's most important point and any key ideas that helped to support or explain it. Write a two- or three-sentence summary on the lines below.

After you preview the article, write one or two preview questions on the lines below:

....

....

....

....

....

MyReadingLab

Reading 2 COMPREHENSION QUESTIONS

The following questions will help you recall the main idea and details of "Liking and Loving: Interpersonal Attraction". Read any parts of the article that you need to find the correct answers.

1. What is the topic, or subject of this selection?
- **a.** why couples form relationships
- **b.** the components of love
- **c.** factors that are involved in attraction
- **d.** Sternberg's theory of love is widely accepted.

MAIN IDEAS

2. What is the authors' overall central point (main point), of this entire selection?
- **a.** There are many reasons why one person may ask another out on a date.
- **b.** Several factors influence the attraction and relationship between two people.
- **c.** Most people are drawn to others on the basis of physical attraction.
- **d.** Liking and Loving: Interpersonal relationships

3. What is the main idea, or most important point, of paragraph 3?
- **a.** Proximity does not guarantee attraction, just as physical attractiveness does not guarantee a long-term relationship.
- **b.** People tend to like being around others who are similar to them in some way.
- **c.** The more people find they have in common with others—such as attitudes, beliefs, and interests—the more they tend to be attracted to those others.
- **d.** When other people hold the same attitudes and beliefs and do the same kinds of actions, it makes a person's own concepts seem more correct or valid.

Continued...

MyReadingLab

Reading 2 COMPREHENSION QUESTIONS

...continued

4. According to the selection, how does low self-worth affect a relationship?

a. People with low self-worth are suspicious of someone who tries to establish a relationship.

b. People with low self-worth rarely want to go out with anyone.

c. Feelings of low self-worth can cause a person to fear relationships.

d. People are rarely attracted to someone with low self-worth.

5. How does passionate, or romantic love, differ from companionate love?

a. There is more intimacy in companionate love.

b. In companionate love, couples are more concerned about physical passion and arousal.

c. Romantic love usually lasts longer than companionate love because it is more fulfilling.

d. Companionate love relies less upon passionate or romantic love, and more upon commitment to each other.

6. One conclusion that can be correctly drawn from this passage is

a. When it comes to love, people are the same all over the world.

b. One culture's idea about the best kind of relationship to have may be different than other cultures' ideas.

c. Couples who fall in love rarely feel the same way after a few years together.

d. It's not possible to predict which relationships will work and which ones will not.

7. According to the selection, a couple's relationship may change over the course of several years.

a. true

b. false

VOCABULARY IN CONTEXT

8. Using vocabulary skills, determine the meaning of the underlined word in this sentence from paragraph 6: In some cases, target students were led to believe that the other students liked them and, in other cases, that the targets disliked them.

a. a goal

b. a point to hit

c. the focus of a study

d. a victim

9. Using vocabulary skills, determine the meaning of the underlined word in this sentence from paragraph 9: In many Western cultures, the ideal relationship begins with liking, then becomes romantic love as passion is added to the mix, and finally becomes a more enduring form of love as a commitment is made.

a. committed

b. to tolerate

c. lasting

d. romantic

10. Some words have more than one meaning. Using vocabulary skills, determine the meaning of the underlined word in the following sentence: Although Mr. Smith has a degree in psychology, his knowledge is so superficial that he was unable to answer any questions requiring a deep understanding of the subject.

a. physical characteristics

b. shallow in character

c. imitative

d. limited

Reading 2
VOCABULARY PRACTICE: CROSSWORD

Read the clues at the bottom of the page and complete the puzzle with words in the Word Bank.

WORD BANK

superficial	proximity	stimuli	validation
complementary	reciprocity	disclose	intimacy
companionate	consummate		

Across Clues

1. one's needs fulfilled by another
6. mutual feelings
8. to share information
9. confirmation

Down Clues

1. ideal love
2. having both intimacy and commitment
3. feelings of closeness to another person
4. visible physical characteristics
5. being physically near
7. things that bring about actions

MyReadingLab

Reading 2 QUESTIONS FOR WRITING AND DISCUSSION

Review any parts of the article you need to answer the following questions.

1. How might a person use proximity to get the attention of someone he or she wants to get to know better?

2. Why do you think people prefer others who are more similar to themselves than those who are dissimilar?

3. Do you think that a match made by a third party such as parents, a dating service, or a computer dating service that matches couples on the basis of their compatibility are reliable ways to meet potential partners? Why or why not?

4. Why do you think the principle of reciprocity influences a person's willingness to disclose personal information to another person?

5. Do you think it is more difficult, the same in difficulty, or easier to meet potential mates in today's society as compared to a generation ago? Explain why.

MyReadingLab

VIEWPOINT FOR CRITICAL THINKING

SOCIAL NETWORKING

In February 2004, Harvard College freshman Mark Zuckerberg created an online student directory which grew into a social networking site that exploded in popularity and later became known as Facebook. Its success was primarily due to the fact that people could make new friends across the country or internationally with the click of a mouse. Despite its efforts to maintain the privacy of its users, some Facebook users have experienced identity theft, stalking, job losses, and various crimes committed by sexual predators, thieves and con artists. Respond to each of the following survey questions, and then discuss your answers with your team or the class.

1. Do you think children still in elementary and middle school should be allowed to have social networking accounts? Why or why not?

2. Do you think social networking Internet companies such as Facebook should be held responsible for damages or injuries that result from criminal abuse of information that is made available online through their website (for example, an identity theft)?

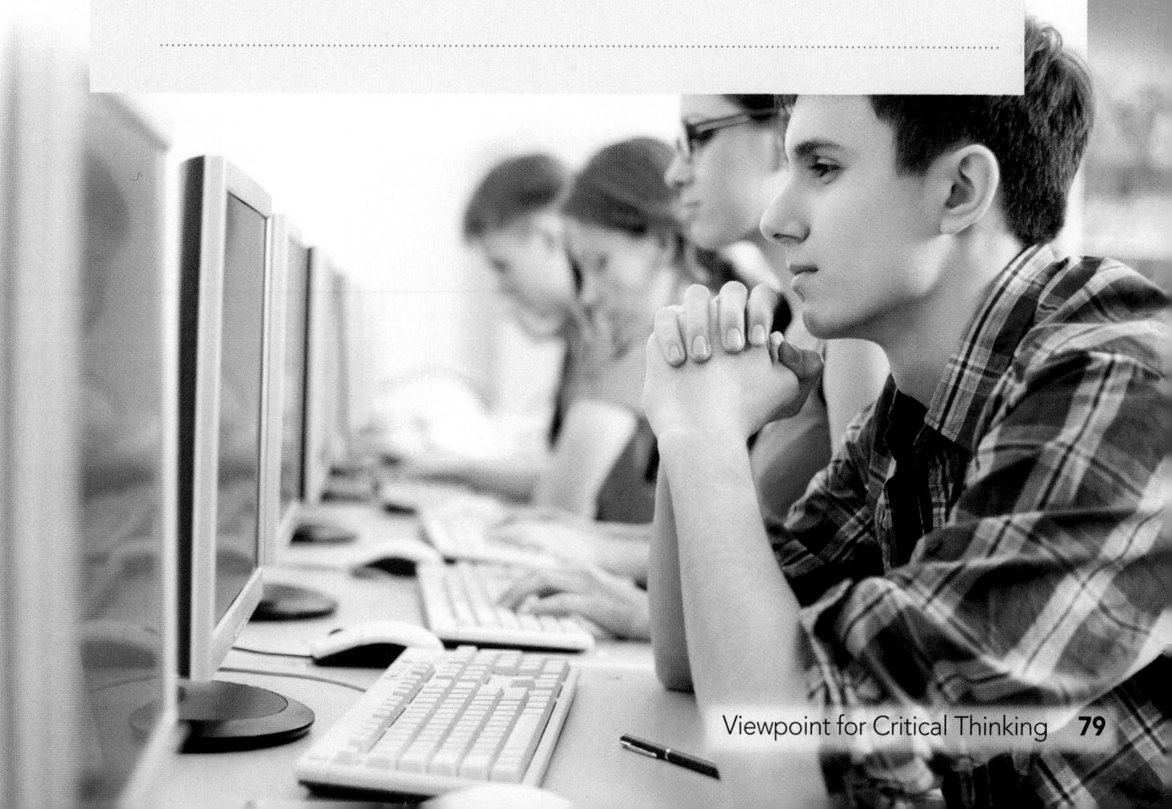

MyReadingLab

VIEWPOINT FOR CRITICAL THINKING

...continued

3. Should a social networking site be restricted in the amount of personal information that it can store about its members? What should those limits be?

4. Most social networking sites make money from their advertising sponsors. Marketing programs sift through members' profiles to determine the advertising programs they will receive through the Internet. Should this practice be eliminated? If so, would you be willing to pay for a social networking site like Facebook that would be more private and secure? Why or why not?

5. Should social networking sites such as Facebook be required by law to ban individuals who have been convicted of certain crimes, such as sexual predators, from using their services? If so, what types of criminals should be banned? Is this something that the government should regulate?

MyReadingLab

REAL-LIFE READING

UNDERSTANDING AUTO INSURANCE TERMS

Although each state has its own requirements for auto insurance, driving without any insurance is illegal. Insurance protects you from lawsuits that could bankrupt you for life. It also helps to pay repair expenses for your car or your medical bills if injured. It covers theft, vandalism, fire, and storm damage. Even if you lease or rent a car, by law you must still have insurance. Here are a few terms you should know before you buy insurance.

A Premium is the amount you pay each month to the insurance company for car insurance.

Liability refers to the amount of damage that you cause on another person's vehicle or person. Most policies show a limit amount for covering bodily injury for each person, and each occurrence.

Personal Injury Protection covers your medical, hospital, funeral, and other such expenses resulting from an accident. It also pays lost income if you are unable to work due to an accident.

Uninsured/Underinsured Motorist Bodily Injury covers injuries that an uninsured driver, or one who doesn't have enough insurance, causes to an insured person. It will cover you if you're injured by a hit-and-run driver.

Uninsured/Underinsured Motorist Property Damage covers damage that an uninsured driver, or one who doesn't have enough insurance, causes to your insured vehicle.

Collision Coverage covers the costs of damage to your car resulting from a collision.

Comprehensive Coverage covers damage to your car resulting from accidents other than collisions (for example, if your car is hit by a tree limb, or damaged in a parking lot.)

Death, Dismemberment and loss of Sight pays for these types of injuries to people who are in your auto accident.

GAP Coverage will cover the difference between the current market value of your car and the amount you still owe on the vehicle if the car is a total loss in an accident.

A Deductible is the amount you will pay for any damages if you are in an accident. The higher your deductible amount is, the less you will pay for your insurance premiums. It's best to choose the highest deductible you can afford when buying car insurance.

Other types of coverage are optional—for roadside assistance, for custom furnishings or equipment (including trailers), for coverage in Mexico, or auto loan/lease coverage—and are covered at an additional cost.

(Source: www.handsonbanking.org)

It pays to shop around for the best price on insurance because there can be a significant difference in insurance costs depending on which company you choose. Also do some checking on an insurance company's customer service

Continued...

MyReadingLab

REAL-LIFE READING

...continued

record. Buying cheaper insurance won't help you if you are in an accident and the company is slow to pay you or avoids paying your expenses. Read every policy thoroughly to make sure there are no unreasonable clauses that provide the insurance company an excuse not to pay you. It's best to use companies that are well known and have good reputations for paying claims.

If you are in an accident and the insurance company offers you a smaller amount than your total expenses, you can try to negotiate for a higher amount. If needed, contact your state's department of insurance (on the Internet) or hire an attorney to represent you. Most attorneys will consult with you for free to determine if you are entitled to a higher payment. You can also get a mediator to help you negotiate for more money if you can't afford a lawyer. Contact your county bar association for more information on mediation.

Use the information in "Understanding Auto Insurance Terms" to answer the following questions.

1. Which types of coverage will cover your costs if you are in an accident with an uninsured motorist?

2. If your property damage liability is set at $50,000 and you are involved in an accident resulting in a total loss of your vehicle, valued at $69,000, what is the maximum amount the insurance company will pay you?

3. If you have GAP coverage and your $69,000 vehicle described in question 2 (on which you still owe $20,000) is totaled, what is the maximum amount your insurance company will pay you?

4. If you have an auto insurance policy with a $500 deductible and the car repair costs for your accident total $1500, how much will the insurance company pay you for these costs?

5. Which type of coverage will cover your car if it is struck by a utility pole during a storm?

MyReadingLab

BUILDING VOCABULARY

Knowing the meanings to many word parts will help you determine the meanings of unfamiliar words. Make a list of English words using the word parts in the table below, and give their meanings. If you are unsure about a word, consult a dictionary. Then use the words to complete the sentences below. (*presented in previous lists)

PREFIXES	ROOTS	SUFFIXES
de-: *to reverse*	vert, vers: *to turn, change*	-tion, -sion: *action, state of**
com-, con-: *with, together*	duct: *to lead, pull*	-ity: *a state or condition*
di-: *from*		-er, -or: *one who, one that*

WORDS

Use one of the words in your word list above in a sentence that reveals its meaning with a context clue. Read the sentence to a classmate and ask him or her to define the word.

MyReadingLab

CHAPTER PRACTICE 1

Using context clues (L.E.A.D.S.), word part clues, and part of speech clues, determine the meanings of the underlined words in the following selection. Choose the definition that fits the context of the sentence or paragraph.

EVOLUTIONARY THEORY AND GENDER

In recent years, evolutionary theory has gained a prominent place in explanations of gender. Support for this approach comes from studies showing that females and males display similar mating patterns across widely varying cultures. To put it [1] succinctly, men tend to prefer youthful, physically attractive mates, whereas women tend to seek men who have the skills to provide for their physical needs (Buss, 1994).

To explain these findings, evolutionary theorists propose that natural selection has shaped both male and female mating strategies to [2] foster the survival of offspring.

Men, they say, use attractiveness as an indicator of health in a [3] potential mate. Moreover, they behave [4] assertively because they know that women are looking for a mate who can protect and provide for them. In contrast, women look for stable, committed mates who are good providers. At the same time, they know that men seek attractive mates, so they focus on that [5] attribute in themselves rather than on developing the skills needed for self-sufficiency.

1. succinctly
   - **a.** briefly and clearly
   - **b.** with great assurance
   - **c.** sadly
   - **d.** oddly
2. foster
   - **a.** to raise
   - **b.** to celebrate
   - **c.** ensure
   - **d.** disapprove of
3. potential
   - **a.** perfect
   - **b.** possible
   - **c.** worthy
   - **d.** preserving
4. assertively
   - **a.** uncertainty
   - **b.** confidently
   - **c.** wealthy
   - **d.** frequently
5. attribute
   - **a.** cause
   - **b.** reason
   - **c.** honor
   - **d.** characteristic

MyReadingLab

CHAPTER PRACTICE 2

Using context clues (L.E.A.D.S.), word part clues, and part of speech clues, determine the meanings of the underlined words in the following selection. Choose the definition that fits the context of the sentence or paragraph.

Note that experiences of romantic relationships are also influenced by cultural expectations (Wang & Mallinckrodt, 2006). At various moments in this chapter, we've [1] alluded to the cultural dimension of independence versus [2] interdependence: Cultures with independent [3] construals of self value the person over the collective; interdependent cultures put greater value on shared cultural goals rather than on individual ones. How does this apply to your love life? If you choose a life partner based on your own feelings of love, you are showing preference for your personal goals; if you choose a partner with an eye to how that individual will [4] mesh with your family's structure and concerns, you are being more [5] attuned to collective goals. Cross-cultural research has led to the very strong generalization that members of independent cultures put much greater emphasis on love (Dion & Dion, 1996).

Members of independent cultures are also more demanding of their potential partners. Because people in these cultures have stronger ideas about personal fulfillment within relationships, they also expect more from marriage partners (Hatfield & Sprecher, 1995).

1. alluded
   - **a.** referred to
   - **b.** permitted
   - **c.** investigated
   - **d.** avoided
2. interdependence
   - **a.** not depending upon
   - **b.** connections
   - **c.** depending upon each other
   - **d.** being independent
3. construals
   - **a.** constructions
   - **b.** interpretations
   - **c.** shared goals
   - **d.** independence
4. mesh
   - **a.** sticking to
   - **b.** fit together
   - **c.** netting
   - **d.** entrap
5. attuned
   - **a.** in tune
   - **b.** in a state of instability
   - **c.** in agreement with
   - **d.** melodic

MyReadingLab

CHAPTER PRACTICE 3

Using context clues (L.E.A.D.S.), word part clues, and part of speech clues, determine the meanings of the underlined words in the following selection. Choose the definition that fits the context of the sentence or paragraph.

> These sexual [1] norms are part of what you acquire as a member of a culture. We already suggested that some general "male" and "female" aspects of sexual behavior may be products of the evolution of the human species. Even so, different cultures define ranges of behavior that are considered to be appropriate for expressing sexual [2] impulses. Sexual [3] scripts are socially learned programs of sexual responsiveness that include [4] prescriptions, usually unspoken, of what to do; when, where, and how to do it; with whom, or with what, to do it; and why it should be done (Krahé et al., 2007; Seal et al., 2008). Different aspects of these scripts are assembled through social interaction over your lifetime. The attitudes and values [5] embodied in your sexual script are an external source of sexual motivation: The script suggests the types of behaviors you might or should undertake.

1. norms
- **a.** ideas
- **b.** upbringing
- **c.** systems
- **d.** standard behaviors

2. impulses
- **a.** natural tendencies
- **b.** muscle signals
- **c.** momentum
- **d.** forward motion

3. scripts
- **a.** manuscripts
- **b.** written rules
- **c.** unwritten rules
- **d.** prescriptions

4. prescriptions
- **a.** medicines
- **b.** rights
- **c.** therapies
- **d.** instructions

5. embodied
- **a.** personalized
- **b.** like a body
- **c.** behaviors
- **d.** incorporated

CHAPTER REVIEW: NOTE CARDS

One way to study your notes is to put them on index cards by topic. Fill in the missing information in the note cards below. On the back of the note card write questions for each topic. After you answer the question, turn the card over to check your answer.

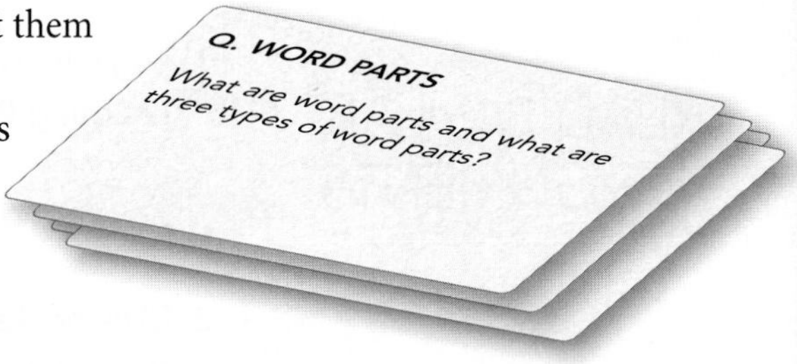

FRONTS OF CARDS	BACKS OF CARDS
A. CONTEXT CLUES Context clues are	**Q. CONTEXT CLUES** What are context clues?
A. L.E.A.D.S. There are five types of context clues to help you determine the meanings of unknown words:	**Q. L.E.A.D.S.** What are five types of context clues to look for?
A. PARTS OF SPEECH Knowing the part of speech can also help determine what type of word an unfamiliar word may be. Four common parts of speech are:	**Q. PARTS OF SPEECH** What are parts of speech and what are four common parts of speech?
A. MONITORING COMPREHENSION Monitor your comprehension by using your .... Think about what you are reading, and if a sentence doesn't make sense, go back and read each word carefully again.	**Q. MONITORING COMPREHENSION** How should you monitor your comprehension?
A. WORD PARTS Words are made up of word parts that help determine their meanings. Three types of word parts are:	**Q. WORD PARTS** What are word parts and what are three types of word parts?

MyReadingLab

READING LAB ASSIGNMENTS

1. Login to **MyReadingLab** and in the menu click on Reading Skills. In the **Learning Path** select **Vocabulary.** Review this skill by reading the brief overview and models. Watch the short animation and then complete any practices or tests to learn the meanings of more words.

2. Click on **Reading Level** and choose two stories to read and answer all of the questions to the best of your ability. Your Lexile level will increase as your reading comprehension improves.

ON THE WEB

You can increase your vocabulary in a fun way with free online games. Websites such as *dictionary.com* and *freerice.com* offer free vocabulary games. Browse the Internet to find other websites with free vocabulary games and activities. You can also find lists of prefixes, roots, and suffixes by searching those terms.

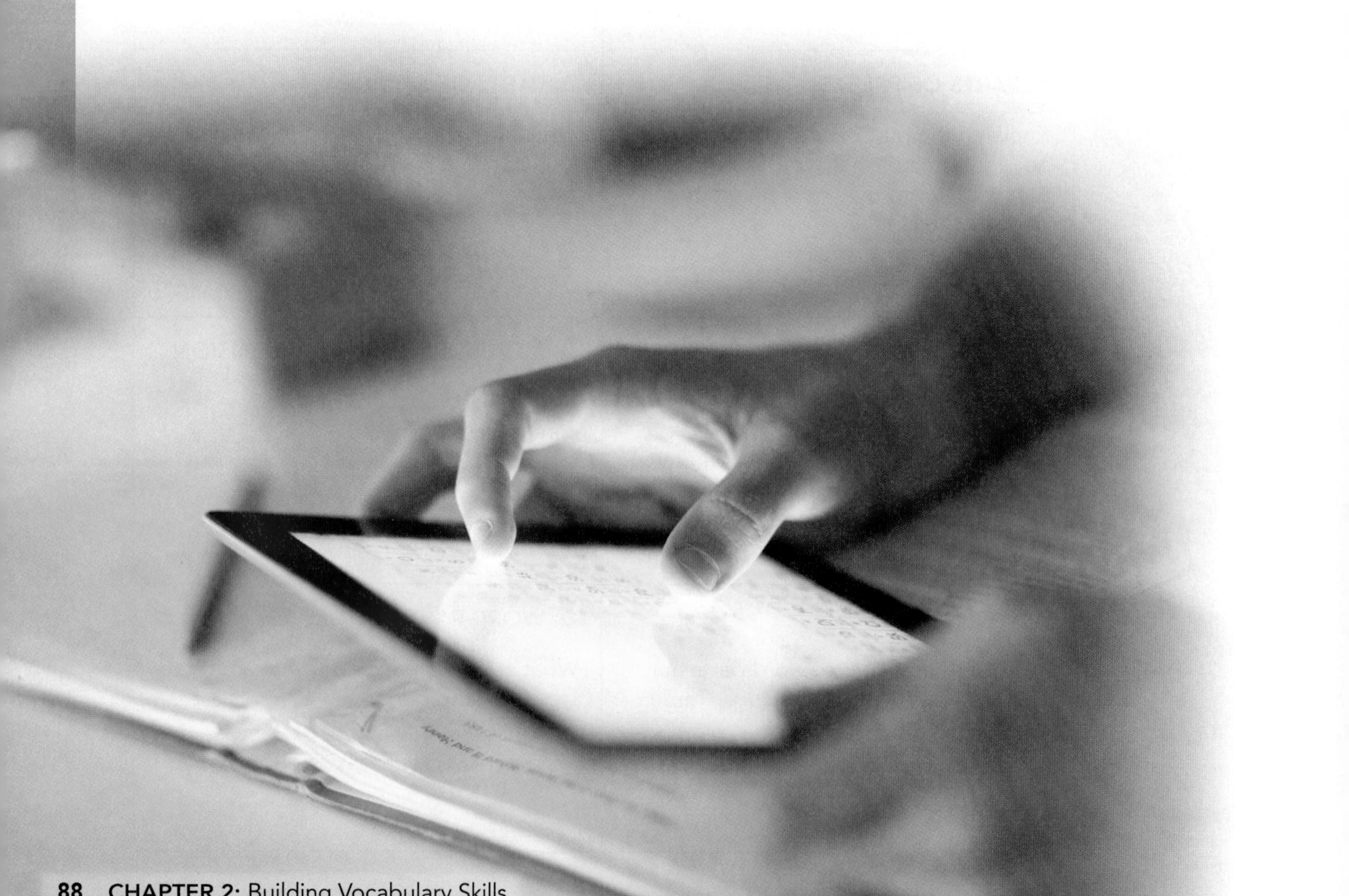

MyReadingLab

MONITOR YOUR LEARNING

In this chapter you learned about using context clues and word part clues to determine the meanings of unfamiliar words. Write a paragraph telling what you learned about these skills, how you learned them, and how you can use them to improve your learning and reading comprehension. When you have finished writing, read your paragraph as if you were reading someone else's paragraph for the first time. Check for missing words, spelling, punctuation, and sentence structure.

3 TOPICS, STATED MAIN IDEAS & SUPPORTING DETAILS

FOCUS ON: Your Health and Fitness

This chapter focuses on ways to get in shape and maintain good health through proper nutrition and exercise. Finding time to eat well and exercise can be difficult when you are busy with school, work, and a family, but learning about some easy diet and fitness strategies that fit your schedule and your budget will help you to develop good habits. Choosing a sport or activity you enjoy, for instance, can make it easier to keep active, keep fit, and enjoy a long, healthy life.

In this chapter you will learn how to:

LEARNING OBJECTIVES

1 identify the topic of a reading selection.

2 identify the stated main idea.

3 identify major and minor details.

WHY STUDY TOPIC AND MAIN IDEA?

Imagine sitting in a college lecture, watching an assigned video, or reading an assignment and trying to take notes for a test. What should you write down? Some students try to record every word the speaker says, or to copy each sentence verbatim (word by word). This is so frustrating that many students give up because they can't keep up with the speaker, or they write too much in their notes. The right way to take notes on anything is to listen or read first, decide what the most important information is, and then paraphrase it in your own words and write it down. Finding the most important information when you are overwhelmed with a lot of data can be extremely difficult unless you know how to spot the main idea and its supporting details. The techniques in this chapter will improve your comprehension and note-taking skills at the same time.

There are three main components to every paragraph: a topic, a main idea, and supporting details. Knowing how to identify these three elements is the key to good reading comprehension. Always begin by focusing on the topic of the paragraph. Identifying the topic will put you in the right direction to find the main idea and its supporting details.

OBJECTIVE **1**

Identify the topic of a reading selection.

IDENTIFY THE TOPIC OF A READING SELECTION

topic: the general subject of the reading selection or lecture.

The **topic** is the general subject of what you are reading, usually expressed in a word or a phrase, such as *Weight-lifting*, or *American College Football Teams*. Finding the topic is the first step to improving your comprehension because it helps you to get on the right track toward finding the main idea. Think of a topic like a pair of shoes. Shoes shouldn't be too small or too large, but just the right fit for your feet. Topics have to be the right fit for the paragraph. If you identify a topic that is too small (too specific) for the paragraph, you'll leave out information that it covers. If you select a topic that is too large (too broad) for the paragraph, it could include information that is not in the paragraph. One way to identify the topic is to look for the subject most often named or referred to in the paragraph. With this in mind, read the paragraph below and decide which topic fits this paragraph perfectly.

> Good nutrition means having a diet that supplies all of the essential nutrients required to maintain a healthy body. Consuming too much or too little of any of the essential nutrients will eventually lead to health problems. In the past, dietary deficiencies of nutrients caused health problems for many people. For example, insufficient intake of vitamin C can lead to **scurvy**, and insufficient iron intake can lead to a form of **anemia**, both of which were once prevalent in much of the world's population (and are still common in the developing world).

scurvy: a disease caused by insufficient vitamin C, resulting in bleeding and weakness.

anemia: a condition of insufficient number of red blood cells resulting from vitamin and mineral deficiencies.

The topic of this paragraph is

a. vitamin deficiencies

b. good health

c. the effects of poor nutrition

d. good nutrition

Explanation:
If you chose *a, vitamin deficiencies*, or *c, the effects of poor nutrition*, these topics are too small—they only cover some of the information in the paragraph. Answer *b, good health* is so broad that it could cover everything from nutrition and exercise to getting medical exams, which are not discussed in this paragraph, so it's too big. The best fit for this paragraph is answer *d, good nutrition*. All of the sentences support the topic by giving you more information about what it means and its importance to good health.

OBJECTIVE **2**

Identify the stated main idea.

main idea: the most important point that the author is making about the topic

IDENTIFY THE STATED MAIN IDEA

A **main idea** is the most important point that the author is making about the topic. A main idea is a concept that is also the author's goal or objective for writing something, and it can be either stated or implied by the details. If the main idea is stated in a sentence, then the sentence containing the main idea is called a **topic sentence**. If the main idea it is not directly stated, but is suggested by the supporting details, it is implied. Here are some tips to keep in mind about main ideas:

1. Main ideas are always complete sentences, never a word, a phrase, or a question because the main idea is a statement of the author's point—a complete thought.
2. Since main ideas state the main point about the topic, the topic is usually found in the topic sentence, or it is referred to in some way. Knowing the topic first will help you identify possible main ideas in a paragraph.
3. Main ideas are general statements about the topic that are broad enough to include all the supporting information in the paragraph.
4. Like topics, main ideas should be just the right fit for the paragraph—not too narrow or too broad.
5. A topic sentence stating the main idea can appear *anywhere* in a paragraph.

Main Idea Styles

There are several styles that are commonly used as main ideas. Becoming familiar with various styles of main ideas can help you spot them more easily.

1. **Main ideas as definitions**: In a definition paragraph, the definition sentence is usually the main idea followed by an explanation of the term and perhaps some examples. In the paragraph below, notice how the details that follow the topic sentence support it by providing more information about what macronutrients are. The topic is in bold print and the topic sentence that states the main idea is underlined.

   Macronutrients are the elements your body uses to provide energy for everyday activities. Substances such as carbohydrates, fats, and proteins are needed in larger amounts than micronutrients, which supply vitamins and minerals. Carbohydrates are the major source for your body's energy, but proteins can also be used for energy. A good balance of macronutrients consists of a diet with about 58% carbohydrates, 30% fat, and 12% protein.

2. **Main ideas that introduce supporting details**: Some main ideas introduce the topic and the major points that the paragraph will address. In the paragraph below about *dietary fiber*, the main idea is supported by the major details that list the several reasons why dietary fiber is important.

   Dietary fiber is important for several reasons. It aids the intestinal tract in eliminating food waste, hastening the digestive process and lowering the risk of colon cancer. Dietary fiber is also helpful in reducing cholesterol because some types of fiber prevent its absorption into the blood. Another benefit of dietary fiber is that it helps to regulate glucose levels, which control the appetite.

3. **Main ideas that summarize**: A main idea can also summarize the most important information of the paragraph into a single broad statement. Notice how the last sentence sums up the supporting details by stressing the importance of water.

   Water enables us to digest food, absorb nutrients into our blood, form blood cells, and regulate body temperature. A loss of even 5% of your body's water can cause fatigue, weakness, and an inability to concentrate. A person cannot live without water for a very long period of time because it is an essential element in nutrition.

4. **Main ideas as discovery**: Main ideas often state something that was learned as a result of a study or an experiment. The supporting details in the following paragraph provide the background information that leads to the main idea. In the following paragraph, notice how the last sentence states what was learned through the study.

    A hundred inmates in a county prison participated in a study to examine the effects of exercise on low back pain. Fifty inmates with chronic back pain were told to continue their regular routines and diet as they normally do. The other fifty with back pain participated in special daily exercises working four muscle groups. At the end of six weeks, the inmates were reexamined and 100% of the group that did not change their routine still complained of low back pain, whereas only 5% of the group that engaged in the special exercise program still suffered from back pain. The results of this study suggest that chronic lower back pain can be decreased or eliminated with exercises that strengthen the back.

Checking the Main Idea

In math, you can check your answers by recalculating the problem using an opposite process. For example, division can be checked with multiplication, and subtraction can be checked using addition. Similarly, you can check your topic sentence to make sure it is the main idea of the paragraph by looking at the major supporting points and asking, "Do most of the supporting details in the paragraph provide more information about this sentence?" If they do, then you have the correct topic sentence.

After reading the paragraph below, decide which one is the correct topic sentence by asking the question, "Do most of the supporting details provide more information about this sentence?"

A Synovial Joint

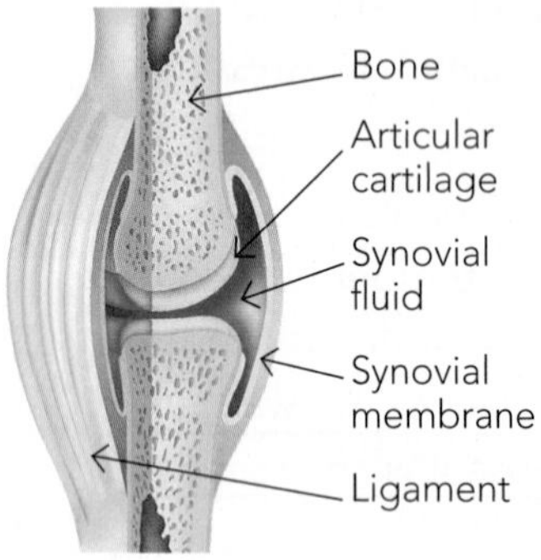

Joint mobility is important for keeping the joint lubricated. Joints contain synovial fluid, which is needed to reduce friction and decrease wear and tear. Moving the joint helps circulate the synovial fluid, which in turn reduces the friction on the cartilage between the bones. Too much friction can damage cartilage, setting the stage for arthritis. Mild stretching can improve the mobility of the joint and promote normal wear on the cartilage covering the ends of the bones.

Which one of these sentences is the main idea that is best supported by the other sentences in the paragraph?

a. Joint mobility is important for keeping the joint lubricated.

b. Joints contain synovial fluid, which is needed to reduce friction and decrease wear and tear.

Explanation:
The major details in the sentences of the paragraph explain why moving joints is important: (1) to improve mobility, (2) to circulate synovial fluid, and (3) to reduce friction on the cartilage. Therefore, the first sentence (answer *a*) is broad enough to cover all the details.

Where to Find Main Ideas

Main ideas can appear **anywhere** in the paragraph.

As you have seen in the examples of paragraphs in the previous sections, main ideas can be found anywhere in a paragraph. Most commonly they are found at the beginning or the end of a paragraph. But they can also be found in the middle of the paragraph if the author begins with details as illustrated in the following paragraph:

Main Idea in middle →

Can a person be both healthy and overweight at the same time? A recent study at the Cooper Clinic in Dallas, Texas, examined the risks of heart-related diseases in men and women including normal-weight and overweight individuals. The study revealed that overweight highly fit men and women had a lower risk for death than men and women who were unfit and of normal weight or overweight. [1] Active overweight individuals can still enjoy the benefits of exercise despite having a higher body mass index than those of normal weight.

Two Topic Sentences

In some paragraphs, the author may repeat the main idea twice in order to emphasize a point. Both topic sentences make the same point but state it differently. Notice the two topic sentences in the following paragraph:

Main Idea →

Obesity can increase the risk of developing numerous diseases, and is a major concern because it has become the most common health problem for Americans. The leading cause of death in the U.S. is cardiovascular disease, or heart disease, and obesity increases the risk of heart attack by 60-80%[1]. Obesity is also linked to hypertension, or high blood pressure, which can cause fatal or debilitating strokes. Another condition related to obesity in many adults is diabetes. Over 80% of people with type 2 diabetes are overweight, including young adults and adolescents[2]. The risks for getting breast, prostate, and colon cancer are also increased among the obese. Clearly, obesity is a major concern for many Americans because it increases the chance of developing serious health problems.

Main Idea →

MyReadingLab

PRACTICE 1

Read the following paragraphs and answer the questions about topics and main ideas. As you read, ask yourself, "What is the topic and the most important point about the topic?"

PARAGRAPH A

Although the mechanism is not well understood, all forms of addiction probably reflect dysfunction of certain biochemical systems in the brain. Addiction is a persistent, compulsive dependence on a behavior or substance, including mood-altering behaviors or activities, despite ongoing negative consequences. Four components are present in all addictions, whether chemical or behavioral:

- Compulsion, or excessive preoccupation with the behavior (drinking, drug use, gambling, etc.) and an overwhelming need to perform it
- Loss of control, or the inability to reliably predict whether any isolated occurrence of the behavior will be healthy or damaging
- Negative consequences, such as physical damage, legal trouble, financial problems, academic failure, or family problems caused by the behavior
- Denial, or the inability to perceive that the behavior is self-destructive

1. What is the topic?
   - **a.** dysfunction
   - **b.** alcohol addiction
   - **c.** addiction
   - **d.** biochemical systems in the brain

2. Which sentence is the topic sentence that expresses the main idea?
   - **a.** Although the mechanism is not well understood, all forms of addiction probably reflect dysfunction of certain biochemical systems in the brain.
   - **b.** Addiction is a persistent, compulsive dependence on a behavior or substance, including mood-altering behaviors or activities, despite ongoing negative consequences.
   - **c.** Four components are present in all addictions, whether chemical or behavioral.
   - **d.** Denial is the inability to perceive that the behavior is self- destructive.

PARAGRAPH B

Addictive substances or behaviors initially provide a sense of pleasure or stability that the addict cannot achieve in other ways. To be addictive, a substance or behavior must have the potential to produce a positive mood change. Chemicals are responsible for the most profound addictions; they produce dramatic mood changes and cause cellular

changes to which the body adapts so well that it eventually needs the chemical in order to function normally. Withdrawal is the variety of symptoms that occur after use of some addictive drugs is reduced or stopped. Other behaviors, such as gambling, spending money, working, and sex, create somewhat milder changes at the cellular level, along with elevating mood, which explains why these behaviors can also be addictive.

3. What is the topic?

a. the causes and effects of addiction
b. withdrawal
c. chemicals and behavior
d. addiction

4. Which sentence is the topic sentence that expresses the main idea?

a. Addictive substances or behaviors initially provide a sense of pleasure or stability that the addict cannot achieve in other ways.
b. To be addictive, a substance or behavior must have the potential to produce a positive mood change.
c. Chemicals are responsible for the most profound addictions; they produce dramatic mood changes and cause cellular changes to which the body adapts so well that it eventually needs the chemical in order to function normally.
d. Withdrawal is the variety of symptoms that occur after use of some addictive drugs is reduced or stopped.

MyReadingLab

PRACTICE 2

Read the following paragraphs and answer the questions about topics and main ideas. As you read, ask yourself, "What is the topic and the most important point about the topic?"

PARAGRAPH A

If you are just beginning an exercise program for fitness, it is often more useful to assess changes in body size and shape as a measurement of your progress, rather than weighing yourself daily on a bathroom scale. The reason: Healthy increases in muscle tissue (achieved by exercise) may cause you to temporarily gain weight, until the process of body fat loss catches up with muscle tissue gains. This is a good thing, but you would not know it if you relied solely on the scale to determine your progress. By monitoring improvements in your body size and shape instead, you can get a more realistic sense of your achievement and stay motivated to stick with an exercise program.

1. What is the topic?

a. exercise program
b. muscle tissue
c. body fat
d. measuring weight loss

Continued...

MyReadingLab

PRACTICE 2

...continued

2. Which sentence is the topic sentence that expresses the main idea?

a. If you are just beginning an exercise program for fitness, it is often more useful to assess changes in body size and shape as a measurement of your progress, rather than weighing yourself daily on a bathroom scale.

b. The reason: Healthy increases in muscle tissue (achieved by exercise) may cause you to temporarily gain weight, until the process of body fat loss catches up with muscle tissue gains.

c. This is a good thing, but you would not know it if you relied solely on the scale to determine your progress.

d. By monitoring improvements in your body size and shape instead, you can get a more realistic sense of your achievement and stay motivated to stick with an exercise program.

PARAGRAPH B

body mass index (BMI): a number calculated from a person's weight and height that is used to assess risk for health problems

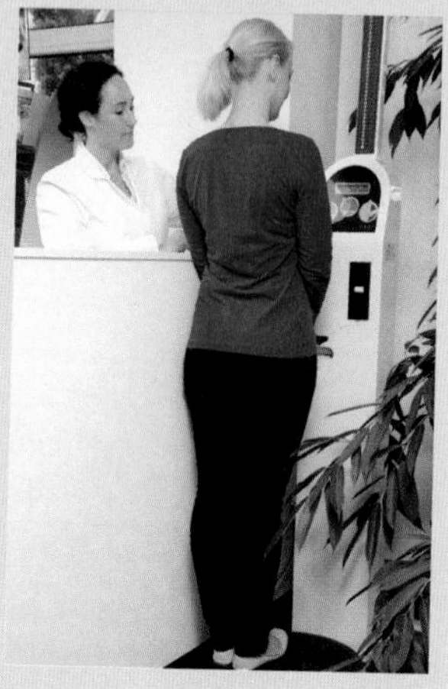

BMI is solely determined by height and weight. While BMI measurements can be helpful for individuals of average muscle and bone density, they can be misleading for athletes, body-builders, and short or petite individuals. The limitation with using BMI scores to assess "fitness" or "fatness" is that they do not differentiate between fat mass and lean mass. For instance, someone who has an exceptionally heavy skeleton and larger-than-average muscle mass may have a BMI score that classifies him or her as "overweight," even if his or her percent body fat is in the "healthy" range. Because of BMI's limitations, it helps to also consider other factors, such as percent of body fat, when assessing the overall picture of a person's fitness.

3. What is the topic?

a. determining weight

b. how to calculate BMI

c. body mass index

d. the limitations of BMI scores

4. Which sentence is the topic sentence that expresses the main idea?

a. The limitation with using BMI scores to assess "fitness" or "fatness" is that they do not differentiate between fat mass and lean mass.

b. BMI is solely determined by height and weight.

c. While BMI measurements can be helpful for individuals of average muscle and bone density, they can be misleading for athletes, body-builders, and short or petite individuals.

d. Because of BMI's limitations, it helps to also consider other factors, such as percent body fat, when assessing the overall picture of a person's fitness.

MyReadingLab

PRACTICE 3

Read the following paragraphs and answer the questions about topics and main ideas. As you read, ask yourself, "What is the topic and the most important point about the topic?"

PARAGRAPH A

The Olympics, the Super Bowl, the World Cup Soccer tournament—people have been competing since before the time of the Ancient Greeks' marathons. What compels us to be the best in sports, business, school, or even cooking? Americans are among the most competitive people on Earth, but they are not alone. Violence at football games in the United Kingdom and Spain are evidence of how seriously they compete. Televisions shows capitalize on this compulsion to be the best with competitions in everything from remodeling houses to making desserts. Whether we aspire to be the best as individuals or as a nation, the urge to stand out from the crowd and be recognized as someone special serves our innate need for approval. Advertising marketers take advantage of this compulsion and sell us products that will make us "winners" by owning the best phone, the best television, or the best car. Competition creates strong motivation economically, socially, and culturally. It is human nature to admire the biggest, strongest and smartest as icons of what we can aspire to achieve. Competition is man's motivation to strive for greatness.

1. What is the topic?
   - **a.** sports competitions
   - **b.** competition
   - **c.** advertising and competition
   - **d.** sporting events

2. Which sentence is the topic sentence that expresses the main idea?
   - **a.** What compels us to be the best in sports, business, school, or even cooking?
   - **b.** Americans are among the most competitive people on Earth, but they are not alone.
   - **c.** Advertising marketers take advantage of this compulsion and sell us products that will make us "winners" by owning the best television or the best car.
   - **d.** Competition is man's motivation to strive for greatness.

PARAGRAPH B

When African-American Jesse Owens arrived in Berlin to compete in the 1936 Olympics, he was allowed to stay at the same hotel as the white athletes because Germany didn't have the same segregation policies that he faced in America. Adolf Hitler, leader of the Nazis, wanted to use the Olympic Games to prove the superiority of his white Germans (the "Aryan race"). However, Owens dominated the track and field events by winning four gold medals, an achievement that disgusted Hitler, and he refused to acknowledge

Continued...

MyReadingLab

PRACTICE 3

...continued

those victories. Although Jesse Owens was the most successful athlete at the 1936 Summer Olympics, he still faced segregation at home. Despite the fact that Owens was hailed as a hero and lauded in a parade in New York City with the other athletes, he had to use the freight elevator at the hotel reception honoring him because blacks were not allowed on public elevators. Nor did the White House invite Owens to congratulate him on his astounding victory, especially for defeating Hitler's "superior" race.

3. What is the topic?

a. 1936 Summer Olympics
b. Gold medal winners
c. Jesse Owens' Olympic victory
d. Jesse Owens

4. Which sentence is the topic sentence that expresses the main idea?

a. When African-American Jesse Owens arrived in Berlin to compete in the 1936 Olympics, he was allowed to stay at the same hotels as the white athletes because Germany didn't have the same segregation policies he faced in America.

b. Although Jesse Owens was the most successful athlete at the 1936 Summer Olympics, he still faced segregation at home.

c. Despite the fact that Owens was hailed as a hero and lauded in a parade in New York City with the other athletes, he had to use the freight elevator at the hotel reception honoring him because blacks were not allowed on public elevators.

d. Nor did the White House invite Owens to congratulate him on his astounding victory, especially for defeating Hitler's "superior" race.

U-REVIEW 1

Review the most important points about main ideas by answering the following questions. Check your answers when you finish.

1. What is a main idea?

....

....

2. What is a topic?

....

....

3. What is a topic sentence?

....

....

4. What two questions should you ask to find the author's main idea?

....

....

OBJECTIVE 3

Identify major and minor details.

SUPPORTING DETAILS

In writing, authors not only have a goal and a main point to convey to readers, they must also support their point with details that help prove, explain, or illustrate the main idea. Supporting details have an important role to play in writing because they complete the picture for the reader. When more details are provided, the author's ideas and messages will be more clear and complete to the readers. Read the following paragraph about the cardiovascular system:

> The cardiovascular system is composed of the heart and blood vessels. It delivers nutrients and oxygen throughout the body. It also helps remove waste products.

The reader is given little information about the cardiovascular system, and many questions remain unanswered, such as *How does it work? What is its structure?*

Supporting details provide all the information that the author feels are necessary for his or her purpose. For instance, a paragraph about the cardiovascular system appearing in a high-school biology textbook will not have as many details as one in a medical school textbook because high school students don't need to know the same amount of information as someone aspiring to become a doctor.

Read the following paragraph about the cardiovascular system containing more supporting details than the first one. The main idea (in bold print) explains what the cardiovascular system is, and the supporting details (underlined) explain its structure and how it works.

> [1] **The cardiovascular system is composed of the heart and a network of blood vessels through which the heart pumps blood and oxygen into the body.** [2] <u>The right side of the heart pumps deoxygenated blood to the lungs through a pulmonary circuit.</u> [3] In the lungs, a gas exchange takes place and carbon dioxide is exchanged for oxygen. [4] <u>The left side of the heart pumps oxygenated blood through the systemic circuit.</u> [5]<u>Arteries carry oxygen-filled blood to the rest of the body and the pulmonary vein carries oxygenated blood to the heart.</u> [6] <u>The veins in the pulmonary circuit carry deoxygenated blood back to the heart.</u> [7] The smallest branches of the blood vessels are the capillaries, with walls only one cell thick that allow nutrients, oxygen, and wastes to easily pass through during the exchange.

Major and Minor Supporting Details

In good writing, the main idea is supported by the major details, and the major details are supported by minor details, as shown in the diagram below.

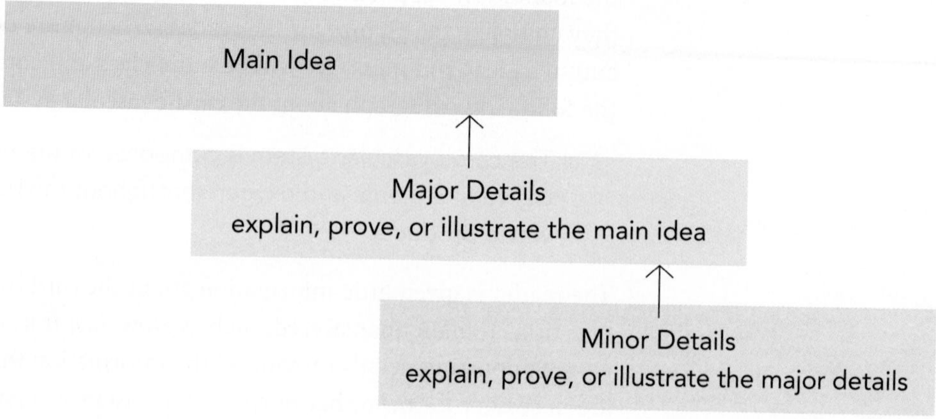

major details explain, prove, or illustrate the main idea.

There are two types of supporting details, each with a specific job to perform. **Major details** explain, prove, or illustrate the main idea. To find the major details, turn the main idea into a question. For example, in the paragraph you read earlier about dietary fiber, the main idea was **Dietary fiber** is important for several reasons. To find the major details, turn this sentence into a question, "What are the reasons why dietary fiber is important?" The reasons are the following major details:

Major Detail #1:

It aids the intestinal tract in eliminating food waste, hastening the digestive process and lowering the risk of colon cancer.

Major Detail #2:

Dietary fiber is also helpful in reducing cholesterol because some types of fiber prevent its absorption into the blood.

Major Detail #3:

Another benefit of dietary fiber is that it helps to regulate glucose levels, which control the appetite.

minor details explain, prove, or illustrate the major details.

Minor details give us more information about the major details. They usually follow major details because they illustrate, prove, or explain the major details. In the paragraph above, blood vessels are a major detail because they are a part of the cardiovascular system. One type of blood vessel is the capillary. Thus, the last sentence provides more information about a major detail—the blood vessels.

To find the major details in the paragraph above about the cardiovascular system, turn the main idea into a question such as, "What is the cardiovascular system?" The four major parts of the system are the major details, found in sentences 2, 4, 5 and 6. They tell us more information about the cardiovascular system, such as what the components are and their functions. Sentences 3 and 7 give us more information about the major details, so they are minor details.

Here is a concept map of how the major and minor details support the main idea about the cardiovascular system:

Topic: The Cardiovascular System

(**Main Idea**) The cardiovascular system is composed of the heart and a network of blood vessels through which the heart pumps blood and oxygen into the body.

Major Details:

- Right side of the heart pumps deoxygenated blood.
- Left side of the heart pumps oxygenated blood.
- Arteries and pulmonary veins carry oxygen-filled blood.
- Veins carry deoxygenated blood back to the heart.

Minor Details:

- In the lungs, carbon dioxide is exchanged for oxygen. (supports: Right side of the heart pumps deoxygenated blood.)
- Capillaries are the smallest blood vessels. (supports: Veins carry deoxygenated blood back to the heart.)

As you read the following paragraph about antibiotics try to spot the major and minor details. The topic is in bold print and the main idea is underlined.

> [1] In the past, doctors treated bacterial infections like ear infections, sinus infections, and tonsillitis with antibiotics that effectively eliminated them. [2] Over time, however, those same antibiotics have become less effective. [3] **Bacteria** can change, or adapt, to resist the medicines developed to kill it. [4] Over the years, more drug-resistant bacteria have developed due in part to the widespread and often improper use of antibiotics. [5] When doctors prescribe antibiotics for infections, they instruct patients to take the drugs until the prescriptions are empty. [6] Instead of following the doctors' orders, some people stop taking the medicine as soon as they feel better. [7] In these cases, the weaker bacteria have been killed, but the bacteria still remaining in patients' bodies is the most drug-resistant strain. [8] Those drug-resistant bacteria multiply and as a result, the infection comes back, but this time it is the drug-resistant strain of the bacteria at work. [9] This is why it's important to take the entire antibiotic as prescribed by your physician—to avoid a relapse by killing *all* the bacteria.

Topic: Bacteria

Main Idea: Bacteria can change, or adapt, to resist the medicines developed to kill it.

Major Detail: (Explain why bacteria is adaptable and how it adapts.) Sentence 4 is a major detail that tells more about the main idea.

Minor Details: (Explain more about sentence 4) Sentences 5–9 are minor details because they provide an example showing *how* bacteria can become drug-resistant.

Introductory Sentences

Introductory sentences are often used to introduce the topic and provide background information for a passage, or to ask questions about the topic to pique the readers' interest. In the paragraph about bacteria, sentences 1 and 2 are introductory sentences (minor details) that point out the problem that antibiotics have become less effective at eliminating bacteria.

Finding Major Details with Transitions

Transitions are words or phrases that show relationships between ideas in a sentence or paragraph, and they can be very useful when identifying major supporting details. Authors sometimes begin major detail sentences with transitional words and phrases. There are many different transitions that show different types of relationships, but for this chapter we will only consider 3 types of transitions. Here are some examples of transition words and their relationships:

1. **Time order transitions** (show a chain of events in the order they occurred): *first, second, third, one, next, later, finally,* and *last of all.*

2. **Listing transitions** (list ideas in no special order): *first, second, third, one, next, later, finally,* and *last of all.*
3. **Addition transitions** (when additional ideas are added on): *also, and, furthermore, another, moreover,* and *in addition.*

Notice how the transitions identify the three major supporting details in the following paragraph. (The main idea is underlined in the first sentence.)

> You can reduce the number of calories and saturated fats in the meals you cook by following several tips. **First**, use low-fat or non-fat milk and cheese when making sauces or casseroles. Low-fat mozzarella, farmer's and ricotta cheeses are less fattening. **Also**, when baking and sautéing, instead of using animal fats, which are saturated, use mono- or poly-unsaturated vegetable oils such as olive oil or canola oil. **Finally**, use wine or vinegar to flavor foods instead of butter, margarine, oils, or mayonnaise to reduce both fat and calorie intake.

MyReadingLab

PRACTICE 4

Read the paragraph and answer the questions that follow. As you read, find the topic and the main idea by asking yourself:

1. What is the topic, and what is the most important point about the topic?
2. Find the major details by turning the main idea into a question.
3. Circle topics, underline main ideas and transitions, and highlight major details.

> One of the most common, and easily interpreted, classification groupings describes individuals as having characteristics that fit into one of four behavior pattern categories: Type A, Type B, Type C, and Type D. People who exhibit Type A Behavior Pattern (TABP) are highly motivated, time-conscious, hard-driving, impatient, and sometimes hostile, cynical, and angry. They have a heightened response to stress, and tendencies toward hostility and anger, placing them at high risk for heart disease. Individuals with Type B Behavior Pattern (TBBP) are easygoing, non-aggressive, and patient, and they are not prone to hostile episodes like their TABP counterparts. People with TBBP are less likely to perceive everyday annoyances as significant stressors and are at low risk for heart disease from stress. People with Type C behavior pattern have many of the positive qualities of TABP because they are confident, highly motivated, and competitive. However, individuals with Type C behavior pattern typically do not express the hostility and anger seen with TABP. People with Type C behavior pattern have the positive characteristics of TABP but do not express their negative emotions and feelings in the same manner. Individuals with Type D behavior pattern also are considered to be at greater risk for stress-related disease because they are prone to worry and anxiety

Continued...

MyReadingLab

PRACTICE 4

...continued

and also tend to be socially inhibited and uneasy when interacting with others. Their social clumsiness results in a chronic state of anxiety, which places them at greater risk for heart disease.

1. Which sentence states the main idea (the topic sentence)?

a. One of the most common, and easily interpreted, classification groupings describes individuals as having characteristics that fit into one of four behavior pattern categories: Type A, Type B, Type C, and Type D.

b. People who exhibit Type A Behavior Pattern (TABP) are highly motivated, time-conscious, hard-driving, impatient, and sometimes hostile, cynical, and angry.

c. Individuals with Type B Behavior Pattern (TBBP) are easygoing, nonaggressive, and patient, and they are not prone to hostile episodes like their TABP counterparts.

d. Individuals with Type D behavior pattern also are considered to be at greater risk for stress-related disease because they are prone to worry and anxiety and also tend to be socially inhibited and uneasy when interacting with others.

2. Write a question using the main idea that helps you to find the major details.

....

....

3. Which of the following sentences is a minor detail? (First identify the topic sentence and major details and then choose the minor one.)

a. Individuals with Type B Behavior Pattern (TBBP) are easygoing, nonaggressive, and patient, and they are not prone to hostile episodes like their TABP counterparts.

b. People with TBBP are less likely to perceive everyday annoyances as significant stressors and are at low risk for heart disease from stress.

c. People with Type C behavior pattern have many of the positive qualities of TABP because they are confident, highly motivated, and competitive.

d. Individuals with Type D behavior pattern also are considered to be at greater risk for stress-related disease because they are prone to worry and anxiety and also tend to be socially inhibited and uneasy when interacting with others.

MyReadingLab

PRACTICE 5

Read the paragraph and answer the questions that follow. As you read, find the topic and the main idea by asking yourself:

1. What is the topic, and what is the most important point about the topic?
2. Find the major details by turning the main idea into a question.
3. Circle topics, underline main ideas and transitions, and highlight major details.

With the rise in rates of overweight and obesity in the United States, it's clear that the balance of "calories in" versus "calories out" has become an issue for many individuals. Several factors are contributing to an increase in calorie consumption. One factor is that people consume a lot of simple sugar, often in the form of sucrose (table sugar) or high fructose corn syrup (a commercial sweetener). The problem with simple sugars is that they often contain many calories but few micronutrients (which is why they're called "empty calories"). Alcohol, if consumed in excess, is another source of empty calories that can undermine an otherwise healthy diet. Chronic alcohol consumption also tends to deplete the body's stores of some vitamins, possibly leading to severe deficiencies. Another factor behind the rise in overweight and obesity in the United States is the high amount of fat in many people's diets. Foods high in fat not only tend to be rich in cholesterol, but also contain more than twice as many calories per gram than foods high in carbohydrate or protein (9 calories/gram versus 4 calories/gram). Limiting fat in the diet helps limit calories and also reduces the risk of heart disease.

1. Which sentence states the main idea (the topic sentence)?
   - **a.** With the rise in rates of overweight and obesity in the United States, it's clear that the balance of "calories in" versus "calories out" has become an issue for many individuals.
   - **b.** Several factors are contributing to an increase in calorie consumption.
   - **c.** Alcohol, if consumed in excess, is another source of empty calories that can undermine an otherwise healthy diet.
   - **d.** Another factor behind the rise in overweight and obesity in the United States is the high amount of fat in many people's diets.

2. Write a question using the main idea that helps you to find the major details.

   ....

   ....

MyReadingLab

PRACTICE 5

...continued

3. Which of the following sentences is a **minor** detail? (First identify the topic sentence and major details and then choose the minor one.)
   a. One factor is that people consume a lot of simple sugar, often in the form of sucrose (table sugar) or high fructose corn syrup (a commercial sweetener).
   b. Alcohol, if consumed in excess, is another source of empty calories that can undermine an otherwise healthy diet.
   c. Another factor behind the rise in overweight and obesity in the United States is the high amount of fat in many people's diets.
   d. Limiting fat in the diet helps limit calories and also reduces the risk of heart disease.

MyReadingLab

PRACTICE 6

Read the paragraph and answer the questions that follow. As you read, find the topic and the main idea by asking yourself:

1. What is the topic, and what is the most important point about the topic?
2. Find the major details by turning the main idea into a question.
3. Circle topics, underline main ideas and transitions, and highlight major details.

The "secondhand" smoke emitted by the lit end of a cigarette, combined with the smoke exhaled by active smokers, is more accurately referred to as environmental tobacco smoke, or ETS. This smoke affects not only the active smoker, who is holding and inhaling from the cigarette, but also non-smoking individuals in the environment. A nonsmoker in an environment high in ETS is called a passive smoker. ETS is similar to the smoke inhaled by an active smoker, but it has some key differences. According to the National Cancer Institute, more than 4500 chemicals have been identified in tobacco smoke, and there may be as many as 100,000 chemicals in this mix of gases and particles. Passive smokers are exposed to the same mix of chemicals as active smokers, although typically in much lower concentrations. Surprisingly, certain chemical compounds are actually higher in concentration in ETS than in actively inhaled smoke. Carbon monoxide, a by-product of incomplete combustion, is the most abundant gas in ETS. In fact, carbon monoxide is approximately five times more abundant in ETS than it is in the smoke inhaled by active smokers. You may have heard of carbon monoxide as a poisonous air pollutant that occurs inside homes with faulty furnaces or other gas-burning appliances. While the levels of carbon monoxide in ETS alone are not deadly to passive smokers, effects of exposure to elevated levels of carbon monoxide can lead to serious consequences. ETS contains high concentrations of airborne particulates (particles with a diameter less than half the width of a human hair) commonly known as tar. Because most active smokers inhale cigarette smoke through a filter tip, the amount of particulates acquired by primary smoking is reduced. However, because neither active nor passive smokers breathe through a filter otherwise, they are both exposed to the full concentration of particulates present in ETS. Chronic exposure to airborne particulates can lead to a number of negative health effects, including emphysema and cancer.

1. Which sentence states the main idea (the topic sentence)?

a. The "secondhand" smoke emitted by the lit end of a cigarette, combined with the smoke exhaled by active smokers, is more accurately referred to as environmental tobacco smoke, or ETS.

b. A nonsmoker in an environment high in ETS is called a passive smoker.

c. According to the National Cancer Institute, more than 4500 chemicals have been identified in tobacco smoke, and there may be as many as 100,000 chemicals in this mix of gases and particles.

d. Chronic exposure to airborne particulates can lead to a number of negative health effects, including emphysema and cancer.

2. Write a question using the main idea that helps you to find the major details.

....

....

3. Which of the following sentences is a minor detail? (First identify the topic sentence and major details and then choose the minor one.)

a. A nonsmoker in an environment high in ETS is called a passive smoker.

b. Surprisingly, certain chemical compounds are actually higher in concentration in ETS than in actively inhaled smoke.

c. You may have heard of carbon monoxide as a poisonous air pollutant that occurs inside homes with faulty furnaces or other gas-burning appliances.

d. ETS contains high concentrations of airborne particulates (particles with a diameter less than half the width of a human hair) commonly known as tar.

U-REVIEW 2

Review the important concepts about supporting details by answering the following questions.

1. What do major supporting details do?

....

....

....

2. What do minor details do?

....

....

....

3. What are two ways to find the major details?

....

....

....

4. How can you tell if a detail is a major one or a minor one?

....

....

....

MyReadingLab

Reading 1
VOCABULARY PREVIEW

"Doping for Gold: The Dangers of Doping" by PBS

Match the words in the Word Bank by writing the letter of the word next to the matching definition. The paragraph numbers in parentheses indicate the location of each word in the reading selection. Read the words in the paragraphs from "Doping for Gold" to determine the correct meanings as they are used in context.

WORD BANK

a. doping (2)	b. synthetic derivatives (4)	c. atrophy (4)
d. masculinizing (4)	e. adenoids (5)	f. stimulates (6)
g. induce (6)	h. therapeutic (7)	i. hemoglobin (8)
j. anecdotal (10)	k. invincibility (12)	

1. .... tissue growth in nose above the throat
2. .... for healing purposes
3. .... chemical compounds produced from similar ones
4. .... the use of performance-enhancing substances
5. .... wasting away; shriveling
6. .... making masculine
7. .... a protein present in the blood of many animals
8. .... to bring about or cause
9. .... the inability to be defeated
10. .... causes an action to occur
11. .... evidence based on observation

MyReadingLab
Reading 1
PREVIEW

Discuss the following questions with a partner or small group.

1. What sports or games do you enjoy playing or watching?
2. Do you think that too much importance is placed upon winning in sports, and not enough emphasis placed on enjoyment? Why or why not?

After you preview the article, write one or two preview questions on the lines below:

....

....

....

....

....

MyReadingLab
Reading 1

"Doping for Gold: The Dangers of Doping" by PBS

"For two years, I took EPO, growth hormone, anabolic steroids, testosterone, amphetamine. Just about everything. That was part of the job." - Erwan Mentheour, Cyclist.

1 Since the beginning of the Olympic Games in Ancient Greece, athletes have taken major steps to become better, faster and stronger than their competitors. Egyptians ingested the ground rear hooves of the Abyssinian mule to improve their performance and Greek athletes ingested mushrooms for their performance-enhancing properties.

What is doping and why is it used?

2 Today, the use of performance-enhancing substances in sports has come to be known internationally as doping. Doping is the use of drugs by athletes in order to achieve a competitive edge, and includes any substance, either natural or synthetic, foodstuff or supplement, legal or illegal, that when introduced to the human body gives the user a competitive advantage, according to the CASA National Commission on Sports and Substance Abuse.

3 The list of performance-enhancing drugs is fairly extensive, according to Dr. Gary Wadler, who serves on the committee that determines The World Anti-Doping Agency's (WADA) banned substances list. Some of the most common drugs used among the elite athletes are the ones we worry about the most, including anabolic steroids, human growth hormones (hGH) and Erythropoietin (EPO), he said. For CASA's 2000 Report "Winning at any Cost:

Doping in Olympic Sports," Dr. Wadler identified their known side effects, but he says that many of the side effects of these drugs are still unknown.

What do anabolic steroids do?

Anabolic Steroids: Physiological/Adverse Effects

4 The anabolic steroids used by athletes are synthetic derivatives of the male sex hormone testosterone. Athletes use steroids to achieve increases in muscle mass and strength and/or to improve recovery from training by decreasing tissue breakdown. Adverse effects of steroid use include liver tumors, testicular atrophy, development of abnormal breast tissue in males and masculinizing effects in females (increased body hair, deepening of voice).

What are the effects of hGH?

Human Growth Hormones (hGH): Physiological/Adverse Effects

5 Human growth hormone is a hormone secreted by the pituitary gland. The release of hGH is controlled by many factors, including diet, exercise, nutrition, drugs and various biological feedback mechanisms. Growth hormone appeals to athletes who are trying to increase their lean body mass and shorten recovery time, but to date there are no well-controlled studies of hGH demonstrating actual improvements in strength and endurance. Side effects that have been reported include headache, enlargement of the adenoids with snoring, and further growth of hands, feet and face.

How does EPO work?

Erythropoietin (EPO): Physiological/Adverse Effects

6 EPO stimulates bone marrow stem cells to produce red blood cells. The additional red cells transport oxygen from the lungs to all organs of the body, including the muscles, and enhance aerobic power. EPO found its way into sports as an alternative to blood doping, the practice of intravenously infusing blood into an individual in order to induce an elevated red blood cell count and increase his or her total aerobic power. This increases the transport of oxygen to the working muscles. The abuse of EPO raises both the red blood count and the thickness of the blood, which can raise the possibility of stroke and heart attack.

7 The athletes are not using these substances for therapeutic purposes. They conjure up their own craziness and use them in massive quantities. A normal dose may be 10 (milligrams), and they may take 100 or 1000 (milligrams). They also combine the drugs, one on top of another—a term known as "stacking," Dr. Wadler said.

8 Doping has definitely been around for a while, but today it seems like you can't follow the Olympic Games without seeing some sort of drug scandal. While there used to be a lack of any effective mechanism to police the use of banned substances in the Olympics, sports governing bodies, such as WADA, are cracking down on doping. Before the iconic opening ceremony of the 2006 Winter Olympics in Turin, Italy, 12 cross-country skiers, including two Americans and a former gold medalist from Germany, were suspended for failed blood tests. The athletes were suspended five days each for elevated levels of hemoglobin, the red blood cell that increases endurance. The test results raised the possibility of blood doping with synthetic hemoglobin to increase oxygen in the muscles. Just last year, Olympic track star Marion Jones was stripped of the record five medals she won in the 2000 Olympics in Sydney, Australia, after she admitted to having used steroids.

What are the effects of doping?

9 "You have to view this as giving yourself a disease," said Dr. Wadler. "In the '80s, I reported a series of deaths from EPO. The cyclists, all in their 20s, 'mysteriously' died after taking EPO."

Continued...

MyReadingLab

Reading 1

...continued

10 One of the problems that still remain is that there is no solid evidence on doping in the Olympics and how many athletes actually use [performance-enhancement] drugs. All of the evidence is anecdotal, according to Sue Foster, CASA's Vice President and Director of Policy Research and Analysis. But there are enough reports and tests to show that it's a serious health and safety issue, she said.

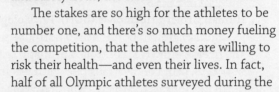

11 The stakes are so high for the athletes to be number one, and there's so much money fueling the competition, that the athletes are willing to risk their health—and even their lives. In fact, half of all Olympic athletes surveyed during the 1996 Summer Olympic Games in Atlanta admitted that they would be willing to take a drug—even if it would kill them eventually—as long as it would let them win every event they entered five years in a row, as reported by *Sports Illustrated*.

12 The mentality of winning at any cost still persists today, according to Dr. Wadler. "Athletes live in a world of invincibility and denial. They'll hear me say it's dangerous, but their risk-reward ratio is so distorted that they disregard the risk even if it means shortening their lives."

918 words divided by .... minutes = ... words per minute

MyReadingLab

Reading 1 REVIEW

A good review strategy to use after reading is to summarize what you just read in your own words. Take a few minutes to think about the author's most important point and any key ideas that helped to support or explain it.

Write a two- or three-sentence summary on the lines below.

....

....

....

....

....

....

....

....

....

MyReadingLab

Reading 1 COMPREHENSION QUESTIONS

The following questions will help you recall the main idea and details of "Doping For Gold." Read any parts of the article that you need to find the correct answers.

MAIN IDEAS

1. What is the topic, or subject of this selection?

a. Doping for Gold
b. athletes who cheat
c. doping in the Olympics
d. doping in sports

2. What is the authors' overall main idea of this selection?

a. Since the beginning of the Olympic Games in Ancient Greece, athletes have taken major steps to become better, faster and stronger than their competitors.

b. Doping has definitely been around for a while, but today it seems like you can't follow the Olympic Games without seeing some sort of drug scandal.

c. Doping is the use of drugs by athletes in order to achieve a competitive edge, and includes any substance, either natural or synthetic, foodstuff or supplement, legal or illegal, that when introduced to the human body gives the user a competitive advantage, according to the CASA National Commission on Sports and Substance Abuse.

d. The stakes are so high for the athletes to be number one, and there's so much money fueling the competition, that the athletes are willing to risk their health—and even their lives.

3. What is the main idea of paragraph 5?

a. Human growth hormone is a hormone secreted by the pituitary gland.

b. The release of hGH is controlled by many factors, including diet, exercise, nutrition, drugs and various biological feedback mechanisms.

c. Growth hormone appeals to athletes who are trying to increase their lean body mass and shorten recovery time, but to date there are no well-controlled studies of hGH demonstrating actual improvements in strength and endurance.

d. Side effects that have been reported include headache, enlargement of the adenoids with snoring, and further growth of hands, feet and face.

SUPPORTING DETAILS

4. Which of the following is a minor detail for paragraph 6?

a. EPO stimulates bone marrow stem cells to produce red blood cells.

b. The additional red cells transport oxygen from the lungs to all organs of the body, including the muscles, and enhance aerobic power.

c. EPO found its way into sports as an alternative to blood doping, the practice of intravenously infusing blood into an individual in order to induce an elevated red blood cell count and increase their total aerobic power.

d. The abuse of EPO raises both the red blood count and the thickness of the blood, which can raise the possibility of stroke and heart attack.

5. According to the article, why is the use of EPO to gain a competitive edge not worth the risk?

a. Drug tests are able to identify athletes who have used EPO.

b. EPO has caused the deaths of numerous young athletes and it can lead to stroke or heart attack.

c. Athletes are willing to do anything to win, even if it means risking their lives.

d. EPO is more effective than blood doping and more difficult to detect in a drug test.

Continued...

MyReadingLab

Reading 1 COMPREHENSION QUESTIONS

...continued

6. Which of the following is the main idea of paragraph 8?

a. Doping has definitely been around for a while, but today it seems like you can't follow the Olympic Games without seeing some sort of drug scandal.

b. Before the iconic opening ceremony of the 2006 Winter Olympics in Turin, Italy, 12 cross-country skiers, including two Americans and a former gold medalist from Germany, were suspended for failed blood tests.

c. While there used to be a lack of any effective mechanism to police the use of banned substances in the Olympics, sports governing bodies, such as WADA, are cracking down on doping.

d. Just last year, Olympic track star Marion Jones was stripped of the record five medals she won in the 2000 Olympics in Sydney, Australia, after she admitted to having used steroids.

DRAWING CONCLUSIONS

7. Which of the following is true according to the information in this article?

a. Few athletes are willing to risk their lives by doping to win competitions.

b. All professional athletes are involved in some sort of cheating because they know their competitors are cheating.

c. Winning Olympic medals by doping is worth the risk of getting caught and losing them.

d. Athletes who have been warned of the serious side effects of doping will not get involved with it.

VOCABULARY IN CONTEXT

8. What is the meaning of the underlined word in this sentence from paragraph 1? Egyptians <u>ingested</u> the ground rear hooves of the Abyssinian mule to improve their performance, and Greek athletes ingested mushrooms for their performance-enhancing properties.

a. ate

b. applied

c. sought after

d. injected

9. What is the meaning of the underlined word in this sentence from paragraph 7? They <u>conjure</u> up their own craziness and use them in massive quantities.

a. calculate

b. institute

c. evaluate

d. create

Reading 1
VOCABULARY PRACTICE: WORD GAME

1. Divide into teams of 2 to 4 people.

2. One team will answer all of the odd numbered questions, and the other will answer the even numbered questions, taking turns after each question. Each team has one minute to answer the question and only one answer is allowed.

3. Answer each question by first filling in the blank in the sentence with one of the words from the Word Bank. Then write the word anywhere on the grid, one letter per square. Words can go across, down, diagonally, or backwards. All words must be spelled correctly.

4. Teams get 5 points for a correct answer and an **additional point** each time they use a letter that is already on the crossword grid by crossing their word over another.

For example:

```
  B
C**R**OSSWORD
  E
  A
  K
```

5. When all the questions have been answered, the team with the most points wins.

1. If you were observing squirrels for a science project and kept a diary of their behavior, your evidence would be ....
2. When Harry was a boy, he had his tonsils and .... removed.
3. The nurse checked the patient's .... levels.
4. Muscles that are not used will begin to .... from disuse.
5. Olympic medallists who test positive for .... lose their medals.
6. People admire fictional action heroes because of their ....
7. Coffee .... the nervous system and wakes you up.
8. Many products made today are .... of other products.
9. Testosterone has .... effects on women athletes.
10. Some drugs may .... hallucinations or anxiety.
11. Marijuana is sometimes used as a .... means to reduce pain.

WORD BANK

doping	masculinizing	induce	synthetic derivatives
adenoids	therapeutic	atrophy	stimulates
hemoglobin	anecdotal	invincibility	

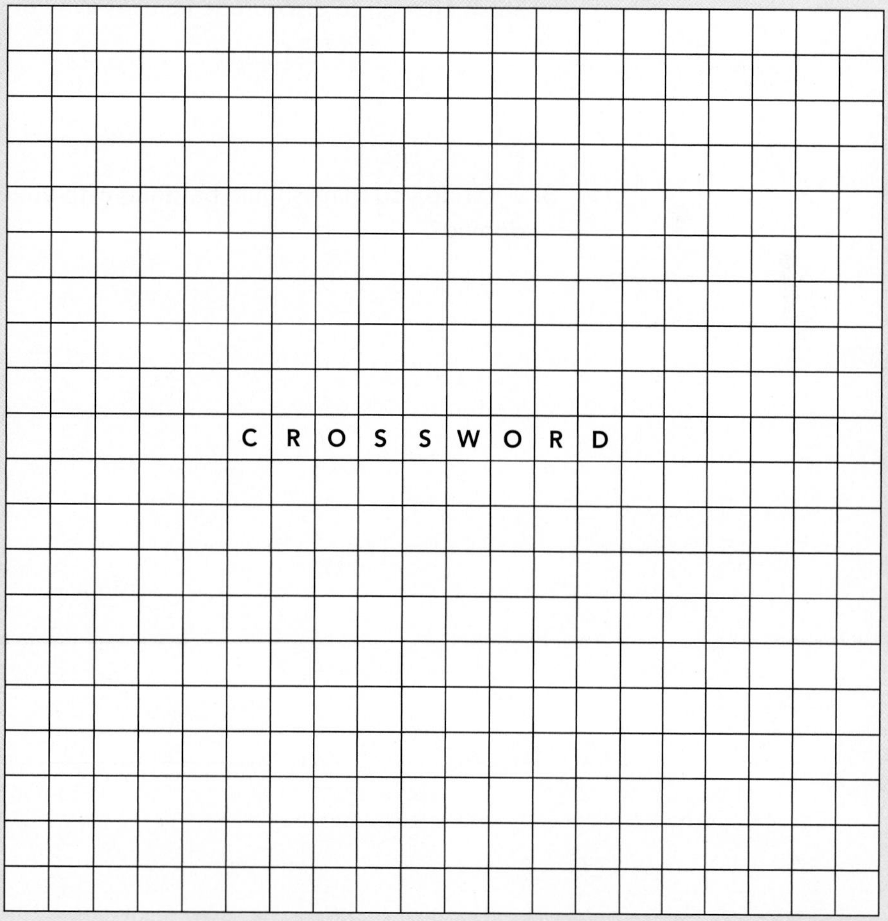

MyReadingLab

Reading 1 QUESTIONS FOR WRITING AND DISCUSSION

Review any parts of the article you need to answer the following questions.

1. Why do you think professional athletes, who have had much success in sports, would take such high risks to indulge in doping when they know the consequences?

2. Which type of doping do you consider the most serious, and why?

3. How would you feel if you found out that an athlete you admired had tested positive for doping, and why?

4. Do you think the penalties for athletes who test positive for doping are harsh enough to discourage its use? Why or why not?

5. What do you think should be done with athletes who test positive for doping?

MyReadingLab

Reading 2
VOCABULARY PREVIEW

"Managing Stress in Your Life" by Janet L. Hopson, Rebecca J. Donatelle, and Tanya R. Littrell

Match the words in the Word Bank by writing the letter of the word next to the matching definition. The paragraph numbers in parentheses indicate the location of each word. Read the words in "Managing Stress in Your Life" to determine the correct meanings as they are used in context.

WORD BANK

a. physiological (3)	b. prone (4)	c. variables (4)
d. negate (4)	e. debilitating (4)	f. eustress (5)
g. metabolic (5)	h. immune (8)	i. supplementation (8)
j. hinders (9)	k. diminishes (10)	

1. .... to undo
2. .... having to do with the physical body
3. .... the adding on of additional things
4. .... harmful
5. .... other factors
6. .... good stress
7. .... relating to the body's defense against illness
8. .... open to; susceptible
9. .... makes less
10. .... of the physical and chemical processes that produce bodily energy
11. .... obstructs, prevents

MyReadingLab

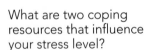

Reading 2
PREVIEW

Discuss the following questions with a partner or small group.

1. What are the causes of stress in your life?
2. What are some things you do to reduce your stress level?

After you preview the article, write one or two preview questions on the lines below:

MyReadingLab

Reading 2

"Managing Stress in Your Life"

by Janet L. Hopson, Rebecca J. Donatelle, and Tanya R. Littrell

What Effective Strategies Can I Use to Manage Stress?

1 Most college students are able to manage their stress and do their best with a low-key, multi-pronged approach.

Internal Resources for Coping with Stress

2 When you perceive that your personal resources are **sufficient** to meet life's demands, you experience little or no stress. By contrast, when you perceive that life's demands exceed your coping resources, you are likely to feel strain and distress.

Self-Esteem and Self-Efficacy

What are two coping resources that influence your stress level?

3 Several coping resources influence your stress appraisal, or how you measure the stress in your life. Two of the most important are self-esteem and self-efficacy. Self-esteem is a sense of positive self-regard, or how you feel about yourself. Self-efficacy is a belief or confidence in personal skills and performance abilities. Researchers consider self-efficacy one of the most important personality traits that influence psychological and physiological stress responses. Low self-esteem or low self-efficacy can lead you to feel helpless to cope with the stress in your life. Conversely, if you work to build your self-esteem and self-efficacy, you will add the benefit of less stress in your life.

What is psychological hardiness?

Hardiness

4 So-called "Type A" personalities are characterized as hard-driving, competitive, time-driven perfectionists. "Type B" personalities, in contrast, are more relaxed, noncompetitive, and more tolerant of others. Historically, researchers believed that people with Type A characteristics were more prone to heart attacks than their Type B counterparts. Researchers today believe that personality types are more complex than previously thought— most people are not one personality type all the time, and other variables must be explored. Psychological hardiness may negate self-imposed stress associated with Type A behavior. Psychologically people are characterized by control, commitment, and an embrace of challenge. People with a sense of control are able to accept responsibility for their behaviors and change those that they discover to be debilitating. People with a sense of commitment have good self-esteem and understand their purpose in life. People who embrace challenge see change as an opportunity for personal growth. The concept of hardiness has been studied extensively, and many researchers believe it is the foundation of an individual's ability to cope with stress and remain healthy.

Exercise, Fun, and Recreational Activity

5 Improving your overall level of fitness may be the most helpful thing you can do to combat stress. Interestingly, research shows that exercise actually stimulates the stress response, but that a well-exercised body adapts to the eustress of exercise, and as a result is able to tolerate greater levels of distress of all kinds. Compared to an unfit person, a fit individual develops a milder stress response to any given stressor. Research also shows that exercise reduces both psychosocial stress and metabolic disturbances leading to belly fat, high blood pressure, high blood cholesterol, and vascular disease.

How does fitness influence stress levels?

6 Many physical activities relieve the feeling of stress and tension, while others—especially those that involve competition, high skill levels, or physical risk—may add to your stress load. Some activities are high in one value and low in the other, but many can build fitness and promote relaxation at the same time. The trick is to balance exercise, fun, and recreational activities in your free time so that you can stay fit and reduce chronic stress.

Basic Wellness Measures

7 Many of the habits you cultivate to improve your wellness can also fight the negative effects of stress.

Eating Well

How does nutrition affect stress levels?

8 Eating nutrient-dense foods rather than fast foods and junk foods gives you more mental and physical energy, improves your immune responses, and helps you stay at a healthy weight. Under-eating, over-eating, or eating nutrient-poor foods can contribute to your stress levels by diminishing your overall wellness. Most claims about vitamins and supplements that reduce

Continued...

MyReadingLab

Reading 2

...continued

stress are unsupported. Vitamin and mineral supplementation beyond your daily requirements may only add to your stress—financial stress, that is!

Getting Enough Sleep

What personal behaviors influence stress levels?

9 Sleep is a central wellness component. Sleep loss hinders learning, memory, academic work, and physical performance. It can also depress mood and prompt feelings of stress, anger, and sadness. Sound sleep is important, too. Some people find that inexpensive earplugs or eye masks from a drugstore block sleep-disturbing sound and light. Others require a quieter, darker room or more considerate roommates to solve their sleep problems.

Avoiding Alcohol and Tobacco

10 Both drinking and smoking can disrupt sleep patterns during the night. Alcohol can disrupt the length of time it takes you to fall asleep as well as the sequence and duration of your sleep states. The nicotine in tobacco is highly addictive and acts as a mild stimulant. Tobacco use also impairs normal breathing and diminishes your ability to fight off colds and other infections.

Change Your Behavioral Responses

11 Realizing that stress is harming your fitness, wellness, relationships, or productivity is often the first step toward making positive changes. Start by assessing all aspects of a stressor, examining your typical response, determining ways to change it, and learning to cope. Often, you cannot change the stressors you face: the death of a loved one, the **stringent** requirements of your major, stacked-up course assignments, and so on. You can, however, change your reactions to them and better manage your stress.

Assess the Stressor

12 List and evaluate the stressors in your life. Can you change the stressor itself? If not, you can still change your behavior and reactions to reduce the levels of stress you experience. For example, if you have a heavy academic workload, such as five term papers due for five different courses during the same quarter or semester, make a plan to start the papers early and space your work evenly so you can avoid panic over deadlines and all-night sessions to finish papers on time.

Change Your Response

13 If something causes you distress—a habitually messy roommate, for example—you can (1) express your anger by yelling; (2) pick up the mess yourself but then leave a nasty note; (3) use humor to get your point across; or (4) initiate an even-tempered, matter-of-fact conversation about the problem. Before you respond, think through the most effective choice. Humor and laughter are surprisingly good ways to **deescalate** tense situations and to benefit your wellness generally. Laughter can boost your immune response, not to mention lightening your mood and even bringing extra oxygen into your lungs! A calm, rational conversation can work well, too.

Cognitive Coping Strategies

How can you change your response to stress?

14 Thinking things through before acting may help you avoid destructive or ineffective responses to potentially stressful events. Forethought and planning can also help you tolerate increasingly higher stress levels while limiting physical and mental wear and tear.

Prepare Before Stressful Events

15 Preparing yourself for an event that you know will be stressful can diminish its impact. For example, practicing in front of friends may help you

find and correct rough spots, and in turn lower your levels of stress during the actual speech.

What can you do to prevent stress?

Downshift

16 You may experience stress because you want to "have it all": a college diploma, a successful career, a family, a wide circle of friends, possessions, status in the community, and so on. But many people are downshifting: stepping back to a simpler life by, for example, moving from a large urban area to a smaller town, changing from a hectic high-pressure career to a low-key one, or scaling back to fewer, less expensive possessions. Consider some immediate and longer-term steps for simplifying your life.

- Avoid unnecessary spending.
- Choose a career that you enjoy for itself, not primarily for the salary it commands. Some lower-paying jobs are less stressful and allow more free time for relaxation.
- Clear out clutter. Having fewer unnecessary, unused items means keeping track and taking care of that much less.

1,223 words divided by .... minutes = ... words per minute

MyReadingLab

Reading 2 REVIEW

A good review strategy to use after reading is to summarize what you just read in your own words. Take a few minutes to think about the author's most important point and any key ideas that helped to support or explain it.

Write a two- or three-sentence summary on the lines below.

....

....

....

....

....

....

MyReadingLab

Reading 2 COMPREHENSION QUESTIONS

1. What is the topic of this selection?

a. Internal resources for coping with stress
b. Self-esteem and self-efficacy
c. How to prepare for stressful events
d. How to manage stress

MAIN IDEAS

2. What is the overall main idea of the entire article?

a. By following several strategies, you can learn to control stress in your life.
b. Most college students are able to manage their stress and do best with a low-key, multi-pronged approach.
c. When you perceive that your personal resources are sufficient to meet life's demands, you experience little or no stress.
d. Preparing yourself for an event that you know will be stressful can diminish its impact.

3. What is the stated main idea of paragraph 13?

a. Before you respond, think through the most effective choice.
b. Humor and laughter are surprisingly good ways to deescalate tense situations and to benefit your wellness generally.
c. Laughter can boost your immune response, not to mention lightening your mood and even bringing extra oxygen into your lungs!
d. A calm, rational conversation can work well, too.

SUPPORTING DETAILS

4. According to the selection, which of the following is NOT affected by a loss of sleep?

a. learning and memory
b. academic work
c. physical performance.
d. blood pressure

5. Which of the following sentences from paragraph 10 is a minor detail?

a. Both drinking and smoking can disrupt sleep patterns during the night.
b. Alcohol can disrupt the length of time it takes you to fall asleep as well as the sequence and duration of your sleep states.
c. The nicotine in tobacco is highly addictive and acts as a mild stimulant.
d. Tobacco use also impairs normal breathing and diminishes your ability to fight off colds and other infections.

DRAWING CONCLUSIONS

6. If you were assigned to give a speech for a class, but hated public speaking, which of the following would reduce your stress over the situation?

a. putting off the speech as long as possible
b. practicing the speech before family and friends several times
c. waiting until the night before the speech to write it and rehearse it
d. thinking a lot about what might go wrong

7. From the article, you could conclude that

a. Everyone suffers from too much stress.
b. All stress is bad for you.
c. People with high self-esteem and self-efficacy can deal with stress better.
d. You can always avoid stressful situations.

VOCABULARY IN CONTEXT

8. Determine the meaning of the underlined word in this sentence from paragraph 2: When you perceive that your personal resources are sufficient to meet life's demands, you experience little or no stress.

a. inadequate
b. too weak
c. enough
d. abundant

9. Determine the meaning of the underlined word in this sentence from paragraph 11: Often, you cannot change the stressors you face: the death of a loved one, the stringent requirements of your major, stacked-up course assignments, and so on.

a. unreasonable
b. strict
c. required
d. specific

10. Determine the meaning of the underlined word in this sentence from paragraph 13: Humor and laughter are surprisingly good ways to deescalate tense situations and to benefit your wellness generally.

a. to decrease
b. to bear
c. to understand
d. to forgive

Reading 1
VOCABULARY PRACTICE: WORD JUMBLE

Use the clues in the first column, and then unscramble the jumbled words in the second column to determine the correct word. Write it in the third column. The first one is done for you.

WORD BANK

physiological	variables	debilitating	prone	negate
eustress	immune	hinders	supplementation	diminishes

CLUES (Clues are not the same as definitions).	**SCRAMBLED WORDS**	**WORD**
1. Taking vitamins, for example	NIATTSPLEUENOPM	S U P P L E M E N T A T I O N
2. changeable factors	SRAEIVLBA	_ _ _ _ _ _ _ _ _
3. not likely to be sickened	NIMEMU	_ _ _ _ _ _
4. bodily	GCLLIYPHSOOAI	_ _ _ _ _ _ _ _ _ _ _ _ _
5. an obstruction does this	DISHREN	_ _ _ _ _ _ _
6. caused by exercise	RESTESUS	_ _ _ _ _ _ _ _
7. Likely to	RENOP	_ _ _ _ _
8. Eliminate	TEGANE	_ _ _ _ _ _
9. As it is used, a soap bar does this	SEDMISINIH	_ _ _ _ _ _ _ _ _ _
10. diseases, for example	GAIBLEDITIN	_ _ _ _ _ _ _ _ _ _ _ _

Write the letters that are highlighted on the following lines. Use them to unscramble the phrase below where some of the letters are given as clues.

L _ _ _ _ _ _ _ _ _ _ _ _ _ _ _ _ _

L _ _ _ H T _ _   _ S   T _ _   _ _ S _   _ _ _ _ _ I _ E

MyReadingLab

Reading 2 QUESTIONS FOR WRITING AND DISCUSSION

Review any parts of the article you need to answer the following questions.

1. According to the descriptions of Type A and Type B people in this article, do you consider yourself to be more of a Type A or a Type B person, and why?

2. What kinds of events do you think are the causes of the most stress for college students?

3. What were some of the causes of stress in this article, and which of these have you experienced?

4. According to the article, what steps can people take to reduce or avoid stress?

5. Which of the strategies mentioned in this article do you use to combat stress? What other strategies do you use to reduce or avoid stress?

MyReadingLab

VIEWPOINT FOR CRITICAL THINKING

COMPETITION IN COLLEGE SPORTS

Each year, athletes are recruited by colleges for their athletic ability, regardless of their academic achievements in high school. Rigorous sports competition among colleges has changed the priorities of many schools. Read about both sides of the issue presented in the following letters and decide what you think should be done to solve this problem.

Dear Editor:

Thanks to the media and the increase of gambling on the Internet, college athletic programs have become a multi-billion dollar business. The annual National Collegiate Athletic Association basketball tournament is known as "March Madness" for a good reason. Players and coaches are under high pressure by their colleges to win because it not only enhances the school's reputation, but also increases revenue from ticket sales and sponsorship. Instead of focusing on their educations, players spend the majority of their time practicing or playing against other schools. Some athletes who are recruited to play lack the academic skills needed to pass foundation courses and these students rarely graduate. High-stakes games pressure students into taking dangerous measures to improve their performances. Coaches often bend rules to keep failing students on their teams, and players with no time for academics find cheating to be their only solution. Restrictions must be placed on college sports which have become too commercialized, too big, and corrupt. It's time to reform college sports and allocate more resources to academics, and to allow more students to participate in intercollegiate sports for the fun of it instead of just the competition.

Signed,

Disgruntled Fan

Dear Editor,

College sports are thriving businesses, and as in any thriving business there will be those who cheat or bend rules to gain advantage. However, that isn't just cause for placing limitations on college athletic teams. Many students on athletic scholarships wouldn't have the opportunity to attend a good school if scholarships were only given to those with intellectual ability. Students often choose schools based on the reputations of their athletic teams. Participation in athletic programs teaches students skills they can't learn in lecture halls, such as leadership, dedication, commitment, and teamwork. A successful sports team boosts a college's reputation and helps to fund other athletic programs that benefit many other students with opportunities for physical activities and fitness. And players from high-profile college teams have a better chance of getting into a professional team even if they never graduate. College sports are good for everyone involved and should not be restricted in any way.

Signed

College Sports Fan

1. If you could attend any college or university you wanted, how much importance would you place on attending a school with a great sports team? Why or why not? Where would you go?

....

....

....

....

2. Do you feel that college athletic programs should be restricted or not, and why or why not?

....

....

....

....

3. The first letter proposes that there is too much emphasis placed on winning in college sports. How has this affected the players, the coaches, and the colleges?

....

....

....

....

Continued...

MyReadingLab

VIEWPOINT FOR CRITICAL THINKING

...continued

4. Some schools charge all students a fee to help pay for athletic programs. Do you think it's fair to require students who do not participate in sports to pay this fee? Why or why not?

5. Do you feel the benefits of college athletic programs outweigh the negative aspects of these programs? Why or why not?

MyReadingLab

REAL-LIFE READING

READING PRESCRIPTION SAFETY INFORMATION

When you receive prescription medicine from a pharmacy, a list of important information is included that should be read carefully. Read the following safety information for a prescription medication and answer the questions.

(*Actronite is a fictional name for a prescription drug.)

Actronite* relieves the symptoms of anxiety and depression in patients 18 years old and over. Elderly patients being treated for dementia-related illness should not use Actronite due to an increased risk of stroke or heart attack. If your symptoms worsen or new side effects occur, call your doctor immediately.

Possible Adverse Side Effects:

- High fever, stiff muscles, sweating, and changes in pulse rate
- Changes in cholesterol (lipid levels) in the blood
- Weight gain
- Uncontrollable body movements, facial tics, or loss of motor skills
- Dizziness, seizures, difficulty swallowing
- Headache, insomnia, or nausea
- Heart problems, irregular heartbeat, or stroke

Notify your physician if you are being treated for diabetes or high blood sugar since this medicine may alter your blood sugar levels. If you are pregnant, you should not take Actronite because the effects on the fetus are unknown. Also, if you are breast-feeding do not take Actronite. Tell your physician about any other medications, supplements, or non-prescription medicines that you are taking, since some may cause adverse reactions when taken with this medication. Do not drink alcoholic beverages while on Actronite.

Take your medication exactly as directed by your physician. Do not change the dosage or stop taking the medicine without first consulting your doctor. Actronite tablets should be taken with food and at least 8 ounces of a non-alcoholic beverage to prevent nausea, and should be swallowed whole, not crushed or broken. For the first week that you are on Actronite, do not drive long distances or use heavy machinery until any possible side-effects are noticed and reported to your doctor. Stay out of the sun while on this medication. Avoid getting overheated and drink plenty of water each day. This medication should be stored at room temperature, 60-88 degrees F. Do not take this medication if the seal on the top of the bottle has been broken or torn. Keep the bottle out of sunlight and out of the reach of children. For more information about this medication, visit our website at Actronite.com.

1. For what condition is Actronite prescribed?

2. Who is restricted from using Actronite?

3. Which side effects can result in serious health problems?

4. How should Actronite be taken?

5. What are some restrictions patients must follow while taking Actronite?

BUILDING VOCABULARY

Knowing the meanings to many word parts will help you determine the meanings of unfamiliar words. Make a list of English words using the word parts in the table below, and give their meanings. If you are unsure about a word, consult a dictionary. Then use the words to complete the sentences below. (* presented in previous lists)

PREFIXES	ROOTS	SUFFIXES
pro-: *forward, in favor of*	ject: *to throw, thrust*	-er, -or: *one who, one that**
in-, im-, en-: *in, into, within*	duc(e): *to lead*	-tion, -sion: *action, state of**
		-ive: *character or quality*

WORDS

Use one of the words in your word list above in a sentence that reveals its meaning with a context clue. Read the sentence to a classmate and ask him or her to define the word.

MyReadingLab

CHAPTER PRACTICE 1

Use the Four Step Reading Process while reading the paragraphs below and answer the questions that follow.

[1] What about people who have a lot of "book smarts" but not much common sense? There are some people like that, who never seem to get ahead in life, in spite of having all that so-called intelligence. It is true that not everyone who is intellectually able is going to be a success in life (Mehrabian, 2000). Sometimes the people who are most successful are those who didn't do all that well in the regular academic setting.

[2] One of the early explanations for why some people who do poorly in school succeed in life and why some who do well in school don't do so well in the "real" world was that success relies on a certain degree of emotional intelligence, the awareness of and ability to manage one's own emotions as well as the ability to be self-motivated, to feel what others feel, and to be socially skilled (Persaud, 2001).

[3] The concept of emotional intelligence was first introduced by Salovey and Mayer (1990) and later expanded upon by Goleman (1995). Goleman proposed that emotional intelligence is a more powerful influence on success in life than more traditional views of intelligence. One who is emotionally intelligent possesses self-control of emotions such as anger, impulsiveness, and anxiety. Empathy, the ability to understand what others feel, is also a component, as are an awareness of one's own emotions, sensitivity, persistence even in the face of frustrations, and the ability to motivate oneself (Salovey & Mayer, 1990).

1. What is the central point (main idea) of this passage?
   - **a.** What about people who have a lot of "book smarts" but not much common sense?
   - **b.** There are some people like that, who never seem to get ahead in life, in spite of having all that so-called intelligence.
   - **c.** Sometimes the people who are most successful are those who didn't do all that well in the regular academic setting.
   - **d.** Goleman proposed that emotional intelligence is a more powerful influence on success in life than more traditional views of intelligence.

Continued...

MyReadingLab

CHAPTER PRACTICE 1

...continued

2. Write a question using the main idea that helps you to find the major details.

....

....

....

3. Which of the following sentences expresses the main idea of paragraph 3?

a. The concept of emotional intelligence was first introduced by Salovey and Mayer (1990) and later expanded upon by Goleman (1995).

b. Goleman proposed that emotional intelligence is a more powerful influence on success in life than more traditional views of intelligence.

c. One who is emotionally intelligent possesses self-control of emotions such as anger, impulsiveness, and anxiety.

d. Empathy, the ability to understand what others feel, is also a component, as are an awareness of one's own emotions, sensitivity, persistence even in the face of frustrations, and the ability to motivate oneself

MyReadingLab

CHAPTER PRACTICE 2

Use the Four Step Reading Process while reading the paragraphs below and answer the questions that follow.

1 Regular resistance training with an adequate load, or amount of weight lifted, will result in an increase in muscle strength. Although men tend to realize greater gains in muscle size due to higher testosterone levels, women often have a larger capacity to improve relative strength over time. Stronger lower- and upper-body muscles benefit both men and women.

Neural Improvements

2 When you start a resistance-training program, you will gain muscular strength before noticing any increase in muscle size. This is because internal physiological adaptations to training take place before muscle enlargement. The strength of a muscular contraction depends, in large part, on effective recruitment of the motor units needed for that contraction. The better your body is at recruiting the necessary motor units through voluntary neural signaling, the stronger your muscles will be. In the first few weeks or months of a resistance-training program, most of the adaptation involves an increased ability to recruit motor units, which causes more muscle fibers to contract.

1. Which sentence states the main idea (the topic sentence) of paragraph 1?

a. Regular resistance training with an adequate load, or amount of weight lifted, will result in an increase in muscle strength.

b. Although men tend to realize greater gains in muscle size due to higher testosterone levels, women often have a larger capacity to improve relative strength over time.

c. Stronger lower- and upper-body muscles benefit both men and women.

2. Write a question using the main idea that helps you to find the major details.

....

....

....

3. Which sentence states the main idea (the topic sentence) of paragraph 2?

a. When you start a resistance-training program, you will gain muscular strength before noticing any increase in muscle size.

b. This is because internal physiological adaptations to training take place before muscle enlargement.

c. The better your body is at recruiting the necessary motor units through voluntary neural signaling, the stronger your muscles will be.

d. In the first few weeks or months of a resistance-training program, most of the adaptation involves an increased ability to recruit motor units, which causes more muscle fibers to contract.

MyReadingLab

CHAPTER PRACTICE 3

Use the Four Step Reading Process while reading the paragraphs below and answer the questions that follow.

[1] Lacrosse is an ancient game that began with the Native Americans of the northeast. The violent nature of the original game can be surmised from the Native American name for the game, baaga àdowe (Ojibway for "bump hips"). In early Native American life, lacrosse served several purposes. The sport was used to resolve intertribal conflicts, to train young warriors, and as a religious ritual or celebration. The games involved 100 to 1,000 men playing on fields from 500 yards to miles in length, with games lasting up to three days. Game objects varied from balls to pieces of bone connected with a leather thong. The name *lacrosse* was coined by French missionaries who saw Native Americans playing the game. Jesuit missionary Jean de Brebeuf brought knowledge of the game to Westerners after seeing Iroquois playing it in 1636. The game's name is a contraction of the phrase *le jeu de la crosse* ("the game of the hooked stick").

[2] In 1856, a Canadian dentist, Dr. William George Beers, founded the Montreal Lacrosse Club and devised rules for the modern game. [2] He shortened the length of the game and reduced the number of players to ten per side. By the early 1900s the game had spread to high schools, colleges, and universities. In recent years the popularity of lacrosse in schools has grown exponentially. According to the U.S. Lacrosse National Federation of High Schools, lacrosse is currently the fastest growing high school sport.

1. Which sentence states the main idea (the topic sentence) of paragraph 1?

a. Lacrosse is an ancient game that began with the Native Americans of the northeast.

b. The sport was used to resolve intertribal conflicts, to train young warriors, and as a religious ritual or celebration.

c. The name *lacrosse* was coined by French missionaries who saw Native Americans playing the game.

d. The game's name is a contraction of the phrase *le jeu de la crosse* ("the game of the hooked stick").

2. Write a question using the main idea that helps you to find the major details of paragraph 2.

....

....

....

3. Which of the following is a minor detail of paragraph 2?

a. In 1856, a Canadian dentist, Dr. William George Beers, founded the Montreal Lacrosse Club.

b. He shortened the length of the game and reduced the number of players to ten per side.

c. By the early 1900s the game had spread to high schools, colleges, and universities.

d. According to the U.S. Lacrosse National Federation of High Schools, lacrosse is currently the fastest growing high school sport.

CHAPTER REVIEW: CONCEPT MAP

Concept Maps are an ideal way to show the relationships between topics, main ideas, and major and minor details. In the concept map below, fill in the correct definition for each term in the boxes.

TOPIC:

....

....

↑

MAIN IDEA:

....

....

↑

MAJOR DETAILS:

....

....

↑

MINOR DETAILS:

....

....

MyReadingLab

READING LAB ASSIGNMENTS

1. Login to MyReadingLab, and in the menu click on Reading Skills. In the Learning Path select **Stated Main Ideas.** Review this skill by reading the brief overview and models. Watch the short animation and then complete any practices or tests. You may also wish to review **Supporting Details** found in the Learning Path.

2. Click on Reading Level, and choose two stories to read and answer the questions to the best of your ability. Your Lexile level will increase as your reading comprehension improves.

ON THE WEB

You can learn more about main ideas and supporting details on the Web by doing an Internet search on the term *understanding main ideas.* Several web sites and videos that may enhance your understanding are available on this topic.

MyReadingLab

MONITOR YOUR LEARNING

In this chapter you learned about how to find the topic, the main idea, and major details of a paragraph, and the central point of longer selections. Write a paragraph telling what you learned about these skills, how you learned them, and how you can use them to improve your learning and reading comprehension. When you have finished writing, read your paragraph as if you were reading someone else's paragraph for the first time. Check for missing words, spelling, punctuation, and sentence structure.

4 DRAWING CONCLUSIONS, IMPLIED MAIN IDEA AND CENTRAL POINT

FOCUS ON: Your Finances

Like it or not, money drives decisions. It forces us to make choices and draw logical conclusions to spend or invest. Often referred to as "the bottom line", money is the reason behind most of the decisions we make. For example, the financial budget at your college determines which courses and amenities the school will keep and which it will eliminate. The federal budget determines how high your taxes will be, and whether or not there will be sufficient financial aid available for college students. Even ideals such as justice and fairness don't impact decision-making as much as money does. Regardless of how exemplary their employees may be, businesses hire or lay off staff based on profits. Learning how to manage your money at an early age will help you make the best decisions throughout your life.

In this chapter you will learn:

LEARNING OBJECTIVES

1. how to draw logical conclusions.
2. how to find the implied main idea.
3. how to determine the central point.

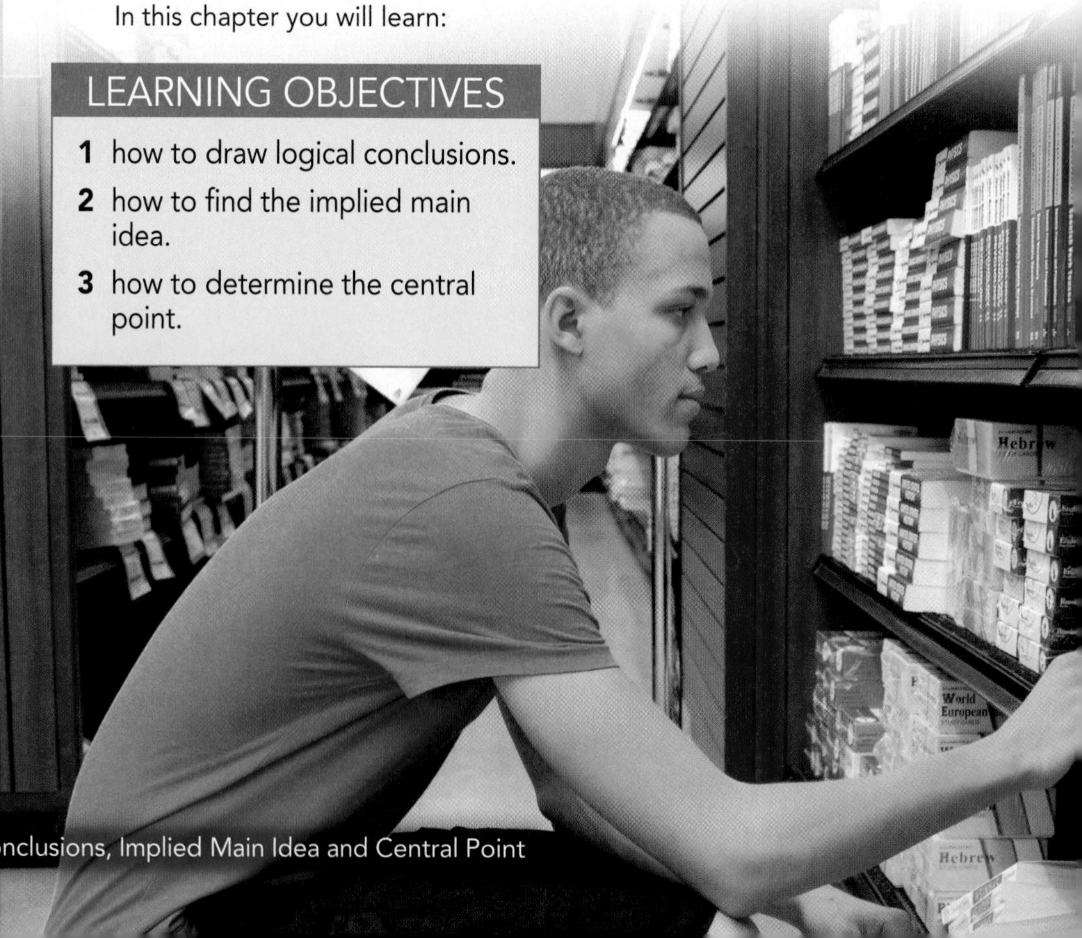

Throughout everyday life you use information around you to draw logical conclusions and make decisions and inferences. While looking outside at the weather you decide whether to take an umbrella. When listening to a lecture in class you decide which information to record in your notes. While studying for a test, you think about what you will most likely be tested on based upon the professor's comments in class.

People who are unable to draw logical conclusions are at a huge disadvantage in life because they can't anticipate an outcome. They make poor choices, use bad judgment that often brings them trouble, or they get into debt. Those who know how to use information to draw logical conclusions are able to make more well-informed predictions. For example, many investors watch the stock prices and business news to determine which stocks are likely to rise so they can make good investments. Scientists who observe phenomena around them are able to make logical inferences and develop experiments to solve problems. Likewise, good readers are able to draw accurate conclusions about the author's intended meaning when reading a textbook or a novel. Your perceptions and predictions are more likely to be accurate and beneficial in all aspects of your life when you can draw logical conclusions.

OBJECTIVE **1**

How to draw logical conclusions.

DRAWING CONCLUSIONS

A **conclusion** is an idea that is inferred based on facts and observations, determined by inductive reasoning.

Unlike literal thinking skills such as finding supporting details and stated main ideas, drawing conclusions relies on the reader's ability to consider all the known facts, on his or her background knowledge, and on the ability to think logically. It also relies heavily upon your ability to make judgments based on facts. A **conclusion** is an idea that is inferred based on facts and observations, determined by inductive reasoning. Inductive reasoning involves learning all the information known about a topic, thinking about the possible implications, and arriving at a logical conclusion. Unlike a guess or an assumption that does not rely on facts, a conclusion is supported by facts and observations. If no evidence is in the passage to support a conclusion, it is a false or invalid conclusion. Drawing a logical conclusion involves several steps that often happen quickly and unconsciously.

For example, if your child has a fever, you begin to assemble the known facts by asking questions such as, is there a rash? If so, it could be measles or an allergic reaction. If not, then you look for other symptoms, such as pain in the abdomen or ears. If there is pain in the abdomen, it could be a gastrointestinal virus, or appendicitis. If there's ear pain, it could be the result of a cold or ear infection. The thinking process you are using is a process of elimination and observation. You're using inductive reasoning by collecting data and making observations to arrive at a conclusion that fits all the facts. This is exactly what good readers do to make logical conclusions while reading.

To Draw Logical Conclusions, Look for **C L U E S**

To help you arrive at correct conclusions while reading, use the following steps with the acronym CLUES. You must think like a detective looking for clues to help you find a logical conclusion.

STEP 1: **Check** *your comprehension of the passage by stating the* ***topic and main idea****.*

STEP 2: **Look** *closely at both* ***major and minor details****.*

STEP 3: **Use the facts** *in the details and don't assume too much even though something may seem to be so.*

STEP 4: **Examine the facts** *to make sure they fit your conclusion.*

STEP 5: **Support your conclusion** *by verifying it with facts from the passage.*

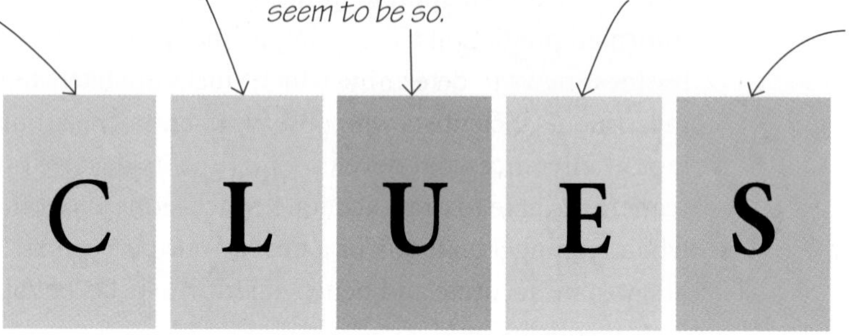

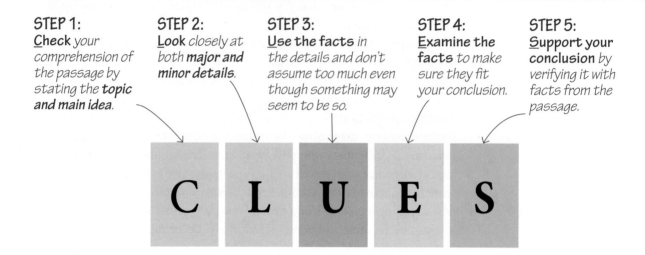

Read the following passage and answer true or false to the statements below. Use the steps in CLUES to answer the questions.

[1] The employees at the Wagner's Department Store were surveyed by the management to find out their overall satisfaction with their employer. [2] The 7,652 workers rated their company highly for several reasons. [3] They are allowed to take off sick days when their children are sick. [4] They get a 20% discount at the store's cafeteria for their meals and 15% off all merchandise. [5] Fresh fruit, granola bars, and water are served at the weekly department meetings. [6] The store pays 100% of all employees' health insurance, and 50% of their dental insurance and their dependents' insurance. [7] Instead of laying off any employees when business is poor, all employee hours are reduced. [8] Once they are hired, employees rarely leave the company.

Directions: As you answer true (T) or false (F) next to the number of the following statements, be ready to prove your conclusions with facts. Write the sentence number(s) after the statements that provided support for your conclusions.

		Supported in sentence numbers
1.	Employees do not have many benefits at Wagner's.	....
2.	Wagner's is flexible and understanding to employees with families.	....

3. .... Wagner's is concerned about the health of its employees. ....

4. .... Wagner's has a high turnover in employees. ....

5. .... Wagner's doesn't want employees to quit once they are hired because it is costly to retrain employees. ....

Guesses and Assumptions

The last question in the exercise above is false not only because the facts are against it, but also because the idea was not discussed in the passage. Whenever a statement about a paragraph relies on information not included in the paragraph, it is a guess or an assumption, not a valid or logical conclusion.

Sweeping Generalizations or Absolute Statements

Statements that contain sweeping generalizations or absolute statements are invalid conclusions. **Sweeping generalizations** apply a particular condition to all members of a group. A sweeping generalization resembles a stereotype, where all members of a group are included or excluded. For example, saying, "Men prefer violent movies to romances" is stereotyping because it implies that *all* men prefer violence to romance.

Absolute statements include words and phrases such as *all, everyone, everybody, none, no one, nobody, always*, or *never*. For instance, the absolute statement that *everyone* loves working at Wagner's Department Store would be a false conclusion. It is unlikely that 100% of the people are totally satisfied in any situation. Another example would be concluding that *no one* likes taking tests, or that *everyone* believes that murder is *always* wrong. If that last statement were true, our prison population would probably be significantly reduced. As you answer the questions for the exercises in this chapter, be on the alert for statements that include sweeping generalizations or absolute statements.

MyReadingLab

PRACTICE 1

Underline the main idea in the paragraph if it is stated. Use the CLUES in the passages below to help you answer true or false to the statements that follow.

What is the national debt and why should individuals be concerned about it? The national debt includes both federal debt and debt held by the public. Debt held by the public is the amount of money the federal government has borrowed to finance its budget deficits. Like a household budget, the government has bills to pay (expenses like national defense, welfare and retirement benefits, loan payments due to other countries, etc.). When there's not enough money to pay for these things, the government borrows from other countries, raises taxes, or prints more cash. Taxes provide some of the money the government needs, and the sale of securities such as savings bonds or interest from loans to other countries provide additional income. During a poor international economy, the government's income from these and other sources declines, leaving a deficit (debt) referred to as *national debt*. The gross national debt in 2000 was about $7 trillion, and by the end of 2013, the national debt exceeded $17 trillion, with the trend increasing. To pay this bill, the government is forced to cut federal programs and increase taxes, leaving less money in your paycheck and fewer benefits for those dependent on government assistance such as financial aid for education.

1. .... When the economy is poor the government sells fewer securities.

2. .... If the national debt continues to increase, more federally funded programs will have to be cut.

3. .... People who are not legal residents of the U.S. do not have to pay income taxes.

4. .... If the national debt continues to grow, the government will have to increase taxes even more.

5. .... If citizens pay more income tax, the national debt will decrease.

MyReadingLab

PRACTICE 2

Underline the main idea in the paragraph if it is stated. Use the CLUES in the passages below to help you answer true or false to the statements that follow.

inflated: (in economics) when prices go higher

Buying a home is the biggest investment in most people's lives. Unfortunately, many make the mistake of buying a house that they can't afford, resulting in unnecessary stress and even devastating financial loss. This happened on a massive scale in 2000 when millions of optimistic home buyers obtained home loans that were higher than they could afford to repay. With the rising demand for home ownership, housing prices became **inflated** and borrowers responded by seeking unrealistically larger loans. They expected market prices would continue to rise indefinitely, thereby providing a profitable investment. Borrowers were aided by lenders using loose credit standards, leading to unrealistic repayment requirements. By 2007 the housing market was oversold and the U.S. economy entered a severe recession. With rising unemployment, borrowers were unable to meet monthly payments, especially when interest rates (and thus payments) on loans increased; housing vacancies increased and property values dropped severely. Some borrowers lost their homes and the equity they had built up in them.

1. .... Lenders will not approve a mortgage to a buyer who is unable to afford it.

2. .... When the demand for housing goes up, home prices increase, as does the amount of mortgage money needed to pay for them.

3. .... The amount of interest you owe on a mortgage can never go higher.

4. .... When home buyers are unable to repay their mortgages, they lose their homes to the lenders.

5. .... Although some people buy houses expecting to sell them for a profit, there is no guarantee that the home will hold its value.

MyReadingLab

PRACTICE 3

Directions: Underline the main idea in the paragraph if it is stated. Use the CLUES in the passages below to help you answer true or false to the statements that follow.

Gasoline prices in 2009 were less than $2.00 per gallon. A year before that they were at $4.00 per gallon before they dropped and then surged upward again. Why do gasoline prices fluctuate so dramatically? What is the basis for the price of gas? A series of interacting complex issues affect the consumer price of gasoline. First, the supply of oil from which gasoline is made is a major contributor to the price. The law of supply and demand dictates that as the availability of an item increases, its value decreases. The production of foreign oil has increased over the past decade, but domestic sources in the U.S. have not kept pace with our demand. The result is an increasing reliance on foreign suppliers who can charge whatever they want for this black gold. At the same time, the demand for petroleum-based products, such as plastics, and for more gasoline fuel have increased. Second, politics also comes into play when a major source of foreign oil is in the Middle East, where governments and nations have been in turmoil for centuries. The uncertainty of whether oil will be available helps to spur higher prices. The transport of oil from a source to the refinery (where gasoline is made) is also another factor that drives up the price. As each of these factors changes on a daily basis it is difficult to predict the price of gasoline.

1. .... Vehicles that need a lot of fuel (fewer miles per gallon) are one cause of higher gasoline prices.

2. .... The U.S. has enough oil to supply its demand without relying on foreign oil.

3. .... Everyone should drive a fuel-efficient vehicle so the price of gasoline will decrease.

4. .... If Americans used more alternative energy sources instead of oil the demand for oil would decrease, lowering prices.

5. .... All auto manufacturers in the U.S. should produce vehicles that meet rigid fuel-efficiency standards.

U-REVIEW 1

Complete the following sentences to review the concepts you have just learned.

1. A logical conclusion is

2. The first step to drawing conclusions is to

3. When drawing conclusions, you should pay attention to

4. Once you have made your conclusion, you should

5. Invalid conclusions often include sweeping generalizations, or words or phrases such as

OBJECTIVE 2

How to find the implied main idea.

IMPLIED MAIN IDEAS

An **implied main idea** is one that is not stated but suggested by the details.

As you recall from the previous chapter, a main idea is the author's overall most important point, which can be either stated or implied. If it is stated, it is found in the topic sentence. If the main idea is not stated, it is implied. An **implied main idea** is one that is not stated but suggested by the details. If the main idea is not stated, how do you determine the author's most important point?

Like drawing a conclusion, determining the implied main idea also relies on inductive reasoning. The steps to find an implied main idea are similar to drawing conclusions:

1. State **the topic** of the passage.
2. Find the **major details** about the topic.
3. **Summarize the major details** in a broad, general statement that includes the topic.

Like stated main ideas, you can check your implied main idea to see if it is correct by asking, "Do most of the major details tell me more about this idea?" If they do, then you have formed an accurate implied main idea.

Conclusions and Implied Main Ideas

A common error that many students make when trying to formulate an implied main idea is drawing a general conclusion that is not the main idea. As you read the following paragraph, think of the topic and the author's most important point.

> Joe was hired by a major telemarketing firm to sell windows over the telephone. He is punctual and rarely misses a day of work. Joe is pleasant to his colleagues and patient with his customers, even when they become angry or hang up on him. Joe does his job well but hopes to have a better job someday where he won't have to do sales over the phone.

Which of these two statements is the main idea, and which one is a conclusion?

a. Telemarketing sometimes involves dealing with angry customers.

b. Joe is a good employee at a telemarketing firm, and he hopes to have a better job someday.

The first statement is a conclusion that is drawn based on how customers become angry or hang up the phone on Joe. The second one is the most general overall point that is made by the supporting details, and is the main idea. To avoid the error of drawing a conclusion that is not the implied main idea always begin with the topic of the passage and ask yourself what the major details are telling you about the topic.

Read the following example:

> If you're thinking of taking a student loan, first consider attending a less expensive college. State colleges and universities usually have lower tuition and fees than privately owned colleges. You can also reduce living expenses by choosing a college in an area where prices are not as high as they are in other areas or cities. To avoid high room and board expenses, consider living with a friend or family member and paying for your rent by helping around the house. Also consider your degree program. For certain majors, such as philosophy, good job prospects are limited, so paying back the debt may be difficult. Expenses vary for different degrees, so research the cost of your degree. Also, before taking a loan, use an online loan calculator to calculate the total amount of debt you will owe by the time you complete your studies. The interest on a student loan may continue to accumulate while you are still in school, adding additional debt, so your loan balance will be higher by the time you graduate. The last thing you need at graduation is a huge mountain of debt that you must now repay.

How to find the implied main idea:

Step 1: **Topic**: Student loan

Step 2: Note the **major details**:

- attend a college with lower fees
- choose a college in an area where prices are lower
- reduce living expenses
- consider your degree program
- calculate how much you'll owe and your prospects for repayment

Step 3: **Summarize** the major details:

Ask yourself, "What are the major details telling me about the topic?" or "What do the major details describe about this topic?" In this case, the major details describe the things to consider when taking student loans, so the main idea should be: There are several factors you should consider before taking a **student loan.**

Read the following paragraph, and answer the questions.

Since the federal government changed the rules for student loan repayment, students with Direct Loans and Federal Family Education Loans are now able to consolidate both loans into one with a lower interest rate. Also, students who are repaying college loans on income-based repayment (IBR) plans can benefit from lower monthly payments which are now capped at 10% of their income instead of 15%. Under this repayment plan, your student loan debt will be forgiven after 20 years instead of the previous 25 years. Also, under this plan teachers and other public servants will have their student loan debt forgiven after 10 years.

1. What is the topic of this paragraph?

a. Direct Loans
b. New federal rules for student loans
c. Educational expenses
d. Federal Family Education Loans

2. What do the major details describe?

a. how to repay loans
b. why loans need to be repaid
c. tips for college students
d. the new rules for student loans

3. Complete the following implied main idea, beginning with the topic.

(Topic:) .... make

it easier for students to ....

MyReadingLab

PRACTICE 4

As you complete the practice below, underline the major details and answer the questions that follow.

When you are surfing the Internet in a public place such as a café or a restaurant you are using an unsecured, shared network which leaves your private information vulnerable to cyber criminals. You can help thwart cyber crime by using strong passwords with unusual combinations of numbers, upper and lower case letters, and symbols. Using your first name and year of birth is an easy one for criminals to figure out. If you're getting ads on your cell phone, you can prevent the sharing of your personal information to these marketing companies by joining the Federal Trade Commission's Do Not Call Registry at www.donotcall.gov. You can also prevent credit card bureaus from sharing your information and avoid identity theft by removing yourself from their marketing lists at optoutprescreen.com. It's also a good idea to check your credit report annually for any unauthorized accounts. To make sure that your credit is safe and secure, you can get a free credit report at annualcreditreport.com.

1. What is the topic of this paragraph?

a. credit card bureaus
b. keeping personal information private
c. unsecured public networks
d. protecting your credit

2. What do the major details describe?

a. tips for keeping personal information private
b. Internet sites that protect your credit
c. keeping passwords safe
d. credit bureaus

3. Complete the following implied main idea:

There are several ways you can ....

....

MyReadingLab

PRACTICE 5

As you complete the practice below, underline the major details and answer the questions that follow.

Unlike credit cards, debit cards do not increase the funds at an individual's disposal but allow users only to transfer money between accounts to make retail purchases. Debit cards are used more than credit cards as payment for U.S. consumer transactions. However, the risk of financial loss is greater for debit cards. Federal law limits the credit card user's liability to $50 for stolen or fraudulent use. However, debit card losses can be higher—ranging up to $500—depending on how quickly the lost card is reported.

1. What is the topic of this paragraph?
   a. credit card losses
   b. financial loss
   c. debit card loss
   d. loss limits on debit and credit cards
2. What do the major details describe?
   a. protecting your credit card from loss
   b. the limits of loss on your debit card
   c. the loss limits of debit and credit cards
   d. the fraudulent use of credit cards
3. Complete the following implied main idea:

   (Topic:) .... are not the same; debit cards .... than credit cards.

MyReadingLab

PRACTICE 6

As you complete the practice below, underline the major details and answer the questions that follow.

In 2002 (business) regulators uncovered a massive $11 billion fraud involving WorldCom—a company that rode the telecom boom to become a darling of the American investment community. What investors did not know was that CEO Bernard Ebbers and CFO Scott Sullivan had been "cooking the books" for years to hide the real story behind the company's finances. In the end, the company collapsed, investors lost billions of dollars, and over 17,000 people lost their jobs. While the WorldCom scheme was masterminded by the company's top executives, people further down the corporate ladder paid a severe price as well. Betty Vinson was a mid-level accountant at WorldCom who accepted instructions from Ebbers and Sullivan to make the accounting adjustments and forge dates to hide the transactions. Over the course of two years, Vinson made almost $4 billion worth of adjustments to the company's books. Almost immediately she felt guilty. She had trouble sleeping, lost weight, withdrew from people at work and, ultimately, tried to quit. But Sullivan convinced her to stay by telling her that she had done nothing illegal and that if anyone asked he would take full responsibility. When the scheme was uncovered, Vinson's testimony helped prosecutors secure lengthy jail terms for both Ebbers and Sullivan. Despite her cooperation, Betty Vincent was still charged and sentenced to five months in jail for criminal conspiracy and securities fraud.

1. What is the topic of this paragraph?
   a. How investors can lose money in business
   b. Betty Vincent
   c. World Com's massive $11 billion fraud in 2002
   d. Businesses with poor ethics

Continued...

MyReadingLab

PRACTICE 6

...continued

2. What do the major details describe?

a. how World Com's $11 billion fraud resulted in financial loss and job losses

b. why Betty Vincent went to jail

c. why people shouldn't lie

d. how big businesses cheat the public

3. Now try writing the implied main idea by beginning with the topic.

....

....

U-REVIEW 2

To review the skill of implied main ideas, answer the following questions.

1. What is an implied main idea?

....

....

2. What is the first step to determine the implied main idea?

....

....

3. What is the second step to determine the implied main idea?

....

....

4. What is the third step to determine the implied main idea?

....

....

5. To check your implied main idea, you should ask,

....

....

OBJECTIVE 3

How to determine the central point.

A **central point** is the main idea of a reading selection longer than one paragraph.

THE CENTRAL POINT

A **central point** is the main idea of a reading selection longer than one paragraph. It is also known as a **thesis** statement or a **central idea**. A central point has many of the same characteristics as a main idea of a paragraph:

- Like a main idea, a central point is the author's overall most important statement about the topic, and it can be either stated explicitly or implied.
- The central point can be found anywhere in the reading selection.
- Sometimes the main idea of a single paragraph will also act as the central point for the entire selection.

To find the central point of a reading selection, you should:

Step 1: **Preview** to find the topic

Step 2: Find the **main idea of each paragraph** (stated or implied)

Step 3: Ask, "What are all these main ideas telling me about the topic?"

Step 4: **Summarize** the central point into a broad statement that includes the topic. To see if it is stated, look for a sentence that expresses the same idea.

Step 5: **Check your central point** by asking, "Do most of the paragraphs tell me more about this idea?"

Read the following example:

> [1] A few years ago, James Davis walked through the doors of the Union Butterfield tool company in Asheville, North Carolina. He had been fired by Union Butterfield just two days before, and now he wanted revenge for what he felt was a grave injustice. To extract that revenge, Davis carried a semiautomatic rifle and a pistol. Once inside the doors, he opened fire, getting off about 50 shots and killing 3 of his former coworkers. After he finished shooting, Davis lit a cigarette and calmly waited for the police to arrive; then he quietly surrendered, and he was led away in handcuffs.
>
> [2] Unfortunately, tragedies such as this one are not all that uncommon. According to recent statistics, 1 employee is killed at a U.S. workplace by a current or former coworker an average of once each week. In addition, another 25 are seriously injured by violent assaults. Overall, some 2 million U.S. workers are victims of some form of workplace violence each year.
>
> [3] The National Institute for Occupational Safety and Health (NIOSH) defines workplace violence as any physical assault, threatening behavior, or verbal abuse that occurs in a work setting. Experts also suggest that U.S. businesses lose billions of dollars each year in lost work time and productivity, litigation expenses, and security measures in the aftermath of

Continued...

workplace violence. Among the most common reasons often given for increasing workplace violence are economic fears regarding job security, heightened concerns for personal safety after the September 11, 2001, terrorist attacks, and generalized stress and anxiety among workers.

Topic: Workplace violence

Paragraph 1 main idea (implied): Jim Davis, a disgruntled former employee of Butterfield Tool Company, shot and killed 3 people at his workplace.

Paragraph 2 main idea (stated): Overall, some 2 million U.S. workers are victims of some form of workplace violence each year.

Paragraph 3 main idea (implied): U.S. businesses lose billions of dollars each year from workplace violence.

The central point of the passage is: **Workplace violence** is a serious threat to U.S. employees and businesses.

Explanation:
Notice how the central point is a broad statement that doesn't repeat the main ideas of each paragraph, but summarizes the ideas by drawing a conclusion about the main points. The first paragraph gave an example of workplace violence using James Davis. The second paragraph discussed the effects of workplace violence on employees. The third paragraph discussed the definition of workplace violence and financial effects of workplace violence. All three paragraphs discussed the seriousness of workplace violence.

In selections with multiple paragraphs, the main ideas act like major details because each paragraph makes an important point about the topic. Sum up the main ideas in the same way that you would summarize the major details in a single paragraph. Next, state broadly what the details (main ideas) are telling you about the topic.

Complete the central point for reading selection about annual percentage rates with the main ideas below:

Topic: An APR

Main Idea #1: An annual percentage rate (APR) is the amount of interest that a lender charges a borrower on a loan.

Main Idea #2: APRs can vary from lender to lender, and are dependent upon factors such as your credit score.

Main Idea #3: An APR can increase after a certain time period if specified in the loan agreement.

Central Point: (Topic): An APR is an annual percentage rate that

....

....

MyReadingLab

PRACTICE 7

Read the reading selection below and answer the questions that follow.

[1] Performance behaviors are the total set of work-related behaviors that an organization expects employees to display. Essentially, these are the behaviors directly targeted at performing a job. For some jobs, performance behaviors can be narrowly defined and easily measured. For example, an assembly-line worker who sits by a moving conveyor and attaches parts to a product as it passes by has relatively few performance behaviors. He or she is expected to remain at the workstation for a predetermined number of hours and correctly attach the parts. Such performance can often be assessed quantitatively by counting the percentage of parts correctly attached.

[2] For many other jobs, however, performance behaviors are more diverse and difficult to assess. For example, consider the case of a research-and-development scientist at Merck Pharmaceuticals. The scientist works in a lab trying to find new scientific breakthroughs that have commercial potential. The scientist must apply knowledge and experience gained from previous research. Intuition and creativity are also important. But even with all the scientist's abilities and effort, a desired breakthrough may take months or even years to accomplish.

1. The main idea of paragraph 1 is

a. performance behaviors
b. Performance behaviors are the total set of work-related behaviors that the organization expects employees to display.
c. Essentially, these are the behaviors directly targeted at performing a job.
d. For some jobs, performance behaviors can be narrowly defined and easily measured.

2. The main idea of paragraph 2 is

a. For many other jobs, however, performance behaviors are more diverse and difficult to assess.
b. For example, consider the case of a research-and-development scientist at Merck Pharmaceuticals.
c. The scientist must apply knowledge and experience gained from previous research.
d. But even with all the scientist's abilities and effort, a desired breakthrough may take months or even years to accomplish.

3. The central point of the entire reading selection is

a. Performance behaviors are the total set of work-related behaviors that an organization expects employees to display.
b. Some performance behaviors are easy to assess.
c. Scientists' work behaviors are more difficult to assess than assembly-line workers' work behaviors.
d. Work behaviors are assessed to determine the value of the employees in a business.

MyReadingLab

PRACTICE 8

Read the reading selection below and answer the questions that follow.

[1] Employees can also engage in positive behaviors that do not directly contribute to the bottom line. Such behaviors are often called organizational citizenship. Organizational citizenship refers to the behavior of individuals who make a positive overall contribution to the organization. Consider, for example, an employee who does work that is highly acceptable in terms of both quantity and quality. However, she refuses to work overtime, won't help newcomers learn the ropes, and is generally unwilling to make any contribution beyond the strict performance requirements of her job. This person may be seen as a good performer, but she is not likely to be seen as a good organizational citizen. Another employee may exhibit a comparable level of performance. In addition, however, she always works late when the boss asks her to, she takes time to help newcomers learn their way around, and she is perceived as being helpful and committed to the organization's success. She is likely to be seen as a better organizational citizen.

[2] A number of factors, including individual, social, and organizational variables, play roles in promoting or minimizing organizational citizenship behaviors. For example, the personality, attitudes, and needs of the individual may cause some people to be more helpful than others. Similarly, the individual's work group may encourage or discourage such behaviors. And the organization itself, especially its corporate culture, may or may not promote, recognize, and reward these types of behaviors.

1. The main idea of paragraph 1 is

- **a.** Employees can also engage in positive behaviors that do not directly contribute to the bottom line.
- **b.** Such behaviors are often called organizational citizenship.
- **c.** Organizational citizenship refers to the behavior of individuals who make a positive overall contribution to the organization.
- **d.** Another employee may exhibit a comparable level of performance.

2. The main idea of paragraph 2 is

- **a.** A number of factors, including individual, social, and organizational variables, play roles in promoting or minimizing organizational citizenship behaviors.
- **b.** For example, the personality, attitudes, and needs of the individual may cause some people to be more helpful than others.
- **c.** Similarly, the individual's work group may encourage or discourage such behaviors.
- **d.** And the organization itself, especially its corporate culture, may or may not promote, recognize, and reward these types of behaviors.

3. **The central point of the entire reading selection is**
   a. Employees can also engage in positive behaviors that do not directly contribute to the bottom line.
   b. Organizational citizenship includes a number of factors that refer to the behavior of individuals who make a positive overall contribution to the organization.
   c. A number of factors, including individual, social, and organizational variables, play roles in promoting or minimizing organizational citizenship behaviors.
   d. An organization itself, especially its corporate culture, may or may not promote, recognize, and reward these types of behaviors.

MyReadingLab

PRACTICE 9

Read the reading selection below and answer the questions that follow.

1 Still other work-related behaviors are counterproductive. Counterproductive behaviors are those that detract from, rather than contribute to, organizational performance. Absenteeism occurs when an employee does not show up for work. Some absenteeism has a legitimate cause, such as illness, jury duty, or death or illness in the family. Other times, the employee may report a feigned legitimate cause that's actually just an excuse to stay home. When an employee is absent, legitimately or not, his or her work does not get done at all, a substitute must be hired to do it, or others in the organization must pick up the slack. In any event, though, absenteeism results in direct costs to a business.

2 Turnover occurs when people quit their jobs. An organization usually incurs costs in replacing workers who have quit—lost productivity while seeking a replacement, training someone new, etc. Turnover results from a number of factors, including aspects of the job, the organization, the individual, the labor market, and family influences. In general, a poor person-job fit is also a likely cause of turnover. There are some employees whose turnover doesn't hurt the business; however, when productive employees leave an organization, it does reflect counterproductive behavior.

3 Other forms of counterproductive behavior may be even more costly for an organization. Theft and sabotage, for example, result in direct financial costs for an organization. Sexual and racial harassment also cost an organization, both indirectly (by lowering morale, producing fear, and driving off valuable employees) and directly (through financial liability if the organization responds inappropriately). Workplace aggression and violence are also a growing concern in some organizations.

Continued...

MyReadingLab

PRACTICE 9

...continued

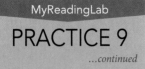

1. The main idea of paragraph 1 is

a. Still other work-related behaviors are counterproductive.

b. Counterproductive behaviors are those that detract from, rather than contribute to, organizational performance.

c. Absenteeism occurs when an employee does not show up for work.

d. In any event, though, absenteeism results in direct costs to a business.

2. The main idea of paragraph 2 is

a. Turnover occurs when people quit their jobs.

b. An organization usually incurs costs in replacing workers who have quit—lost productivity while seeking a replacement, training someone new, etc.

c. Turnover results from a number of factors, including aspects of the job, the organization, the individual, the labor market, and family influences.

d. There are some employees whose turnover doesn't hurt the business; however, when productive employees leave an organization, it does reflect counterproductive behavior.

3. The main idea of paragraph 3 is

a. Other forms of counterproductive behavior may be even more costly for an organization.

b. Theft and sabotage, for example, result in direct financial costs for an organization.

c. Sexual and racial harassment also cost an organization, both indirectly (by lowering morale, producing fear, and driving off valuable employees) and directly (through financial liability if the organization responds inappropriately).

d. Workplace aggression and violence are also a growing concern in some organizations.

4. The central point of the entire reading selection is

a. Still other work-related behaviors are counterproductive.

b. Counterproductive behaviors are those that detract from, rather than contribute to, organizational performance.

c. Absenteeism and turnover are two of the most counterproductive behaviors of an organizational performance.

d. Counterproductive behaviors are bad for business.

U-REVIEW 3

With a partner, take turns answering the following questions as true or false. If the answer is false, tell why.

1. A central point is the main idea of a reading selection longer than one paragraph.

....

....

2. To find the central point you should begin by determining the topic of the entire selection.

....

....

3. The central point is usually found in the first sentence.

....

....

4. The central point may be stated or implied.

....

....

5. You can check your central point by asking, "What are all these details telling me about the topic?"

....

....

MyReadingLab

Reading 1
VOCABULARY PREVIEW

"How to Deal With a Bad Boss"

by Steve Tobak

Match the words in the Word Bank by writing the letter of the word next to the matching definition. The paragraph numbers in parentheses indicate the location of each word in "How to Deal With a Bad Boss" (and the insert (I), "Seven Signs of a Dysfunctional Boss"). Read the words in the paragraphs to determine the correct meanings as they are used in the context of the selection.

WORD BANK

a. manipulate (2)	e. intact (4)	i. retaliation (9)
b. pit (2)	f. objectivity (5)	j. ensuing (14)
c. condescending (2)	g. benignly (6)	k. minutiae (I-2)
d. demoralizing (3)	h. confrontational (7)	l. repercussions (I-4)

1. .... in the kindest way
2. .... taking revenge
3. .... to place into competition with
4. .... consequences
5. .... treating someone in an inferior manner
6. .... a lack of emotion or bias
7. .... discouraging
8. .... argumentative
9. .... small insignificant details
10. .... whole; not separated
11. .... following; subsequent
12. .... to deviously control

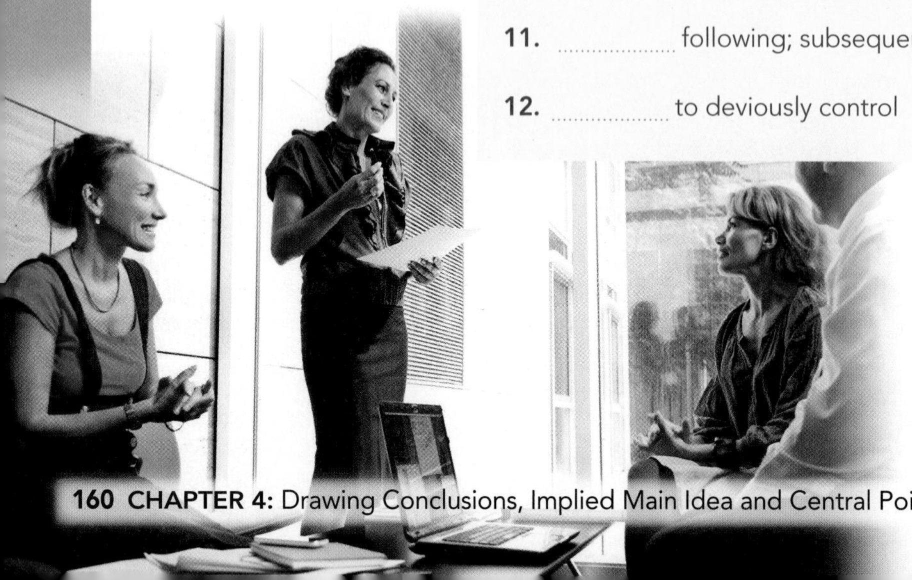

MyReadingLab

Reading 1 PREVIEW

1. Even if you've never had a job, have you ever had to work with someone you didn't like? Describe the situation and how you handled it.
2. What do you think makes a person a good boss or a bad boss? Describe each of these from your own perspective.

After you preview the article, write one or two preview questions on the lines below:

....

....

....

....

MyReadingLab

Reading 1

"How to Deal With a Bad Boss"

by Steve Tobak

Even if you never have to work for a boss in your life, you will inevitably have to deal with difficult people who have some power over you. They could be college professors, customers, landlords, spouses, or in-laws. Learning how to handle dysfunctional people is a skill that can help you succeed in any situation.

1 Of all the emails I get asking for advice, the most common by far is people wanting to know how to handle a bad or dysfunctional boss. Just last week, for example, a manager contacted me about a VP (vice president) who badmouths employees and gossips about peers behind their backs.

What kinds of behaviors signal a dysfunctional boss?

2 Other examples include business owners who play mind games to manipulate employees, executives who pit managers against each other, managers doing things that are unethical or against company policy, and bosses that are just plain abusive, condescending or inconsiderate.

3 The situations have striking similarities. Employees try to look the other way or just sort of live with it, but the situation is chronically disturbing, demoralizing and stressful. Eventually, they feel compelled to do something about it or confront the offender head on, but they're not sure how to approach it. That's when they contact me.

4 Having pretty much seen it all, I've found that the method for dealing with this sort of thing is pretty much consistent across the board. Here's

Continued...

MyReadingLab

Reading 1

...continued

what you do, in order, starting with making sure it isn't you or just a misunderstanding and ending, hopefully, with you moving on with your career and your sanity intact.

Make Sure it isn't you or a Misunderstanding

5 Your first step should always be to take a cold, hard look in the mirror and try to achieve some level of perspective and objectivity. Or you can talk to someone you trust who knows both you and your boss. You might very well be blowing things way out of proportion for reasons that have nothing to do with him. It happens all the time.

What are the first steps you should try to deal with a bad boss?

6 If that fails, then schedule a casual, private one-on-one with your boss. Give him the benefit of the doubt. As benignly as possible, tell him what's bugging you and suggest that perhaps there's been some misunderstanding or maybe there's something he'd like you to do differently. Be open to his response. Try to put yourself in his shoes.

7 The idea here is to perhaps resolve the issue or conflict without being confrontational or bringing out any heavy artillery.

Don't Go Head-to-head With Your Boss

8 I'm afraid you're not going to want to hear this, but it's the bottom-line truth and you need to deal with it: If you go head-to-head—meaning a heavy-duty confrontation—with the boss, you'll probably lose. The same thing goes for going to Human Resources (HR) or going over his head. That's because you'll more than likely lose your job over it. That said, if you feel that you must, there is a way to go about it that'll minimize your risk, but that's a last resort we'll get to in a minute.

It's a Free country and You Have Choices—Exercise Them

9 If you've had enough, you can try to get out from under your boss by transferring to another group within your company. I've seen it done dozens of times, even done it myself, back in the day. It works quite effectively. If you're afraid about retaliation if your boss finds out, it's up to you to assess that risk. Is it worth it to at least try? If, on the other hand, you've pretty much had it with the company, then get your résumé out there, find a job elsewhere and quit.

What are your options if things don't improve?

10 Usually, just making that mental commitment to get out provides some relief from the stress. As for finding a job in this market, sure, it may take awhile, but the sooner you start looking, the sooner you'll find something. Just don't do anything stupid like saying you're looking for a job on LinkedIn or Facebook. Use your head.

11 Whatever you do, leave in peace and without burning any bridges. Do not vent in the exit interview. In all likelihood, it won't do any good and it may come back to haunt you down the road. I don't care what anyone else says—spilling your guts is never a good move. Just move on.

The Last Resort: Taking it Head-on

12 If there's something inside you that screams you've got to take some sort of action to address the problem head-on, here's what you do. Just remember that, one way or another, this path may very well cost you your job. It might be worth it, but only you can make that call.

13 Do not go to HR or go over your boss's head. Not yet. First, meet with him or her in private, one-on-one, and as professionally, respectfully and directly as possible, express your concerns. Keep it brief and don't go overboard or get hysterical. One or two examples of what you've observed

will do fine. Then wait patiently for her to respond. Listen carefully, openly and as objectively as you can.

14 If the ensuing conversation is congenial and open, then go with it. If it heats up, then back down.

15 If, for whatever reason, that doesn't work out and you still have fight left in you, again, understanding the risks, go ahead and go to HR or go over the boss's head. You can even do that with coworkers, as a group, if a whole bunch of you are fed up. Maybe others have already complained and it might work out in your favor. I've rarely seen that happen, but you never know.

What are the possible consequences of a confrontation?

16 Something else to keep in mind: Whether the last resort works out or not, there's actually a good chance you're burning a bridge that may come back to haunt you down the road. Never underestimate what people in power may do when they feel wronged, threatened, or rejected, even by the little guy. Bad references hurt and they never go away. Remember that.

17 One more important thing. If you're burned out or getting depressed over it, get some help and consider just quitting, even without a new job. Seriously, it's not worth risking your health and well-being.

Seven Signs of a Dysfunctional Boss by Steve Tobak

[1] **The game has rules, but the rules keep changing.** It's a relatively common but insidious game I call "chaos and control." If they sense you becoming disloyal, too comfortable, or too powerful, they'll want to knock you off the pedestal they've put you on. By bringing you down, it boosts their position relative to yours. One day you're the golden boy, a trusted advisor who can do no wrong. The next day you're a bumbling idiot.

[2] **Major focus on minutiae**. One Fortune 500 CEO was obsessed with my clothes and appearance. He wasn't alone in that peculiarity; it's a sign of a controlling person. And whatever details get their maniacal attention, whatever the object of their obsessive compulsion, it's really just a way to distract their brains from facing their own sadness, fear or depression. That's why it's often triggered by stress and bad news.

[3] **A "man of the people."** They thrive on attention and adoration from the masses to feed their deep-seated insecurity but are rarely capable of any true emotional connection with others.

[4] **Hypersensitive and vindictive when rejected**. Everything's about them—you're just a tiny little asteroid revolving around their planet-sized ego. Anything you do that they perceive as rejection, even if you're just not letting them be the center of attention, is a personal **affront**. There will be repercussions. Some are direct, bullying or verbally abusive; others are more subtle, underhanded or passive-aggressive.

[5] **Failure is not an option**. They're always pointing fingers, making excuses, and blaming others because they can never really be wrong in their own eyes. They will say they're not perfect, that they make mistakes, but you'll never get them to admit to one in real time. To do so would potentially fracture that fragile **façade** of being special and Godlike. Deep inside, they're really frightened children, which is why the pretense is so critical to maintain.

Continued...

diversions: time-wasting activities that entertain or amuse

6 **Loves distraction, hates surprises**. They revel in the tiniest distraction. They can be entertained or even entertain themselves with surprisingly silly **diversions**. Anything to take them away from the depressing reality of boring, mundane, day-to-day life which mere mortals must endure. But surprise them with serious news, especially bad news in front of others, and you're in big, big trouble.

7 **Sees conspiracy everywhere**. Since the world revolves around them, they see conspiracy in coincidence and deep meaning in incidental remarks. That's why they so often overreact or even panic over what appears to be nothing. Little things become life-threatening. Why? Even though it's stressful for them, it also affirms their self-importance and makes them feel big. Grandiosity is often a response to depression.

1,429 words divided by .... minutes = ... words per minute

MyReadingLab

Reading 1 REVIEW

A good review strategy to use after reading is to summarize what you just read in your own words. Take a few minutes to think about the author's most important point and any key ideas that helped to support or explain it.

Write a two- or three-sentence summary on the lines below.

....

....

....

....

....

....

MyReadingLab

Reading 1 COMPREHENSION QUESTIONS

The following questions will help you recall the main idea and details of "How to Deal with a Bad Boss." Read any parts of the article that you need to find the correct answers.

1. What is the authors' central point of this selection?
   - **a.** Bad bosses can make your life miserable.
   - **b.** Bad bosses are dysfunctional people who use their power to intimidate other people.
   - **c.** Of all the emails I get asking for advice, the most common by far is people wanting to know how to handle a bad or dysfunctional boss.
   - **d.** There are some steps you can take if you have to deal with a bad boss.

2. Broadly, the major details of the insert section, "Seven Signs of a Dysfunctional Boss" tell

a. what a bad boss does

b. how to handle a bad boss

c. the behaviors of bad bosses

d. how bad bosses control people

3. What is the main idea of paragraph 9?

a. If you've had enough, you can try to get out from under your boss by going to his or her supervisor to complain.

b. If you are fed up with your boss, you can find another position elsewhere.

c. If you have a bad boss, you should quit your job.

d. You may risk retaliation if you try to transfer in your job.

SUPPORTING DETAILS

4. According to the passage, why shouldn't you confront your boss and tell how you feel about him or her?

a. You may face repercussions and get yourself fired.

d. You may regret what you said later but the damage will be done.

c. Your boss will post bad comments about you on Facebook or LinkedIn.

d. Your coworkers will resent you for speaking out and causing trouble.

5. Why shouldn't you go over your boss's head or report the problem to Human Resources?

a. You may get a bad reputation that can harm your career even if you try to go elsewhere.

b. The supervisor over your boss is not interested in your problems.

c. The supervisor will report your complaint to your boss and make things worse.

d. Going to the supervisor won't change the behavior of your boss.

DRAWING CONCLUSIONS

6. What does the author mean when he says, "there's actually a good chance you're burning a bridge that may come back to haunt you down the road"?

a. You will come to a point in your career when you will want to go back but you won't be able to return.

b. You are doing something that cannot be undone and may hurt your career in the future.

c. Your future depends on doing something now that won't hurt your future opportunities.

d. You are harming your boss and there may be repercussions.

7. Why does the author recommend leaving your job if it is making you very unhappy?

a. Life is too short and you should find a job that makes you happy.

b. Bad managers show the poor character of the company.

c. You cannot win a battle against a bad boss.

d. Too much stress can affect both your physical and mental health.

Continued...

MyReadingLab

Reading 1 COMPREHENSION QUESTIONS

...continued

8. Why does the author recommend that you never post comments on Facebook or LinkedIn about your boss or the fact that you're looking for another job?
   a. Your friends on the social networks will think you're complaining needlessly.
   b. Your friends on the social networks may try to influence your decision to leave.
   c. Someone at work may see your comments and report them to your boss.
   d. Future employers may see your comments and not want to hire you.

VOCABULARY IN CONTEXT

9. What is the meaning of the underlined word in this sentence from insert paragraph 4? Anything you do that they perceive as rejection, even if you're just not letting them be the center of attention, is a personal affront.
   a. matter
   b. confrontation
   c. insult
   d. forward

10. What is the meaning of the underlined word in this sentence from insert paragraph 5? To do so would potentially fracture that fragile façade of being special and Godlike.
    a. false pretense
    b. idea
    c. structure
    d. question

Reading 1 VOCABULARY PRACTICE: WORD DRAWING GAME

Practice the words from the reading selection with this fun game played by four or more players in teams.

WORD BANK

manipulate	intact	retaliation	pit
objectivity	ensuing	condescending	benignly
minutiae	demoralizing	confrontational	repercussions

1. Write each of the words above on a slip of paper, fold in half, and put into an envelope or container.

2. Form two teams of partners. Decide which team will go first.

3. One partner on the first team will take one of the slips (do not show it to anyone) and draw a picture on a piece of paper to represent the idea or a clue for the word. The artist may include words on the drawing, but no form of the word, definitions, or word clues to the definition may be used. Examples or illustrations of a word may be used.

4. The artist will then show the drawing to his or her partner, who will have one minute to guess the word. The other team will keep time and keep score.

5. If the partner correctly names the word, the team receives one point. If the answer is incorrect or time runs out, no points are given. Only three guesses are allowed. Players are allowed to look at the word list when answering.

6. The play goes to the second team and one partner will draw the word while the first team keeps time and score. Each member of each team will take turns drawing.

7. When all the words have been drawn, the team with the most points wins.

MyReadingLab

Reading 1 QUESTIONS FOR WRITING AND DISCUSSION

Review any parts of the article you need to answer the following questions.

1. Of all the descriptions in "Seven Signs of a Dysfunctional Boss", which do you think are the worst characteristics that a boss could have, and why?

2. The author recommends avoiding confrontations with your boss. If a confrontation occurs, he recommends backing down. Do you think this is good advice? Why or why not?

3. In some ways, the article implies that it is almost impossible to get rid of a bad boss. Why do you think some companies allow bad bosses to continue managing?

4. If you like your boss, it is easy to become his or her friend. Do you think this is a good idea or a bad one? Why or why not?

5. How might some of the advice in this article help you in your chosen profession?

MyReadingLab

Reading 2 VOCABULARY PREVIEW

"Protecting Your Identity" by Corinne Fennessy

Match the words in the Word Bank by writing the letter of the word next to the matching definition. The paragraph numbers in parentheses indicate the location of each word in "Protecting Your Identity." Read the words in the paragraphs to determine the correct meanings as they are used in the context of the selection.

WORD BANK

a. incurred (1)	b. taunt (1)	c. wreak havoc (1)
d. fraudulent (1)	e. vulnerable (3)	f. appropriate, *v.* (4)
g. imperative (7)	h. procrastinate (8)	

1. .... cause chaos

2. .... to delay unnecessarily

3. .... open to attack

4. .... to mock or jeer

5. .... to seize

6. .... acquired

7. .... crucial

8. .... false or misrepresented

MyReadingLab

Reading 2 PREVIEW

Discuss the following questions with a partner or small group.

1. Why would it be important to monitor your financial records and keep copies of your bank statements?
2. What are some of your goals that require money to achieve, and what is your financial plan to earn the money?

After you preview the article, write one or two preview questions on the lines below:

....

....

....

....

....

MyReadingLab

Reading 2

"Protecting Your Identity"

by Corinne Fennessy

1 Back in 1998, a very notorious identity theft criminal who was also a convicted felon stole a man's identity and used it to buy homes, motorcycles, and handguns. He incurred over $100,000 in credit card debt, and then filed for bankruptcy in his victim's name. If this wasn't bad enough, he also phoned his victim to taunt him saying that he could continue to wreak havoc on his life as much as he wanted because identity theft wasn't a crime at that time. It took the victim and his wife over four years and $15,000 to restore their credit and reputations. In Florida, a woman obtained a fraudulent driver's license in the name of her victim and used it to withdraw more than $13,000 from the victim's bank account. She also opened five department store credit cards in her victim's name and charged approximately $4,000 on the cards before she was stopped.

2 Identity theft and cyber crime have become a mainstream problem around the world. As of 2012, 10% of Americans have been victims of credit card fraud, and an additional 7% have experienced debit or ATM fraud. Credit card fraud makes up 40% of all financial fraud, with combined worldwide losses totaling $5.5 billion. Interestingly, almost half of all credit card fraud begins with email as its source.

What are some of the crimes committed by identity thieves?

3 Anyone who has a driver's license, an email account, a bank account, or a credit card is vulnerable to identity theft. Someone steals your personal information and uses it without your permission or your knowledge to purchase expensive items or take out huge loans in your name. Identity thieves can open credit card accounts in your name, get medical treatments on your health insurance, open cell phone accounts, wipe out your bank accounts, or even file an income tax return in your name and steal your refund. Victims are unaware that their personal information is being used to commit fraudulent acts until significant damage has occurred. In some cases, innocent victims have been arrested because they didn't show up at a court date of which they had no knowledge.

4 Identity theft crimes are committed by **resourceful** criminals using a variety of strategies, which continue to multiply daily. The easiest ways to steal information are by dumpster diving (rummaging through trash for information such as account numbers), or by stealing a wallet, purse, or cell phone to steal passwords to financial accounts. Some cyber thieves work for legitimate companies and appropriate your personal information from their databases. Every year incidents of data theft are reported by major financial institutions or businesses that maintain records on millions of customers. Others deceive victims by pretending to represent a familiar and trustworthy institution or business through emails (phishing) or phone calls (pretexting).

What do pretexters do?

5 Pretexters are people who pretend to represent a business or research firm. They ask for information such as your name, date of birth, or even

Continued...

your social security number. Pretexters use this information to access your financial accounts posing as you or someone you have authorized to have access to them. Once they have access, they can steal money from your accounts or make unauthorized charges to them.

What Are the Signs of Identity Theft?

What are some signs of identity theft?

6 If you receive phone calls from bill collectors representing companies where you don't have accounts, if your personal checks are refused by a merchant, or if there are charges on your credit cards or checking account that were not authorized by you, you may be a victim of identity theft. If your health insurance company rejects your claim for a prescription or service because you have reached or exceeded your benefits limit, your health insurance is possibly being used by someone else. When your monthly credit card statements fail to appear in the mail, you should call the company and ask if they have been sent out, or go online to check them. An identity thief may have stolen statements from your mailbox to get the account information, or changed your billing address to hide fraudulent activity.

What You Should Do

Why should you file an Identity Theft Report?

7 If you find that you are a victim of fraud, it is imperative that you file an Identity Theft Report with your local police immediately. If possible, file a report in person instead of over the phone so you can receive a copy of the report. When you do this, credit reporting companies will block fraudulent information from appearing on your credit report. Your credit report shows your credit score, which is used by banks and other lenders to determine whether you qualify for loans or mortgages, and by potential employers who often check a person's credit as part of the pre-employment background check. If your credit score is lowered due to fraudulent activities, it can not only affect your ability to get credit, but also your employment opportunities. Filing an Identity Theft Report can also protect you from debt collectors, and an extended fraud alert will appear on your credit report. Once a fraud alert is placed on your file, you can request a free credit report.

8 Next, you should send copies of this report to all the businesses and credit reporting companies involved who may place a freeze on your accounts. The cost of placing a freeze varies from state to state, and the fee may cost you from $0 to $10. You can request that the freeze be lifted at a later date once the problem has been resolved. If businesses request more details about your case, you must respond within a limited time frame or be held liable, so don't procrastinate. Also, send copies of your report along with a cover letter to the fraud departments of the three major credit reporting companies: TransUnion, Equifax, and Experian. Don't try to solve your credit problems by requesting a new Social Security number because credit bureaus often combine credit records from old and new social security numbers. Or if no credit history is shown under your new number, it may hinder your ability to get credit if you need it. Also, the new number can be stolen just as easily as the first one.

What should you do if you are a victim of identity theft?

9 Third, close any credit accounts or financial accounts with the companies involved by notifying them in writing and keeping copies of your letters. Send these by email or registered mail so you have proof of your correspondence. Make copies of all fraudulent activity and keep detailed,

organized files. If your identity theft case is taking longer than anticipated, you can file a complaint or request help from the Federal Trade Commission (FTC) hotline (1-877-ID-THEFT) and consult with one of their counselors. All of these actions can be handled by a professional credit security company, but it will cost hundreds of dollars. You should first try to handle the problem yourself for free and only hire a professional if things become too much for you to handle.

Deterring Identify Thieves

10 Never carry your Social Security card or number in your wallet. Carry only one credit card in your wallet at a time. Store additional credit cards and personal information and in a secure place at home such as in a safe, and keep your purse in a locked drawer when you're at work. Avoid giving your social security number to businesses or other agencies unnecessarily. Shred any papers that have personal or financial information before discarding them. Cut up expired credit cards and hotel room cards with magnetic strips on the back. Hotel room cards can hold your credit card number on the strips. To prevent credit card offers from arriving in your mailbox, call the federal opt-out numbers. When doing business online, create passwords that are combinations of random letters, numbers, and special characters instead of names, dates, or places related to you. Conduct business only with **reputable** firms and stay away from unfamiliar websites. Many cyber crimes are committed over the Internet by individuals outside of your jurisdiction, even across the globe, which makes finding and arresting them extremely difficult.

11 Educate yourself about identity theft and your rights as a victim by going online to one of the federal agency websites such as the Consumer Protection Agency, the Department of Justice, or the FBI. Report suspicious activities and do background checks on any business with your local Better Business Bureau before you give them your credit card numbers. Taking some precautions and safeguarding your information are your best defense against identity theft.

1,398 words divided by .... minutes = ... words per minute

MyReadingLab

Reading 2 REVIEW

A good review strategy to use after reading is to summarize what you just read in your own words. Take a few minutes to think about the author's most important point and any key ideas that helped to support or explain it.

Write a two- or three-sentence summary on the lines below.

....

....

....

....

....

MyReadingLab

Reading 2 COMPREHENSION QUESTIONS

The following questions will help you recall the main idea and details of "Protecting Your Identity." Read any parts of the article that you need to find the correct answers.

MAIN IDEAS

1. What is the implied central point of this reading selection?

a. Identity theft is a crime with serious consequences, but it can be avoided and resolved by taking action.

b. Identity theft can ruin your financial situation and hinder your career.

c. It is difficult to prevent identity theft.

d. What should you do if you are a victim of identity theft?

2. What is the implied main idea of paragraph 6?

a. If you receive phone calls from bill collectors representing companies where you don't have accounts, if your personal checks are refused by a merchant, or if there are charges on your credit cards or checking account that were not authorized by you, you may be a victim of identity theft.

b. There are several signs that indicate that identity theft may have occurred.

c. Identity thieves can prevent you from using your own credit or health insurance.

d. You must take action to prevent identity theft from happening to you.

3. What is the implied main idea of paragraph 10?

a. Never carry your Social Security card or number in your wallet.

b. Don't obtain more credit cards than necessary.

c. Avoid giving out your social security number to anyone.

d. You can protect yourself from becoming an identity theft victim by taking some precautions.

SUPPORTING DETAILS

4. According to the passage, what are pretexters?

a. They send emails to potential victims to collect information about them, and use the data to obtain access to their credit card or bank accounts.

b. They call people pretending to represent a reputable business or agency to gain information which is used to access people's financial accounts so they can steal from them.

c. They surf the Internet looking for access to active financial accounts while people are using them.

d. They steal customer information from businesses and banks and then appropriate money from their customers' accounts.

5. All of the following are signs that identity theft may have occurred except

a. Your health insurance claim is denied because you have reached your benefits limit.

b. Your credit card is denied when you go to use it because you have exceeded your credit limit.

c. Your phone line is unexpectedly shut off.

d. Your credit card statement does not arrive in the mail.

DRAWING CONCLUSIONS

6. From this selection, you can conclude that

a. It's unwise to respond to emails from people or businesses that are not familiar to you.

b. Social security numbers are protected by the federal government.

c. If you are a victim of identity theft, you are never responsible for any debts that you did not authorize.

d. Identity theft is a crime that is often committed against the elderly.

7. According to this selection, who is responsible for doing all the work to restore good credit and to get fraudulent activity erased from a credit report?

a. the police

b. federal government agencies

c. businesses where unauthorized charges were made

d. the victim

8. According to the reading selection, you can conclude that

a. People should never use credit cards on the Internet.

b. Identity thieves will not be able to continue their schemes once everyone takes precautions to protect their identity.

c. Phishing only occurs when a computer is on and someone is using the Internet.

d. Identity thieves operate from all parts of the world.

VOCABULARY IN CONTEXT

9. What is the meaning of the underlined word in the following sentence? Identity theft crimes are committed by <u>resourceful</u> criminals using a variety of strategies—which continue to increase daily.

a. evil

b. experienced

c. creative

d. hungry

10. What is the meaning of the underlined word in the following sentence? Conduct business only with <u>reputable</u> firms and stay away from unfamiliar websites.

a. trustworthy

b. illicit

c. stable

d. recognizable

Reading 2 VOCABULARY PRACTICE: WORD SEARCH

Complete the following sentences using the vocabulary words in the Word Bank. If you want a challenge, compete with another player or team to find the words in the word puzzle and circle them. The words may be horizontal, vertical, diagonal, or backwards. Once you have circled the word in the puzzle, write the coordinates of the word's first letter after the sentence.

Example:

Phishing .... is soliciting information from someone by email. *B-4* ....

WORD BANK

incurred	taunt	wreak havoc	fraudulent	vulnerable
appropriate	imperative	procrastinate		

1. People who bully others may .... them because they have low self-esteem and need to feel superior. ....
2. Thieves who commit .... activity over the Internet from foreign countries are difficult to find. ....
3. If you .... on doing something, you may wait until it's too late to accomplish it. ....
4. People who are easily deceived are more .... to identity theft. ....
5. Once a cyber criminal acquires customer data, it is easy to .... funds from their financial accounts. ....
6. The Weather Channel reported that the hurricane will continue to .... along the Eastern coastline for the next 12 hours. ....
7. It is .... that you monitor your bank statements and credit card statements each month for unauthorized charges. ....
8. While attending college, many students have .... so much debt that it will take decades to pay it back. ....

	A	B	C	D	E	F	G	H	I	J	K	L	M
1	V	U	L	N	E	I	A	B	L	E	A	V	A
2	U	N	C	L	E	N	S	A	M	X	L	M	P
3	L	H	A	V	O	C	A	P	P	P	R	O	P
4	N	P	E	P	R	U	M	O	O	E	D	S	W
5	E	H	T	A	P	R	S	A	U	R	X	R	O
6	R	I	M	P	E	R	A	T	I	V	E	P	R
7	A	S	W	O	M	E	O	N	I	A	C	E	U
8	B	H	D	A	D	D	Y	P	K	C	U	P	S
9	L	I	N	S	T	E	I	H	R	A	G	A	L
10	E	N	F	U	R	I	A	T	I	I	N	G	L
11	**A**	G	P	I	C	V	L	T	W	N	A	Y	Q
12	**S**	A	N	P	O	T	C	H	G	I	R	T	R
13	**L**	U	N	C	H	A	L	L	I	A	W	E	E
14	F	R	A	U	D	U	L	E	N	T	G	O	T
15	**R**	E	N	O	U	N	C	E	S	E	R	U	M
16	E	T	A	N	I	T	S	A	R	C	O	R	P

MyReadingLab

Reading 2 QUESTIONS FOR WRITING AND DISCUSSION

Review any parts of the article you need to answer the following questions.

1. Why do you think that identity thieves are so difficult to apprehend?

2. Which steps are you currently taking to protect your credit, or what steps do you plan to take to protect it?

3. Besides the effect that identity theft has on individual victims, what other institutions or groups are affected by it, and how?

4. Which groups of people do you think are most vulnerable to identity theft, and why?

5. What actions do you think law enforcement should take to prevent identity theft from occurring?

MyReadingLab

VIEWPOINT FOR CRITICAL THINKING

PRIVACY IN THE WORKPLACE

Dear Editor:

Some employers are installing video cameras and monitoring employees' computers on the pretense that they are offering security. Providing a safe and secure environment sounds beneficial, but when employers start snooping on your every move, they need to be reminded of the Fourth Amendment, which affirms "the right of the people to be secure in their persons, houses, papers, and effects against unreasonable searches and seizures." This means employers do not have the right to monitor your personal emails, conduct searches of your Internet browsing history, or search your desk or office when you are not there. If employees are doing their jobs, employers have no right to trespass on privacy. Some employers go so far as to monitor your habits and tell you that you shouldn't smoke, or that you need to join Weight Watchers if you want to keep your health insurance or your job. Background checks scrutinize everything from criminal history to credit history. Employers monitor blogs and social network posts like Facebook. Video cameras spy on employees. New GPS chips in cell phones can monitor where you are at any minute of the day and many employers use them to keep tabs on their workers. It's bad enough that the government watches everything we do. Now our employers are doing the same thing. When will this invasion of our personal lives end?

Signed,

Sybil Liberty

Dear Editor:

In response to Ms. Liberty's concerns about the invasion of our privacy at work, I am supportive of anything my employer does to keep the work place a safe place. Every day we hear about workplace violence in the news. Disgruntled employees who carry guns or call in bomb threats are everywhere. There are laws in most states that protect workers against unnecessary searches. If employers want to monitor emails, search lockers, desks and offices, or even search a person to ensure the safety of their workers, I believe they have not only the right but the responsibility to do so. Background checks protect the company and the safety of the employees. If people have a history of violence or drug abuse, the company has the right to know that before they invest time and money training people and providing them benefits. If someone blogs about getting even with a boss or coworker, the company can take action before something tragic happens. If someone is doing something to harm the company or its employees, it has a right to know. Innocent people have nothing to hide. As far as I am concerned, the company can monitor anything about me that they wish.

Signed,

Contented Coworker

1. What is the point of view of the first letter regarding workplace privacy?

2. What is Ms. Coworker's viewpoint regarding workplace privacy?

3. Which viewpoint do you support, and why?

4. Which types of surveillance or monitoring do you feel are acceptable, and which are not?

5. Do you think the Fourth Amendment applies to the workplace or to how the government should treat citizens? Explain why.

MyReadingLab

REAL-LIFE READING

BUYING A USED CAR

When buying from a dealer or a private owner, you may not get the full truth about the vehicle you want to buy. To avoid disappointment or getting cheated, keep the following tips in mind:

- Check the reputation of the seller. If it is at a dealership, go online to the Better Business Bureau or a private reporting company such as Angie's List to find out their history. If buying from a private owner, you can enter a name into your Internet browser's search box to see if any police records turn up.
- Avoid getting emotional over a particular car. Regardless of what a salesperson tells you, this deal will never be the last chance to own one. Be ready to walk away if the seller seems too anxious to sell, or if something is suspicious. Be open-minded about the model you want, keeping two or three other possibilities in mind. People who must have a particular car often end up paying too much or getting a lemon.
- Before you go to see the car, make arrangements with a mechanic you trust who will look the car over before you buy it.
- Arrive 15 minutes early to see the car to look for any last-minute fixing that might be going on.
- Take a list of what to inspect on a car. These lists are available online. If this is your first car, first practice doing an inspection on a friend's car.
- Take the car for a test drive. Start it yourself and notice how the engine sounds, or if there is smoke coming out of the tailpipe. If there are any flaws, point these out to the seller and deduct the repair costs from the price you pay. If the car needs major repairs, don't buy it.
- Ask to see receipts showing the maintenance performed on the vehicle over the past year or two. Look for records of regular oil changes (about every 3-6 months depending on the miles it is driven).
- Read the owner's vehicle registration and write down the Vehicle Registration Number (VIN #). Confirm that the person selling it is the legal owner by asking to see the vehicle title (proof of ownership paper) and a photo ID. If the seller doesn't have these, walk away; it may be a stolen vehicle. You can check the VIN number for free at the National Insurance Crime Bureau at https://www.nicb.org.
- Go online to a service such as Carfax to learn the vehicle's history, including accidents and theft. It will also tell you the fair value for this vehicle. You will need the VIN number to use Carfax.
- Ask if there is an existing lien on the vehicle (if it is being used as collateral on a loan). Don't buy it if it has a lien.
- If you want to buy the vehicle, insist on being allowed to take the car to a mechanic you trust for an inspection. The seller may go with you, but if he or she refuses, you shouldn't buy the car.
- If you purchase from a dealer, consider adding an extended warranty. Read the warranty carefully to know what is covered and ask if it includes both parts and labor on repairs.

- Always try to get a lower price. Sellers set a high price and expect buyers to negotiate. Look online at Blue Book or Carfax for the fair value of the vehicle, and for other cars for sale with the same model and year. Know what the car is worth before you see it.
- Be sure to get a receipt signed by the seller showing the date, sale price, model, year, and VIN number of the car. Also, get the title paper because you cannot register the car without both of these papers.

1. Why is it important to not be too passionate about a particular vehicle?

2. If the owner cannot provide the title for the vehicle, what might this mean?

3. Why should you research the vehicle's history before you buy it?

4. Why is it important to get a receipt and the title when you buy the car?

5. Why is it important to research the seller and the vehicle before you buy?

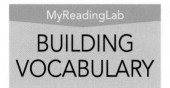

MyReadingLab

BUILDING VOCABULARY

Knowing the meanings to many word parts will help you determine the meanings of unfamiliar words. Make a list of English words using the word parts in the table below, and give their meanings. If you are unsure about a word, consult a dictionary. Then use the words to complete the sentences below. (* presented in previous lists)

PREFIXES	ROOTS	SUFFIXES
inter-: *between*	mis: *to send*	-tion, -sion: *action, state of**
dis-: *away*	rupt: *to burst*	-ive: *character or quality**
e-, ex-: *out**		

WORDS

....

....

....

....

....

Use one of the words in your word list above in a sentence that reveals its meaning with a context clue. Read the sentence to a classmate and ask him or her to define the word.

....

....

....

....

....

....

....

....

MyReadingLab

CHAPTER PRACTICE 1

Directions: Read the passages below from a business textbook and answer the following questions.

[1] Trade between countries historically occurred to allow each country to exploit its particular areas of competitive advantage, which generally resulted in a "win-win" situation for both parties. In the twenty-first century, however, questions are being raised about the impact that global trade has on less-developed countries when they become involved in trade with powerful multinational corporations (MNCs). Even when trade is taking place between relatively equal trading partners, some critics argue that globalization has some potentially serious drawbacks.

[2] Critics argue that multinational corporations cause serious harm when they extend their business practices around the globe. Too often, MNCs destroy the livelihoods of home-country workers by moving jobs to developing countries where workers are willing to labor under poor conditions for less pay (outsourcing). In Canada, for example, the last surviving fruit-processing facility, located outside of Niagara-on-the-Lake in southern Ontario, is slated for foreclosure. The facility produced canned peaches and pears under familiar labels such as Del Monte and Aylmer. It is expected that the factory's owner, CanGro Foods, will outsource production to China, where costs are much lower. The plant closure affects not only the employees of the facility, but also the farmers who supply the fruit. About 900 acres of peach trees are expected to be destroyed by farmers who no longer have a market for their product. Critics of globalization question whether the benefit of slightly cheaper products on store shelves is worth the bigger price that is being paid—namely, the loss of local jobs and the erosion of domestic industries.

1. What is the central point of this passage?

a. Trade between countries historically occurred to allow each country to exploit its particular areas of competitive advantage, which generally resulted in a "win-win" situation for both parties.

b. Global trade has a negative effect on some businesses and economies.

c. Global trade has serious impacts on less-developed countries when they become involved in trade with powerful multinational corporations.

d. The last surviving fruit-processing facility, located outside of Niagara-on-the-Lake in southern Ontario, is slated for foreclosure due to outsourcing to China.

Continued...

MyReadingLab

CHAPTER PRACTICE 1

...continued

2. What is the implied main idea of paragraph 1?

- **a.** Global trade has serious impacts on less-developed countries when they become involved in trade with powerful multinational corporations.
- **b.** Multinational corporations are exploiting less-developed countries for profit.
- **c.** Less-developed countries cannot compete in global trade because they end up losing jobs.
- **d.** Multinational corporations should be restricted from global trading to protect the less-developed countries.

3. From the passage you can conclude that

- **a.** multinational corporations are responsible for damaging the economies of smaller countries.
- **b.** global trade has such a negative impact on less-developed countries that it should be stopped.
- **c.** global trade has not always been regarded negatively.
- **d.** multinational corporations use global trade as a means to exploit smaller, less-developed countries.

4. From the passage you can conclude that

- **a.** outsourcing work to other countries has an effect on local economies because corporations no longer need as many employees or suppliers.
- **b.** Del Monte and Aylmer will send Canadian workers to China to process and pack fruit before it is shipped to warehouses.
- **c.** outsourcing to other countries will cause an increase in the price of goods at the markets.
- **d.** more local industries will spring up if multinational corporations outsource jobs to other countries.

5. From the passage you can conclude that

- **a.** less-developed countries will benefit from companies who will outsource work to their countries where labor costs are cheaper.
- **b.** labor costs in large, well-developed countries like Canada or the U.S. are too high.
- **c.** if more companies would outsource to other countries, there would be less competition for jobs in their home countries.
- **d.** when corporations send work to other countries to save costs, jobs and businesses in their home countries are negatively affected.

MyReadingLab

CHAPTER PRACTICE 2

Directions: Read the passages below from a business textbook and answer the following questions.

1 The negative effects of globalization are felt by developing countries as well. Critics argue that traditional lifestyles and values are being weakened, and sometimes destroyed, as global brands foster a global culture of North American movies, fast food, and cheap mass-produced consumer products. Still others claim that the demand of MNCs (Multinational Corporations) for constant economic

growth and cheaper access to natural resources do irreversible damage to the physical environment, especially in light of the weak environmental regulations found in many developing nations. The environmental consequences of shipping goods long distances to their ultimate markets raise additional concerns about global warming and environmental sustainability.

2 All these negative consequences, critics maintain, stem from the abuses of international trade—from the policy of placing profits above people on a global scale. These views surfaced in street demonstrations in Quebec City in 2001 when protesters gathered outside the Summit of the Americas conference—a gathering of 34 governments to discuss economic integration in the Western Hemisphere. Since then, meetings of the International Monetary Fund (IMF) and World Bank have regularly been assailed by large crowds of protestors who have succeeded in catching the attention of the worldwide media.

1. What is the central point of this passage?

a. The negative effects of globalization are felt by developing countries as well.

b. All these negative consequences, critics maintain, stem from the abuses of international trade—from the policy of placing profits above people on a global scale.

c. Many people are protesting the negative effects of globalization.

d. Multinational corporations are causing traditional cultures to disappear.

2. What is the implied main idea of paragraph 2?

a. Multinational corporations are guilty of contributing to global warming and polluting the environment.

b. Protesters are drawing attention to the negative effects of globalization.

c. Multinational corporations are abusing their power and causing economic disaster for developing countries.

d. People in Quebec City protested against the unfair practices of multinational corporations.

3. From the passage you can conclude that

a. traditional values and culture are replaced with another country's values, brands, and culture by multinational corporations.

b. shipping goods outside of a company's own country has little effect on the environment.

c. multinational corporations are likely to reduce their globalization if more people protest.

d. globalization is successful because people pay less for products made elsewhere.

Continued...

MyReadingLab

CHAPTER PRACTICE 2

...continued

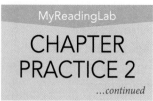

4. From the passage you can conclude that
   a. local traditions are preserved when local economies decide to restrict global trade.
   b. people should always buy from local producers and businesses instead of multinational corporations.
   c. most governments are not concerned by globalization.
   d. developing countries do not have strong environmental regulations to protect the environment.

5. From the passage you can conclude that
   a. globalization has negative effects on the environment.
   b. the International Monetary Fund (IMF) and World Bank are trying to stop globalization.
   c. companies who do not become large multinational corporations cannot survive.
   d. globalization always improves less-developing countries' economies by providing employment opportunities.

MyReadingLab

CHAPTER PRACTICE 3

Directions: Read the passages below from a business textbook and answer the following questions.

1 Meanwhile, supporters of MNCs respond that huge corporations deliver better, cheaper products for customers everywhere, create jobs, and raise the standard of living in developing countries. They also argue that globalization increases cross-cultural understanding. Anne O. Kruger, first deputy managing director of the IMF, had this to say about globalization: "The impact of the faster growth on living standards has been phenomenal. We have observed the increased well-being of a larger percentage of the world's population by a greater increment than ever before in history. Growing incomes give people the ability to spend on things other than basic food and shelter, in particular on things such as education and health. This ability, combined with the sharing among nations of medical and scientific advances, has transformed life in many parts of the developing world. Infant mortality has declined from 180 per 1000 births in 1950 to 60 per 1000 births. Literacy rates have risen from an average of 40 percent in the 1950s to over 70 percent today. World poverty has declined, despite still-high population growth in the developing world."

2 Business people who find themselves in the midst of international ventures for the first time are often shocked at how much there is to learn. The differences between the foreign landscape and the one they are familiar with are often huge and multifaceted. Some are quite obvious, such as differences in language, currency, and everyday habits (say, using chopsticks instead of cutlery). But others are subtle, complex, and sometimes

even hidden. Success in international business means understanding a wide range of cultural, economic, legal, and political differences between countries.

1. What is the central point of this passage?

- **a.** Globalization has improved poor nations.
- **b.** Globalization offers several benefits and increases cross-cultural understanding.
- **c.** Knowing other country's cultures can help a multinational corporation to be successful.
- **d.** Globalization has transformed life in many parts of the developing world.

2. What is the implied main idea of paragraph 1?

- **a.** Multinational corporations deliver better, cheaper products for customers everywhere, create jobs, and raise the standard of living in developing countries.
- **b.** Globalization by multinational corporations offers many benefits.
- **c.** Higher incomes improve a country's overall health and education.
- **d.** World poverty has declined despite an increase in population in the developing world.

3. From the passage you can conclude that

- **a.** multinational corporations do not benefit developing countries as much as they benefit highly-developed countries such as the U.S. and Canada.
- **b.** globalization is preferred by the IMF and World Bank.
- **c.** globalization protects multinational corporations from having to pay more employees.
- **d.** globalization has raised the standard of living for many people living in developing countries.

4. From the passage you can conclude that

- **a.** medicines and advanced treatments were never available in some developing countries before globalization.
- **b.** an increase in literacy is due entirely to globalization.
- **c.** everyone living in developing countries appreciates their culture better now than before globalization.
- **d.** higher incomes improve a developing country's overall health and education.

5. From the passage you can conclude that

- **a.** all international business is beneficial to developing countries.
- **b.** if not for globalization, no one would have an understanding of how to do business in another culture.
- **c.** to be successful in international business, you must have a complete understanding of other nations' cultures, languages, and traditions.
- **d.** globalization improves every country's health and education.

U-REVIEW

Answer each of the following questions.

1. A conclusion is ....

....

2. An implied main idea is ....

....

3. A central point is ....

....

CHAPTER REVIEW: IMPLIED MAIN IDEA FLOW CHART

Fill in the missing information in the flow chart below. A flow chart shows the steps of a process in sequential order. To find an implied main idea, you should:

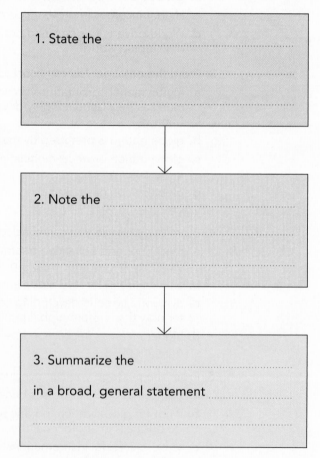

1. State the ....

....

....

↓

2. Note the ....

....

....

↓

3. Summarize the ....

in a broad, general statement ....

....

MyReadingLab

READING LAB ASSIGNMENTS

1. Login to **MyReadingLab** and in the menu click on Reading Skills. In the **Learning Path** select **Inferences**. Review this skill by reading the brief overview and models. Watch the short animation and then complete any practices or tests to learn the meanings of more words. You may also wish to review **Implied Main Ideas** found in the Learning Path.

2. Click on **Reading Level** and choose two stories to read and answer the questions to the best of your ability. Your Lexile level will increase as your reading comprehension improves.

ON THE WEB

You can learn more about drawing conclusions on the Web by doing an Internet search on the terms *drawing conclusions* or *making inferences*. Several Web sites and videos are available on this topic, which may enhance your understanding.

MyReadingLab

MONITOR YOUR LEARNING

In this chapter you learned about how to draw conclusions as well as how to determine implied main ideas and central points. Write a paragraph telling what you learned about these skills, how you learned them, and how you can use them to improve your learning and reading comprehension. When you have finished writing, read your paragraph as if you were reading someone else's paragraph for the first time. Check for missing words, spelling, punctuation, and sentence structure.

5 PATTERNS OF ORGANIZATION

FOCUS ON: Your Entertainment

"Humanities" refers to a broad category of subjects, including art, architecture, music, theatre, literature, dance, photography, and cinema. It includes everything that brings beauty and enjoyment to life; without the humanities, life would have little meaning. Even people who say they have no interest in the arts do watch television, go to movies, or play video games, which are all artistic media. The arts not only develop our emotions and creative expression, they communicate across cultural boundaries about our highest aspirations and values. Humanities enable us to share our humanness. Most of us can remember hearing a piece of music, or seeing a picture that evoked a strong emotion. At that moment we were feeling what the artist wanted to share when he or she created that piece. The humanities allow us to communicate our deepest, most profound emotions—those things for which there are no words to express.

In this chapter you will learn how to:

LEARNING OBJECTIVES

1. identify various patterns of organization and which transitions are associated with each of the patterns.
2. recognize relationships within and between sentences.
3. recognize overall patterns of organization.

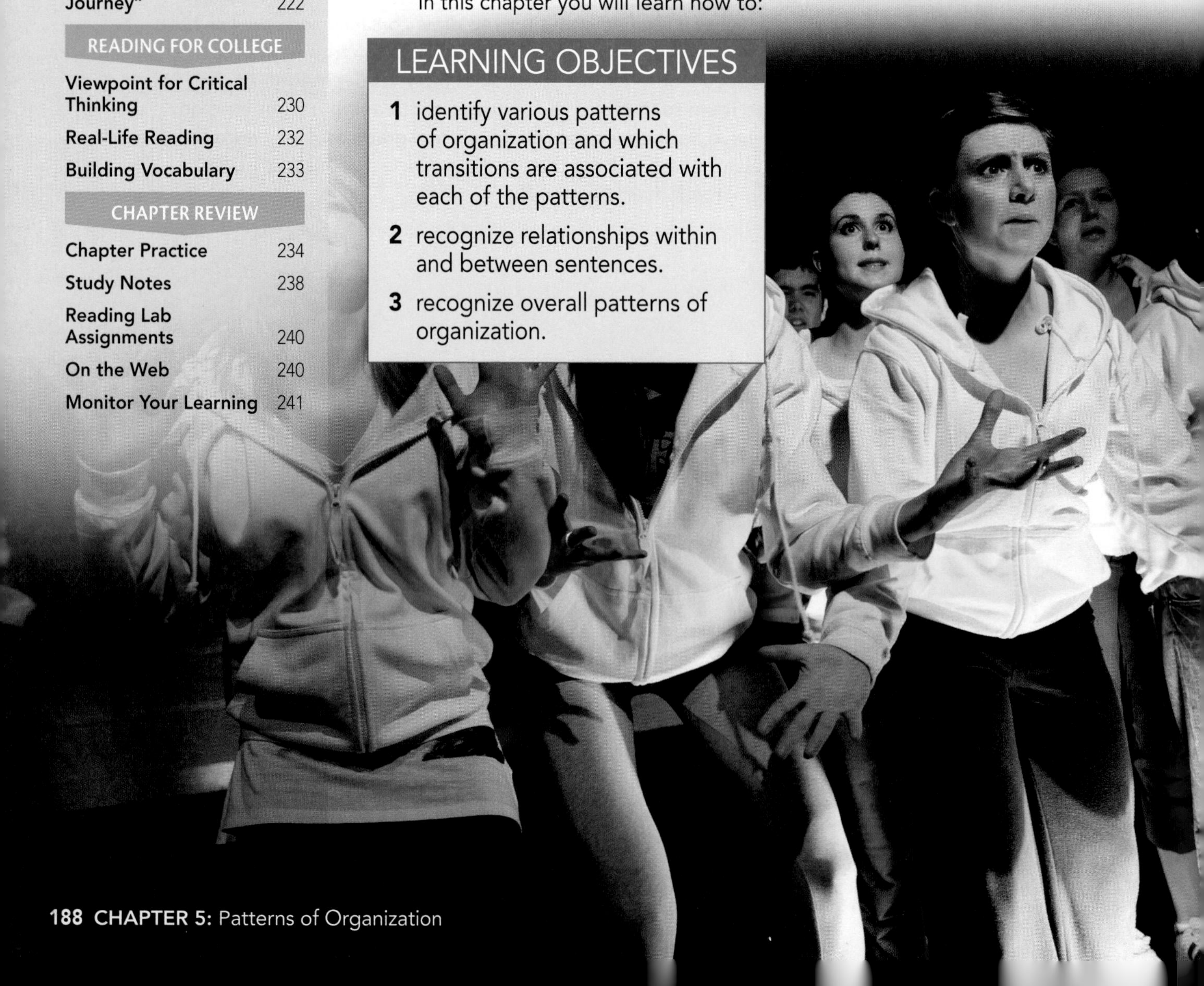

PATTERNS AND TRANSITIONS

OBJECTIVE 1

Identify various patterns of organization and which transitions are associated with each of the patterns.

The human brain loves patterns. It appreciates **symmetry** in objects and living things, and the repetition of melody, words, and rhythm in music. Even our numerical system is based on a pattern of tens. There are also patterns present in the way authors present ideas. Recognizing the pattern that an author is using to present details helps us to anticipate what will come next, and to organize the information to comprehend and remember it better. Recognizing the author's pattern also enables you determine the main idea and the author's purpose, or goal. In addition, becoming familiar with patterns and transitions will improve your writing skills tremendously as you learn to utilize them in your own writing in college.

symmetry: balanced in form or shape where one side is a mirror image of the other.

Patterns of organization refer to the way that authors arrange the supporting details in a sentence, paragraph, or longer reading selection. Knowing the pattern that an author is using helps us to clarify our thinking. Patterns provide an organized framework for the supporting details. Seeing the big picture in the pattern will help you understand the relationships between the main idea, the major details, and minor details. You will better understand how ideas relate to one another. For example, if you recognize that an author is using a cause and effect pattern, presenting the major details as the effects of something, you will start looking for more effects as you read and see them as the result of one or more causes.

patterns of organization: the way that authors arrange the supporting details in a sentence, paragraph, or longer reading selection.

Likewise, when you use patterns in your own writing, your writing is more organized, and as a result your message will become clearer to readers. This chapter will teach the most common patterns and the transition words that accompany each pattern.

You are probably already familiar with many of the patterns that authors use. For example, if an author is describing a chain of events in the order in which they occurred, the pattern is known as *time order*. If an author is describing how to do something in sequential steps, the pattern is *steps in a process*, or *process pattern.*

Each pattern makes use of **transitions**—words or phrases that show relationships of one idea to another. Learning the transitions associated with each pattern will also help you identify what pattern the author is using. In the appendix of this book you will find a chart of all the patterns of organization and their most common transitions.

transitions: words or phrases that show relationships between ideas.

To illustrate the use of transitions, read the following sentences:

> Some of the oldest examples of art are prehistoric cave paintings, *followed by* painted objects found in *early* Egyptian tombs.

(The transitions in this sentence in italics show when the examples of art were created in **time order**.)

> One stringed instrument of ancient Egypt *is known as* the tamboura.

(The transition in italics shows that a **definition** is about to be presented.)

Learning transitional words and phrases that go with each pattern will help you understand the relationship of ideas being shown in the paragraphs or sentences. However, not all sentences have transitions, and the transitions that you find may *not* signal the actual pattern being used. In these cases, you must rely on your ability to examine the details and draw a conclusion about the pattern of organization or relationships being shown. Read the following example.

> Dances in ancient cultures were performed for various purposes. Some of them were to enrich the harvest; others were for fertility, for victory in battle, or for bountiful hunting.

(There are no transitions in these two sentences. However, the second sentence provides examples of the various purposes of ancient dances. The relationship shown is known as the ***generalization and example*** pattern.)

OBJECTIVE **2**

Recognize relationships within and between sentences.

RELATIONSHIPS WITHIN AND BETWEEN SENTENCES

When looking at patterns in sentences, we refer to their *relationships* to each other. How do two parts of a sentence or two sentences *relate* to each other? To help you learn the various patterns and their transitions, we will begin with looking at relationships within sentences and between them. The transitions associated with each pattern are in boxes followed by sentences that use some of those transitions.

When looking for relationships within sentences, pay close attention to the punctuation in the sentence. A comma and coordinating conjunction or a semicolon may separate two ideas. Ask yourself, "How does the second idea in the sentence relate to the first one?" Read the following example:

> African music uses rhythms similar to those in Western music, *but* it has different microtones in its musical scales.

(Notice after the comma, a contrasting idea is presented and the transitions *but* and *different* indicate a difference. This relationship is one of contrast.)

When looking for transitions between sentences read both sentences and ask, "How does the second sentence relate to the first one?" Focus on the second sentence, paying close attention to its beginning. Many sentence pairs that show a relationship between two ideas will use a transition at the beginning of the second sentence, such as in the following example:

> One characteristic of African vocal music is the call and response, wherein the leader sings a phrase and other singers repeat it. *Another* feature is the use of heterophony, where both singers and instruments play the same melody at the same time.

(The relationship of the second sentence to the first is one of addition because the author is adding on another idea on the same topic and uses the transition word *another*.)

PATTERNS OF ORGANIZATION—PART 1

Complete the sentences below using the transitions in the boxes to show the correct relationships within or between ideas. Try to use a variety of transitions when completing the sentences. There may be more than one transition that can complete a sentence correctly.

1. The Definition Pattern

In a **definition pattern** the author defines a word or term. It may be a short one-sentence definition, or a long and detailed one. As you learned in Chapter 2, definitions are often given between commas, dashes, parentheses or brackets. Authors often use definition patterns in textbooks when they give a definition of a term and further explain its meaning, or give examples. Look for **example transitions** such as:

for example	such as	to illustrate
for instance	including	like

DEFINITION PATTERN TRANSITIONS

are	are known as	defined	definition	describes
is (are)	is (are) known as	means	refers to	is (are) called
that is	term(ed)			

1. *Trompe l'oeil* is a French term meaning "trick of the eye" and it .... a two-dimensional artwork designed to appear three-dimensional.

2. A *rebus* .... a riddle composed of symbols that suggest the sounds they represent.

3. Artworks composed of pieces of colored material set in plaster or cement .... *mosaics.*

4. The word *Romanesque* .... "in the Roman manner."

5. The artistic style that represents ideas or objects in a style true to life .... *realism.* **For instance**, a landscape of a scene that appears as it does in real life is an example of realism.

2. The Listing Pattern

The **listing pattern** (also known as *simple listing*) presents a random list of ideas. An example of a listing pattern would be a description of all the different majors that your college offers. The order of the details is not important, so the author simply lists them in no particular order.

LISTING PATTERN TRANSITIONS

one	final	furthermore	third	finally
last	then	also	and	in addition
moreover	include(s)	another	next	first
additionally	second	for one thing		

1. The Romantic Movement was a period in time when the arts incorporated themes of nature, beauty, death, and love. ______________________, it illustrated supernatural, mystical, and magical places.
2. Mozart began composing music at age five. ______________________, he composed his first symphony by the time he was eight.
3. Learning to play music can improve your logical thinking skills, __________ provide enjoyment. ______________________, it can help to develop creativity.
4. There are several ways to enjoy music. ______________, it can soothe or stimulate your senses. ______________, it can evoke powerful emotions, and ______________, it can create an association with something familiar, such as a wedding march.
5. In the 19th century, two women artists emerged as important contributors to impressionism. Berthe Morisot painted contemporary life and family. ______________ female artist who focused on family in her paintings was Mary Cassat.

3. The Cause and Effect Pattern

The **cause and effect pattern** shows the causes or the effects of one or more actions. It can show how one or more effects can have several causes, or how one or several causes can have several effects. The cause and effect pattern would be used to show the causes and effects of a disease, for example. This pattern answers the question as to *why* something happens.

(*Note: the word *affect* is a verb, meaning "to cause." The word *effect* is a noun, meaning "a result.")

CAUSE TRANSITIONS

affect*	due to	leads, leads to	cause	because
reason	since	if…then	explanation	

EFFECT TRANSITIONS

as a result	consequently	result	consequence
effect*	so	therefore	thus

1. The effects of two world wars on humanity made us question our existence. ………………………… a new approach to art known as existentialism emerged.
2. The British Invasion of the 1960's ………………………… the influence of British pop music on American music.
3. Nationalism was popular in the late 19th century and ………………………… ………………………… many composers began writing music to celebrate nations and cultures.
4. The process of creating something original ………………………… many artists to experiment with various media.
5. ………………………… Adolf Hitler and some of his top generals in the Nazi party were avid art collectors, many famous and priceless works of art were saved from destruction during World War II.

4. Compare and Contrast Pattern

The **compare and contrast pattern** shows how things are alike or different. When you compare things, you notice their similarities. When contrasting things, you observe their differences. Authors sometimes use only one of these patterns or both together, so this pattern is referred to as "compare and contrast" or "compare and/or contrast." For instance, the compare and contrast pattern would be used to show the similarities and differences between two versions of *Hamlet*.

COMPARISON TRANSITIONS (SHOW LIKENESSES)				
alike	as	both	in the same way	same
similar	like	likewise	in a similar way	

CONTRAST TRANSITIONS (SHOW DIFFERENCES)			
although	as opposed to	but	contrast
contrary to	differ	different	even though
however	in contrast	instead	in spite of
less than	more than	nevertheless	on the contrary
on the other hand	rather than		

1. After World War II, just as music styles changed from predictable lines and harmonies, ______________ art diverged from traditional styles.
2. ______________ many people enjoy watching plays and movies, they often don't read the books upon which they are based.
3. ______________ visual art and literature link each of us to cultural, philosophic, and religious ideas.
4. ______________ reading literature, try listening to it from an audio book to expand your appreciation of classic works.
5. In the early twentieth century, sound recordings were crude and indistinguishable. ______________, by mid-century, recordings were sharp and much-improved in quality.

Order Patterns

Two patterns deal with the order of things and therefore share the same transitions. Time order pattern deals with the chronological sequence of events, whereas the process pattern shows the sequence of steps, stages, or phases. The transitions for these patterns help us determine *when* something happens.

5. The Time Order Pattern

The **time order pattern** (chronological order) shows ideas in the order in which they occur in a chain of events. To illustrate, a summary of the major battles of the Civil War would be written in the time order pattern if the battles are presented in the order they occurred. In addition to the transitions below, dates that are listed in chronological order are also considered signals of the time order pattern.

TIME ORDER TRANSITIONS

first	second	third	next
finally	later	meanwhile	during
then	after(ward)	before	until
current(ly)	last	often	now
while	previous(ly)	over time	when
as	begin	beginning	
start, (ed), (s), (ing)	prior to	subsequent(ly)	

1. Leonardo da Vinci completed one of his most famous paintings in 1485, *The Madonna of the Rocks*, and ten years .... he created his renowned painting *The Last Supper.*

2. Degas produced two of his most famous paintings in the late nineteenth century: *The Dance Class* in 1874, ... *The Absinthe Drinkers* in 1876.

3. Sound films .... in 1927. .... then, musicians played live music to accompany silent movies.

4. Michelangelo was born in Florence, Italy in 1475, and is famous for his sculpture, *The Pieta* (1498), and the Sistine Chapel ceiling, which he completed .... 1534 to 1541.

5. The British rock group known as *The Who* had only modest success in the U.S. .... they produced the first rock opera, *Tommy,* in 1968, which gave them international acclaim.

6. The Process Pattern

The **process pattern** is similar to the time order pattern, but it is used to show steps, stages, or phases of an action that is repeatable. Some examples of when the process pattern would be used are instructions about how to register for a college course, or a description of the series of stages in a child's development, or the phases of an illness. Whereas time order usually describes a specific event, a process implies that the actions are repeatable each time it happens. **The transitions are the same as the time order pattern,** but the details focus on *how* and *in what order* something should happen.

1. To prepare a canvas for painting with acrylic paint, you should .... apply an undercoat in a neutral color.
2. When developing a roll of film, you must .... by presoaking the film in water for one minute. Mix the developing chemicals together in the developing tank, and .... place the film inside for ten seconds.
3. .... the film is inside the developing tank, gently move the film around. .... remove the film and rinse it gently under water.
4. A play begins with a script, and .... the actors are chosen to play the roles of the characters.
5. To make glass art, ... sand and other ingredients are heated until they become molten. .... , the glass is either poured into a mold or blown into a shape by a glassblower using a pipe.

OBJECTIVE 3

Recognize overall patterns of organization.

Overall Patterns of Organization

To find the overall pattern of organization in a paragraph or longer selection, begin by finding the topic and main idea, which often provides a clue to the pattern of organization. Read, for instance, the following topic sentences and the patterns they suggest.

The history of rock music *began* with African-American songs and rhythms. (**Pattern: Time order**)

Syncopa tion *is* a complex rhythm that accents a part of a beat that is not usually accented. (**Pattern: Definition**)

There are several *differences* between the styles of impressionist painting and cubist painting. (**Pattern: Contrast**)

When trying to decide which organizational pattern is used in a particular piece of writing, always start by referring to the main idea and ask, what was the author's purpose or intent? Then, move through the rest of the process (to remember the steps, think of the word REAL):

STEP 1: *Read to find the topic and main idea.*

STEP 2: *Examine the major details.*

STEP 3: *Ask, "What pattern do most of the sentences follow?"*

STEP 4: *Look for transitions to confirm the pattern of organization.*

R E A L

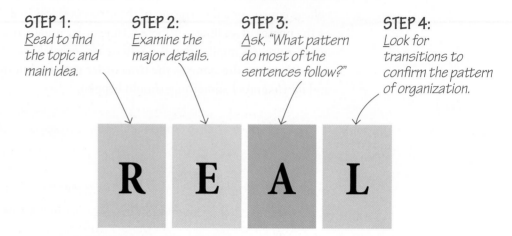

When asking, "What pattern do most of the sentences follow?" you must analyze the supporting details. For example, if most of the details in the paragraph explain the steps of how to do something, they are in a process pattern. The key to identifying the correct pattern of organization is to know all of the patterns and their most common transitions. You can also find clues to the pattern in the main idea. Read the following examples:

Example #1:

In 1955, guitarist and singer Chuck Berry had his first hit single, "Maybellene." *During* the 1950's, Berry's rock and roll tunes were hits as popular dance music; in fact, he was one of the first African-American musicians to dominate the pop music charts. His music *later* inspired British groups such as the Beatles and the Rolling Stones, who recorded some of his songs in the 1960's. In 1986, Chuck Berry was inducted into the Rock and Roll Hall of Fame.

The overall pattern of organization for this paragraph is time order because most of the sentences describe events in sequential order. The first event begins in 1955 and the last one ends in 1986.The transitions *during* and *later*, and the use of dates are clues to the time order pattern.

Example #2:

As you read the following paragraph, use the 4 steps in R.E.A.L. to determine the overall pattern of organization.

Flemish: adjective for people of Flanders, now known as the country of Belgium. Synonym: Dutch

Part of the drastic change in **Flemish** painting stemmed from a new development in painting media—oil paint. The versatile properties of oil paints gave Flemish painters new opportunities to vary surface texture and brilliance, and to create far greater subtlety of form. Oils allowed the blending of color areas because they remained wet and could be worked on the canvas for a while. Egg tempera, the earlier medium, dried almost immediately upon application.

The topic is Flemish painting, and the main idea is in the first sentence. The phrase *stemmed from* in this context means *resulted from*. You may have noticed contrasting ideas in the last two sentences, but this is not the author's purpose or goal for writing the paragraph. The main idea states that there was a drastic change in Flemish painting resulting from the introduction of oil paint. Thus, this passage uses a cause and effect pattern.

MyReadingLab

PRACTICE 1

Directions: Follow the four steps in R.E.A.L. to determine the overall pattern of the following paragraph. Underline any transitions that help you determine the overall pattern of organization. You may find the chart of Patterns of Organization in the **Appendix** of this book helpful when completing the practices.

tempera: a water-based type of paint used in art

Acrylics, in contrast with tempera, are composed of modern synthetic products, including an acrylic polymer that acts as a binding agent for their pigments. Most acrylics can be dissolved in water (but are water-impermeable when dry) and offer artists a wide range of possibilities in both color and technique. Acrylic paint can be opaque or transparent. It dries fast and thin, and it is resistant to cracking under extremes of temperature and humidity. Perhaps less permanent than some other media, it adheres to a wider variety of surfaces and does not darken or yellow with age, as do oil-based pigments.

1. What is the main idea of this paragraph?
   - **a.** Acrylics are synthetic paints.
   - **b.** Acrylics are synthetic paints that differ from other media.
   - **c.** Acrylics offer artists a wide range of possibilities in both color and technique.
   - **d.** Acrylic paint can be opaque or transparent.

Continued...

MyReadingLab

PRACTICE 1

...continued

2. What is the relationship within this sentence? Acrylics, in contrast with tempera, are composed of modern, synthetic products.
   a. definition and example
   b. cause and effect
   c. compare/contrast
   d. time order
3. What is the relationship within this sentence? Perhaps less permanent than some other media, it adheres to a wider variety of surfaces.
   a. definition
   b. time order
   c. cause and effect
   d. compare/contrast
4. What is the relationship within this sentence? It does not darken or yellow with age, as do oil-based pigments.
   a. cause and effect
   b. compare
   c. contrast
   d. listing
5. What is the overall pattern of organization for this passage?
   a. cause and effect
   b. compare/contrast
   c. definition
   d. listing

MyReadingLab

PRACTICE 2

Directions: Follow the four steps in R.E.A.L. to determine the overall pattern of the following paragraph. Underline any transitions that help you determine the overall pattern of organization. You may find the chart of Patterns of Organization in the Appendix of this book helpful when completing the practices.

> Rhyme—the coupling of words that sound alike—constitutes the most common sound structure in poetry. In the best poetry, rhyme ties the sense together with the sound. Rhyme can be masculine, feminine, or triple. Masculine rhyme uses single-syllable words such as "hate" and "mate." Feminine rhyme uses sounds forming accented and unaccented syllables: for example, "hating" and "mating." Triple rhyme has a correspondence over three syllables, such as "despondent" and "respondent."

1. What is the main idea of this paragraph?
   a. Rhyme—the coupling of words that sound alike—constitutes the most common sound structure in poetry.
   b. In the best poetry, rhyme ties the sense together with the sound.
   c. Rhyme can be masculine, feminine, or triple.
   d. Rhyme is used in many varieties of poetry.

2. What is the relationship between the following sentences? Masculine rhyme uses single-syllable words such as "hate" and "mate." Feminine rhyme uses sounds forming accented and unaccented syllables: for example, "hating" and "mating."
   a. cause and effect
   b. compare/contrast
   c. listing
   d. time order
3. What is the relationship within the following sentence? Feminine rhyme uses sounds forming accented and unaccented syllables: for example, "hating" and "mating."
   a. definition and example
   b. listing
   c. cause and effect
   d. process
4. What is the relationship within the following sentence? Triple rhyme has a correspondence over three syllables, such as "despondent" and "respondent."
   a. cause and effect
   b. listing
   c. process
   d. definition and example
5. What is the overall pattern of organization for this passage?
   a. cause and effect
   b. compare/contrast
   c. definition and example
   d. process

MyReadingLab

PRACTICE 3

Directions: Follow the four steps in R.E.A.L. to determine the overall pattern of the following paragraph. Underline any transitions that help you determine the overall pattern of organization. You may find the chart of Patterns of Organization in the Appendix of this book helpful when completing the practices.

Lithography (the term's literal meaning is "stone writing") rests on the principle that water and grease do not mix. To create a lithograph, artists begin with a porous stone—usually limestone—and grind one side until absolutely smooth. They then draw an image on the stone with a greasy substance. They can control the darkness of the final image by varying the amount of grease used: the more grease, the darker the image. After drawing the image, the artist treats the stone with gum arabic and nitric acid, and then rinses it with a petrol product that removes the image. However, the water, gum, and acid have impressed the grease on the stone, and when wetted it absorbs water only in the ungreased areas. Finally, a grease-based ink is applied to the stone. It, in turn, will not adhere to the water-soaked areas, but only where the artist has drawn. As a result, the stone can be placed in a press and the image will be transferred to the waiting paper.

Continued...

MyReadingLab

PRACTICE 3

...continued

1. What is the implied main idea of this paragraph?
   a. Lithography (the term's literal meaning is "stone writing") rests on the principle that water and grease do not mix.
   b. To create a lithograph, artists begin with a porous stone—usually limestone—and grind one side until absolutely smooth.
   c. Lithography is a print-making process that consists of several steps.
   d. Lithography was created to help artists sell multiple copies of their work.
2. What is the relationship within the following sentence? To create a lithograph, artists begin with a porous stone—usually limestone—and grind one side until absolutely smooth.
   a. time order
   b. process
   c. listing
   d. cause and effect
3. What is the relationship within the following sentence? They can control the darkness of the final image by varying the amount of grease used: the more grease, the darker the image.
   a. definition and example
   b. listing
   c. time orde
   d. cause and effect
4. What is the relationship between the following sentences? It, in turn, will not adhere to the water-soaked areas, but only where the artist has drawn. As a result, the stone can be placed in a press and the image will be transferred to the waiting paper.
   a. compare/contrast
   b. process
   c. cause and effect
   d. time order
5. What is the overall pattern of organization for this passage?
   a. process
   b. time order
   c. cause and effect
   d. compare/contrast

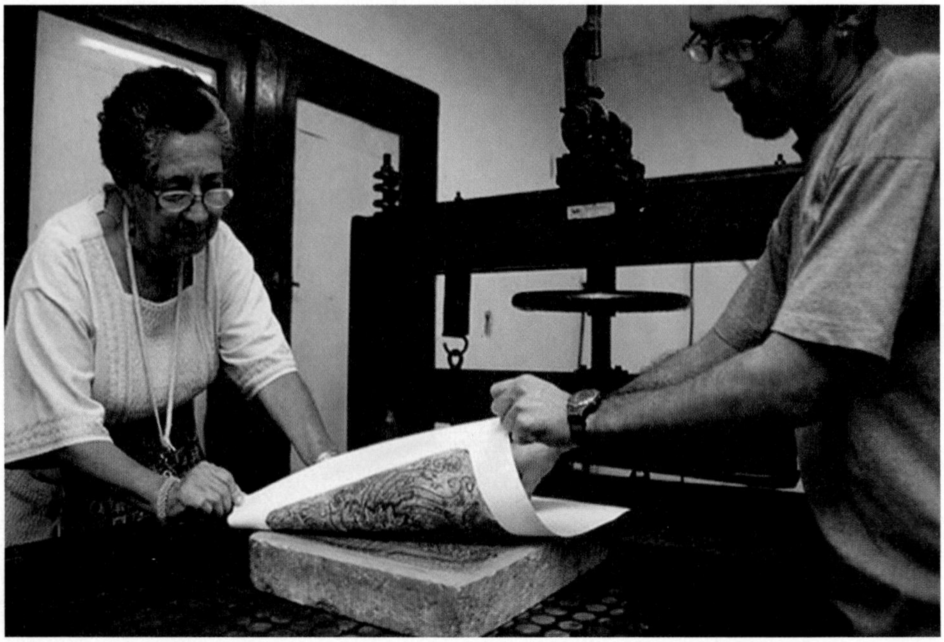

U-REVIEW 1

To review the patterns of organization you have learned so far, match the following patterns to the correct descriptions and transitions. Some answers are used more than once. The first one is completed for you.

PATTERN OF ORGANIZATION	DESCRIPTION	TRANSITIONS
Definition pattern: C and J	A. Shows the causes and/or the effects of one or more actions	G. like, similar, both, same, likewise, also, rather, however, but, yet, instead of, on the other hand
Listing pattern: ______ and ______	B. Shows how things or ideas are alike or different	H. consequently, as a result, due to, because, therefore, thus, so
Cause and effect pattern: ______ and ______	C. Defines a term and may offer an explanation or example(s).	I. first, second, third, next, finally, also, then, another, and, last
Compare and/ or contrast pattern ______ and ______	D. Shows a chain of events in the order in which they occurred	J. means, is, are, is called, is known as, refers to, term
Time order pattern ______ and ______	E. Shows details as steps, phases, or stages	
Process pattern ______ and ______	F. Presents details in random order.	

PATTERNS OF ORGANIZATION—PART 2

Review the information about patterns and transitions in Part 1 of this chapter before continuing with the remaining five patterns. Complete the sentences below using the transitions in the boxes to show the correct relationships within or between ideas. Try to use a variety of transitions when completing the sentences. There may be more than one transition which can complete a sentence correctly.

7. Space Order Pattern

Details arranged in **space order** (spatial order) show locations. Space order could be used to show the different geographical areas of a country, for example. The transitions for this pattern answer the question, "*Where?*"

SPACE ORDER (SPATIAL ORDER) TRANSITIONS

on	over	next to	up	beneath
top	bottom	beyond	left	right
between	north	south	east	west
through	beside	upward	at	within
outside of	around	center	along	parallel to
adjacent to	from	near	outer	inner
in	under	front	back	inside

1. In St. Paul's Cathedral in London, the wide, open nave of the church draws the worshippers' attention toward the altar at the .... of the cathedral.

2. At the center of the cathedral, the eyes are directed .... to the peak of the great dome, decorated with paintings celebrating the life of St. Paul.

3. Mesopotamia, located .... the Tigris and Euphrates Rivers, was the site of one of the earliest civilizations.

4. Trade routes of the ancient world ran .... the shorelines of the Mediterranean Sea.

5. The prehistoric cave paintings of Lascaux are found .... the caves near Montignac, France.

8. Classification Pattern

The **classification pattern** organizes details into groups or categories that share similar characteristics, such as types or kinds of things. If a textbook describes the different types of crimes committed in the U.S., it is using the classification pattern. Using the transitions in the box below to complete the following sentences will help you learn some transitions for the classification pattern. There may be more than one transition which can complete a sentence correctly.

CLASSIFICATION TRANSITIONS

class	classification	type	kind(s)
classify	category	categories	group

1. Several different .... of musical instruments make up the instrumentation of a typical orchestra.

2. In the woodwinds .... there are flutes, oboes, clarinets, and bassoons.

3. Walt Disney Productions made many award-winning films in different .... such as animated films, documentaries, and live-action films.

4. We can .... the compositions of John Williams into several categories: film scores, concertos, orchestral compositions, and chamber music.

5. Director Steven Spielberg has achieved success in several .... of films: adult-themed films, such as *Saving Private Ryan*, science fiction films, such as *Close Encounters*, and action-adventure films, such as the *Indiana Jones* series.

9. The Generalization and Example Pattern

When an author states a point and provides a specific example to illustrate the point, this is known as the **generalization and example** pattern. It is characterized by a broad statement that is usually the main idea of the paragraph followed by one or more examples. The pattern is often signaled by the example transitions found in the box below.

GENERALIZATION AND EXAMPLE TRANSITIONS

for example for instance such as to illustrate including like

1. The struggle against evil by a small, brave hero is a common theme in popular cinema. .... young Luke Skywalker in the *Star Wars* films, Harry in the *Harry Potter* films, or Bilbo Baggins in the *Lord of the Rings* series, play small heroes battling gigantic evil foes.

2. The works of the 19th century composer Peter Tchaikovsky have remained popular today. His orchestral works .... *The Nutcracker* and the *1812 Overture* are performed every Christmas and Fourth of July, respectively.

3. Romanticism developed as a literary style that evoked powerful feelings. ...., the *Lyrical Ballads* of William Wordsworth and the poetry of Samuel Taylor Coleridge express passion for natural beauty.

4. In the late 19th century, a group of artists created a new way of seeing reality, called impressionism. Claude Monet's *On the Seine at Bennecourt* .... is one of the finest examples of the style.

5. With the development of computer graphics, a new artistic media was born. Many of the earliest digital animation films, ... *Render Man* and *Luxo Jr.*, were among the first to be nominated for an Academy Award.

10. The Statement and Clarification Pattern

The **statement and clarification pattern** begins with a broad statement followed by an explanation. The author seeks to bring clarity to his pronouncement by providing more details. This pattern may use some transitional phrases such as the ones in the box below, but transitions are not always present.

STATEMENT AND CLARIFICATION TRANSITIONS

in other words	to explain	one explanation
to clarify	essentially	basically

1. Around 1600, the music director of the Basilica of St. Mark in Venice, Italy, made church services more interesting. ...., he placed the musical instruments and the singers in different areas throughout the church.

2. Postmodernism in theatre reflects a departure from the traditional values of society. ...., it portrays the alternative social lifestyles of feminist, lesbian, and gay groups who had long been ignored in theatre.

3. In *Rear Window*, Director Alfred Hitchcock relied on the viewer's ability to infer a complete landscape from isolated details. He relied .... on the two essential narrative functions that editing performs.

4. Primary structures differ from other types of sculpture. ...., viewers walk around and through a three-dimensional sculpture.

5. After two world wars, art was redefined. ...., art was no longer just an expression of beauty, but also an expression of reality in its ugliest truth.

11. Addition Pattern

The **addition pattern** is similar to the listing pattern in that the details follow no specific order. However, the addition pattern is evident when the details add more information about the same topic. It is used to express multiple points about something. For instance, a description of a new sports car may use this pattern to show all the interesting features of the car. The addition pattern is characterized by transitions like those found in the box below.

in addition	and	also	additionally
moreover	furthermore		

1. In the 21st century, the Internet has broadened the exposure of new musical talent. .... it has influenced the variety of musical styles that have developed as a result of sharing music internationally.

2. Max Steiner, one of the most famous film composers of modern times, scored the music for *King Kong* in 1933. .... he scored the music for *Gone with the Wind* in 1939 and *Citizen Kane* in 1941.

3. In the 1950's, Pop Art emerged as an expression of the popular culture of that era. .... it utilized elements of the visual environment that surround us every day.

4. Minimalism, another artistic style of the 1950s and 1960s, doesn't seek to communicate a message or an emotion. .... it presents geometric shapes and forms in neutral colors to allow viewers to develop their own interpretations.

5. Leonardo da Vinci was a renowned 15th century artist. .... he was an inventor of musical instruments, military weapons, and practical devices.

MyReadingLab

PRACTICE 4

Follow the four steps in R.E.A.L. to determine the overall pattern of the following paragraph. Read the passage and underline any transitions that help you determine the overall pattern of organization. You may find the chart of Patterns of Organization in the Appendix of this book helpful when completing the practices.

In *Psycho* (1960), Hitchcock's narrative problem was to keep the audience from realizing midway through the film—when Norman moves her body from the upstairs bedroom to the basement—that the mother is dead. Hitchcock attached his camera to the ceiling and filmed from directly overhead as Norman carries the corpse down to the cellar. The extremely high angle, coupled with the jostling movement as Norman goes down the stairs, prevents the audience from realizing that he is carrying a corpse. The viewer is even fooled into thinking that the mother is kicking in protest.

1. What is the main idea of this paragraph?
   - **a.** Hitchcock's *Pyscho* was a triumph because of its camera angles.
   - **b.** Hitchcock was the director of *Pyscho* in 1960.
   - **c.** Hitchcock used camera angles to fool viewers and hide an important clue as to what Norman was carrying down the stairs.
   - **d.** Hitchcock didn't want viewers to realize that the mother was dead.
2. What is the relationship within this sentence? Hitchcock attached his camera to the ceiling and filmed from directly overhead as Norman carries the corpse down to the cellar.
   - **a.** space order
   - **b.** listing
   - **c.** addition
   - **d.** classification
3. What is the relationship within this sentence? The extremely high angle, coupled with the jostling movement as Norman goes down the stairs, prevents the audience from realizing that he is carrying a corpse.
   - **a.** generalization and example
   - **b.** classification
   - **c.** addition
   - **d.** cause and effect
4. What words and transitions help to signal the overall pattern?
   - **a.** from, which, to, carries
   - **b.** is, are, was, with
   - **c.** from, to, down to, overhead
   - **d.** coupled with, is even
5. What is the overall pattern of organization for this passage?
   - **a.** classification
   - **b.** space order
   - **c.** compare/contrast
   - **d.** addition

MyReadingLab

PRACTICE 5

Follow the four steps in R.E.A.L. to determine the overall pattern of the following paragraph. Read the passage and underline any transitions that help you determine the overall pattern of organization. You may find the chart of Patterns of Organization in the Appendix of this book helpful when completing the practices.

Casablanca (1942) is a Hollywood classic wartime adventure film about heroic resistance against the Nazis, and it is also a lush, romantic melodrama. Rick (Humphrey Bogart), a nightclub owner, has come to Casablanca to get over a disastrous love affair with Ilsa Lund (Ingrid Bergman). Ilsa turns up unexpectedly one night in Rick's café and sets in motion the romantic fireworks that move the plot along to its exciting conclusion.

1. What is the main idea of this paragraph?

a. *Casablanca* (1942) is a Hollywood classic wartime adventure film about heroic resistance against the Nazis, and it is also a lush, romantic melodrama.

b. In Casablanca, a nightclub owner has a romantic affair with a woman named Ilsa Lund.

c. In the film Casablanca, the hero fights against the Nazis and rekindles a romance.

d. Ilsa turns up unexpectedly one night in Rick's café and sets in motion the romantic fireworks that move the plot along to its exciting conclusion.

2. What is the relationship within this sentence? *Casablanca* (1942) is a Hollywood classic wartime adventure film about heroic resistance against the Nazis, and it is also a lush, romantic melodrama."

a. space order **c.** addition

b. time order **d.** classification

3. What is the relationship within this sentence? Rick (Humphrey Bogart), a nightclub owner, has come to Casablanca to get over a disastrous love affair with Ilsa Lund (Ingrid Bergman).

a. generalization and example **c.** space order

b. cause and effect **d.** addition

4. What is the relationship between the following sentences? Rick (Humphrey Bogart), a nightclub owner, has come to Casablanca to get over a disastrous love affair with Ilsa Lund (Ingrid Bergman). Ilsa turns up unexpectedly one night in Rick's café and sets in motion the romantic fireworks that move the plot along to its exciting conclusion.

a. time order

b. classification

c. space order

d. compare/contrast

5. What is the overall pattern of organization for this passage?

a. statement and clarification **c.** classification

b. generalization and example **d.** cause and effect

MyReadingLab

PRACTICE 6

Follow the four steps in R.E.A.L. to determine the overall pattern of the following paragraph. Read the passage and underline any transitions that help you determine the overall pattern of organization. You may find the chart of Patterns of Organization in the Appendix of this book helpful when completing the practices.

History resounds with examples of new artistic attempts that met with terrible reception from so-called experts, whose idea of what an artwork ought to be could not allow for experimentation or departure from accepted practice. In 1912, for instance, when Vaslav Nijinsky (1889-1950) choreographed the ballet *Rite of Spring* to music by Igor Stravinsky (1882-1971), the unconventional music and choreography actually caused a riot: audiences and critics could not tolerate that they did not conform to accepted musical and balletic standards. Today, both the music and choreography are considered masterpieces.

1. What is the main idea of this paragraph?

a. History resounds with examples of new artistic attempts that met with terrible receptions from so-called experts, whose idea of what an artwork ought to be could not allow for experimentation or departure from accepted practice.

b. In 1912, for instance, when Vaslav Nijinsky (1889-1950) choreographed the ballet Rite of Spring to music by Igor Stravinsky (1882-1971) audiences and critics could not tolerate that they did not conform to accepted musical and balletic standards.

c. Critics and audiences are often wrong about new artistic styles.

d. Nijinsky's choreographed ballet *Rite of Spring* was not accepted by critics because it didn't conform to accepted musical and balletic standards.

2. What is the relationship within this sentence? In 1912, for instance, when Vaslav Nijinsky (1889-1950) choreographed the ballet *Rite of Spring* to music by Igor Stravinsky (1882-1971), the unconventional music and choreography actually caused a riot: audiences and critics could not tolerate that they did not conform to accepted musical and balletic standards.

a. space order
b. classification
c. compare/contrast
d. cause and effect

3. What is the relationship between the following sentences? History resounds with examples of new artistic attempts that met with terrible reception from so-called experts, whose idea of what an artwork ought to be could not allow for experimentation or departure from accepted practice. In 1912, for instance, when Vaslav Nijinsky (1889-1950) choreographed the ballet *Rite of Spring* to music by Igor Stravinsky (1882-1971), the unconventional music and choreography actually caused a riot: audiences and critics could not tolerate that they did not conform to accepted musical and balletic standards.

a. time order
b. statement and clarification
c. generalization and example
d. addition

MyReadingLab

PRACTICE 6

...continued

4. What is the relationship between the following sentences? In 1912, when Vaslav Nijinsky (1889-1950) choreographed the ballet *Rite of Spring* to music by Igor Stravinsky (1882-1971), the unconventional music and choreography actually caused a riot: audiences and critics could not tolerate that they did not conform to accepted musical and balletic standards. Today, both the music and choreography are considered masterpieces.
   a. classification
   b. space order
   c. statement and clarification
   d. compare/contrast
5. What is the overall pattern of organization for this passage?
   a. statement and clarification
   b. time order
   c. generalization and example
   d. cause and effect

U-REVIEW 2

To review the patterns of organization you have learned so far, match the following patterns to the correct descriptions and transitions. Some answers are used more than once. The first one is completed for you.

PATTERN OF ORGANIZATION	DESCRIPTION	TRANSITIONS
Space Order pattern: D and G	A. Groups ideas into categories with similar characteristics	F. class, group, type, kind, category
Classification pattern: .... and	B. A broad statement is followed by 1 or more specific examples.	G. under, over, above, beyond, on, in, at, north, south, east, west
Generalization & Example pattern: .... and	C. Details add on more information about the topic.	I. for example, for instance, such as, to illustrate
Statement & Clarification pattern .... and	D. Shows details by their location. Transitions tell where something is.	J. in other words, to explain, one explanation, to clarify, essentially, basically
Addition pattern .... and	E. A broad statement followed by an explanation	K. also, and, in addition, additionally, moreover, furthermore

MIXED PATTERNS

Students should be aware that sometimes authors mix two patterns in a paragraph. For example, an author may contrast the differences between theater in the past and the present and mix a contrast pattern with a time order pattern. Or, you may see a definition and example pattern mixed with a space order pattern, such as definitions of each part of the digestive system and their locations. There are no rules regarding what patterns can be mixed together. Read the following example and identify the two patterns that you see in the paragraph.

> To solve their debt crisis, British Parliament began a series of acts in *1764* that would raise money through taxation in the American colonies. The *first* was the Sugar Act, which reduced the duty on molasses in order to discourage smuggling while increasing the power of the courts to punish smugglers. It also prohibited the importation of foreign molasses, which forced colonists to buy it from the British. In the *same year*, Parliament enforced the Currency Act, which forbade colonists from printing their own currency. In *1765* the Stamp Act required that all official documents and printed materials must have stamps on them. This was a form of taxation, since the colonists had to buy the stamps, which *caused* an increase in costs. *As a result*, colonists protested by boycotting all imports from Britain, *causing* much economic distress for British merchants, who begged Parliament to repeal the act.

Topic: Parliament's Acts against the American colonies.

Main Idea: To solve their debt crisis, British Parliament began a series of acts in 1764 that would raise money through taxation in the American colonies.

Patterns of Organization: Time order and cause and effect
The main idea shows the author's intention, or purpose, was to show the series of acts that Parliament enforced to solve their debt crisis (which is the *cause* of the acts), and list them in chronological order, beginning in 1764. The *effects* of the acts are also described in the paragraph (the cost increases, protesting by boycotting, and economic distress).

Additional Patterns
The summary pattern and order of importance pattern are explained in the Appendix of this book, but they are not included in the practices for this chapter.

MyReadingLab

Reading 1
VOCABULARY PREVIEW

"Pyramus and Thisbe" (Greek Mythology) (Adapted from Thomas Bulfinch. *Myths of Greece and Rome*)

Match the words in the Word Bank by writing the letter of the word next to the matching definition. The paragraph numbers in parentheses indicate the location of each word in the reading selection, "Pyramus and Thisbe." Read the words in the paragraphs to determine the correct meanings as they are used in the context of the selection.

WORD BANK

a. ardor (1)	b. bosoms(1)	c. lamenting (5)	d. edifice (5)
e. reeking (6)	f. slake (6)	g. rent (7)	h. hapless (8)
i. peril (8)	j. imprinting (12)	k. scabbard (14)	l. retain (15)
m. ratified (16)	n. sepulcher (16)		

1. .... to keep; maintain

2. .... passion

3. .... satisfy

4. .... a sword sheath

5. .... a structure (a building, monument, etc.)

6. .... stinking

7. .... danger

8. .... tomb

9. .... to have torn; ripped apart

10. .... putting; placing

11. .... consented to

12. .... hearts

13. .... grieving over

14. .... unlucky

MyReadingLab

Reading 1
PREVIEW

Discuss the following questions with a partner or small group.

1. Many of today's super heroes are based on mythology. What super heroes do you enjoy reading about or watching in movies or television? What super powers do they have?
2. What are some myths that are you already familiar with? What mythical characters have you heard about?

After you preview the article, write one or two preview questions on the lines below:

MyReadingLab

Reading 1

"Pyramus and Thisbe" (Greek Mythology) (Adapted from Thomas Bulfinch. *Myths of Greece and Rome*)

Ancient Greek and Roman mythology are among the oldest forms of literature that have been handed down orally through generations. To these ancient people, their gods and goddesses were religious idols whom they worshipped in temples and prayed to daily. Ancient Greeks and Romans created many myths, or stories, to explain how things occurred in nature that they didn't understand, or to warn about the consequences of immoral actions. They also taught morality through mythical characters whose good deeds were rewarded and wrongful actions were punished. The story of Pyramus and Thisbe is the story of two lovers who share an ironic destiny. If the story seems familiar, this plot idea has been repeated in other literary works, including Shakespeare's *Romeo and Juliet.*

Why were Pyramus and Thisbe kept apart?

1 Pyramus (PEER-a-mus) was the handsomest youth, and Thisbe (THIZ-bee) the fairest maiden, in all Babylonia (Bab-a LONE-ee-ya), where Semiramis reigned. Their parents occupied adjoining houses; and being neighbors

Continued...

MyReadingLab

Reading 1

...continued

brought the young people together, and acquaintance ripened into love. They would gladly have married, but their parents forbade it. One thing, however, they could not forbid- that love should glow with equal ardor in the bosoms of both. They conversed by signs and glances, and the fire burned more intensely for being covered up.

2 In the wall that parted the two houses there was a crack, caused by some fault in the structure. No one had remarked it before, but the lovers discovered it. What will not love discover! It allowed a passage of the voice; and tender messages used to pass backward and forward through the gap. As they stood, Pyramus on this side, Thisbe on that, their breaths would mingle.

3 "Cruel wall," they said, "why do you keep two lovers apart? But we will not be ungrateful. We owe you, we confess, the privilege of transmitting loving words to willing ears."

4 Such words they uttered on different sides of the wall; and when night came and they had to say farewell, they pressed their lips upon the wall, she on her side, he on his, as they could come no nearer.

What did Pyramus and Thisbe plan to do?

5 The next morning, when **Aurora** had put out the stars, and the sun had melted the frost from the grass, they met at the accustomed spot. Then, after lamenting their arduous fate, they agreed that next night, when all was still, they would slip away from the watchful eyes of their parents, leave their dwellings and walk out into the fields. To ensure a meeting, they'd go to a well-known edifice standing outside the city's bounds, called the Tomb of Ninus, and the one who came first should await the other at the foot of a certain tree. It was a white mulberry tree, and it stood near a cool spring. All was agreed on, and they waited impatiently for the sun to go down beneath the waters and night to rise up from them.

Aurora: the Roman goddess of the dawn

What did the lioness do?

6 Then cautiously Thisbe went forth, unobserved by the family, her head covered with a veil, made her way to the monument and sat down under the tree. As she sat alone in the dim light of the evening she saw a lioness, her jaws reeking with recent slaughter, approaching the fountain to slake her thirst. Thisbe fled at the sight, and sought refuge in the hollow of a rock. As she fled, she dropped her veil. The lioness, after drinking at the spring, turned to retreat to the woods, saw the veil on the ground, and tossed and tore it with her bloody mouth.

7 Pyramus, having been delayed, now approached the place of meeting. He saw in the sand the footsteps of the lion, and the color fled from his cheeks at the sight. Presently he found the veil all rent and bloody.

What did Pyramus do when he found Thisbe's veil?

8 "O hapless girl," said he, "I have been the cause of your death! You, more worthy of life than I, have fallen the first victim. I will follow. I am the guilty cause, in tempting you forth to a place of such peril, and not being myself on the spot to guard you. Come forth, lions, from the rocks, and tear this guilty body with your teeth."

9 He took up the veil, carried it with him to the appointed tree, and covered it with kisses and with tears.

10 "My blood also shall stain your veil," said he, and drawing his sword, plunged it into his heart.

11 The blood spurted from the wound, and tinged the white mulberries of the tree all red; and sinking into the earth reached the roots, so that the red color mounted through the trunk to the fruit.

12 By this time Thisbe, still trembling with fear, yet wishing not to disappoint her lover, stepped cautiously forth, looking anxiously for the youth, eager to tell him the danger she had escaped. When she came to the spot and saw the changed color of the mulberries she doubted whether it was the same place. While she hesitated she saw the form of one struggling in the agonies of death. As she started back, a shudder ran through her frame like a ripple on the face of the still water as when a sudden breeze sweeps over it. But as soon as she recognized her lover, she screamed and beat her breast, embracing the lifeless body, pouring tears into its wounds, and imprinting kisses on the cold lips.

13 "O Pyramus," she cried, "what has done this? Answer me, Pyramus, it is your own Thisbe that speaks. Hear me, dearest, and lift that drooping head!"

14 Hearing the name of Thisbe, Pyramus opened his eyes, and then closed them again. She saw her veil stained with blood and the scabbard empty of its sword.

15 "Your own hand has slain you, and for my sake," she said. "I too can be brave for once, and my love is as strong as yours. I will follow you in death, for I have been the cause; and death which alone could part us shall not prevent my joining you. And you unhappy parents of us both, deny us not our united request. As love and death have joined us, let one tomb contain us. And you, mulberry tree, retain the marks of slaughter. Let your berries still serve forever as memorials of our blood."

What did Thisbe do when she found Pyramus?

16 Saying this, she plunged the sword into her breast. Her parents ratified her wish, and the gods also consented to it. The two bodies were buried in one sepulcher, and the tree ever after brought forth purple berries, as it does to this day.

1,083 words divided by .... minutes = ... words per minute

MyReadingLab

Reading 1 REVIEW

A good review strategy to use after reading is to summarize what you just read in your own words. Take a few minutes to think about the author's most important point and any key ideas that helped to support or explain it.

Write a two- or three-sentence summary on the lines below.

....

....

....

....

....

....

....

....

MyReadingLab

Reading 1 COMPREHENSION QUESTIONS

The following questions will help you recall the main idea and details of "Pyramus and Thisbe." Read any parts of the article that you need to find the correct answers.

MAIN IDEAS

1. What is the implied main idea of paragraph 1?

a. Pyramus was the handsomest youth, and Thisbe the fairest maiden, in all Babylonia, where Semiramis reigned.

b. Their parents occupied adjoining houses; and being neighbors brought the young people together, and acquaintance ripened into love.

c. Pyramus and Thisbe were neighbors who fell in love but their love was forbidden by their parents.

d. Pyramus and Thisbe were lovers.

2. What is the implied main idea of paragraph 12?

a. By this time Thisbe, still trembling with fear, yet wishing not to disappoint her lover, stepped cautiously forth, looking anxiously for the youth, eager to tell him the danger she had escaped.

b. Thisbe discovered the lifeless body of Pyramus and the mulberry bush soaked with his blood.

c. When she came to the spot and saw the changed color of the mulberries she doubted whether it was the same place.

d. Thisbe didn't believe that Pyramus was dead but only wounded and begged him not to die.

SUPPORTING DETAILS

3. According to the story, why did Pyramus believe that Thisbe was dead?

a. He saw the lioness attack her.

b. He found her veil all torn and bloody.

c. He held her lifeless body in his arms and kissed her lips.

d. She was not there at their appointed meeting place.

4. According to the myth, which of the following is the reason for the color of the mulberry tree?

a. It was a white mulberry tree, and it stood near a cool spring.

b. He took up the veil, carried it with him to the appointed tree, and covered it with kisses and with tears.

c. The blood spurted from the wound, and tinged the white mulberries of the tree all red; and sinking into the earth reached the roots.

d. As love and death have joined us, let one tomb contain us.

DRAWING CONCLUSIONS

5. From paragraph 5 you can conclude that

a. The town's people had built the Tomb of Ninus because he was honored as a god.

b. The ancient Greeks believed that the goddess Aurora extinguished the stars every morning.

c. The sun was worshipped by the Ancient Greeks.

d. The ancient Greeks believed that night was caused by Aurora setting the sun into the water.

PATTERNS OF ORGANIZATION

6. The overall patterns of organization for this story are

a. time order and cause and effect

b. time order and compare/contrast

c. statement and clarification

d. steps in a process and addition

7. What is the relationship within the following sentence? They would gladly have married, but their parents forbade it.
   a. compare/contrast
   b. cause and effect
   c. addition
   d. time order

8. What is the relationship between the following sentences? As she sat alone in the dim light of the evening she saw a lioness, her jaws reeking with recent slaughter, approaching the fountain to slake her thirst. Thisbe fled at the sight, and sought refuge in the hollow of a rock.
   a. time order
   b. statement and clarification
   c. space order
   d. cause and effect

VOCABULARY IN CONTEXT

9. What is the meaning of the underlined word in the following sentence? The blood spurted from the wound, and tinged the white mulberries of the tree all red; and sinking into the earth reached the roots, so that the red color mounted through the trunk to the fruit.
   a. resisted
   b. absorbed
   c. sat upon
   d. disappeared

10. What is the meaning of the underlined word in the following sentence? Then, after lamenting their arduous fate, they agreed that next night, when all was still, they would slip away from the watchful eyes of their parents, leave their dwellings and walk out into the fields.
   a. crooked
   b. passion
   c. difficult
   d. curious

Reading 1
VOCABULARY PRACTICE: CONCENTRATION

For two to three players

1.

Write the 14 vocabulary words and 14 definitions from the Vocabulary Preview word bank on 28 small cards or pieces of paper so there is one word card and a matching definition card for each word. Shuffle them and place them face down in four rows.

2.

The first player turns over two cards but doesn't pick them up. If the two cards are a word and its matching definition, the player picks up both cards and keeps them. The player gets another turn. If the two cards do not match, the cards are turned face down in the exact same spots and the play goes to the next person.

3.

The next player turns over any two cards, and the game continues in the same way as described above.

The object of the game is to memorize the positions of the cards and to match up as many correct words with definitions as you can. The player with the most matching cards wins.

MyReadingLab

Reading 1 QUESTIONS FOR WRITING AND DISCUSSION

1. Situational irony is when something happens that is totally unexpected and often the opposite of what the reader expects to happen. What irony is found within this myth?

2. As evident in this myth, in what ways were the ancient Greeks similar to people today in our society?

3. What are some moral lessons that this myth might have intended to teach?

4. In literature, objects sometimes become symbols for concepts. For example, a dove symbolizes peace. What do you think the mulberry tree symbolized in this myth?

5. What conclusions can you draw about Pyramus based on his actions in this story?

MyReadingLab

Reading 2
VOCABULARY PREVIEW

Steven Spielberg's Epic Journey

by Corinne Fennessy

Match the words in the Word Bank from "Steven Spielberg's Epic Journey" by writing the letter of the word next to the matching definition. The paragraph numbers in parentheses indicate the location of each word in the reading selection. Read the words in the paragraphs to determine the correct meanings as they are used in the context of the selection.

WORD BANK

a. synonymous (1)   b. gross (1)   c. deistic (1)
d. colossal (1)   e. chaotic (2)   f. discordant (2)
g. papier maché (3)   h. saltpeter (7)   i. philanthropists (8)
j. unparalleled (9)

1. .... supporters of charities
2. .... the same as; equal to
3. .... huge
4. .... a fireworks chemical
5. .... earnings before expenses
6. .... confusing; with turmoil
7. .... a paper, flour, and water mixture that hardens
8. .... unmatched; superior
9. .... god-like
10. .... quarrelsome

MyReadingLab

Reading 2
PREVIEW

Discuss the following questions with a partner or small group.

1. What are some of your favorite movies?
2. What do you think are the characteristics that make a good movie? How important is having a skilled director for the success of a movie?

After you preview the article, write one or two preview questions on the lines below:

....

....

....

MyReadingLab

Reading 2

"Steven Spielberg's Epic Journey"

by Corinne Fennessy

Steven Spielberg is one of those fortunate individuals who knew from the time he was a child what he wanted to do in life. His passion and determination have given him an outstanding career, but he has also found fulfillment in his personal life through family and philanthropy.

What are some of Spielberg's most successful movies?

1 The name Spielberg is synonymous with entertainment. Over the past few decades, director, producer and screenwriter Steven Spielberg has created blockbuster films that have earned him 3 Oscars and many other awards, including Golden Globes and Emmys. His films have been some of the highest-grossing in history: *E.T.: The Extra-Terrestrial* (1982) grossed $435,110,554; ***Jurassic Park*** (1993) $357,067,947; and *Indiana Jones and the Kingdom of the Crystal Skull* (2008) $317,101,119. Twenty-seven of his movies have earned a lifetime gross total of over $4 billion, making him one of the most successful director/producers in history. These figures almost make him seem deistic. So how did someone who has created such a colossal body of work become so successful?

2 Spielberg was born in Cincinnati, Ohio in 1947. His father was a computer executive who owned several patents for his programs, and his mother was a classical pianist. Steven was the oldest, with three younger sisters. "It was creative and chaotic at our house," says Steven's father. Because of Mr. Spielberg's career, the family moved several times, from New Jersey to Arizona and eventually to California. Although he moved frequently and his parents' discordant marriage eventually ended in divorce, Steven Spielberg still has fond memories of his formative years. One of his earliest childhood memories gave him a sense of fear, wonder and hope, emotions that often resonate in his film characters.

What was Steven's life like growing up in the Spielberg family?

3 "My dad took me out to see a meteor shower when I was a little kid," he said, "and it was scary for me because he woke me up in the middle of the night. My heart was beating; I didn't know what he wanted to do. He wouldn't tell me, and he put me in the car and we went off, and I saw all these people lying on blankets, looking up at the sky. And my dad spread out a blanket. We lay down and looked at the sky, and I saw for the first time all these meteors. What scared me was being awakened in the middle of the night and taken somewhere without being told where. But what *didn't* scare me, and was very soothing, was watching this cosmic meteor shower. And I think from that moment on, I never looked at the sky and thought it was a bad place."

4 What goes on in the mind of a creative mastermind like Spielberg? He explains, "Sometimes I think I've got ball bearings for brains; these ideas are slipping and sliding across each other all the time. My problem is that my imagination won't turn off. I wake up so excited I can't eat breakfast. I've never run out of energy. It's not like **OPEC** oil; I don't worry about a premium going on my energy. It's just always been there. I got it from my

OPEC: Organization of the Petroleum Exporting Countries, a multinational group of oil-producing countries.

Continued...

MyReadingLab

Reading 2

...continued

mom." His film-making began when he was in elementary school, and usually involved the entire Spielberg family. His father helped him construct movie sets with toys and papier maché. Their living room was often cluttered with cables and lights as young Spielberg filmed scenes with his 8 mm camera, enlisting his friends, his sisters, and just about anyone who came to visit the house. His sisters still remember the crazy antics they did as child stars in young Steven's movies.

How did Spielberg show his passion for movie-making?

5 His love of making movies led to a life-changing experience when he was 17 years old. He took a studio tour at Universal Studios, Hollywood, but the tour tram didn't stop at the sound stages. During a bathroom break, he sneaked into one of the sound stages to watch movies being made. There he met a man who turned out to be the head of the editorial department. They talked and Spielberg told him about his 8 mm films that he had made. The editor said that he'd like to see them, so he gave Spielberg a gate pass to get on the studio lot the next day. Spielberg returned and showed him four of his films and the editor was very impressed. Spielberg came back on his own again the next day, dressed in a suit and carrying his father's brief case, which held a sandwich and two candy bars. Looking as if he belonged there, he waved at the same guard who had seen him the previous day and walked right in. Every day that summer he hung out with movie makers on the studio lots. He even found a closet to make into his "office" and put his name on the building directory. At Universal he had found the place and people who would shape his future.

How did Spielberg get his start in making movies?

6 Spielberg enrolled at California State University at Long Beach and attended classes two days a week and spent three days a week at the Universal studio lot. He kept showing his films to anyone who would see them, and worked at the college to earn money to buy 16 mm film and rent a new camera. With his new 16 mm camera, he wrote and directed a film called "*Amblin*" in 1967 about two hitchhiking teens. After showing it to some people at Universal, he was offered a seven-year contract to direct television series episodes. He was 20 years old then, and 7 years later he directed his first full-length feature movie, *The Sugarland Express* (1974), which grossed $7.5 million.

7 Besides being immersed in film-making, Spielberg is a dedicated husband and father of seven children, including two adopted African-American children. "Fathering is a major job," he's said, "but I need both things in my life: to be a director, and for my kids to direct me." His morning ritual includes making pancakes and waffles for the kids' breakfasts and transporting them to school. He makes a point to be home for dinner with his family, and when he films on location, his family comes along. He says that his children keep him grounded and remind him that he is foremost a dad who just happens to be a film-maker. "If I'm feeling pretty good about myself, I just go home for a dose of saltpeter," Spielberg said.

In what ways does Spielberg help others?

8 In addition to his career and family life, Spielberg is one of the entertainment industry's most generous philanthropists. Because of his empathy and his influence, the world is a better place. He has donated more than $85 million to Jewish groups, and he founded the Righteous Persons Foundation and the Shoah Visual History Foundation, which creates video histories of Holocaust survivors around the world. He is also co-chairman of the Starbright Foundation, which aids seriously ill children. His donations built the Steven Spielberg Pediatrics Research Center at the Cedars-Sinai

Medical Center, the largest nonprofit hospital in the western United States. Following the events of Hurricane Katrina in 2006, Spielberg donated $1.5 million to the American Red Cross and the Bush-Clinton fund for hurricane victim aid. He continues sharing his bounty wherever there is a need.

9 Spielberg's life is his legacy. As long as Spielberg has ideas and a film crew, he'll be creating new movies. "I dream for a living," Spielberg says. "Once a month the sky falls on my head, I come to, and I see another movie I want to make." Dreamers like Spielberg inspire the rest of us to dream bigger dreams and to find the passion in our own lives that motivates us to break through the boundaries of our own self-induced limitations to become more than we believe we can. His unparalleled success demonstrates that we never know what we are capable of achieving unless we try.

1,264 words divided by .... minutes = ... words per minute

How Many of these Spielberg movies have you seen?

(This list does not include Spielberg's television or screenwriting projects.)
Jurassic Park IV *(2014)*
Men in Black 3 *(2012)*
Lincoln *(2012)*
War Horse *(2011)*
The Adventures of Tintin *(2011)*
Indiana Jones and the Kingdom of the Crystal Skull *(2008)*
Munich *(2005)*
War of the Worlds *(2005)*
The Terminal *(2004)*
Catch Me If You Can *(2002)*
Minority Report *(2002)*
A.I. Artificial Intelligence *(2001)*
Saving Private Ryan *(1998)*
Amistad *(1997)*
The Lost World: Jurassic Park *(1997)*
Schindler's List *(1993)*
Jurassic Park *(1993)*
Hook *(1991)*
Always *(1989)*
Indiana Jones and the Last Crusade *(1989)*
Empire of the Sun *(1987)*
The Color Purple *(1985)*
Indiana Jones and the Temple of Doom *(1984)*
Twilight Zone - The Movie *(1983)*
E.T. The Extra-Terrestrial *(1982)*
Raiders of the Lost Ark *(1981)*
1941 *(1979)*
Close Encounters of the Third Kind *(1977)*
Jaws *(1975)*
The Sugarland Express *(1974)*

MyReadingLab

Reading 2 REVIEW

A good review strategy to use after reading is to summarize what you just read in your own words. Take a few minutes to think about the author's most important point and any key ideas that helped to support or explain it.

Write a two- or three-sentence summary on the lines below.

MyReadingLab

Reading 2 COMPREHENSION QUESTIONS

1. **What is the main idea of paragraph 4?**
   - **a.** His love of making movies led to a life-changing experience when he was 17 years old.
   - **b.** Spielberg returned and showed him four of his films and the editor was very impressed.
   - **c.** Every day that summer he hung out with movie makers on the studio lots.
   - **d.** At Universal he had found the place and people who would shape his future.

MAIN IDEAS

2. **What is the implied main idea of paragraph 3?**
   - **a.** Spielberg's mind is always thinking of new ideas.
   - **b.** Spielberg's passion for movie-making was supported by his family members.
   - **c.** Spielberg's family moved frequently, so Steven made movies.
   - **d.** The Spielberg family was chaotic and the parents' marriage ended in divorce.

3. **What is the central point of the entire article?**
   - **a.** Steven Spielberg is one of history's most successful film makers.
   - **b.** Steven Spielberg is a family man and philanthropist.
   - **c.** Steven Spielberg's life is evidence of his love of films, family, and helping mankind.
   - **d.** As long as he has ideas and a film crew, Steven Spielberg will never stop making movies.

SUPPORTING DETAILS

4. **When did Spielberg get his first break in the business?**
   - **a.** When he was in elementary school, Spielberg made home movies with an 8 mm camera.
   - **b.** Spielberg wrote and filmed "*Amblin*" in 1967 and showed it to people at Universal studios.
   - **c.** When he was 17, Spielberg sneaked into one of the sound stages at Universal Studios to watch movies being made.
   - **d.** Spielberg showed an editor at Universal Studios four of his films and he was very impressed.

5. **From paragraph 5, you can conclude that**
   a. Spielberg was determined to get hired as a director.
   b. Spielberg believed that success is about being lucky.
   c. Spielberg never worked a regular job outside of television or movies.
   d. Spielberg didn't want to be a television director.

PATTERNS OF ORGANIZATION

6. **What is the relationship within the following sentence from paragraph 2? "Because of Mr. Spielberg's career, the family moved several times from New Jersey to Arizona and eventually to California."**
   a. space order
   b. listing
   c. cause and effect
   d. addition

7. **What is the overall pattern of organization for the article?**
   a. cause and effect
   b. generalization and example
   c. statement and clarification
   d. time order

VOCABULARY IN CONTEXT

8. **What is the meaning of the word in bold print in the following sentence?**
   "Although he moved frequently and his parents' discordant marriage eventually ended in divorce, Steven Spielberg still has fond memories of his **formative** years."
   a. unhappy
   b. developing
   c. life-changing
   d. parental

9. **What is the meaning of the word in bold print in the following sentence?**
   One of Spielberg's earliest childhood memories gave him a sense of fear, wonder and hope, emotions that often **resonate** in his film characters.
   a. are reflected
   b. sound like
   c. visited
   d. related

10. **What is the meaning of the word in bold print in the following sentence?**
   Because of his **empathy** and his influence, the world is a better place.
   a. passion
   b. understanding
   c. sympathy
   d. wealth

Reading 2
VOCABULARY PRACTICE: CROSSWORD PUZZLE

Complete the crossword puzzle below using words from the Word Bank. Some words will be left over.

WORD BANK

chaotic	empathy	deistic	gross
resonate	formative	discordant	papier mache
philanthropist	saltpeter	synonymous	unparalleled

Across Clues

4. confusing; with turmoil
6. paper, flour, & water mixture
8. equal to; same as
9. earnings before expenses
10. god-like

Down Clues

1. unmatched; superior
2. fireworks chemical
3. supporter of charities
5. quarrelsome
7. huge

MyReadingLab

Reading 2 QUESTIONS FOR WRITING AND DISCUSSION

1. How did Steven Spielberg's childhood influence his career as an adult?

2. What qualities make someone like Steven Spielberg so successful?

3. When Spielberg pretended to work at Universal Studios, what does this tell us about his dedication to his future career and his networking?

4. Do you think Spielberg's success is a result of luck or his own initiative? Explain.

5. What kinds of films do you think Spielberg strives to create? Why do you think his movies are so popular?

MyReadingLab

VIEWPOINT FOR CRITICAL THINKING

VIOLENT VIDEO GAMES

Read the letters below to the editor about the sale of violent video games and answer the following questions.

Dear Editor:

I am very disturbed by the amount of graphic violence and murder in video games. Recent mass killings and random shootings in the news illustrate the excessive violence in our society that is encouraged by video games and other media like these. The Supreme Court ruled in 2012 that a law to ban minors from buying violent video games was unconstitutional. The writers of the U.S. Constitution never foresaw the atrocities that some young people would commit in the future. Besides, the Constitution was written for adults, not minors, so it doesn't apply to children under 18. The law needs to regulate the sale of violent video games to children and provide stiff penalties to merchants who break it. Our representatives in Congress should take the lead in banning the sales of violent video games to anyone under age 18.

Signed,

Mad Mother

Dear Editor:

I find the argument in the letter about banning the sale of violent video games to minors absurd. First of all, who is going to enforce this law, the video game police? Secondly, even if there were a law banning the sale of violent games, minors who want to play these games can get them from older siblings or friends. It's impossible to keep them out of young players' hands. Third, lots of people have played violent video games as kids and have not turned out to be mass murderers. The violence committed by some people is the product of their own twisted minds and not the result of playing violent video games. There could be many reasons why some people kill others, but taking violent video games from minors will not solve the problem of violence in our society. It's much bigger than that, and the Supreme Court was smart enough to know that the law to ban the sale of violent games to minors was a bad idea.

Signed,

Reality Check

1. What is the viewpoint of the writer of the first letter regarding the sale of violent video games?

2. What is the viewpoint of the writer of the second letter regarding the sale of violent video games?

3. With which viewpoint do you most agree, and why?

4. Do you believe that Mad Mother is correct in assuming that the U.S. Constitution does not apply to minors, only adults? Why or why not?

5. Do you think that some video games are excessively violent or pornographic, and if so, how should they be restricted?

MyReadingLab

REAL-LIFE READING

U.S. COPYRIGHT LAW

Under the U.S. Copyright laws, it is illegal to copy or use the work of another individual without permission from the holder of the copyright. This applies to reference works, general books (fiction and non-fiction, creative works), periodicals (newspapers, magazines, journals, etc.), Web sites, all forms of art, photos, movies, music, speeches, choreography, architectural designs, visual aids, or any other work created by someone other than yourself. Regardless of where you found the information, if someone else created it, you must acknowledge the creator's ownership. Presenting someone else's ideas or words without giving them credit is called *plagiarism*, a form of theft and a serious offense.

To avoid plagiarism, you must provide the source of your material, listing the place where you found it, the creator's name(s), the publishing date and publisher (if there is one). There are several styles for presenting this information and your instructor or librarian can help you learn how to cite your sources correctly. Under *fair use*, you may reprint a small section of copyrighted material of less than 50 words without the author's permission as long as the source of the material is cited.

Most college and high school instructors use computer software to detect plagiarism, so it is easily traceable, and the consequences for committing plagiarism are serious. Instructors can search for online essays and papers for sale as easily as students can, so buying a paper online that someone else wrote is not only cheating, but a waste of money.

Expressing someone else' ideas in your own words without citing the source of the ideas is also plagiarism. Whether you are paraphrasing another person's ideas in your own words, or using a direct quote, you must cite the source. However, you do not have to cite information that is considered common knowledge. Common knowledge includes

- historical events (example: what happened on 9/11/2001)
- folk literature that cannot be traced to a specific writer (Ex.: *Snow White*)
- common sense observations (overspending causes debt)

1. What is plagiarism?

....

....

....

2. How can you avoid plagiarism if you want to use images or music from an online resource in a PowerPoint presentation for a college course?

....

....

....

3. Would it be plagiarism if you took notes on a section from a book or Web site, and then reworded the information in your own words for a term paper? Why or why not?

....

....

4. If you used information that someone else wrote in a blog for a Web page you created for a digital media assignment, would this be considered plagiarism? Why or why not?

....

....

5. Would you need to get permission from an author to quote 25 words in your term paper for psychology class?

....

....

MyReadingLab

BUILDING VOCABULARY

Knowing the meanings to many word parts will help you determine the meanings of unfamiliar words. Make a list of English words using the word parts in the table below, and give their meanings. If you are unsure about a word, consult a dictionary. Then use the words to complete the sentences below. (* presented in previous lists)

PREFIXES	ROOTS	SUFFIXES
uni- mono-: *one*	chrom-, chromat: *color*	-ic: *state, condition, or quality of*
bi-, di-: *two*	cycle: *circle, wheel*	-y: *relating to*
tri-: *three*	gam-: *union; marriage*	-ist: *one who**

WORDS

....	....	....
....	....	....
....	....	....
....	....	....
....	....	....

MyReadingLab

CHAPTER PRACTICE 1

Read the following passage and follow the four steps in R.E.A.L. to determine its overall pattern. Underline any transitions that help you determine the overall pattern of organization. You may find the chart of Patterns of Organization in the Appendix of this book helpful when completing the practice.

gait: a way of walking

UNIQUE BODY LANGUAGE

Many stars have distinctive, highly identifiable ways of moving. Denzel Washington, for example, has a centered, rolling **gait** that projects calmness and power. Film makers often capitalize on the body language of an established star so that it becomes part of the visual design of a film. John Wayne had a peculiar manner of walking that, in time, became famous. A large and very graceful man, his feet were quite small in relation to his bulk, and he developed an easy, fluid gait that riveted attention—such a large man moving so easily on small feet. Actress Katharine Hepburn (with whom he worked in *Rooster Cogburn,* 1975) was impressed with "the light dancer's steps he took with them." Wayne's graceful, catlike movements became a justly famous part of his screen persona, evident in scores of films over many decades. In *Red River,* Wayne walks through a herd of cattle, and they scatter to get out of his way. It's an impressive thing to see.

1. What is the main idea of this paragraph?

a. Many stars have distinctive, highly identifiable ways of moving.

b. Denzel Washington, for example, has a centered, rolling gait that projects calmness and power.

c. Film makers often capitalize on the body language of an established star so that it becomes part of the visual design of a film.

d. John Wayne had a peculiar manner of walking that, in time, became famous.

2. What is the relationship between the following sentences? Many stars have distinctive, highly identifiable ways of moving. Denzel Washington, for example, has a centered, rolling gait that projects calmness and power.

a. generalization and example

b. cause and effect

c. compare and contrast

d. definition and example

3. The major supporting details of this paragraph are
   a. the ways film makers use body language in movies
   b. examples of actors whose body language is a part of their persona
   c. films that show actors using body language
   d. directors who use actors with identifiable body language in their films

4. The overall pattern of organization for this passage is
   a. time order
   b. cause and effect
   c. statement and clarification
   d. generalization and example

MyReadingLab

CHAPTER PRACTICE 2

Read the following passage and follow the four steps in R.E.A.L. to determine the overall pattern. Underline any transitions that help you determine the overall pattern of organization. You may find the chart of Patterns of Organization in the Appendix of this book helpful when completing the practice.

1 The Earth Harp is a gigantic harp made of multiple wires that stretch out over the audience during a performance. The wires, running from 100 to 1,000 feet long, are tuned to harmonic tones emitting ethereal, magical sounds, filling the air with beautiful, rich harmonic music.

2 The inventor of the Earth Harp, William Close, experimented with several versions of his harp before he created his present model. He runs 16 to 22 wires ("strings") from the huge bridge of the harp on stage out over the audience, and anchors them to different places in the theatre. To play the harp, Close wears gloves covered in powdered resin (a material used on stringed instruments to reduce friction). He then pinches the string and slides his gloved hand along the string to produce a vibration much like running a finger around the brim of a wine glass. Other strings begin to vibrate, creating resonating harmonies that fill the entire auditorium. The Earth Harp is also often accompanied by other stringed instruments or vocals.

3 William Close has performed with his Earth Harp in various concert halls around the world as well as outdoor venues, including the Space Needle in Seattle, the Kennedy Center, and outside the Colosseum in Rome. He also played his Earth Harp on the top of a mountain, and the sounds resonated deep down into its caves. Each place the Earth Harp is played provides a unique musical experience due to the acoustic characteristics of the location.

Continued...

1. **What is the central point of this passage?**
   a. The Earth Harp is a gigantic harp with strings up to 1000 feet long.
   b. William Close invented the Earth Harp.
   c. The Earth Harp has been used in performances all over the world.
   d. The Earth Harp has from 16 to 22 strings made of wire.

2. **What is the relationship within the following sentence? Each place the Earth Harp is played provides a unique musical experience due to the acoustic characteristics of the location.**
   a. compare and contrast
   b. space order
   c. time order
   d. cause and effect

3. **What is the relationship between the following sentences? Other strings begin to vibrate, creating resonating harmonies that fill the entire auditorium. The Earth Harp is also often accompanied by other stringed instruments or vocals.**
   a. cause and effect
   b. addition
   c. generalization and example
   d. definition and example

4. **The pattern of organization in paragraph 2 is**
   a. classification
   b. statement and clarification
   c. process
   d. listing

5. **The pattern of organization in paragraph 3 is**
   a. time order
   b. space order
   c. definition
   d. statement and clarification

MyReadingLab

CHAPTER PRACTICE 3

Read the following passage and follow the four steps in R.E.A.L. to determine the overall pattern of each paragraph. Underline any transitions that help you determine the overall patterns of organization. You may find the chart of Patterns of Organization in the Appendix of this book helpful when completing the practices.

1 The most important musical influences on the Beatles were rhythm and blues and American rockabilly. With the advent of the Beatles in the early 1960s, the character of popular music changed in fundamental ways. First, rock music became an international phenomenon. Second, every rock group developed its own identifiable sound and its own specific look. In the early days, for example, the Beatles all wore the same clothes and matching haircuts.

2 The Beatles' career as a group can be divided into two periods: the public and the private. The public period is represented by the first half of the decade, when they toured and made records of songs they could sing on stage. In contrast, the private period, the second half of the Sixties, was devoted exclusively to recording, using the technology of the studio in novel ways that could not be reproduced in a live performance. These technologically advanced records had an enormous influence on recording techniques for the whole of the later history of rock music.…In seven years, they changed the entire course of popular music.

1. What is the central point of this selection?

- **a.** The most important musical influences on the Beatles were rhythm and blues and American rockabilly.
- **b.** The Beatles' career as a group can be divided into two periods: the public and the private.
- **c.** Over seven years, the Beatles changed the entire course of popular music.
- **d.** These technologically advanced records had an enormous influence on recording techniques for the whole of the later history of rock music.

2. What is the relationship within the following sentence? With the advent of the Beatles in the early 1960s, the character of popular music changed in fundamental ways.

- **a.** cause and effect
- **b.** compare and contrast
- **c.** time order
- **d.** listing

3. **What is the relationship between the following sentences? The public period is represented by the first half of the decade, when they toured and made records of songs they could sing on stage. In contrast, the private period, the second half of the Sixties, was devoted exclusively to recording, using the technology of the studio in novel ways that could not be reproduced in a live performance.**

a. cause and effect
b. statement and clarification
c. process
d. compare and contrast

4. **The overall patterns of organization for the entire selection are**

a. time order and compare and contrast
b. statement and clarification
c. space order and time order
d. generalization and example

CHAPTER REVIEW: STUDY NOTES

Fill in the missing information for the following study notes for patterns of organization.

1. Patterns of Organization are the way that the .... are organized in a paragraph.

2. .... are words or phrases that show relationships between ideas.

3. Order patterns such as .... and .... both use the same transitions that tell when something happens (*first, second, third, next, then, finally*, etc.)

4. The transitions that tell where something is (*next to, below, above, adjacent to, parallel to, inside*, etc.) indicate that the supporting details follow the .... pattern.

5. In the definition pattern, the details explain .... and may provide one or more examples of the term.

6. The .... pattern provides the reasons why something happened and/or the consequences or results of those actions.

7. The .... pattern shows how things are similar and the .... pattern shows how things are different.

8. In the .... pattern, the supporting details are arranged into groups or categories according to their shared characteristics.

9. The supporting details in the .... pattern are in no particular order, whereas the details in the .... or .... patterns must be in a special sequence.

10. In a .... pattern a general point is followed by an explanation, whereas in the .... pattern, a broad point is followed by one or more specific examples of the point.

Studying Transitions

To review the transitions for each pattern, you can make flash cards using the patterns and transitions chart in the Appendix. You can also play a sorting game or matching activity to match the transitions with the correct patterns. For more ideas, have your instructor consult the Instructor's Manual that accompanies this text.

To review some of the transitions and their patterns, write the pattern(s) that are suggested by each of the following transitions:

1. before, during, while, simultaneously, meanwhile, later...

....

2. reason, result, consequence, therefore, thus, yields, produces, leads to...

....

3. furthermore, also, moreover, additionally

....

4. similar to, but, yet, likewise, nevertheless, both...

....

5. category, type, kind, group, branch....

....

MyReadingLab

READING LAB ASSIGNMENTS

1. Login to **MyReadingLab** and in the menu, click on Reading Skills. In the **Learning Path**, select **Nine Patterns of Organization (Combined)** to review nine of the patterns in this chapter. To review individual patterns, click in the Learning Path on the title of the pattern(s) you wish to review, such as **Patterns of Organization: Time Order.** Review this skill by reading the brief overview and models. Watch the short animation and then complete any practices or tests.

2. Click on **Reading Level** and choose two stories to read and answer the questions to the best of your ability. Your Lexile level will increase as your reading comprehension improves.

ON THE WEB

You can learn more about patterns by doing an Internet search on the terms *patterns of organization* or *thought patterns.* Several Web sites and videos are available on this topic, which may enhance your understanding.

MyReadingLab

MONITOR YOUR LEARNING

In this chapter you learned about various patterns of organization and their transitions. Write a paragraph telling what you learned about these skills, how you learned them, and how you can use them to improve your learning and reading comprehension. When you have finished writing, read your paragraph as if you were reading someone else's paragraph for the first time. Check for missing words, spelling, punctuation, and sentence structure.

6 CRITICAL THINKING

FOCUS ON: Your Science and Technology

Most of us take science and technology for granted. But stop to think for a moment where we would be without them: there would be no cell phones, no computers, no television, media, or Internet. This is, of course, because scientific principles led to inventions like these and others, such as the automobile, the airplane, the microwave, the refrigerator and freezer, and even the foods we eat. Chemistry is used in making medicines, toiletries, foods, beverages, clothing, and beauty products. Agriculture enables us to produce abundant food products and crops to feed more people around the world. But advances in technology and science also have consequences for the environment. Thinking critically about how technology and science affect our world can help us make good decisions for the future. We must be responsible about how we use resources today to leave a better world for tomorrow.

In this chapter, you will:

LEARNING OBJECTIVES

1 apply critical thinking strategies.
2 distinguish facts from opinions.
3 identify the author's purpose and tone.
4 identify the intended audience.
5 detect bias.

OBJECTIVE 1

Apply critical thinking strategies.

WHAT IS CRITICAL THINKING?

Think about the last time you had to make a big decision. Perhaps it was whether to go to college, or where to attend school. Perhaps it was choosing a major or finding financial aid to help pay for school. Sometimes life's decisions are even more critical, like when you have to decide whether to marry or divorce, or what doctor or treatment to choose when you, or perhaps a loved one, are seriously ill. When there is a legal issue that you must face or even while serving on jury duty, you must make important decisions that affect other people's lives. Someday you may have a business to run or money to invest. How will you invest it? Where will you invest it?

Critical thinking is learning to think in a reasoned and logical way according to specific criteria or standards.

Whenever you have big problems or serious questions like these to answer, critical thinking comes into play. **Critical thinking,** learning to think in a reasoned and logical way according to specific criteria or standards, is required in almost every college course you take, and is the foundation for logical problem solving on the job. The term *critical* in this context means based on criteria, or specific standards that guide the process. The process of critical thinking involves three parts: asking questions, finding answers, and accepting results that are based on logical conclusions.

An author's **argument** (or claim) is the author's viewpoint on an issue.

Critical thinking is used to solve problems, make decisions, and to evaluate arguments, or claims. An author's **argument** (or claim) is his or her viewpoint on an issue. It is a statement that expresses the author's opinion about something and is often the main idea of the paragraph. For example, some authors' arguments are:

People should not be allowed to text while driving.

Pesticides used on crops can cause cancer.

Aliens from outer space have been visiting this planet for centuries.

When an author makes a claim such as one of these, you expect the claim or argument to be supported with good, solid facts and reasoning. Your job as a critical reader is to evaluate the support for the author's claim and conclude whether you agree or disagree.

In problem solving, using critical thinking can help you make decisions under given circumstances to arrive at the best solution to the problem. By following the basic steps of critical thinking, solutions to problems can be understood more efficiently and clearly because the process eliminates confusion and non-productive thinking. Several important reading skills are a major part of critical thinking. As you read through the four steps of critical thinking, notice the reading skills (in bold print) that you use when working through the process.

The Critical Thinking Process

STEP 1

Identify the problem, claim, or argument.

What are the **topic** and the **main idea?**

STEP 2

Examine the **supporting details.**

On what premise (**supporting details**) is the claim based?

What is the **author's purpose?** Who is the **intended audience?**

Is the author **biased?**

Is the support weak or strong? **(facts or opinions?)**

Is there sufficient (enough) support?

Is the support relevant to the argument?

Is the support accurate?

Does the argument rely on **inductive** or **deductive reasoning?**

What is the **author's tone?**

Is **figurative** language used?

STEP 3

Ask questions to determine what additional information is needed to make the argument or problem clear and to discover new facts.

What are the various possible interpretations?

What facts are needed to form a complete picture of the argument?

What other implications might this have on other things?

Are there other viewpoints to consider?

Does the conclusion meet the standards of critical thinking, or must it be reconsidered?

STEP 4

Draw a logical **conclusion** based on your analysis of the support by examining the supporting details for the following:

- data collected from reliable and accurate sources
- accurate interpretations of data
- comparisons to similar situations
- relevant examples

To be a critical thinker, you must

- be open-minded (willing to consider any idea or question)
- think objectively (without bias or judgment of any kind)
- be persistent
- be an independent thinker (not influenced by others' opinions)
- be broad-minded (considering all viewpoints, including your own)
- be willing to dig deeper into problems and stay with them longer

Critical Thinking in Problem Solving

In addition to evaluating arguments, the critical thinking process helps to find solutions to practical problems. Read the following example of how the critical thinking process helped to solve an airline company's mysterious illness.

1. **Identify the problem, claim, or argument:**

    In 1980, flight attendants working for Eastern Airlines developed a 24-hour skin rash on their arms, hands, and faces

2. **Examine the supporting details:**

    The same number of attendants developed the rash on every flight.

    Not every flight attendant developed the rash.

    No passengers developed the rash.

    The rash only appeared on attendants who worked flights over large bodies of water.

    The rash did not appear on every flight over large bodies of water.

3. **Ask questions** based on the support to determine what information is needed to make the argument or problem clear and to discover new facts:

    What was different about the attendants who developed the rash and those who did not? Could the rash be caused by environmental conditions such as pollution? Were items brought on board for some of the flights but not all of them? Is the support based on facts or opinions? Is there bias in the support? What is the author's purpose and tone?

Digging Deeper

To answer these questions and others, the inspectors closely examined each plane where the rash occurred and each plane where it did not. Their inspections revealed that the rash occurred on newer planes only. They began drawing some conclusions from the facts:

> The rash probably resulted from coming into contact with certain materials on flights over large bodies of water.
>
> The only items that flight attendants used when flying over large bodies of water that were different from other flights were the life vests.
>
> The life vests on the newer planes were made of different material than the vests on the older planes.

4. Draw a logical **conclusion** based on your analysis of the support.

Based on these facts, what would you conclude about the cause of the rash? You probably reasoned that the newer life vests were the cause of the rash on the flight attendants who demonstrated their use before each flight over a large body of water. This is what the inspectors concluded and they made a recommendation to Eastern Airlines to replace the life vests, which eliminated the occurrences of the rash.

EXERCISE:

Follow the four steps for critical thinking for the following:

- How to reduce transportation costs, parking fees, and air pollution from vehicles on campus
- How to recycle more products from the campus

Evaluating Arguments with Critical Thinking

The same process is followed when reading about an issue to evaluate the support for an author's argument. Read the example below about global climate change.

1. **Identify the problem, claim, or argument.**

> The Earth is undergoing a climate change wherein warming trends are increasing more rapidly than in the past.

2. **Examine the supporting details:**

> The average surface temperature of the Earth increased 1.33 degrees F in the past 100 years and if the trend continues, will increase 3.2 - 7.2 degrees F in the 21st century. The 12 warmest years on record occurred from 1995 to 2006. The sea level has risen an average of 7 inches during the 20th century and will rise 7-21 inches in the 21st century. Summer Arctic Sea ice has thinned by 7.4% per decade since 1978. Since 1980, major glaciers have lost an average of 31.5 ft in vertical thickness. In

Glacier National Park alone, only 27 of the park's original 150 glaciers still remain. Scientists estimate that these will also disappear by 2030.

3. **Ask questions** based on the support to determine what information is needed to make the argument or problem clear and to discover new facts:

   Where did this data come from? Is the source reliable? Is the information accurate? Is the data current or outdated? What is the author's purpose and tone, and who is the intended audience? Is there bias in the support? Is the data based on facts or opinions?

To dig deeper we need to also ask questions about the supporting details:

> What could be causing the warming trend of the Earth? Have there been similar warming and cooling trends in the past? Is this part of a natural cycle of Earth's climate? Are air temperatures rising in proportion to melting ice? Were there any changes in the sun or in the Earth's atmosphere before the warming trend escalated? What might be the consequences of this warming trend? Can it be controlled?

Consider the Source

When gathering data, it is important to know the reliability of the source of your information. Simply hearing something on the news doesn't make it reliable data. You need to find reliable, trustworthy sources for information. Research your sources to find out if they have a good record of providing the truth and if they use **primary** and **secondary sources** for information.

primary source: firsthand accounts, such as historical documents, letters, speeches, eyewitness reports, or research reports.

secondary sources: reported and analyzed information from other sources, such as primary sources.

The facts presented in the paragraph on global warming came from a report by the Intergovernmental Panel on Climate Change (IPCC) consisting of hundreds of scientists and government officials who released this report in 2007 based on climate research reports from around the world. In order for this report to be considered a valid source, we would need to compare these figures to other reports from similar organizations that are reliable sources. Most of the data has been corroborated by other reliable sources. Their predictions are based on the models from past measurements, but they are actually *opinions* and not facts.

4. **Draw a logical conclusion** based on your analysis of the support.

   Based on the data that has been established by reliable resources, we can conclude that the Earth is undergoing a climate change wherein warming trends are increasing more rapidly than in the past. This conclusion concurs with the author's claim based on facts because this passage had valid, reliable, factual support. If the results of your inquiry had shown that the facts were misinterpreted or inaccurate, then your conclusion would have been different or inconclusive.

Reading Skills in Critical Thinking

All of the reading skills that you have learned in this book are important components of critical thinking. You must identify the argument, claim, or problem (usually the main idea), and examine the support for the argument in the supporting details. You must draw logical conclusions and consider the pattern of organization through which the details are presented. Are the supporting details providing causes? Effects? Or comparing and contrasting ideas?

In this chapter you will learn additional skills to help you evaluate the evidence in your critical thinking: determining facts and opinions, identifying the author's argument, the author's purpose and tone, and identifying bias. Each skill is a tool that you can use to help you think critically.

Invalid Support

When evaluating support for an argument, you are judging the type of support that is given to determine its validity. To be valid, the support must be logical, sufficient, reliable, and accurate. There are many names for different types of *invalid* (not valid) support, known as **logical fallacies.** If you are interested in finding out more about logical fallacies, you can go to MyReadingLab, click on Reading Skills and Critical Thinking to learn more.

EXERCISE:

Which of the following would be considered relative support for this argument? Cell phones should be turned off during class.

1. When cell phones ring or buzz, they cause a distraction to others.
2. Instead of focusing on the lecture, students are using their phones and miss important information.
3. Not all students can afford expensive cell phones.
4. When some students receive calls, they answer them in class and disturb others.

If you chose statements 1 and 2 and 4 as relevant support, you were right. Statement 3 makes a point that is not related to the argument.

OBJECTIVE 2

Distinguish facts from opinion.

DISTINGUISHING FACTS FROM OPINIONS

The term "fact" can be misleading because it is often equated with things that are true, but this is not always the case. Facts can also be false. In critical thinking a **fact** is anything that can be proven true or false by some observable or measurable means. Read the following facts and discuss how they might be proved as true or false:

fact: Something that can be proven true or false by observable or measurable means.

1. Russia and surrounding countries in Eastern Europe have doubled in their numbers of HIV cases in the past decade.
2. Retrograde amnesia is the loss of memory from the point of an injury backwards in time.

Opinions, on the other hand, cannot be proven. They include attitudes, beliefs and feelings that may or may not be true. In addition, all future events and predictions are opinions. Giving advice is also a form of opinion, since the author is expressing a feeling or belief about what should be done. Opinions can be found everywhere, even in textbooks.

opinions: Attitudes, beliefs and feelings that cannot be proven, including advice, future events, and predictions.

Opinions are an important part of our body of knowledge, especially when they are based on known facts or given by experts. **Expert opinion** is still an opinion but it has more validity because the source of the opinion is someone with knowledge of and experience in the subject. An example of an expert opinion is a weather forecast. An expert in meteorology studies the weather conditions and patterns of weather movement and makes predictions about the weather forecast. Good meteorologists are often able to predict the weather with fair accuracy, but all predictions are future events and not provable; therefore, they are still opinions.

expert opinion: An opinion given by an expert or a group of experts in a particular field.

Opinions often rely on adjectives that describe an attitude or feeling and may use positive or negative words. Look for words that imply judgment such as "best" or "worst." Read the following opinions and discuss why they are not facts.

> Based on recent figures, the U.S. economy is expected to grow by 2 to 3 percent in the coming year.
>
> Astronomers believe there may be billions of galaxies in the universe, some with plants like our own.

In the last chapter, you learned about absolutes, or generalizations. When deciding if something is a fact or an opinion, consider phrases such as "all," "none," "no one," or "everyone." For instance, can it be proved that "all Americans love coffee"? Or, that "everyone believes that murder is wrong"? It would be impossible to prove either of these statements, so they cannot be labeled as facts, only as opinions.

Opinion Phrases

As you read, be aware of opinion phrases that indicate the author is expressing an opinion. Opinion words and phrases include:

it appears that	apparently	it seems that	believe
guess	surmise	presumably	in my opinion
in my view	it's likely that	possibly	this suggests
should	ought to	may	could

Keep in mind that the word's context in the sentence is important to consider when deciding if a sentence is a fact or an opinion. For example, the word *may* can be used to indicate a future event (e.g., it *may* rain tomorrow: opinion), or to mean "allow" or "make possible" (e.g., this rock cycle *may* occur either beneath or above the Earth's surface: fact).

Sentences with Both Fact and Opinion

Occasionally you will encounter sentences containing both fact and opinion. If you are only offered "fact" *or* "opinion" as choices, use "opinion" to describe sentences that contain both fact and opinion. However, if you are completing an exercise or practice that offers the choice "fact *and* opinion", then use that choice if it applies.

MyReadingLab

PRACTICE 1

For each sentence in the following paragraph from a science textbook, decide whether the statement is fact or opinion and write F or O on the space provided. Underline any words or phrases that signal an opinion.

1. .... Debris such as discarded fishing nets, plastic bags and bottles, fishing line, buckets, floats, and other trash harm aquatic organisms.

2. .... Aquatic mammals, seabirds, fish, and sea turtles may mistake floating plastic debris for food and can die as a result of ingesting material they cannot digest or expel.

3. .... In recent years scientists have learned that plastic trash is accumulating in certain regions of the oceans where currents converge.

4. .... One such area is the "Great Pacific Garbage Patch" in the northern Pacific.

5. .... The site is often estimated as being twice the size of Texas, and one study documented 3.3 plastic bits per square meter in its waters.

6. .... In 2006, the U. S. Congress responded to such ocean pollution by passing the Marine Debris Research, Prevention, and Reduction Act.

7. .... However, more is needed.

8. .... We can all help by reducing our use of unnecessary plastic, reusing the plastic items we do use, and recycling the plastic we discard.

U-REVIEW 1

With a partner, list the definitions for facts and opinions below:

Facts ....

....

Opinions ....

....

OBJECTIVE 3

Identify the author's purpose and tone.

IDENTIFY THE AUTHOR'S PURPOSE AND TONE

One of the first steps to thinking critically is to determine why the author wrote something. Knowing the author's motive can provide a great deal of insight about the author's viewpoint.

Identify the Author's Purpose

author's purpose: explains why the author wrote the reading selection; the goal for writing.

Begin by stating the topic and main idea, which usually tells the author's argument or claim. Next, ask, "Why did the author write this? What goal(s) did he or she have in mind?" The **author's purpose** explains why the author wrote the reading selection. An author may have very a very specific purpose in mind, or a general one. The most common general purposes are:

to persuade the reader

to entertain the reader

to inform the reader

to advise the reader

to criticize something or someone

to offer a solution to a problem

to analyze something

Read the following paragraph to determine the author's argument and purpose.

> The Virginia State Board of Game and Inland Fisheries asked game officials today to consider exerting tighter control over fox penning. Fox penning is putting foxes into large, wooded, fenced areas—prohibiting the fox's ability to escape—and then training dogs to chase and trap them. The foxes are eventually caught by the dogs and sometimes are killed. Fox hunting is a centuries-old practice that is now banned in many countries but still is practiced in Canada, France, Australia, and Italy. In the United States the practice is called "fox chasing," which allows the foxes to be trapped and released unharmed, but in reality many are killed. Fox penning is a cruel, inhumane practice that should not be allowed anywhere.

Topic: Fox Penning

Main Idea (Argument): Fox penning is a cruel, inhumane practice that should not be allowed anywhere.

Author's goal or purpose: To persuade readers that fox penning should not be allowed.

Identify the Author's Tone

Author's tone refers to the feelings that the author reveals in the reading selection.

The **author's tone** refers to the feelings that the author reveals in the reading selection. Through the use of specific words such as adjectives, an author can signify his or her feelings about a topic. To determine the author's tone, ask, "What is the author's feeling about this topic?" Remember that it is the author's attitude or feeling and not your own viewpoint about the topic that is to be considered here. Keep this in mind as you read the following examples.

1. It is commendable that the Virginia State Board of Game and Inland Fisheries has requested tighter control over fox penning.

(Notice the word *commendable*, which means worthy of praise. The author sounds as if he is admiring the Virginia State Board of Game and Inland Fisheries for its action against fox penning. In this sentence, the author's tone is admiring.)

2. Fox penning is a cruel, inhumane practice that should not be allowed anywhere.

(Notice the words *cruel* and *inhumane*. This author has negative feelings about fox penning. The author's tone is critical.)

Read the following passage to determine the author's purpose and tone:

> Every year we put out birdseed for our feathered friends who come to feast and provide us with a close-up view of nature. Inevitably, our furry friends with long, bushy tails also show up to steal the seed and create havoc. I used to get really angry at them, going so far as to use a squirt gun to spray the little sneaks stealing the bird seed, but it was all in vain. As soon as I left the house, the squirrels cleaned out the feeder in no time flat and left it in tatters, swinging on a breeze. I pictured them up in the trees with little communication devices talking to each other.
>
> *"Charley, this is Bravo-1. The witch is riding her SUV, heading west."*
>
> *"Copy that, Bravo-1. Rendezvous at the feeder."*
>
> *"This is Bravo-1. On my way."*
>
> Then the squirrels all attacked the feeder with gusto, fighting over the seed, spilling it on the ground, tearing the feeder into a wreck of twisted wires and shredded plastic. Careful examination of the leftovers revealed that the only seeds they ate were the sunflower seeds. So I bought 2 feeders and filled one with sunflower seeds for the squirrels and one with birdseed for the birds. The two groups now feed peacefully, unless the sunflower seeds run out before the

Continued...

birdseed. Again, I hear their voices taunting me:

"Hey, lady...you'd better get out here and fill this thing or your little birdies will be eatin' dirt!"

I know better than to ignore their threats. I've seen what they will do and it isn't pretty. Like a harried victim of extortion, I pay up.

What is the author's general purpose?

....

What is the author's tone?

....

What words or phrases in the passage were clues to the purpose and tone?

....

....

....

When deciding upon an author's tone, it may help to refer to the list below of some of the most common tone words and their meanings.

absurd: ridiculous	admiring: cherishing
apathetic: not caring; indifferent	approving: commending, praising
angry: mad	bitter: critical
compassionate: sympathetic	celebratory: celebrating
cynical: expecting the worst	cautionary: warning
disapproving: not approving	distressed: upset
earnest: being honest	evasive: avoiding the issue
formal: official-sounding	frustrated: aggravated
ghoulish: evil, monstrous	grim: sad, depressing
humorous: amusing, funny	incredulous: not believing
indignant: outraged at injustice	impassioned: with intense feeling
ironic: the opposite of what's expected	irreverent: mocking
light-hearted: amusing, humorous	neutral: objective, straightforward
nostalgic: thinking fondly of the past	objective: straightforward; factual
optimistic: hopeful	outspoken: frank
pathetic: pitiful	pessimistic: negative
reverent: respectful	righteous: morally correct
sarcastic: condescending	satiric: ridiculing
sensational: overly dramatized	sentimental: emotional
sincere: being truthful	solemn: serious
tragic: terrible, awful	uncertain: not certain
vindictive: seeking revenge	whimsical: fun

Tone and Figurative Language

figurative language is the use of expressions that are different than their actual literal meaning.

Figurative language is the use of expressions that are different than their actual literal meaning. It is used when authors want to express something indirectly by using similes and metaphors. Figurative language can suggest an author's tone by using comparisons or illustrations. When an author compares two similar things using the words *like* or *as*, it is known as a **simile**. Two examples of similes are:

She looks *like* an angel when she sleeps.

He's *as* sharp *as* a tack when it comes to calculations.

When an author compares less-similar ideas or things without using *like* or *as*, it is known as a **metaphor.**

All the world's a stage and all the men and women merely actors.

—*As You Like It,* William Shakespeare

Money is the fuel that drives the economy.

In the first quote, comparing life to a play and all people as the actors implies that life is something entertaining, like a drama, comedy, or tragedy (or likely all three). The second quote implies that money is necessary to keep the economy running, like fuel runs an engine.

Denotation and Connotation

To determine tone, it is also important to consider the author's choice of words when describing something. Words have meanings, or dictionary definitions, known as their **denotations.** For example, a *crowd* is a large group of people, as is a *gang* or a *mob*. The latter two words, however, evoke a negative feeling in the reader. Why? Because each of these words comes with an underlying or implied meaning, known as a **connotation**. Which of the following words have a more negative connotation?

slender	skinny
fat	husky
odor	stench
tragic	sad
fired	terminated

MyReadingLab

PRACTICE 2

acetaminophen: a chemical compound used to relieve pain and reduce fever.

As you complete the practices for author's purpose and tone, begin with the author's topic and main idea to find the argument, and then identify the author's purpose and tone by underlining words or phrases with positive or negative connotations. To think critically, you should write questions that you would like to have answered regarding the topic.

The United States Department of Agriculture (USDA) Wildlife Services plans to airdrop **acetaminophen**-laced dead mice on the island of Guam in an attempt to control unwanted brown tree snakes. Acetaminophen will cause renal and liver failure in animals who take the bait, resulting in a slow, agonizing death that can take days or even weeks for snakes and others with slow metabolisms. Not only is this method exceedingly cruel, it is also indiscriminate, posing a danger to the owls and other large birds and small carnivorous animals that also eat mice. This in turn threatens other parts of the food chain, including scavengers and aquatic life. This mass poisoning initiative is being undertaken to keep snakes from being transported to Hawaii, yet a brown tree snake has not been detected on those islands in 17 years. Please scrap this cruel and dangerous initiative. If brown tree snake control is necessary, then find a more responsible plan.

1. What is the author's argument, or claim, about poisoning brown tree snakes?

a. Brown tree snakes are not harmful and should be left alone.
b. The USDA Wildlife Services should stop the plan to drop dead mice laced with acetaminophen to control the brown tree snakes in Guam.
c. Poisoning brown tree snakes is a cruel practice.
d. The USDA is irresponsible in its treatment of wildlife.

2. What is the author's purpose in this paragraph?

a. to inform about the USDA's plan to stop the poisoned mice drop in Guam
b. to criticize the USDA
c. to persuade readers that the USDA should not drop poisoned mice in Guam
d. to analyze the reasons why the USDA is dropping poisoned mice in Guam

3. What is the author's tone in this paragraph?

a. disapproving
b. angry
c. satiric
d. nostalgic

4. Identify the following sentence from the paragraph: Acetaminophen will cause renal and liver failure in animals who take the bait, resulting in a slow, agonizing death that can take days or even weeks for snakes and others with slow metabolisms.

a. fact
b. opinion
c. expert opinion

5. What questions do you have that would help you know more about this issue?

....

....

....

....

MyReadingLab

PRACTICE 3

As you complete the practices for author's purpose and tone, begin with the author's topic and main idea to find the argument, and then identify the author's purpose and tone by underlining words or phrases with positive or negative connotations. To think critically, you should write questions that you would like to have answered regarding the topic.

In recent experiments, researchers at Duke University developed a brain-to-brain link between two rats. The researchers trained the one rat to distinguish between a wide chute and a narrow one by feeling it with its whiskers, and to match the different chutes with corresponding holes by poking them with its nose.

In one experiment, a rat correctly matched the chute width with a corresponding hole 96% of the time. This rat became the encoder. A second rat (the decoder) was fitted with tiny electrodes and was given the recorded brain activity of the first rat. The second rat depended entirely on the signals sent to its brain by the electrodes to make a correct match for the same activity and was able to choose the right hole 62% of the time, a figure much higher than would be obtained by choosing randomly. The researchers then repeated the experiment by sending the recorded brain activity of the encoder rat over the Internet to another rat in Brazil. The rat in Brazil also matched chutes and holes correctly 62% of the time. Researchers hope to use the brain link interface technology to develop organic computers that communicate over networks to solve problems.

1. What is the author's argument, or claim, about the brain link experiment?
   - **a.** Researchers at Duke University developed a successful brain-to-brain link between two rats in one lab, and to another rat over the Internet.
   - **b.** Researchers hope to use brain link interface technology to develop organic computers that communicate over networks to solve problems.
   - **c.** The decoder rats were able to match the chutes and holes correctly 62% of the time.
   - **d.** Animals should not be used to test brain interface with computers.

Continued...

MyReadingLab

PRACTICE 3

...continued

2. What is the author's purpose in these paragraphs?

- **a.** to persuade readers that rats should not be used in brain-computer interface experiments
- **b.** to advise readers about the experiments conducted on animals at Duke University
- **c.** to explain why rats are being used for brain link experiments
- **d.** to inform readers about Duke University's experiments in brain linking

3. What is the author's tone in these paragraphs?

- **a.** persuasive
- **b.** distressed
- **c.** objective
- **d.** pessimistic

4. Identify the following sentence from the paragraph: The second rat depended entirely on the signals sent to its brain by the electrodes to make a correct match for the same activity and was able to choose the right hole 62% of the time, a figure much higher than would be obtained by choosing randomly.

- **a.** fact
- **b.** opinion
- **c.** expert opinion

5. What questions do you have that would help you know more about this issue?

....

....

....

....

....

....

MyReadingLab

PRACTICE 4

As you complete the practices for author's purpose and tone, begin with the author's topic and main idea to find the argument, and then identify the author's purpose and tone by underlining words or phrases with positive or negative connotations. To think critically, you should write questions that you would like to have answered regarding the topic.

Animal rights protesters want to prohibit the use of live animals in research altogether, but if such research benefits suffering humans, it is too valuable to be prohibited. Recently, researchers at Tufts University successfully implanted working eyeballs on the tails of tadpoles to find answers to important questions. Could the optic nerve be the only route for incoming visual signals? Could different parts of the nervous system further down on the spinal cord process those signals on their own without help from the brain?

To test their ideas, scientists transplanted tadpole eyeballs on the tails of over 200 tadpoles. Next, they designed an experiment to determine if the tail eyes had visual ability by using red and blue lights at the sides of each bowl. The results of the experiment were impressive. Seven tadpoles with tail eyes demonstrated that their tail eyes worked. The scientists then questioned why some tadpoles could see and others couldn't. The answer was that the 7 tadpoles with vision had developed nerve growth all the way to their spinal cords, which enabled them to see. The results of this experiment led to new questions. Could the spinal cord be used to do other tasks normally associated with the brain? Could it be used to restore movement to paralyzed limbs?

1. What is the author's argument, or claim, about using animals for experiments?

a. Using tadpoles to determine how the spinal cord works is an acceptable form of experimentation with live animals.

b. Researchers at Tufts University have successfully implanted working tadpole eyeballs on the tails of tadpoles to find answers to important questions about the nervous system.

c. Experiments with living things are inhumane even if they provide new information to scientists.

d. Animal rights protesters want to prohibit the use of live animals in research altogether, but the benefits of such research outweigh the use of animals.

2. What is the author's purpose in these paragraphs?

a. to persuade readers that using live animals in research is too valuable to prohibit

b. to persuade the reader that using live animals in research is inhumane

c. to inform readers about an experiment that put working eyes on the tails of tadpoles

d. to criticize the researchers who performed experiments on live tadpoles.

Continued...

MyReadingLab
PRACTICE 4
...continued

3. What is the author's tone in these paragraphs?
   a. ghoulish
   b. righteous
   c. admiring
   d. reverent
4. Identify the following sentence from the paragraph: Animal rights protesters want to prohibit the use of live animals in research altogether, but if such research benefits suffering humans, it is too valuable to be prohibited.
   a. fact
   b. opinion
   c. expert opinion
5. What questions do you have that would help you know more about this issue?

....

....

....

....

....

OBJECTIVE 4

Identify the intended audience.

intended audience: explains for whom the reading selection was written.

IDENTIFY THE INTENDED AUDIENCE

Critical thinkers not only ask why an author wrote something but also for whom it was written. Knowing the **intended audience** can help you determine the author's purpose and tone. When thinking about the intended audience, it is also helpful to consider the source of the information. For instance, a scientific description of a disease in a medical textbook for medical students would be much more detailed than one in a high-school biology textbook. To determine the intended audience, ask, "For whom was this passage written? Who would find this information useful? What is the source of this material?"

Read the following example and choose the intended audience.

> Within your body, millions of cells must divide every second to maintain a total number of about 60 trillion cells. The replacement of lost or damaged cells is just one of the important roles that cell reproduction, or cell division, plays in your life. Another function of cell division is growth. All of the trillions of cells in your body result from repeated cell division that began in your mother's body with a single fertilized egg cell. (*Essential Biology* by Neil A. Campbell and Janet B. Reece)

The intended audience is

a. physicians
b. physiologists
c. biology students

If you noticed the source of the selection was from a biology textbook, *Essential Biology* by Neil A. Campbell and Janet B. Reece, you probably correctly chose answer C. Both physicians and physiologists would most likely already know this material and not find it useful.

MyReadingLab

PRACTICE 5

Read the following topic sentences from various sources and determine the intended audience.

1. Business entities that are disregarded as separate from their owner, including qualified subchapter S subsidiaries, are required to withhold and pay employment taxes and file employment tax returns using the name and employer identification number (EIN) of the disregarded entity. (www.irs.gov)

   ....

2. When operating this digital scale, use the AC adapter provided by the manufacturer to avoid damaging the electronics of the device. (DigitAm Scale Users Manual p. 4)

   ....

3. The **relative minor** of a major key, or the **relative major** of a minor key, has the same key signature but a different tonic; as opposed to *parallel* minor or major, which shares the same tonic. (Smith, K.L *Music for Educators*. 2013. p.12)

   ....

4. If you've ever been interested in traveling to Alaska make plans now to see the newest documentary film, "Ask for Alaska!" (Miller, Ann. "An Alaskan Spectacle." *Travel Rover Magazine*. September/October, 2011. p. 49)

   ....

5. The angle at which (the blood splatter) was projected can be determined by measuring the length and width of the blood drop and then applying the following formula: Angle of Impact = arc sin W/L. (Sullivan, Wilson T. *Crime Scene Analysis*. Pearson. 2007. p. 244.)

   ....

U-REVIEW 2

Answer the following questions by writing the correct questions and compare your answers with your partner or team.

1. To determine whether something is a fact or an opinion, you should ask,

....

....

2. To find the author's purpose for writing something, you should ask,

....

....

3. To find the author's tone, you should ask,

....

....

4. To find the intended audience, ask,

....

....

OBJECTIVE **5**

Detect bias.

DETECTING BIAS

bias: the author's attitude or opinion about something

When authors reveal their opinions about a topic, they are showing us their point of view from their own perspective. **Bias** is present when an author reveals his or her attitude or opinion (positive or negative) about something. We often refer to bias as a type of prejudice. For instance, saying, "I have always thought that a BMW is a better car than a Mercedes" shows bias. When the author's attitude about the topic is not evident and there is no negative or positive spin about something, the writing is **unbiased.**

Opinions are present in biased writing, so be aware of opinion words and phrases. But not every opinion is a biased statement. In the sentence, "Inhaling toxic substances will cause brain damage," there is no bias because the author doesn't reveal his or her opinion about the topic. However, in the sentence, "Companies that are guilty of allowing toxic materials into the environment should be severely punished," the author is stating his or her opinion about the topic, so this is a biased statement.

Bias is present in many different situations, and can even be found in textbooks. If you are able to recognize bias, then you will be aware when someone is trying to influence your thinking. Critical thinkers look for facts and make their own decisions about what they believe. Non-critical thinkers let other people do their thinking for them, and frequently suffer the consequences for it.

Are You Biased?

Everyone has some type of bias. We all have our favorite brands of clothing, cars, sports teams, music, or restaurants. What are some product brands that you prefer? What are some brands that you would never buy? Clearly, some bias is normal; however, it is appropriate in some circumstances, but not in others. For instance, we do not expect news reports to be biased; they should be factual, without showing the reporter's personal attitudes about the topics. We also want our instructors to be fair and without bias toward any students. We expect our police to be unbiased, treating everyone the same. On the other hand, we expect advertisers to be biased in favor of their products and political candidates to be biased about their ability to lead.

Read the following sentences. Which sentence below is biased in favor of pesticides? Which one is biased against pesticides? Which one is neutral, or unbiased?

1. Thanks to pesticides, crop losses have been significantly reduced.
2. Pesticides include insecticides but they can also control fungi and bacteria.
3. Pesticides are harmful chemicals that can poison wildlife and birds, and should not be used in agriculture.

When Bias Is Factual

Bias is also present when the facts support only one side of an issue. For instance, if a car manufacturer advertises how economical and fuel efficient its cars are, this is also a form of expected bias. Retailers rarely tell you both the good and bad points about the products they sell. Therefore, it is important to consider the author's purpose when looking for bias. Always ask yourself if the author is trying to persuade you or influence your thinking in some way.

When looking for bias, ask, "What is the author's attitude about this topic?" If the author reveals a positive or negative attitude about the topic, or gives an opinion, then the author is showing bias. If the author is presenting the facts in a balanced manner by showing the positive and negative sides about the topic, then the writing is unbiased. When you come to a word which you think may be biased, ask yourself if the word reveals the author's attitude, or if it describes a provable fact.

If an author expresses only one opinion or uses only one biased word or phrase in the passage, it is still considered biased. As you read the following sentences, look for bias.

1. Climate change is due to many factors, including the impact of humans on the environment.
2. Careless humans have had a negative impact on the environment and are responsible for climate change.

In the first sentence, it can be proved that climate change is due to many factors, including humans. Therefore, it is a fact and unbiased.

In the second sentence, the word "careless" indicates the author's opinion, so it is biased.

Identify the following sentences as either biased (B) or unbiased (U). Underline any words or phrases that reveal the author's bias.

1. .... Hydrogen is the best fuel to use in motor vehicles because it doesn't pollute the air.

2. .... Hydrogen fuel is produced from water or other substances.

3. .... Hydrogen is currently too expensive to produce on a large scale to meet our energy needs.

4. .... Hydrogen fuel reduces the need for fossil fuels.

5. .... When compared to hydrogen fuel engines, battery operated engines cost less and are a more efficient way to produce clean energy.

MyReadingLab

PRACTICE 6

As you read the following passage, apply all of the critical thinking skills you have learned so far. Write questions that you would like to have answered about the topic.

Mazda has successfully managed to reduce fuel costs and pollution with its new diesel engine design. The new engines boast approximately 44 mpg highway while meeting strict emission standards. The two-stage engine contains a small turbine and a larger turbocharger to increase high-end horsepower. These 2.2- or 2.5-liter diesel engines have lighter, lower-friction components, including an aluminum cylinder block that reduces engine weight by 55 pounds. A lighter engine means better mileage. New fuel injectors and exhaust valve designs allow for a lower compression ratio, which lowers exhaust pollutants and eliminates the need for expensive exhaust emission treatments. The new Skyactive-D diesel engine is a long-awaited innovation that will become the new diesel engine standard.

("How Mazda Reinvented the Diesel Engine" Lawrence Ulrich, Popular Science, May 8, 2013.)

1. What is the author's argument or claim?

a. A new diesel engine, the Skyactive-D was built by Mazda.
b. The new Skyactive-D engine is the best engine available in autos.
c. The new Skyactive-D diesel engine is a long-awaited innovation that will become the new diesel engine standard.
d. The Skyactive-D diesel engine reduces pollution and increases fuel efficiency.

2. Which of the following statements is an opinion?

a. Mazda has successfully managed to reduce fuel costs and pollution with its new diesel engine design.
b. A lighter engine means better mileage.
c. New fuel injectors and exhaust valve designs allow for a lower compression ratio which lowers exhaust pollutants and eliminates the need for expensive exhaust emission treatments.
d. The new Skyactive-D diesel engine is a long-awaited innovation that will become the new diesel engine standard.

3. What is the author's purpose in this passage? (Choose all that apply.)

a. to persuade readers that the Skyactive-D diesel engine is a good engine
b. to inform readers about the Skyactive-D diesel engine
c. to explain why the Skyactive-D engine is fuel efficient
d. to assess the fuel economy and pollution standards of the Skyactive-D engine

4. In this passage, the author's tone is

a. objective
b. admiring
c. ironic
d. grim

5. This passage is

a. biased
b. unbiased

Continued...

MyReadingLab

PRACTICE 6

...continued

6. What questions do you have about this topic?

MyReadingLab

PRACTICE 7

As you read the following passage, apply all of the critical thinking skills you have learned so far. Write questions that you would like to have answered about the topic.

Once great apes were killed for bush meat but now they are captured live and put onto private airplanes in the African bush and shipped to China. This trade in wild apes is now a greater threat to their survival than hunting or the destruction of their habitat. The wild ape trade is banned under the Convention on International Trade in Endangered Species (CITES), but wildlife protection workers recently uncovered an ape trading network operating out of Guinea, West Africa. Wild apes were captured and sent to Asia, where live gorillas can sell for up to $400,000. The apes had originated in the Democratic Republic of the Congo. Recently a drug smuggler in West Africa was caught with a live baby chimpanzee wedged between sacks of marijuana in his (car) trunk. Animals that are saved in rescue operations are sometimes killed because of fears of disease, or they end up in animal sanctuaries thousands of miles from their original habitats. With new DNA testing, more retrieved animals such as these could be traced to their origin and returned home. If conservation efforts fail to stop the trade of live apes, they will soon face extinction in the wild.

("Trafficking now the Greatest Threat to Wild Apes," Fred Pearce, New Scientist, March 6, 2013)

1. What is the author's argument or claim?
   - **a.** Once great apes were killed for bush meat but now they are captured live and put onto private airplanes in the African bush and shipped to China.
   - **b.** This trade in wild apes is now a greater threat to their survival than hunting or the destruction of their habitat.
   - **c.** Animals that are saved in rescue operations are sometimes killed because of fears of disease or they end up in animal sanctuaries thousands of miles from their original habitats.
   - **d.** With new DNA testing, more retrieved animals such as these could be traced to their origin and returned home.

2. Which of the following statements is an opinion?
   a. Once great apes were killed for bush meat but now they are captured live and put onto private airplanes in the African bush and shipped to China.
   b. This trade in wild apes is now a greater threat to their survival than hunting or the destruction of their habitat.
   c. Animals that are saved in rescue operations are sometimes killed because of fears of disease or they end up in animal sanctuaries thousands of miles from their original habitats.
   d. If conservation efforts fail to stop the trade of live apes, they will soon face extinction in the wild.
3. What is the author's purpose in this passage? (Choose all that apply.)
   a. to inform readers about the wild live ape trade
   b. to persuade readers that ape trading is dangerous
   c. to advise readers against trading in wild apes
   d. to persuade readers of the consequences of ape trafficking
4. In this passage, the author's tone is
   a. cynical
   b. apathetic
   c. cautionary
   d. righteous
5. This passage is
   a. biased
   b. unbiased
6. What questions do you have about this topic?

....

....

....

....

....

MyReadingLab

PRACTICE 8

As you read the following passage, apply all of the critical thinking skills you have learned so far. Write questions that you would like to have answered about the topic.

The discovery of antibiotics, drugs that kill certain nonhuman (primarily bacterial) cells, revolutionized tuberculosis treatment in the1940s. Since then, infected patients with active tuberculosis (TB) are typically kept in isolation for only 2 weeks until antibiotics kill off most of the *M. tuberculosis* in the lungs. At this point, the patient is no longer contagious and can return to the community. However, because the *M. tuberculosis* can hide inside immune system cells for long periods, antibiotic treatment must be maintained for 6 to 12 months to completely eliminate the organism.

Since the 1980s, however, scientists have chronicled a disturbing rise in the number of antibiotic-resistant tuberculosis infections—ones that cannot be cured by the standard drug treatment. According to the Center for Disease Control, from 2000 to 2004, 20% of reported TB cases did not respond to standard treatments (and thus are called multi-drug-resistant TB, or MDR-TB), and 2% were resistant to treatment with second-line drugs (called extensively drug-resistant TB, or XDR-TB). Even in the United States, with abundant access to resources and drugs, one-third of individuals diagnosed with active XDR-TB have died of the disease.

As control has become less effective, the number of cases of TB in both developed and developing countries has begun to rise. In countries with fewer resources, the toll of XDR-TB could be much greater. In a recent XDR-TB outbreak in South Africa, 52 of 53 individuals diagnosed with the strain died within a month of showing signs of active disease. The resurgence of tuberculosis has now been declared a global health emergency by the World Health Organization.

(From "Science for Life with Physiology 3e," Colleen Belk and Virginia Borden, Pearson, 2010, pp.257-258)

1. What is the author's argument or claim?

a. The discovery of antibiotics, drugs that kill certain nonhuman (primarily bacterial) cells, revolutionized tuberculosis treatment in the 1940s

b. Since the 1980s, however, scientists have chronicled a disturbing rise in the number of antibiotic-resistant tuberculosis infections—ones that cannot be cured by the standard drug treatment.

c. Even in the United States, with abundant access to resources and drugs, one-third of individuals diagnosed with active XDR-TB have died of the disease.

d. The resurgence of tuberculosis has now been declared a global health emergency by the World Health Organization.

2. Which of the following statements is an opinion?

a. The discovery of antibiotics, drugs that kill certain nonhuman (primarily bacterial) cells, revolutionized tuberculosis treatment in the 1940s.

b. In countries with fewer resources, the toll of XDR-TB could be much greater.

c. Even in the United States, with abundant access to resources and drugs, one-third of individuals diagnosed with active XDR-TB have died of the disease.

d. As control has become less effective, the number of cases of TB in both developed and developing countries has begun to rise.

3. What is the author's purpose in this passage? (Choose all that apply.)

a. to inform readers about drug-resistant XDR-TB

b. to warn readers about drug-resistant XDR-TB

c. to criticize the CDC for not taking measures sooner to prevent XDR-TB

d. to instruct students about XDR-TB

4. In this passage, the author's tone is

a. indignant

b. optimistic

c. impassioned

d. straightforward

5. This passage is

a. biased

b. unbiased

6. What questions do you have about this topic?

....

....

....

....

....

....

U-REVIEW 3

Answer true (T) or false (F) to each of the following statements.

1. .... Reading selections are biased when authors reveal their attitudes about topics.

2. .... Bias is never found in textbooks or newspapers.

3. .... Bias often contains opinion.

4. .... Factual reading selections are always unbiased.

5. .... If the author does not reveal an attitude in favor or against something, he or she is unbiased.

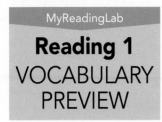

MyReadingLab

Reading 1
VOCABULARY PREVIEW

"No-Fly Zone: Denied Their Natural Habits, Millions of Pet Parrots Lead Bleak, Lonely Lives" by Charles Bergman

Match the words in the Word Bank by writing the letter of the word next to the matching definition. The paragraph numbers in parentheses indicate the location of each word in the reading selection, "No Fly Zone." Read the words in the paragraphs to determine the correct meanings as they are used in context.

WORD BANK

a. embodied (3)	b. pewter (3)	c. ubiquitous (3)
d. self-mutilation (4)	e. unprecedented (7)	f. morphed (8)
g. bleak (8)	h. vetted (12)	i. tsunami (17)
j. partisan (18)	k. sketchy (21)	l. dysfunctional (33)
m. moral dilemma (26)		

1. .... a giant sea wave

2. .... to have brought to life;

3. .... harsh; grim

4. .... changed; transformed

5. .... suspicious

6. .... injuring oneself

7. .... a metal (or its color)

8. .... verified one's credentials

9. .... never before seen

10. .... moral or ethical problem

11. .... supporting a particular group or ideal

12. .... badly functioning

13. .... found everywhere; common

MyReadingLab

Reading 1 PREVIEW

Discuss the following questions with a partner or small group.

1. Have you ever had any pets or know of animals that have seemed clever or intelligent? What behaviors made them seem intelligent?
2. What are your feelings about keeping wild animals in captivity?

After you preview the article, write one or two preview questions on the lines below:

....

....

....

....

....

MyReadingLab

Reading 1

"No-Fly Zone: Denied Their Natural Habits, Millions of Pet Parrots Lead Bleak, Lonely Lives"

by Charles Bergman

Some parrots and parrot-family birds are as intelligent as apes or dolphins. As a result, they often suffer from isolation, boredom, and neglect while in captivity. Rescued from a hoarder, this parrot had pulled out all his feathers. Such self-mutilation is common in birds unable to engage in natural behaviors.

1 Sofia popped off her perch, climbed up my arm, and leaned into my face. A Moluccan cockatoo, among the world's most stunning birds, Sofia's most distinctive feature is her huge round head—big, white, and inviting as a fluffy pillow. She fanned her crest in a spectacular blush of pink, coral, and salmon. I looked into Sofia's black eyes and held her close. As she dropped her head and burrowed in tight, I was overcome by the intimacy of the moment, like cuddling a baby.

2 "They can really turn on the charm," said Betsy Lott, smiling.

3 That combination of beauty and charm has helped make parrots like Sofia the fourth most popular pet in America—behind only dogs, cats, and the ubiquitous freshwater fishes. But there's a dark side to our passion for parrots, and Sofia embodied that too. Once an elegant bird in white feathers,

Continued...

MyReadingLab

Reading 1

...continued

she's now a tattered beauty, her feathers ragged and her chest plucked bare, showing a big patch of wrinkled pewter-gray skin.

4 Sofia's good friend and perch mate, Mango, wears a cone-shaped collar to keep her from even more aggressive self-mutilation. Only captive parrots pluck and wound themselves like this.

5 "I get calls every day from people looking to dump their parrots," Lott says.

6 The owners of these parrots finally gave up on them and placed them in Mollywood, Lott's home-based organization for surrendered parrots. They're two of about 350 parrots she and her husband tend to just outside of Bellingham, Washington, near the Canadian border.

7 Sofia and Mango represent a category of parrot that's grown over the last 20 years: the unwanted, abandoned, and disposable bird. In 1992, the Wild Bird Conservation Act made it illegal to import most wild-caught parrots into the United States. While a victory for wildlife conservation, it fueled a captive breeding boom of unprecedented proportions.

8 Once, parrots were icons of the tropical good life. Now they have morphed into figures of increasing controversy and crisis. The truth is, most pet parrots are only a few generations removed from the wild, and few owners are prepared to fulfill even their most basic instincts: flying, flocking, and finding mates. These highly social creatures are usually kept alone and rarely allowed to fly—many parrots' wings are clipped. Often their relatively small cages have little in the way of stimulation and "enrichment," or toys. For an animal as emotionally complex as a chimpanzee or dolphin, it amounts to an unimaginably bleak existence. In fact, parrot advocate Mira Tweti estimates that some 75 percent of birds "live a life of abuse or neglect."

Why do parrots often become aggressive or begin to mutilate themselves?

9 With no outlet for the chronic frustration of living in an environment expressly unsuited to them, these intelligent creatures often develop destructive behaviors like screaming, aggression to their owners, and the self-mutilation that Sofia and Mango have displayed.

10 Understandably, all of this takes a toll on birds' owners. Often the human caretakers feel out of their depth, similarly frustrated, and even guilty about the daily trial of living with an animal who is traumatized and psychologically damaged—and who may outlive them by decades.

11 Some resort to confining their birds to the closet, basement, or garage, where the dark silences them and hides the mess. Other owners simply unload their high-maintenance charges with friends or family members (many parrots pass through multiple homes in their lifetimes) or at places like Mollywood, which have sprouted up like mushrooms in response to the fallout.

12 The problem is so large that Tweti, Lott and other rescuers, and organizations such as The Humane Society of the U.S., don't recommend parrots as pets in the first place. Because they are so long-lived, there will likely be a need for responsible, carefully vetted home care for many birds for many years. But the best situation for most, these groups maintain, is an accredited sanctuary environment.

13 Sofia nudges me with her head, and I rub the back of her neck. She's one of many such parrots—literally hundreds—I've met in rescues and sanctuaries around the country. They became my inspiration to try to figure out what's really happening to their kind and what that means for our rapidly changing relationship.

14 "These parrots are like people—like children," Lott says. "It's like adopting a 2-year-old special needs child. One that will never grow up."

"A Tsunami of Unwanted, Disposable Parrots"

15 There are about 350 species of parrots—a sprawling group of birds that includes huge macaws and cockatoos, Amazons and African grey parrots, conures, and smaller cockatiels and budgies (sometimes known as parakeets). Nearly a third of the species are endangered or threatened in the wild, in large measure because we've wanted them for pets.

16 Karen Windsor and Marc Johnson run Foster Parrots in Rhode Island, one of the oldest captive parrot sanctuaries in the country. "We're experiencing a failure of parrots as pets," says Windsor. "Every sanctuary turns down birds every day. You hear every reason and excuse from owners. You bet it's a crisis."

What happens to parrots that are no longer wanted?

17 Tweti, author of *Of Parrots and People* and an expert on parrot welfare, predicts a "tsunami of unwanted, disposable parrots" yet to come from the millions of sales over the last three decades, since parrots often live as long as people.

Inside a Parrot Mill

18 Howard Voren has been a national leader in captive breeding for more than three decades. He was a top importer of wild-caught parrots when it was legal, and he developed many of the breeding techniques that made mass production of parrots possible and profitable. And he's an outspoken partisan in the parrot wars. Crisis? "That's just a bunch of fat ladies in polyester suits who call themselves animal behaviorists," he says. "I call them ARFs—Animal Rights Fanatics."

19 I wanted to learn from Voren how commercial breeders produce their chicks, how the birds are treated in the process, and how he feels about his animals. He has a large personality, leaning in close to make his points. I was surprised to learn that he sees himself as the misunderstood, slightly alienated hero of parrot conservation.

20 "I'm the pioneer," he says. "I wrote the book on hand-rearing and hand-feeding of parrots. I showed how to mass-produce them, how to do it. It's always the pioneers who take all the arrows."

21 "There are some sketchy breeders," he tells me. "They may have parrots in deplorable conditions. There are lots of backyard breeders, hobbyists. But they all go out of business. The nature of parrots won't allow it. Parrots in mills will die. If you run a facility that's awful, the parrots won't reproduce. Those breeders will go by the wayside."

What do Mr. Voren's comments reveal about his attitude toward parrots?

22 Out back, we walk through long rows of hundreds of cages, wire rectangles elevated off the ground. Each cage is perhaps 3 x 3 x 4 feet (large by some standards) and holds a breeding pair. No toys. No distractions. On the wooden back of the nest box in each cage, inky notes track every egg laid that season. The eggs are removed as they are laid. The babies never see their parents: Voren experimented with real chickens as brooding birds but found it more efficient to invent an "artificial chicken" device to heat and hatch the eggs. Voren tells me his goal is to be able to completely control the birds and their breeding process. "If I'm successful, I can make them breed whenever I want or turn them off with a snap of the finger."

Continued...

23 "Do you have personal relationships with your parrots?" I ask. "I'm a capitalist," he says. "I'm in business. No personal relationship with the parrots." He pauses. "That maybe gives the wrong impression. It's just that you can't have a personal relationship with 1,500 adult birds." The old breeder parrots are sold at auction. "When a pair reaches the end of their productivity, they go to a broker," he says, "to be sold to other breeders. Only not with my name on them."

24 We enter a room in a long, low building. It's windowless. A woman from Honduras is working with baby parrots inside, feeding them, I think. This is where the hatched birds come to be raised and weaned, where they learn to feed themselves.

25 Stacked wire cages line two of the walls. They are full of green nanday and fiery-orange sun conures—small long-tailed parrots originally from South America. They're increasingly popular as the market for larger birds declines. From a bank of shelves, Voren pulls out one of many plastic storage containers, the kind you can buy at Home Depot. He opens the top, revealing 16 baby conures, some nearly covered in green feathers, others still mostly naked. They stand in a layer of wood shavings and sawdust, craning to look up at me. Voren is proud of them, likening the container to their early life in a hole in a tree in the forest.

26 Voren says he feels no moral dilemma about any part of his operation. On the contrary, he believes it contributes to conservation, since by knowing parrots in the home we'll be motivated to save parrots in the wild. (Many advocates feel otherwise, noting it's the pet trade that contributed to wild birds' decline.)

What kinds of living conditions do parrots have in parrot mills?

27 The image of the baby parrots in the plastic storage boxes has stayed with me. They were not so much parrots as products. Not so much babies as profits with feathers.

Captive Breeding Has Declined, but Problems Persist

28 As one of the most respected parrot breeders in the world, E. B. Cravens writes frequently on parrots and their care. He has great insight into their nature. I wanted to talk to him about the psychology of parrots—especially the babies and parents in big breeding operations.

29 "Absolutely, they are factory farms, pumping out parrots. There are also conscientious breeders, and lots have stopped breeding too, like me." At captive breeding height, he says, maybe 750,000 parrots per year were being produced in the United States. Now that number is maybe 100,000 per year as people learn more and more about how difficult parrots can be in the home.

30 "All these parrots, the babies, they're orphans," he says. "My breeder friends hate it when I say this. But that's what they are, orphans."

31 Cravens has been letting his own parrot-parents follow their "strongest impulse": raising their offspring themselves. Baby parrots need closeness. In the wild, they'll spend months and months in constant contact with their parents. But in a factory-style breeding operation, they never see their parents or are removed early on to be raised by people. The result is young

parrots who don't know who they are, who spend their lives in a no-birds land between human and animal.

32 At first, the young parrots are cuddly and affectionate. "People are smitten," Cravens says. "They think, 'Oh, this parrot really loves me, just like a baby.' And you want to be loved like that. But the truth is, it's just lonely. It's needy."

33 In a few years the parrot hits puberty and develops intense needs for bonding with a mate. "It gets sexual, and the problems really begin. It may attach to one person in the family and grow hostile to others. It may even bite or attack others. ... The parrots become dysfunctional because they have not been allowed to have a childhood."

What are some of the needs that baby parrots have?

34 The owners of Santa Barbara Bird Farm in California, Phoebe Linden and her husband have not bred parrots in 11 years, out of concern for what breeding does to the birds' mental health.

35 "There are so many crazy, whacked-out parrots," she says, emotion filling her voice. "Every domestically raised bird is traumatized. To some extent all are. Some birds respond to trauma, like some people, and have no effects. Some drag their trauma around with them all their lives."

(Retrieved from http://www.humanesociety.org/news/magazines/2013/03-04/no-fly-zone-millions-of-pet-parrots-lead-bleak-lonely-lives.html#id=album-181&num=content-3272.)

1,993 words divided by .... minutes = ... words per minute

MyReadingLab

Reading 1 REVIEW

A good review strategy to use after reading is to summarize what you just read in your own words. Take a few minutes to think about the author's most important point and any key ideas that helped to support or explain it.

Write a two- or three-sentence summary on the lines below.

....

....

....

....

....

....

....

MyReadingLab

Reading 1 COMPREHENSION QUESTIONS

The following questions will help you recall the main idea and details of "No Fly Zone." Read again any parts of the article that you need to find the correct answers.

MAIN IDEA AND CENTRAL POINT

1. What is the overall implied central point of this selection?

a. Parrots in captivity are unable to fulfill their basic needs for flight, flocking, and mating.

b. Domestically raised parrots are traumatized and react with self-mutilation and aggression.

c. Parrots in captivity are intelligent, complex animals facing a crisis of neglect and abandonment, and should not be sold as pets.

d. Most owners don't realize the needs of parrots and abandon them when their behavior becomes intolerable.

2. What is the main idea of paragraph 8?

a. Once, parrots were icons of the tropical good life.

b. Now they have morphed into figures of increasing controversy and crisis.

c. The truth is, most pet parrots are only a few generations removed from the wild, and few owners are prepared to fulfill even their most basic instincts: flying, flocking, and finding mates.

d. For an animal as emotionally complex as a chimpanzee or dolphin, it amounts to an unimaginably bleak existence.

SUPPORTING DETAILS

3. According to the passage, young parrot chicks in the wild

a. spend months and months in close contact with their own parents.

b. are left by their parents as soon as they can fly.

c. live in tree holes until they can fly away.

d. are baby orphans.

DRAWING CONCLUSIONS

4. Many breeders who are still raising parrots in parrot mills believe

a. parrots are happy living in cages in homes.

b. parrots are a profitable commodity and their needs are irrelevant.

c. parrots have social needs that must be met.

d. parrots are able to adapt to any living situation.

PATTERNS OF ORGANIZATION

5. The overall pattern of organization for this selection is

a. time order

b. spatial order

c. compare and contrast

d. cause and effect

CRITICAL THINKING

6. Identify the following statement from paragraph 25: "They're increasingly popular as the market for larger birds declines."

a. fact

b. opinion

c. fact and opinion

7. The author's claim or argument in this reading selection is

a. Parrots in captivity suffer because they are kept in unsuitable environments, and they should not be sold as pets.

b. The numbers of wild parrots are decreasing due to human predation.

c. Federal laws should be made to prohibit the possession and breeding of parrots.

d. Parrots in captivity should only be sold to responsible owners.

8. The author's purpose and tone in this article are:
   a. to inform readers about parrots in a neutral tone
   b. to persuade readers that parrots don't belong in captivity in a concerned tone
   c. to advise readers not to buy parrots in a cautionary tone
   d. to criticize parrot owners in a critical tone

9. The information in this article is
   a. biased in favor of owning parrots as pets.
   b. biased against owning parrots as pets.
   c. unbiased.

Reading 1 VOCABULARY PRACTICE

Use the words in the Word Bank to complete the story below. The part of speech for each word is given as a clue. Not all of the words will be used in the story.

WORD BANK

embodied (v)	pewter (n)	ubiquitous (adj)
self-mutilation (n)	unprecedented (adj)	morphed (v)
bleak (adj)	vetted (v)	tsunami (n)
partisan (n)	sketchy (adj)	dysfunctional (adj)
moral dilemma (n)		

THE SEA DOG

Hitching a ride on a freighter to a tropical island had always been one of my fantasies. However, I wasn't prepared for the reality of my .... (adj) existence aboard a ship. A musty, hard cot chained to a wall in a tiny rust-ridden cubicle no larger than the back seat of a Chevy truck was my new home. The captain had thoroughly .... (v) my passport and credentials before leaving port in the rusting hulk. I was a little apprehensive about sharing quarters with such a bunch of rugged and .... (adj) shipmates. One with a scar across his cheek stared at me as if I were his next victim. Their prolific and .... (adj) tattoos and body piercings bore evidence of fearless .... (n) . Over the weeks on board I .... (v) from a naïve and cultured young man to a swarthy sea-dog. My hands became leathery from coiling ropes, and my skin bronzed under the blazing Pacific sun. As we approached Fiji, we heard warnings of an undersea earthquake and a possible .... (n) of .... (adj) size that could swamp our ship. There was no .... (n) about who would get the life raft—it would be every man for himself. Fortunately, the quake's aftershocks only gave us rough seas for a while and we reached our destination safely. My experience has made me a .... (n) of sailing on freighters, and I plan to sail home the same way, if I ever leave this tropical paradise.

MyReadingLab

Reading 1 QUESTIONS FOR WRITING AND DISCUSSION

1. This article presents the issue of parrots in captivity from the author's point of view. If someone were writing it from a parrot breeder's point of view, what points would most likely be made in favor of breeding and selling parrots?

2. Although laws make it illegal to import most wild-caught parrots into the United States, breeders are still allowed to breed and sell parrots. Do you think this should be allowed? Why or why not?

3. Do you think animals with intelligence such as parrots, dolphins, or dogs should be treated differently than animals with less intelligence? Why or why not?

4. The article states that parrots are often abandoned or given up by owners who can't deal with their aggression or self-mutilation. What are some other ways that abandoned birds could be cared for? Should they be released into the wild? Why or why not?

5. People bring exotic animals into their homes as pets. What impact does this have on wildlife? On the animals? On the environment? On the community?

Reading 1
CRITICAL THINKING ANALYSIS CHART

To solve problems and reach logical conclusions using critical thinking, it is often helpful to use a chart such as the one below. Fill in the points made in the article to support each side of the issue and then label each one as fact or opinion. Write questions you still have in the third column and a conclusion at the end.

Points in favor of having parrots as pets	Points against having parrots as pets	Questions still unanswered

Conclusion: Your conclusion about whether parrots should be allowed as pets:

MyReadingLab

Reading 2 VOCABULARY PREVIEW

"Quiet Down Below" by Sara B. McPherson

Match the words in the Word Bank from "Quiet Down Below" by writing the letter of the word next to the matching definition. The paragraph numbers in parentheses indicate the location of each word in the reading selection. Read the words in the paragraphs to determine the correct meanings as they are used in the context of the selection.

WORD BANK

a. racket (2)	b. compensate (3)	c. echolocation (3)
d. bisonar (3)	e. dorsal bursae (4)	f. denser (5)
g. anthropogenic (6)	h. habitat (10)	i. frequency (11)
j. wavelengths (11)	k. mitigate (19)	

1. .... more tightly packed together
2. .... a dolphin organ
3. .... noise
4. .... lessen
5. .... echolocation
6. .... natural environment
7. .... the distance between two points in a wave
8. .... to make up for
9. .... rate of sound vibrations generated
10. .... human-made
11. .... a method of locating objects

MyReadingLab

Reading 2 PREVIEW

Discuss the following questions with a partner or small group.

1. What kinds of human-made vehicles or devices generate loud sounds under water?
2. How might loud sounds affect marine animals or their environment?

After you preview the article, write one or two preview questions on the lines below:

....

....

....

MyReadingLab

Reading 2

"Quiet Down Below" by Sara B. McPherson

Is an increasingly noisy ocean making life harder for whales and dolphins?

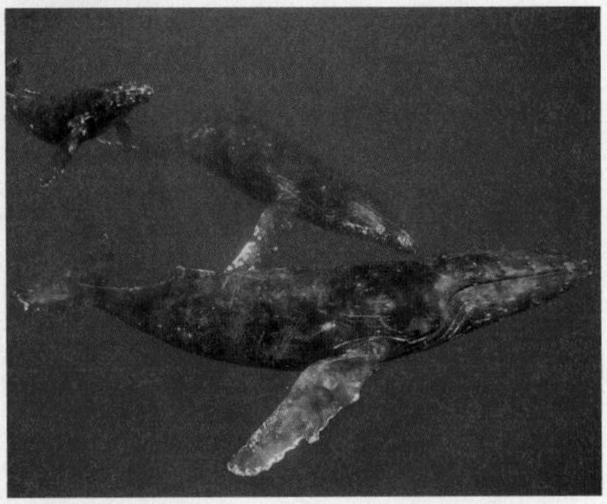

1 You might not think of the ocean as a noisy place. But since the 1950s, there's been a sharp increase in commercial shipping, oil exploration, and military-testing activities—all of which are noisy operations.

2 Some scientists liken the recent undersea racket to a rock concert. And just as your hearing can be temporarily affected by loud music, noisy oceans might be affecting marine animals—such as dolphins and whales—that rely on their hearing for survival. The question is, to what extent?

"Seeing" with Sound

Why do marine animals use biosonar?

3 Very little light makes its way deep into the ocean's waters, making it hard for marine animals to rely solely on their eyesight to get around or find food. Dolphins, porpoises, and other *toothed whales* compensate by using sophisticated natural sonar, called *echolocation*, or *bisonar*, to help them "see" underwater.

4 A dolphin echolocates using sound waves produced by two vibrating organs located below its blowhole. The vibration of these organs—the *dorsal bursae* and *phonic lips*—creates a series of clicks. A fat-filled organ in the animal's forehead, called the *melon*, acts like a lens that narrows and directs the sounds. The signal travels through the water until it strikes an object and bounces back to the dolphin. The returning sound waves travel through fatty deposits in the animal's lower jaw that connects to its ears.

How does biosonar work?

5 Dolphins can tell how far away an object is by how long it takes the sound waves to return. They can also tell the shape, size, and speed of the object—whether it's a predator, a ship, or its next meal. And because water is denser than air, sound travels almost five times faster in the ocean than it does in the atmosphere. It also travels farther, enabling dolphins to hear sounds that originated many miles away.

Turning Up the Volume

6 Scientists are concerned that increasing *anthropogenic*, or human-made, sounds in the seas may be negatively affecting whales and dolphins.

7 According to Shannon Rankin, a wildlife biologist at the National Oceanic and Atmospheric Administration, ocean noise can cause a number of problems for these animals. "In extreme cases, sounds can cause direct injury and permanently damage their hearing," she says. "Hearing loss can also be temporary. But enough temporary damage can lead to permanent hearing damage," says Rankin.

8 Excessive noise can also mask the sounds animals make to communicate with one another. For instance, noise that interrupts whale songs can make it hard for whales to find mates.

Continued...

MyReadingLab
Reading 2
...continued

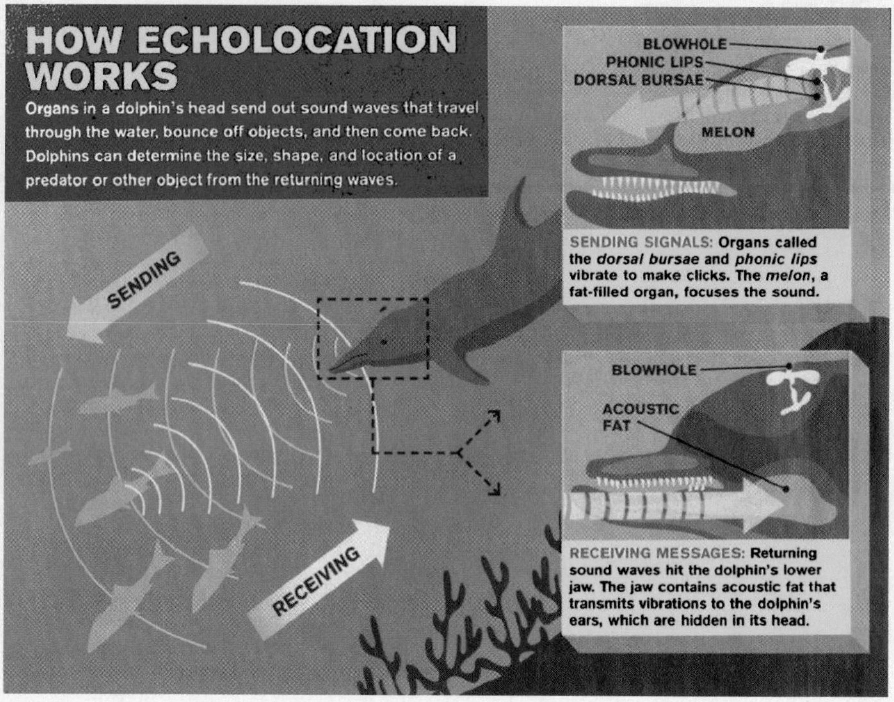
HOW ECHOLOCATION WORKS
Organs in a dolphin's head send out sound waves that travel through the water, bounce off objects, and then come back. Dolphins can determine the size, shape, and location of a predator or other object from the returning waves.
SENDING
RECEIVING
BLOWHOLE
PHONIC LIPS
DORSAL BURSAE
MELON
SENDING SIGNALS: Organs called the dorsal bursae and phonic lips vibrate to make clicks. The melon, a fat-filled organ, focuses the sound.
BLOWHOLE
ACOUSTIC FAT
RECEIVING MESSAGES: Returning sound waves hit the dolphin's lower jaw. The jaw contains acoustic fat that transmits vibrations to the dolphin's ears, which are hidden in its head.

9 Studies have shown that loud noise causes some whales to raise or alter their voices in an attempt to be heard—just as you might shout in a crowded room. Scientists don't know what the long-term effects of all that "shouting" might be.

10 Whales and dolphins may also have trouble finding food if noise pollution interferes with their echolocation signals. And Rankin notes that whales and dolphins could even abandon prime habitat to escape from noise and end up living in a less desirable environment.

Tuning It Out

11 Fortunately, whales have some ability to muffle or tune out unpleasant noise. Sound travels in a series of waves that are measured in terms of *frequency* (rate of sound vibrations generated). Higher-frequency sounds have smaller *wavelengths*—the distance between a wave's peaks—and a higher pitch. Lower-frequency sounds have larger wavelengths and a lower pitch.

12 Different animals hear and communicate in different pitches, according to Ted Cranford, a professor at San Diego State University who studies biosonar. For example, the biological structures that dolphins use to hear can accept only certain sound waves. If the frequency is too high or too low, they naturally tune out the sound.

13 Studies have also shown that some toothed whales can muffle noise by reducing their hearing sensitivity when they anticipate a loud sound. "The effect is similar to a person sticking their fingers in their ears trying to block out loud noise," says Cranford.

How do different marine animals respond to high and low frequency sounds?

14 These remedies are only temporary, however, and it's unknown whether they're all that helpful. "The ability of toothed whales to block unwanted noise depends on how much noise is filtered out and how well they can adjust their sensitivity," Cranford explains. "Right now, we don't know how the noise is muffled, or how long the whales can maintain it."

How Much Is Too Much?

15 For Rankin, the big question is just how much anthropogenic noise is too much for whales and dolphins. "We need to figure out at what point noise in the ocean interferes with the animals' ability to function," she says.

16 This is a difficult question to answer. Because of whales' immense size and the fact that their habitats are offshore, it's extremely hard and expensive for researchers to study them in their natural environment.

17 Scientists do know that the majority of human-made ocean noise produces low-frequency sounds.

18 Toothed whales use higher frequencies for echolocation, so researchers think that noise pollution may not affect them as much as it does their toothless cousins—*bateen whales*—which tend to rely on lower frequencies. However, scientists acknowledge that more research is needed to better understand how noise pollution affects whales and dolphins.

19 "Ocean noise is rising in intensity," says Cranford, "so we should be concerned. We need to put our resources together to figure out how sound affects wildlife and how we can mitigate the impact."

881 words divided by .... minutes = ... words per minute

MyReadingLab

Reading 2
REVIEW

A good review strategy to use after reading is to summarize what you just read in your own words. Take a few minutes to think about the author's most important point and any key ideas that helped to support or explain it.

Write a two- or three-sentence summary on the lines below.

....

....

....

....

....

MyReadingLab

Reading 2 COMPREHENSION QUESTIONS

The following questions will help you recall the main idea and details of "Quiet Down Below." Read any parts of the article that you need to find the correct answers.

MAIN IDEAS

1. What is the author's argument, or claim, about noise pollution?

a. Whales and dolphins are becoming endangered because of noise pollution in the oceans.

b. More research is needed to better understand how noise pollution affects whales and dolphins.

c. But since the 1950s, there's been a sharp increase in commercial shipping, oil exploration, and military-testing activities—all of which are noisy operations.

d. Noise pollution is not healthy for any living thing and must be stopped.

2. What is the main idea of paragraph 4?

a. A dolphin echolocates using sound waves produced by two vibrating organs located below its blowhole.

b. Echolocation works much like sonar.

c. Dolphins use echolocation to locate objects in their environment.

d. The signal travels through the water until it strikes an object and bounces back to the dolphin.

3. What is the main idea of paragraph 7?

a. Animals affected by noise pollution suffer permanent hearing loss.

b. Hearing loss from noise pollution is always temporary.

c. Shannon Rankin is a wildlife biologist at the National Oceanic and Atmospheric Administration.

d. The effects of noise pollution can cause a number of problems for marine animals.

SUPPORTING DETAILS

4. According to the article, which of the following statements is true?

a. Dolphins are more sensitive to sound pollution than whales.

b. Sound travels faster and farther under water.

c. Not all dolphins use biosonar to find food.

d. The majority of anthropogenic sound is high frequency.

DRAWING CONCLUSIONS

5. Scientists are concerned about anthropogenic noise pollution because

a. if it continues, dolphins will disappear forever.

b. sharks may not be able to find food if there is too much noise pollution.

c. it affects the number of offspring that marine mammals produce.

d. it can affect how marine mammals find their food and escape predators.

PATTERNS OF ORGANIZATION

6. What is the overall pattern of organization for this article?

a. time order

b. compare/ contrast

c. cause and effect

d. generalization and example

CRITICAL THINKING

7. Identify the following sentences from paragraph 19. "Ocean noise is rising in intensity," says Cranford, "so we should be concerned. We need to put our resources together to figure out how sound affects wildlife and how we can mitigate the impact."

a. facts

b. opinions

c. expert opinion

8. What is the author's purpose and tone for this article?
- **a.** The author's purpose is to persuade and the tone is concerned.
- **b.** The author's purpose is to inform and the tone is objective.
- **c.** The author's purpose is to criticize and the tone is sarcastic.
- **d.** The author's purpose is to analyze and the tone is whimsical.

9. In this article the author is
- **a.** biased against harming wildlife.
- **b.** biased against noise pollution.
- **c.** biased in favor of studying the effects of noise pollution on marine animals.
- **d.** unbiased.

10. Which of the following sentences provides the best support for the argument that more research is needed to better understand how noise pollution affects whales and dolphins?
- **a.** The signal travels through the water until it strikes an object and bounces back to the dolphin.
- **b.** In extreme cases, sounds can cause direct injury and permanently damage their hearing.
- **c.** Studies have shown that loud noise causes some whales to raise or alter their voices in an attempt to be heard—just as you might shout in a crowded room.
- **d.** Fortunately, whales have some ability to muffle or tune out unpleasant noise.

Reading 2
VOCABULARY PRACTICE: CROSSWORD PUZZLE

Use the clues to complete the answers to the crossword puzzle below. Refer to the vocabulary preview for definitions.

WORD BANK

racket	compensate	echolocation	bisonar
habitat	dorsal bursae	denser	anthropogenic
frequency	wavelengths	mitigate	

Across Clues

2. A dolphin organ used in biosonar
6. Environment
7. How dolphins find food
10. To lessen
11. Distance between wavelengths

Down Clues

1. Distances between peaks of waves
3. Man-made
4. How some animals locate food
5. Noise
8. Make up for
9. More tightly packed

MyReadingLab

Reading 2 QUESTIONS FOR WRITING AND DISCUSSION

1. What are some of the causes of noise pollution in the oceans? Think of those mentioned in the article plus any others that you can imagine.

2. How might some of these causes be modified or changed so that there would be less noise pollution of the oceans?

3. Based on the information in this article, do you think that marine biologists have a valid concern for the well-being of marine life? Why or why not?

4. How might noise pollution affect marine life?

5. What are some things that you and others can do to make more people aware of the problem of noise pollution in the ocean and its possible consequences?

MyReadingLab

VIEWPOINT FOR CRITICAL THINKING

GUN OWNERSHIP

Ownership of guns and assault weapons in the United States remains a controversial issue. Read the following letters to the editor about gun control and answer the critical thinking questions.

Dear Editor:

It was ten days before Christmas in 2012 when 26 school children attending Sandy Hook Elementary School were killed by a teenage gunman on a violent rampage. Their families had no Merry Christmas that year, and probably will not be able to ever see another holiday decoration without thinking about their tragic loss. The issue of gun control rose above every other national concern for the next six months. To protect themselves from losing reelection, elected officials avoid passing serious gun control laws while our young people are murdered daily. When will Congress stop talking about gun control and actually DO something? We need to stop the sales of all guns in this country and make them illegal to own. No one needs a gun to survive in this country, and hunters don't need to shoot innocent animals. If people gave up their weapons, there would be no more massacres like the one at Sandy Hook. I urge everyone to write to your state senator or congressional representative and demand that guns be outlawed.

Signed,

Ms. Disarmed

Dear Editor:

What happened at Sandy Hook was a real tragedy, but what Ms. Disarmed doesn't realize is that guns don't kill people, people kill people. If guns were outlawed, it would only increase the black market demand for illegal weapons, making criminals even wealthier. When bills were introduced to Congress for gun control after the Sandy Hook shooting, there was a mad rush by the general public to get gun permits before the government increased restrictions on getting guns. This proves that many Americans would still want to own a gun even if they were illegal. If that young man who attacked Sandy Hook Elementary School couldn't get his hands on a gun, he probably would have made a bomb and still killed them. People who want to commit murder will find a way to do it. How can we possibly ban all the various ways you can kill somebody? Ban knives? Bows and arrows? Sling shots? Rope? Poison? How about baseball bats, because those can be used as weapons, too? The issue we need to address is not gun control-- it's people control. Yes, there is too much violence in our society, but unless we can eliminate the causes of violence, gun control will not stop the killings. There are better ways to stop violence than banning guns, Ms. Disarmed. Why not look at the real issues behind all the violence and address those first?

Signed,

Mr. Ennar Ray

1. What is the author's argument, or point of view, in the first letter? Do you agree with her support for her argument? Why or why not?

The AUTHORS ARGUMENT IS TO STOP The Sale of GUN. I do not support her argument because there are other weapons that are used to commit crime what we need is crime prevention.

2. What is the author's argument, or point of view, in the second letter? Do you agree with his support for his argument? Why or why not?

The author's argument.

3. With which argument do you agree, and why?

4. What facts support your argument on gun control? (You may find resources online to support your argument.) What information do you need to know before you can make a well-supported argument for or against gun control?

5. What technological devices could be used in public buildings to keep the general public safe from mass murderers?

MyReadingLab

REAL-LIFE READING

READING LABELS

Read the following label from a pesticide (insect killer) product and answer the questions that follow.

BUG-KILL

PESTICIDE SPRAY

Kills bugs inside and outside of your home.

Storage:
Store product in a cool, dry place, away from children and pets. Protect from freezing. Be sure nozzle is in the OFF position before storing.

Warning:
Harmful if swallowed. Can also cause eye and skin irritation. Avoid contact with skin or clothing. Wear long-sleeved shirt and long pants, socks, shoes, and gloves when spraying product.

First Aid:
If swallowed, call poison control center immediately for advice on treatment. Sip a glass of water but do not induce vomiting unless instructed to do so by doctor. If spray gets in the eyes, hold eyes open and rinse with water gently for 15-20 minutes. Call the emergency hotline for treatment at 1-800-999-0000.

Directions:
Remove pets from area before spraying. Turn nozzle on container to ON position before spraying.

Indoor Application
In kitchens and other rooms: Remove food, pets, and children from the area before spraying.
Cover counters, tables, chairs, and utensils before spraying. Shake container well and squeeze spray gun handle to dispense pesticide along floor under cabinets and along baseboards. Pets and people may re-enter area once spray has dried. Wash all surfaces (except sprayed areas) with soap and water after spraying.

Outdoor Application
Do not spray into the air or into a water supply. Hold spray nozzle 8-10" from the surface. Apply along the exterior of the home at ground level. Spot treat other areas such as in the garage or on a patio.

After Spraying: Wash hands and exposed skin with soap and water. If the container is empty, rinse thoroughly with water. Do not pour any unused product down any indoor or outdoor drains. Take unused product to a hazardous waste facility.

Hazard Statement
This product is hazardous to humans and animals. Read and follow application instructions carefully before using. Product may cause an allergic reaction in some individuals. Product is toxic to fish, reptiles, bees, and invertebrates. Do not use this product where it may run into ponds, gutters, storm drains, or ditches. Apply only when rain is not forecast for the next 24 hours. Do not spray when windy. Do not apply near blooming plants if bees are in the area.

Notice: Consumer assumes all risk of use, storage and handling of this product when not used according to instructions.

1. What precautions must be taken before using Bug Kill?

2. If Bug Kill gets in someone's eyes or mouth, what should be done?

3. What precautions should be taken after spraying?

4. Why is this product hazardous to humans? What should be done to avoid contamination to wildlife and water sources?

'G FOR COLLEGE

MyReadingLab

BUILDING VOCABULARY

Knowing the meanings to many word parts will help you determine the meanings of unfamiliar words. Make a list of English words using the word parts in the table below, and give their meanings. If you are unsure about a word, consult a dictionary. Then use the words to complete the sentences below. (* presented in previous lists)

PREFIXES	ROOTS	SUFFIXES
trans-: *across*	mis-, mit-: *to send* *	-tion, -sion-: *action, state of**
sub-: *under*	fer-: *to carry*	-ology: *the study of*
bio-: *life*	neur-: *nerve*	-ist: *one who*

WORDS

Use one of the words in your word list above in a sentence that reveals its meaning with a context clue. Read the sentence to a classmate and ask him or her to define the word.

MyReadingLab

CHAPTER PRACTICE 1

Read the passage and answer the critical-thinking-skills questions that follow.

pesticides (PEST-i-sides): chemicals that kill insects and are often harmful to the environment

pristine (pris-TEEN): without flaws or blemishes

unsustainable (un-sus-TANE-able): not able to be maintained or continued

[1] Farmers are only one-half of the food production equation. Consumers also determine how and what food is produced. If consumers consistently select certain types of foods, farmers will try to supply them. In many cases, consumer demand encourages some of the more damaging environmental consequences of modern agriculture.

[2] Most of the **pesticides** sprayed on vegetable and fruit crops are applied to reduce crop "losses" that are caused by consumers who do not purchase fruits and vegetables with superficial signs of pest damage. The only way to produce **pristine** products is to apply hundreds of pounds of pesticides to completely eliminate pest insects. If consumers were willing to accept a visible but small amount of pest damage to fresh vegetables, then the amount of pesticides used on these crops could drop tremendously.

[3] Consumer demand for meat also fuels **unsustainable** farming practices. Most of the beef, pork, and poultry produced in the United States come from animals that are fed field-grown grain in enormous feed lots, called factory farms. The same production process holds for hogs, chickens, and turkeys. In fact, 66% of the cereal grain consumed in the United States, including 80% of the corn and 95% of the oats, is used to feed these animals. Because much of the energy consumed by an animal is used for maintenance rather than growth, the grain used as animal feed yields fewer calories in the form of meat. Put another way, a 10-acre field of corn can support 10 people if they eat the corn directly, but only 2 people if the corn is fed to cattle and then eaten as beef.

(Belk & Borden, *Biology Science for Life with Physiology* 3e. Pearson 2010. pp. 588-589)

1. The central point and argument of this passage is:

a. Farmers are only one-half of the food production equation.

b. Consumers also determine how and what food is produced.

c. Both farmers and consumers determine what food will be grown in U.S. agriculture.

d. Consumer demand encourages some of the more damaging environmental consequences of modern agriculture.

Continued...

MyReadingLab

CHAPTER PRACTICE 1

...continued

2. The author's purpose and tone for this passage is

a. to criticize how farmers use excessive amounts of pesticides to produce perfect-looking vegetables and fruits, and the tone is critical.

b. to inform readers about how meat production uses more grain products than eating the food directly, and the tone is objective.

c. to persuade consumers that they can help the environment by making better choices when choosing foods to eat, and the tone is persuasive.

d. to warn readers about dangerous chemicals used in their food production, and the tone is cautionary.

3. In this passage, the author is

a. biased in favor of buying fruits and vegetables without blemishes.

b. biased in favor of reducing the demand for meat, poultry, and perfect fruits and vegetables.

c. biased against eating meat, poultry, or dairy foods.

d. unbiased

4. Which of the following sentences is an opinion?

a. If consumers were willing to accept a visible but small amount of pest damage to fresh vegetables, then the amount of pesticides used on these crops could drop tremendously.

b. In fact, 66% of the cereal grain consumed in the United States, including 80% of the corn and 95% of the oats, is used to feed these animals.

c. If consumers consistently select certain types of foods, farmers will try to supply them.

d. Most of the beef, pork, and poultry produced in the United States comes from animals that are fed field-grown grain in enormous feed lots, called factory farms.

5. The intended audience for this passage is

a. Congressmen.

b. agricultural biologists.

c. consumers who are concerned about the future of our environment.

d. manufacturers of pesticides.

MyReadingLab

CHAPTER PRACTICE 2

Read the passage and answer the critical-thinking-skills questions that follow.

unbeknown (un-be-KNOWN): without one's knowledge

[1] The interests of both the employer and the public often coincide, as seen in the following case. Automobile manufacturers are required by the 1970 Clean Air Act to submit the results of 50,000-mile emissions tests on any new engine to the Environmental Protection Agency (EPA). Only one tune-up may be performed on each engine during these tests. In 1972, test results were submitted by the Ford Motor Company in its new 1973 model engines. Unfortunately, **unbeknown** to top-level management, four employees had ordered or directly performed illegal maintenance on the engines during testing. This maintenance included repeated replacement of spark plugs and resetting of ignition timing.

[2] A computer specialist discovered this illegal maintenance while examining computerized records of the testing. He wrote a memorandum outlining his findings to Lee Iacocca (then president of the Ford Motor Co.). Mr. Iacocca immediately informed the EPA and withdrew Ford's application for certification of its engines.

[3] Production schedules were delayed while new tests were conducted on an emergency basis. Ford also received a significant amount of negative publicity and was fined $7 million for both civil and criminal violations.

[4] The overzealous employees who were responsible for these illegal acts of engine maintenance failed to meet their obligations both to their employer and to the general public. Although they may have perceived themselves as loyal employees acting in the best interests of the company, in fact they were disloyal in their actions.

(Voland, Gerard. *Engineering by Design*, 2e. Pearson, 2004. p. 328.)

1. **The central point and argument of this passage is**

a. The interests of both the employer and the public often coincide, as seen in the following case.

b. Automobile manufacturers are required by the 1970 Clean Air Act to submit the results of 50,000-mile emissions tests on any new engine to the Environmental Protection Agency (EPA).

c. The employees who performed illegal maintenance on Ford's 1973 engines during EPA testing failed to meet their obligations both to their employer and to the general public.

d. A computer specialist discovered this illegal maintenance while examining computerized records of the testing.

MyReadingLab

CHAPTER PRACTICE 2

...continued

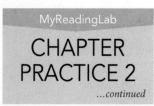

2. The author's purpose and tone for this passage is

a. to inform readers about an incident at the Ford Motor Co. in 1973, and the tone is objective.

b. to persuade readers that the illegal maintenance performed by the employees at the Ford Motor Co. in 1973 was disloyal and the tone is critical.

c. to criticize the Ford Motor Co. for performing illegal maintenance during a test for the EPA, and the tone is indignant.

d. to inform readers about how the president of Ford Motor Co. informed the EPA about the illegal maintenance done on the engines to be tested even though the consequences would be severe, and the tone is admiring.

3. In this passage, the author is

a. biased against employees who are unethical because their illegal actions can be harmful.

b. biased in favor of the Ford Motor Company for telling the truth about their engines to the EPA despite the severe consequences.

c. biased in favor of the employees who performed illegal maintenance because they were trying to help the Ford Motor Company look good to the EPA.

d. unbiased

4. Which of the following sentences is an opinion?

a. Automobile manufacturers are required by the 1970 Clean Air Act to submit the results of 50,000-mile emissions tests on any new engine to the Environmental Protection Agency (EPA).

b. Unfortunately, unbeknown to top-level management, four employees had ordered or directly performed illegal maintenance on the engines during testing.

c. A computer specialist discovered this illegal maintenance while examining computerized records of the testing.

d. Ford also received a significant amount of negative publicity and was fined $7 million for both civil and criminal violations.

5. The intended audience for this passage is

a. people interested in buying cars

b. engineering students

c. newspaper reporters

d. the Environmental Protection Agency

MyReadingLab

CHAPTER PRACTICE 3

fossil fuels: non-renewable energy sources such as coal and oil

Read the passage and answer the critical-thinking-skills questions that follow.

1 Because of human dependence on fossil fuels, urban areas produce large amounts of gaseous waste. These air emissions include carbon dioxide as well as combustion by-products, including nitrogen and sulfur oxides, small airborne particulates, and fuel contaminants such as mercury. Exposure to sunlight and high temperatures can cause some of these by-products to react with oxygen in the air to form ground-level ozone or smog. For individuals with asthma, heart disease, or reduced lung function, smog exposure can lead to severe illness, even death. When gaseous pollution enters the upper reaches of Earth's atmosphere, it can be carried on air currents to less-settled areas throughout the globe. Air emissions from coal-fired power plants throughout the Midwest cause severe acid rain in lightly settled regions of the northeastern United States, and air-borne toxins such as benzene and PCBs (polychlorinated biphenyls) have been found in high levels in animals in the Arctic.

2 Air pollution is a problem in both developed and less-developed countries. In less-developed countries, pollution control is weak or lacking altogether; in more developed countries, the sheer volume of fossil fuel use contributes to poor air quality. In the United States, the number of miles driven by car per household has nearly doubled in the last 25 years, partially due to an increase in the distance that individuals live from their workplaces. Development of suburban settlements outside the geographical limits of cities has been termed *urban sprawl*. Urban sprawl not only contributes to an increase in fossil fuel consumption but also affects wildlife through habitat destruction and fragmentation. Urban sprawl also impairs water quality via the destruction of wetlands and the increasing amount of paved surfaces, which funnel pollutants and warmed water into lakes, streams, and rivers.

(Belk & Borden, *Biology Science for Life with Physiology* 3e. Pearson 2010. pp. 415–416.)

1. The central point and argument of this passage is

a. Urban sprawl not only contributes to an increase in fossil fuel consumption but also affects wildlife through habitat destruction and fragmentation.

b. Because of human dependence on fossil fuels, urban areas produce large amounts of gaseous waste.

c. For individuals with asthma, heart disease, or reduced lung function, smog exposure can lead to severe illness, even death.

d. Air pollution, caused by the combustion of fossil fuels, can create problems for the environment in both developed and less-developed countries.

Continued...

MyReadingLab

CHAPTER PRACTICE 3

...continued

2. The author's purpose and tone for this passage is

- **a.** to warn readers that air pollution can be harmful to humans, and the tone is pessimistic.
- **b.** to advise readers against burning fossil fuels, and the tone is righteous.
- **c.** to inform readers about the effects of air pollution, and the tone is straightforward.
- **d.** to persuade readers that air pollution is bad for human health, and the tone is grim.

3. In this passage, the author is

- **a.** biased against the burning of fossil fuels.
- **b.** biased in favor of urban sprawl.
- **c.** biased against less-developed countries.
- **d.** unbiased.

4. Which of the following sentences is an opinion?

- **a.** Because of human dependence on fossil fuels, urban areas produce large amounts of gaseous waste.
- **b.** These air emissions include carbon dioxide as well as combustion by-products, including nitrogen and sulfur oxides, small airborne particulates, and fuel contaminants such as mercury.
- **c.** In the United States, the number of miles driven by car per household has nearly doubled in the last 25 years, partially due to an increase in the distance that individuals live from their workplaces.
- **d.** In less-developed countries, pollution control is weak or lacking altogether; in more developed countries, the sheer volume of fossil fuel use contributes to poor air quality.

5. The intended audience for this passage is

- **a.** biology students
- **b.** the general public
- **c.** environmental scientists
- **d.** government officials

CHAPTER REVIEW: OUTINE

The outline below is a summary of all the important points in this chapter. Review the learning objectives and complete the missing information on the outline.

I. Critical Thinking

A. Learning to think ....

....

B. Critical thinking is used to ....

....

1. An argument, or claim, is ....

....

C. Four steps of Critical Thinking:

1. Identify the ....
2. ....
3. ....
4. ....

II. Elements of Critical Thinking

A. Distinguishing Facts from Opinions

1. A .... can be proven true or false by observable or measurable means.
2. Opinions include ....

....

B Author's Purpose and Tone

1. .... explains why the author wrote the reading selection.
2. Author's tone refers to the ....

....

3. .... is the use of expressions that are different than their literal meanings (Ex: metaphors, similes, and connotations).

Continued...

CHAPTER REVIEW: OUTINE

...continued

C. The Intended Audience

1. The author's intended audience explains ....

D. Detecting Bias

1. Bias is present when an author ....

2. When the author's attitude about the topic is not evident and there is no negative or positive spin about something, the writing is ....

MyReadingLab

READING LAB ASSIGNMENTS

1. Login to **MyReadingLab** and in the menu click on Reading Skills. In the **Learning Path** select **Critical Thinking** to review the skills by reading the brief overview and models. Watch the short animation and then complete any practices or tests as needed or as directed by your instructor.

2. Click on **Reading Level** and choose two stories to read and answer the questions to the best of your ability. Your Lexile level will increase as your reading comprehension improves.

ON THE WEB

You can learn more about critical thinking on the Web by doing an Internet search on the term *critical thinking* or *critical reading skills.* Several Web sites and videos are available on this topic, which may enhance your understanding.

MyReadingLab

MONITOR YOUR LEARNING

In this chapter you learned about critical thinking skills. Write a paragraph telling what you learned about these skills, how you learned them, and how you can use them to improve your learning and reading comprehension. When you have finished writing, read your paragraph as if you were reading someone else's paragraph for the first time. Check for missing words, spelling, punctuation, and sentence structure.

7 STUDY SKILLS

FOCUS ON: Your World

Today's world is much different than the one in which your parents and grandparents lived. Due to innovations in technology, we are much more in touch with the international community than ever before, changing the world into a "global village." We encounter people from all nations and ethnic groups on a daily basis at school, at work, and on our computers or phones. Although we may differ in language and cultural practices, many of the same problems affect all societies: poverty, hunger, human rights abuses, and war, to name a few. Each generation makes a contribution toward solving these problems. Your own generation will be looking for answers and each of you has an opportunity to do something to make the world a better place. Learning about these and other national and international issues will give you a better understanding of these issues, thus equipping you to face them more readily.

By the end of this chapter, you will

LEARNING OBJECTIVES

1. know how to take good notes.
2. learn how to study for tests and take tests.
3. understand how to evaluate and use Web sites.

GETTING THE MOST BANG FOR YOUR BUCK

Getting the most bang for your buck means getting the most value from something you paid for. In your case, it's a college education that has probably cost you a lot of time and money. Why not get the most out of it and pass all of your courses on the first try? Why not get at least Bs in all of your courses and qualify for scholarships? You can accomplish both of these goals by learning some ways to study and take tests efficiently. However, you must be willing to take the time to learn them and then use them. Most students who learn study techniques don't apply them, and so they never see any improvement. Knowing how to study and applying the study skills you learn can help you earn higher grades.

There is very little reason for anyone to fail a course in college and have to pay for it a second time. The main reason why students fail is because they don't put in the amount of time or effort needed to pass. They give up, they decide it's too hard and that they would rather do other things with their time. The result is failure, dropping out, and wasting time and money. As discussed in Chapter 1, college is a huge commitment, and students who are not ready or willing to make a big effort will not succeed. Chances are that if you are still in this course at this point, you are willing to work toward success. Attaining success is like planting an orchard: you plant the seeds, you take time to water, fertilize, and treat for bugs and fungi. After you've watched them grow year after year, the trees finally bear fruit and the crop is ready for picking. Similarly, any long-term goal requires patience and persistence.

OBJECTIVE 1

Know how to take good notes.

HOW TO TAKE GOOD NOTES

In the first chapter of this text you learned how to use the Four Step Reading process to gain better comprehension and recall for your reading assignments. A fifth step, note-taking, should also be included in your study program. Research done on the effectiveness of note-taking have shown that students who took notes in addition to listening to lectures scored an average of one letter grade higher than students who used a highlighter on printed copies of the PowerPoint slide notes.

Another reason why you should take notes is that it helps you stay focused during class or while reading. You are less likely to drift off into daydreams if you are actively engaged in writing. Note-taking not only gives you a more complete account of the information, but it also reinforces your memory with a kinesthetic action. As mentioned in Chapter 1, we all have different learning styles that address different learning modes: visual, audio, and kinesthetic. The more ways you can rehearse the information using all three modalities, the more likely you will remember it. Also, many students are now using electronic resources such as e-texts, and taking notes is essential if annotating and highlighting features are not available. There are some easy steps to follow when taking good notes from a lecture or a reading selection that will improve your learning.

STEP 1

Always complete the reading assignment before class begins.

Complete your assignments following the four-step reading process described in Chapter 1. This will provide the background information that you need to make sense of the new information you will learn in class. It is also necessary to help you decide what to take notes on because you will already know the major and minor ideas. You will be able to take fewer notes in class, thus focusing on the important ideas and leaving out the minor details.

STEP 2

During class, pay attention.

If you have trouble staying with the instructor or keeping up in class, bring a digital recorder and record the lecture so you can play it back at your own pace. You should still take notes in class but skip lines so you can add details later that you missed during the lecture. This will cut down on the amount of time needed to take the notes after class.

STEP 3

Focus on the big ideas first.

Use your reading assignment before the lecture or class to make an outline of the major topics that will be discussed. During the lecture, fill in the minor details. Use any style of note-taking that is best for you, but the most popular styles are informal outlines, concept maps, and Cornell notes. Whichever method you use, remember to state ideas in your own words so you can review as you are taking notes.

STEP 4

Revise and review your notes after class.

Remember that studying is something you must do every day in order to move information from your short-term memory into your long-term memory. Review your notes as soon as possible on the same day as the class lecture. The longer you wait, the more your memory will fade. During your daily study sessions, go through your notes and make additions, corrections, diagrams, charts, or any other details that will help you remember the information. If you recorded the lecture or if it is available online, play it and check your notes to make sure they are complete and accurate. Each day, start by reading through the section you wrote for the previous day and then revise your notes from today's class. This will reinforce your memory and understanding of the major ideas. If you think you missed something important, consult another student or your professor for the information. (Don't worry that your professor will think you weren't listening; he or she will be delighted that you are interested!)

How to Take Notes

Here are some important tips on how to take good notes:

- **Come to class 5 minutes early with an outline of the topics** that will be discussed already written in your notebook. You may find this in the assigned reading or in a professor's course outline for the class. Use time before class to get your note-taking materials ready. If you are using a computer, get it open to the place where you will begin your note-taking. Use a large notebook and leave space to make additional notes, diagrams, charts, or drawings during your review session later. Skip lines and make a wide margin—at least 2 1/2 inches—for adding information later.
- **Don't try to write down everything the professor says**. Listen for key ideas, such as terms, processes, or important events. Underline or highlight terms so you can find them easily, and be sure to annotate them in the margins.
- **Copy anything the professor writes on the board**, including diagrams or charts.
- **If the visual aids** (like graphs) **are available online, write down where they can be found** so you can add them to your notes later.
- **Listen carefully for major details and jot them down quickly but legibly**. Try to listen for the most important information. For example, if the professor describes an experiment, note the name or source of the research and the information learned from it rather than every step of the experiment. You can find out those details later if needed.
- **Use abbreviations as much as possible**. Use phrases, not sentences.
- **Choose a seat in class where you will not be distracted**. Sitting toward the front of the class makes it easier to stay focused. Stay away from talkers. They can still be your friends outside of class, but they may destroy your grade if you sit next to them in class.
- **Ask questions about anything that is not clear**, but be respectful of other

people's time. Asking one or two questions to clarify a point is okay, but if you are really lost, make an appointment to see the professor during office hours instead of using a lot of class time.

- **When taking notes from a reading assignment, podcast, video, e-text, or PowerPoint presentation, follow the same techniques described above,** and write down the source and page numbers where the information was found in case you need to refer back to it later.

Cornell Notes

You used Cornell notes at the conclusion of Chapter 1 to review the most important concepts. This system was developed by Walter Pauk at Cornell University in the 1950s and it remains popular today. It is the best way to prepare for tests and learn material because it requires students to create questions and answer them. To create Cornell Notes, you should:

1. Divide your paper into two columns: a question/cue column on the left and a notes column on the right.
2. Take notes on a lecture or reading assignment in the notes column.
3. Later, write questions or general topics in the left side from the notes.
4. To study, cover the right column and read the questions in the left column, reciting the answers.

Use the Cornell Note system to take notes on a mini-lecture found online at MyReadingLab. In the menu on the home page, click on Study Skills, and then Learning Path. Click on "Effective Note Taking" and click "Overview" to fill in the Cornell Notes below as you follow the lecture online. Remember to use the tips you learned while taking notes and to pause the presentation or slide back if you need to see a slide again. If you don't have access to this online lecture, do an Internet search for a similar mini-lecture on note-taking or a Web site page and complete your own Cornell Notes for the mini-lecture.

QUESTION/CUE	NOTES
Why are good notes important?	• .... • Taking notes makes you pay attention
What are the characteristics of good notes?	• .... • .... • .... • Write questions in margins & to study, try to answer without looking at notes
3 Stages of note-taking	Before class: • .... • .... • .... During class: • .... • .... • .... After class • .... • Ask questions and add information

To use your Cornell Notes as a study guide, cover the notes column with your hand and try to answer the questions in the question or cue column. If you wrote general topics instead of questions (as in the last cue, "3 Stages of note-taking"), turn the topics into questions and try to answer them. For example, you might ask "What are the 3 stages of note-taking?"

Formal and Informal Outlines

Many students prefer to use outlines when taking notes from a reading selection. Outlines show relationships between major and minor ideas, so you can see what elements belong to a larger group. It's a good idea to write down page numbers when taking notes on an outline so you can find the information easier if needed.

Formal outlines use Roman numerals, letters, and numbers to show a hierarchy of ideas. The most general concepts are listed first next to the margin, and the more specific concepts are indented under the major ones. The writing is very succinct on an outline, using only words or phrases instead of sentences. The most common formal outlines follow the format below. Notice how each level down the hierarchy is indented to show that it is a subclass, or part, of the topic above it. The length of an outline depends on how much information you wish to record. You can use as many Roman numerals, letters, or numbers as you need in the order shown below.

Formal Outline Format

Central Idea or Thesis Statement

Roman numerals —— **I.** Topic of a section or division

Upper case letters —— **A.** Major detail

Numbers —— **1.** Minor detail

Lower case letters —— **a.** a detail relating to the minor detail

Example:

Read the following example of an outline on religion in the United States.

Central Idea: → Religion in the United States remains an important part of social life.

I. Religion is a major social institution (p. 403)

- **A.** Types of religions[1]
  - **1.** Churches
    - **a.** state churches
    - **b.** denominations
  - **2.** Sects
    - **a.** charismatic leaders and suspicion of the larger society.
  - **3.** Cults
    - **a.** unconventional beliefs and practices
- **B.** U.S. is one of the most religiously diverse nations[2]
  - **1.** 73% Christian
  - **2.** 2% Jewish

([1] Source: Macionis, John. *Society: The Basics*, 12e. Pearson 2013. p. 403.). ([2] Source of data: Wikipedia.org.)

3. 0.8% Muslim
4. 0.7 % Buddhist
5. 0.4% Hindu
6. 23.1% Other religions and non-religious people

Informal Outlines

An **informal outline** is a simpler way to take notes from a reading selection because it doesn't rely on a strict format using letters or numbers. The indentations on each line show which ideas belong together. Sometimes bullets are used instead of numbers for lists. For example:

Religion is a major social institution (p. 403)

  Types of religions

   • Churches

     state churches

     denominations

   • Sects

     charismatic leaders and suspicion of the larger society.

   • Cults

     unconventional beliefs and practices

Making an Informal Outline

Directions: Read the following selection from a sociology book and complete the missing notes in the informal outline.

Majority and Minority: Patterns of Interaction

Social scientists describe interaction between majority and minority members of a society in terms of four models: pluralism, assimilation, segregation, and genocide.

Pluralism

Pluralism is a state in which people of all races and ethnicities are distinct but have equal social standing. In other words, people who differ in appearance or social heritage all share resources roughly equally.

The United States is pluralistic to the extent that almost all people have equal standing under the law. In addition, large cities contain countless "ethnic villages" where people proudly display the traditions of their immigrant ancestors. These include New York's Spanish Harlem, Little Italy, and Chinatown; Philadelphia's Italian "South Philly"; Chicago's "Little Saigon"; and Latino East Los Angeles. New York City alone has more than 300 magazines, newspapers, and radio stations in more than ninety languages (Paul, 2001; Logan, Alba, & Zhang, 2002; New York Community Media Alliance, 2011).

But the United States is not truly pluralistic, for three reasons. First, although most people value their cultural heritage, few want to live exclusively with others exactly like themselves (NORC, 2011: 667–70). Second, our tolerance for social diversity goes only so far. One reaction to the growing proportion of minorities in the United States is a social movement to make English the nation's official language. Third, as you will see later in this chapter, people of various colors and cultures do not have equal social standing.

(Macionis, John. *Society: The Basics*, 12e. Pearson 2013. pp. 282-283.)

MAJORITY AND MINORITY: PATTERNS OF INTERACTION p. 282

Social scientists describe interaction between majority and minority members of a society in terms of four models:

....

Pluralism: ....

....

....

....

Large U.S. Cities contain "ethnic villages"

- New York's Spanish Harlem, Little Italy, and Chinatown
- ....
- ....
- ....

U. S. is not truly pluralistic for three reasons (p. 283)

- ....
  ....
- our tolerance for social diversity is limited
- ....
  ....

Notice how the second bulleted item in the last section was reworded to save writing. Whenever possible, try to express ideas in the shortest form without leaving out the most important point. Also, notice the term *pluralism* was underlined. Remember to underline or highlight terms you must learn so you will remember to pay close attention to them and find them more easily.

Taking Notes Digitally

If you are using an e-text in a college course, you can still take notes using the online note-taking feature available in most e-text programs. The same principles apply to note-taking as described above. However, you must click on the notes icon, type in your notes and remember to save them. You should double-space notes and leave wide margins. Printing your notes and keeping them filed in your notebook will allow you to study anytime and not just when you're online or on your computer. Remember to write down page numbers and the source from where your notes were taken so you can refer back to the text when needed. If you need to add additional notes you can hand write them between the lines or in the margins if you leave enough space.

To make outlines, you can use an outline template on your computer. Templates are preset format programs and most word document programs have them. In Microsoft Word, for example, you can create an outline by going under the Format menu and clicking on Bullets and Numbering, and then click Outline Numbered tab. As you fill in notes, the program will automatically set up the information in an outline format.

QUESTION/CUE	NOTES
	Remember to skip lines when taking notes so you can add information later if needed.

To do Cornell notes, make your own template using a table. Using the Table tool in your word document toolbar, make a table that is 2 columns wide and 2 rows long. Copy the template as shown in the sample exercise above for Cornell notes and take notes in the bottom right column. Later you can type questions in the cue column on the left and use those to study the material.

MyReadingLab

PRACTICE 1

Directions: Fill in the missing information on the Cornell Notes below.

LOW-INCOME COUNTRIES

agrarian: rural or agricultural societies dependent upon the land.

Low-income countries cover 18 percent of the planet's land area and are home to 17 percent of its people. Low-income countries, where most people are very poor, are mostly **agrarian** societies with some industry. Fifty-three of these nations are spread across Central and East Africa and Asia. Population density is generally high, although it is greater in Asian countries (such as Bangladesh) than in Central African nations (such as Chad and the Democratic Republic of the Congo).

In poor countries, 36 percent of the people live in cities; a majority inhabit villages and farms as their ancestors have done for centuries. In fact, half the world's people are farmers, most of whom follow cultural traditions. With limited industrial technology, they cannot be very productive—one reason that many endure severe poverty. Hunger, disease, and unsafe housing shape the lives of the world's poorest people.

Those of us who live in rich nations such as the United States find it hard to understand the scope of human need in much of the world. From time to time, televised pictures of famine in very poor countries such as Ethiopia and Bangladesh give us shocking glimpses into the poverty that makes every day a life-and-death struggle for many in low-income nations.

(Macionis, John. *Society: The Basics*, 12e. Pearson 2013. pp. 228-229.)

QUESTION/CUE	NOTES
What characterizes low-income countries?	Low-income Countries: • most people very poor & agrarian (farming) • 53 nations in .... • .... • .... majority live in villages & farms • limited .... • ...., and unsafe housing
agrarian	agrarian: rural or agricultural societies dependent upon the land.

MyReadingLab

PRACTICE 2

Directions: Read the following selection about education and complete the formal outline below.

SCHOOLING AND ECONOMIC DEVELOPMENT

The extent of schooling in any society is tied to its level of economic development. In low- and middle-income countries, which are home to most of the world's people, families and local communities teach young people important knowledge and skills. Formal schooling, especially learning that is not directly connected to survival, is available mainly to wealthy people who can afford to pursue personal enrichment. The word *school* is from a Greek root that means "leisure." In ancient Greece, famous teachers such as Plato, Socrates, and Aristotle taught aristocratic, upper-class men who had plenty of spare time. The same was true in ancient China, where the famous philosopher K'ung Fu-tzu (Confucius) shared his wisdom with just a privileged few.

Today, schooling in low-income countries reflects the national culture. In Iran, for example, schooling is closely tied to Islam. Similarly, schooling in Bangladesh (Asia), Zimbabwe (Africa), and Nicaragua (Latin America) has been shaped by the distinctive cultural traditions of these nations.

All low-income countries have one trait in common when it comes to schooling: There is not much of it. In the poorest nations (including several in Central Africa), more than one-fourth of all children never get to school (World Bank, 2012); worldwide, one-third of all children never make it as far as the secondary grades. As a result, about one-sixth of the world's people cannot read or write.

(Macionis, John. *Society: The Basics*, 12e. Pearson 2013. pp. 406–407.)

SCHOOLING AND ECONOMIC DEVELOPMENT (pp. 406–407)

I. Schooling in any society is tied to ....

....

A. In low- and middle-income countries families and local communities ....

....

B. Formal schooling- ....

....

1. Historical examples: ....

....

C. Today, schooling in low-income countries reflects the national culture.

1. Iran: ....

2. School shaped by the distinctive cultural traditions in ....

....

D. All low-income countries do not have much schooling

1. In poorest nations (several in Central Africa), more than one-fourth of all children ....

....

2. ....

....

3. ....

....

....

....

MyReadingLab

PRACTICE 3

Directions: Read the following selection about education and complete the informal outline below.

THE CAUSES OF WORLD HUNGER

Although there is technically enough food to feed the entire world population, one out of every 8 people goes hungry daily. There are many causes of hunger that explain why some areas of the world experience more hunger than others. First, natural disasters have tragic consequences for low-income countries that do not have the resources to deal with a calamity such as a flood or earthquake and to provide enough food for victims. Some areas experience severe drought that causes crop failure and loss of livestock. A second cause of hunger is war. During war, millions of people are displaced from their homes where many have farms. Starvation is often used as a means to force opponents into submission by seizing food and livestock or by mining fields and wells. A lack of supplies for farming and keeping livestock make it difficult to conduct agriculture during times of conflict. Roads, warehouses, and markets are all impacted by war, preventing food and supplies from reaching those most needy. A third cause of hunger is overuse of natural resources. In low-income countries, agricultural practices do not make best use of the land and resources. Overuse of land and deforestation result in erosion, salinization (salt in the soil), and desertification (forming deserts). In Africa, for example, soil degradation over the next 40 years could reduce crop yields by half.[1]

([1] Withgott & Brennan, *Essential Environment*, 3e. Pearson. 2009. p. 138.)

CAUSES OF WORLD HUNGER (p. 138)

There is enough food to ....

....

....

Causes of hunger:

- ....

  cause loss of crops and livestock

- War
    - ....

      ....
    - ....

      ....

- ....
  ....
- ....
  ....
- ....
  - Low-income countries: agricultural practices mis-use land and resources
  - ....
    ....

U-REVIEW 1

Review the concepts for note-taking by completing the self-test below.

1. Why is it important to take notes on material you must learn?

a. Note-taking is expected by most professors.

b. The notes taken in class have different information than the textbook.

c. Taking notes will help you understand and recall the information better than just reading, highlighting, and annotating.

2. Why should you complete all reading assignments before the class lecture?

a. Reading ahead will keep you from getting behind.

b. Reading the information first will provide the background information you need so you can understand more and know what to take notes about.

c. If you read about the topic first you will not have to take notes during the lecture.

3. Which of the following is NOT an important step in note-taking?

a. focus on big ideas first and major details

b. state ideas in your own words

c. use complete sentences

4. The best note-taking system to use for studying a subject is

a. concept mapping

b. Cornell note system

c. formal outlines

5. When taking notes from an online source such as an e-text, you should

a. double-space, leave wide margins, and print your notes.

b. save the online resource on a device such as a USB flash drive or cloud.

c. read only the sections at the beginning and end of the selection.

OBJECTIVE 2

Learn how to study for tests and take tests.

STUDYING FOR TESTS AND TAKING TESTS

Getting good grades in college often depends on achieving good test grades. It is surprising that many students believe that the students who get the highest test scores are the smartest people. This may be true sometimes when a test involves logical thinking and problem-solving, but usually the highest-scoring students are those who have taken the time to prepare for the test. In fact, colleges are filled with very intelligent students who do not have high grades due to their lack of effort. So you don't have to be the smartest student in the class to score well on a test—you just have to be well prepared mentally and physically.

Very few students like taking tests, but tests are one of the most efficient ways to find out what students have learned and whether they can apply their new skills. Many students become so nervous before a test that they have a difficult time remembering what they have learned. Some exhibit all the common signs of stress: rapid heartbeat, sweating, dry mouth, dizziness or a headache. All of these symptoms are reactions to the brain's perception of something fearful.

The brain sends out messages that something bad is about to happen. The body responds to these messages by producing hormones that increase blood pressure and produce some of the aforementioned symptoms. The brain then goes into overload, making it difficult to think. This kind of testing anxiety is a real phenomenon and anyone who has experienced it knows it can have a very negative effect on performance. The keys to avoiding test anxiety are to be well prepared academically and physically and to have a positive mental attitude.

Academically Well Prepared

Students are often very busy people with part-time or full-time jobs, family commitments, and daily responsibilities. Finding enough time to study can be a real challenge, but the key to academic preparedness is to allow yourself ample time to absorb the material. As such, studying for all tests in a course begins on the first day of class. It is an on-going, daily process (as described in Chapter 1) that enables you to move information from your short-term memory into your long-term memory. This includes completing reading or writing assignments by their due dates, attending class, keeping up with homework and reviewing your notes on a daily basis. Waiting until the day before the test to study will not prepare you adequately. You must learn the material as you receive it, reviewing it frequently. This is why it's so important to use a reading-study strategy such as the four-step reading process or SQ3R as you are reading. Note-taking is also an important part of preparing for tests because the action of writing the information will help your brain to remember it better. In fact, try to use a variety of strategies as described in the first chapter, as the more ways you can rehearse something, the better you will remember it.

Students often ask, "How long should I study?" The amount of time you study depends on how long it takes you to really learn the material and the difficulty of the material itself. Some subjects require a great deal of time to learn, and not everyone learns at the same rate.

Studying means reading your notes, the material you highlighted in your textbooks, looking up answers to questions in your texts, reviewing old tests and quizzes, and self-testing over and over and over again. Your goal should be to "overlearn" it so well that you could recite the information while doing something else, like playing basketball! If your instructor goes over the answers of a test or quiz, pay close attention. Chances are you will see the same or similar questions on unit tests or your final exam. Get the right answers so you can use them to study with later in the course. If your professor doesn't go over the test, look up the correct answers and write them down. Keep all test papers filed in your notebook and use them as study guides during the semester.

Learn the Terms

When studying, be sure to pay special attention to terms used in the subject you are studying. For instance, in sociology, you may have to know the meanings of terms like *counterculture* or *ethnocentrism*. If you are asked a question on a test with a term in it that you don't know, you can only try to guess at the correct answer. Clearly, knowing the terms of your subject is essential to doing well on a test, so write them into your notes and highlight or underline them.

Preparing for Tests

In addition to your usual daily review of your notes, you should begin preparing for big tests at least a week ahead of time. Here are some tips on how to prepare for a test:

- Set up a schedule of what you will study and when you will study it.
- Divide large units into chapters or topics and cover one area in each study session.
- Review the previous material briefly before tackling the next section.
- Say important concepts out loud and repeat them.
- Look for relationships between ideas.
- Group things together that are parts of larger concepts and study them as a "bundle." (For example: The causes of poverty: natural disasters, war, overuse of resources).
- Recite answers to questions and check your answers.
- Look up anything you don't know or find the answers using your course materials, your professor, and the online resources included in your course.
- Ask the professor which topics you should study.
- Think like a teacher and create questions on the most important topics, or use questions your professor asked in class.
- Make drawings, charts, diagrams, concept maps, or tables to summarize information.
- Form a study group or find a study partner so you can teach each other the information.

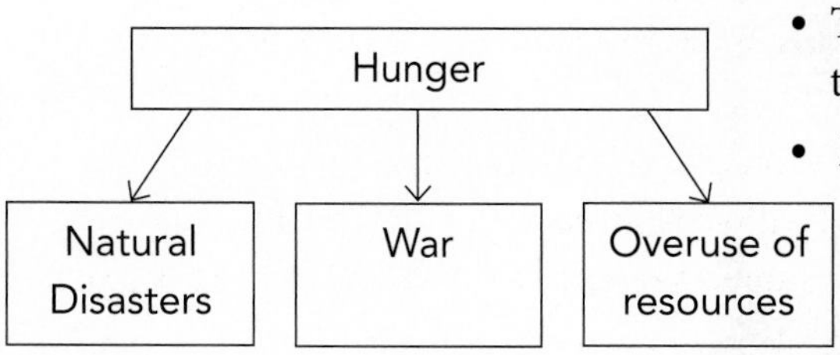

- Study in a quiet place, away from distractions.
- Turn off your phone to avoid interruptions.
- Study when you're alert, not when you're too tired to think.
- Take a 5-minute break every 45–55 minutes to get a drink and walk around.
- Read through all the material as many times as it takes to learn it. Frequent self-tests will let you know what you still need to study.
- Get help if you need it! Meet with your professor or a tutor at least a week before the test so you have time to study afterward

Physically Well Prepared

1. **Rest:** You can't do well on any test when you haven't had enough sleep and have skipped breakfast. *Always* get a good night's sleep the night before a test—at least 7 hours—so you'll feel alert and rested. Cramming until late at night will NOT help you do well on the test, so stop studying early enough to get adequate sleep. Listen to music or watch television if that helps you to relax, but don't think about the test. Set your alarm to give yourself extra time to get there if the test is in your first class. If you run late, the added stress will negatively affect your performance. If you have extra time while waiting for class to begin you can review, but don't begin studying new material. Use the time to strengthen what you already know.
2. **Food:** Eating a light, healthy breakfast that includes some protein and glucose (natural sugar found in fruits and juices) will help sustain your energy for the duration of the test and provide the chemicals your brain needs to function at its best. Whole-grain cereals and granola bars have protein, as does milk or soymilk. Skipping breakfast or just drinking coffee is not a good strategy. Have a fruit smoothie if you're not into solid foods in the morning. Limit your caffeine to one cup. Too much caffeine and sugar may make you unable to focus and think clearly. If your test is later in the day, eat a healthy snack (protein and glucose) and drink water at least 15 minutes before the test.
3. **Setting:** Sit away from distractions like other students who annoy you and avoid windows or doors where noise is loudest. Remember to turn off your phone. Come on time and prepared with whatever materials your professor told you to bring. Nothing is more frustrating to professors than students who come without pencils, pens, paper, answer sheets, or other required materials on test day. Your professor is not your school supply source, so don't even ask.

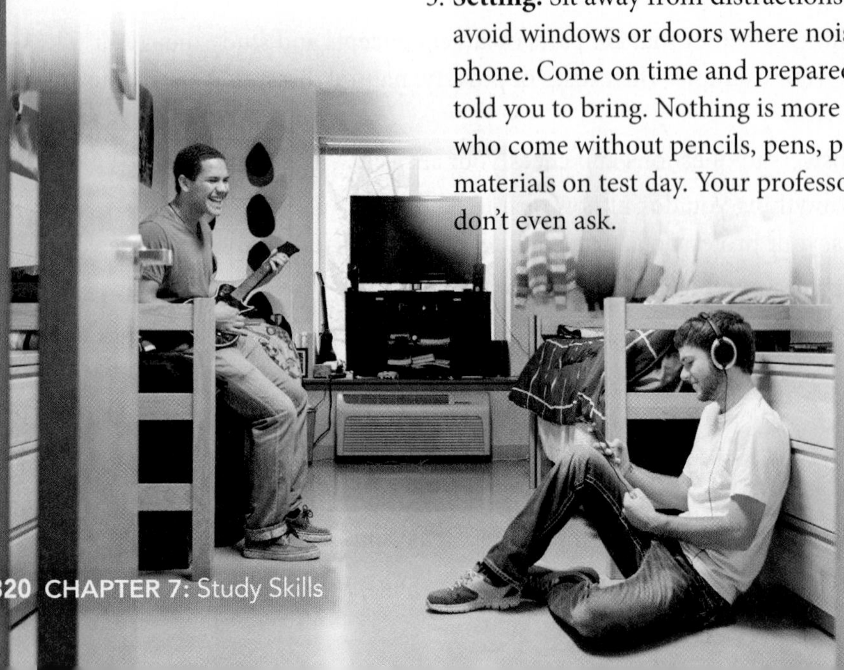

The Right Attitude

It's natural to be nervous before a test, and being on edge a little can help you be more alert. But worrying, fretting, and going into panic mode are not helpful. To release tension, take some deep breaths and let them out slowly. Try taking a deep breath, tightening all the muscles in your body and holding for 30 seconds; then, release them and take another deep breath. Think of a place where you would love to be and go there mentally for a few minutes. Tell yourself that you are prepared for this test and will do your absolute best. Visualize yourself answering each question carefully, confidently, and correctly. If you think positively about your performance you'll do better than if you think negatively during the test.

During the Test

Here are some pointers on what to do during the test:

- Before you start, look over the test to note how many questions there are and what topics are covered.
- Note the time the test ends, write it down, and keep an eye on the clock. Get started right away and stay on task.
- Make sure you have the correct test and all the pages to the test.
- Read the directions carefully! Note whether your answers must be in ink or pencil and if you must write on one side of the paper or both sides.
- If you are allowed scratch paper, make a 2-minute concept map or a *general* topical outline of the material. This may help you recall the details later.
- If there are passages to read, glance through the questions first to see what topics you should pay closest attention to while reading.
- Read the questions very carefully. Skipping one word or misreading a word can make a big difference in the answer that you choose.

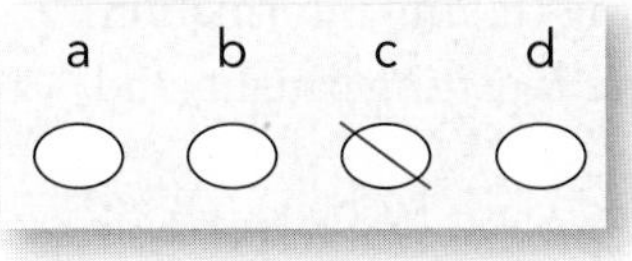

- Don't get stuck on any one question. Make a guess and move on to the next one. If you are using an electronically scanned answer sheet, mark the answer with a slash (/) so you can come back to it later. If you run out of time, at least you will have answered the question.
- Don't leave smudges on your answer sheet. Bring a good eraser and don't mark your answers too heavily so you can erase cleanly if needed.
- Don't make stray marks like question marks in the margins of your answer sheet. The scanner will read these as incorrect answers and mark them wrong. Use a slash as described above.
- Don't over-analyze questions. Often the answer that seems obvious is the correct one.
- Narrow down answer choices to the best two answers, and then choose the one you believe is correct based on what you know.
- Complete every question, even if you are not sure of an answer. Any you skip will be counted wrong. Besides, you might just guess correctly.
- For multiple-choice questions, read ALL of the answer choices; do not choose the first one that looks correct.

- Try adding each of the answer choices to a stem question (an incomplete sentence) to see which one seems best.
- Look for absolutes or generalizations like "always" or "never." These are often false statements.
- Watch for negative words in questions like "all of the following *except*," or "which of these is *not*." The answer you choose should be the false one.
- Sometimes you can get information from questions to help you with answers to other questions. Look for key terms in the questions.
- When you finish the test, go back to the beginning and check all your answers again to make sure you didn't skip any or marked the wrong answer. Spend additional time one the ones you marked with a slash.
- DO NOT CHANGE ANSWERS unless you are positive that the answer you have marked is incorrect. Usually your first choice is the correct one.
- Make sure you have ended up on the same question number as on your answer sheet. If you find it's off by one number, work backward from the end of the test to the beginning to find the mistake.
- If you are taking a test online, don't forget to SAVE your answers or SUBMIT them before logging out.

Cheating on Tests

Cheating on a test includes many different types of behaviors such as getting access to answers beforehand, getting unauthorized copies of a test in advance, looking at someone else's paper during the test, or using notes or other "cheat sheets" during a test. Cheating is much more common today than it was in the past. With phone cameras and access to electronic files, cheating has become an art form for some students. Appealing to students' ethical values is of little use. Those who cheat see absolutely nothing wrong with it, even though it is a form of lying (letting the professor think the answers are your own) and stealing (taking information without permission). The only concern that cheaters have is getting caught, and the consequences for cheating can be serious.

Students caught cheating on exams can be given a zero for that test or be given an F in the course. On one college campus, a student stole a final exam for a course and sold copies of it for $100 each. He didn't get very far because one of the honest students made the professor aware that the test was being sold. The test was immediately replaced with a new one and everyone who paid $100 ended up taking a totally different test. The student who was selling the tests was given an F in the course and withdrawn. Think twice before you cheat. Getting an F can lower your grade point average, and most colleges now keep records of crimes committed on campus by students. Students who repeat those kinds of acts are usually expelled. This also means losing the tuition or financial aid that was paid for the course, as well as the time that was invested.

MyReadingLab

PRACTICE 4

Directions: Circle the letters of the correct answers for the following questions without looking back for the answers. After you have completed the test, go back and look up the information. Correct your answers by marking the right answer with a check mark. On the lines after the questions, analyze why you missed some of the questions.

MULTIPLE CHOICE QUESTIONS

1. The process of studying for a test begins

a. when you have all your notes organized for the test.

b. after you have completed your Cornell notes for the material being tested.

c. the day before the test.

d. the first day of class by doing all the assignments and attending all the classes.

2. When preparing to study for a test, you should do all of the following except

a. Set up a schedule of what you will study and when you will study it.

b. Divide large units into chapters or topics and cover one area each study session.

c. Ask the professor about what questions will be on the test.

d. Turn off your phone to avoid interruptions.

TRUE OR FALSE QUESTIONS

3. You should get help if your understanding of a concept is unclear by meeting with a tutor or a professor one day before the test.

a. true

b. false

4. The amount of time you should study for a test varies because some subjects require a great deal of time to learn, and not everyone learns at the same rate.

a. true

b. false

SHORT ANSWER QUESTIONS

5. Group things together that are parts of larger concepts and study them as a ....

6. Make .... to summarize information.

7. Read through all the material as many times as it takes to learn it. Frequent .... will let you know what you still need to study.

READING STRATEGIES

MyReadingLab

PRACTICE 4

...continued

MATCHING QUESTIONS

Directions: Write the letter of the matching definition on the line after the term.

a. a note-taking format that uses 2 columns
b. The indentations on each line show which ideas belong together.
c. General topics and subtopics are linked to show relationships.

8. Concept map ....

9. Cornell Notes ....

10. informal outline ....

QUESTION ANALYSIS

The most common reasons why answers are wrong are:

- student didn't read the question correctly
- student didn't read all of the answer choices carefully
- student misunderstood the question or didn't understand it at all
- student didn't know the information
- student rushed through the test too quickly

After you complete this practice, look up the answers and mark the ones you missed with a check. Determine why you chose the wrong answers (the list above may help) and make a few notes about what happened below.

....

....

....

....

....

MyReadingLab

PRACTICE 5

Directions: Circle the letters of the correct answers for the following questions without looking back for the answers. After you have completed the test, go back and look up the information. Correct your answers by marking the right answer with a check mark. On the lines after the questions, analyze why you missed some of the questions.

1. To be physically well-prepared for a test, you should

a. do some exercises or go running on the night before the test.
b. cram for the exam for most of the night before the test.
c. take 5 minute breaks and do some sit-ups or yoga.
d. get at least 7 hours of rest the night before the test.

2. On the day of the test you should

a. stop at the bookstore to buy your supplies immediately before the test begins.
b. get to the test early to study the material you haven't covered yet.
c. set your alarm to give yourself plenty of extra time to get to the test.
d. eat a big breakfast with meat, eggs, and plenty of coffee with sugar.

TRUE OR FALSE QUESTIONS

3. Having a few cups of coffee with sugar before the test will help you stay alert and focused.

a. true
b. false

4. Eating some protein and glucose and drinking water will provide your brain with the chemicals it needs to function its best.

a. true
b. false

5. Granola bars, cereal, or fruit smoothies are good breakfast options.

a. true
b. false

ANSWER COMPLETION QUESTIONS

6. When choosing a seat, you should try to sit ....

....

....

7. You should arrive at the test 5 minutes early with ....

....

8. To relieve tension you should ....

....

....

9. You should visualize yourself answering each question ....

....

Continued...

MyReadingLab

PRACTICE 5

...continued

10. If you have extra time before the test begins, you should review ....

....

....

QUESTION ANALYSIS

After you complete this practice, look up the answers and mark the ones you missed with a check. Determine why you chose the wrong answers and make a few notes about what happened below.

....

....

....

....

....

MyReadingLab

PRACTICE 6

Directions: Circle the letters of the correct answers for the following questions without looking back for the answers. After you have completed the test, go back and look up the information. Correct your answers by marking the right answer with a check mark. On the lines after the questions, analyze why you missed some of the questions.

MULTIPLE CHOICE QUESTIONS

1. When you receive the test you should do all of the following *except*

a. notice the time the test ends and write it down.
b. sharpen your pencil or look through your book bag for pens or paper.
c. notice how many questions are on the test and what topics are covered.
d. make sure you have all the pages to the test.

2. If there are reading passages to read, you should

a. read the directions carefully.
b. glance through the questions to see what topics you should pay closest attention to while reading.
c. read the passages very carefully.
d. all of the above.

3. Which of the following testing strategies is *not* recommended?

a. If you think an answer may be incorrect, you should change it.
b. Don't spend too much time on one question. Come back to it later.
c. Make a guess by putting a slash through an answer choice that you need to check later.
d. Don't leave smudges on an electronic answer sheet and use a good eraser.

TRUE OR FALSE QUESTIONS

4. On electronic answer sheets, a scanner will see stray marks as incorrect answers and mark them wrong.
   a. true b. false

5. Often the answer that seems obviously to be the right one is the correct one.
   a. true b. false

6. A good testing strategy is to narrow down your answer choices to the best two answers and then make a guess about which one is correct.
   a. true b. false

7. Absolutes or generalizations like "always" or "never" are often false statements.
   a. true b. false

SHORT ANSWER QUESTIONS

8. When you finish the test, go back to the beginning and ....

   ....

   ....

9. If you are answering a stem question (an incomplete sentence), you should try adding .... to the stem question to see which one is the most likely to be true.

10. Sometimes you can get information from .... to help you with answers to other questions. Look for .... in the questions.

QUESTION ANALYSIS

After you complete this practice, look up the answers and mark the ones you missed with a check. Determine why you chose the wrong answers and make a few notes about what happened below.

....

....

....

....

....

....

....

U-REVIEW 2

Answer true or false to the following questions. If an answer is false, change the statement to make it true.

1. Read through all the material you will be tested on three times to learn it.

....

....

2. In formal outlines, the most general concepts are listed first next to the margin, and the more specific concepts are indented under the major ones.

....

....

3. Asking one or two questions to clarify a point during class is okay, but if you are really lost, you should make an appointment to see the professor during office hours instead of using a lot of class time.

....

....

4. You should complete the reading assignment for the lecture after the lecture so you will know what the reading is about.

....

....

5. For questions with phrases like "all of the following *except*," or "which of these is *not*" you should choose the false answer choice.

....

....

OBJECTIVE 3

Understand how to evaluate and use Web sites.

EVALUATING WEB SITES

Students depend on the Internet to help them learn and study in college. It is important to consider the reliability of the Web sites you are using for study or research. Generally, any Web site recommended by your instructor or college librarian will be trustworthy. However, if you're looking for Web sites on your own, you must evaluate them critically.

Why You Need to Evaluate Web Sites

When you open a Web site, you should notice who is publishing and writing the Web site. Educational institutions, national or international news organizations, textbook publishers, Web sites published by states or the U.S. government, and well-known organizations such as the International Red Cross are all trustworthy sources for Web sites. However, the majority of Web sites on the Internet are run by privately owned companies or individuals, and they are not authorized by anyone but themselves. As a result, the information they provide may be skewed or downright false. If a Web site is unfamiliar to you, you should use the following criteria and your critical thinking skills to evaluate the site for accuracy and current information.

Web Site Questions to Ask

1. Look at the URL to determine the source of the information. Sometimes unauthorized Web sites use the name of another source as a link and will claim to provide the same information as the original source, but often this is not what happens. For instance, if you search for the National Gallery of Art, it yields a whole list of sources. But only the **www.nga.gov** will take you to the authentic site of the National Gallery. The others are secondary sites that make reference to the gallery and may provide information such as reviews, but they are not as reliable as the primary source: the gallery itself. For reliable information, always go to the original source and the official Web site rather than a secondary source.
2. Most reliable Web sites provide a date to let you know when the information was last updated. Web sites without dates can be years old since many of the less reliable sites are often neglected or abandoned. If you need current facts, the data on the Web site may be too old and no longer true.
3. Remember to think critically. Who is the author of the information? What is his or her purpose for writing? Is the author trying to persuade you or influence your thinking? Is the site really just an advertisement to sell a product or service? Is the author biased? Does the author use facts that are true, accurate, and current? Are the sources of information provided?
4. Does the Web site have a professional appearance? Is the Web site sponsor clearly named? Web sites with spelling and grammatical errors indicate that the authors are not the experts they claim to be.

5. Look for a bibliography of sources at the end of the page. Check on the references that are provided to see if the information has been accurately reported.

Always check your facts with three or more sources to verify that the information is correct before you use it in a paper or research project. Blogs are written by anyone who wants to comment and are not reliable sources for information.

MyReadingLab

PRACTICE 7

Visit this Web site to evaluate it according to the criteria below by placing a check mark in the column under the appropriate description. When you complete your evaluation, add up the total points for each Web site and compare their results.

Visit the following Web site to complete the evaluation below: **www.nga.gov**

CRITERIA	Strongly Agree (3 points)	Somewhat agree (2 points)	Disagree (1 point)
The Web site provides current, up-to-date information.			
The Web site provides factual data that is provable as true or false.			
The Web site does not have biased or persuasive language.			
There are no products or services offered for sale on this Web site.			
The organization, institution, or company that produces the Web site is legitimate.			
The Web site has a professional appearance and the information is written correctly in standard English.			
There is a list of sources or a bibliography where more information can be found.			
Total Points:	....	....	....

MyReadingLab

PRACTICE 8

Visit this Web site by searching MIT Open Courseware Architecture to complete the evaluation below. Search: MIT Open Courseware Architecture

CRITERIA	Strongly Agree (3 points)	Somewhat agree (2 points)	Disagree (1 point)
The Web site provides current, up-to-date information.			
The Web site provides factual data that is provable as true or false.			
The Web site does not have biased or persuasive language.			
There are no products or services offered for sale on this Web site.			
The organization, institution, or company that produces the Web site is legitimate.			
The Web site has a professional appearance and the information is written correctly in standard English.			
There is a list of sources or a bibliography where more information can be found.			
Total Points:	....	....	....

MyReadingLab

PRACTICE 9

Choose one of the following Web sites and evaluate it using the criteria below. After your evaluation, compare your results with someone who evaluated a different Web site. Discuss what features you liked and disliked based on your evaluation scores.

Search using:
Conspiracy Theories
Rootsweb Alien Ancestors
Mystery Pile Crop Circles

CRITERIA	Strongly Agree (3 points)	Somewhat agree (2 points)	Disagree (1 point)
The Web site provides current, up-to-date information.			
The Web site provides factual data that is provable as true or false.			
The Web site does not have biased or persuasive language.			
There are no products or services offered for sale on this Web site.			
The organization, institution, or company that produces the Web site is legitimate.			
The Web site has a professional appearance and the information is written correctly in standard English.			
There is a list of sources or a bibliography where more information can be found.			
Total Points:	....	....	....

Which Web site earned the highest score for reliability? Why?

....

....

....

....

U-REVIEW 3

Answer true or false to the following questions or ask a partner and take turns answering them. Check your answers with the instructor.

1. .... All Web sites are reliable sources of information
2. .... If a Web site looks professional, it is probably a reliable source.
3. .... For reliable information, always go to the original source and the official Web site rather than a secondary source.
4. .... Web sites that are unbiased provide more balanced and factual information.
5. .... Blogs are reliable sources for information.

READING SELECTIONS

MyReadingLab

Reading 1
VOCABULARY PREVIEW

"Sexual Attitudes in the United States" by John Macionis

Match the words in the Word Bank by writing the letter of the word next to the matching definition. The paragraph numbers in parentheses indicate the location of each word in the reading selection, "Sexual Attitudes in the United States." Read the words in the paragraphs to determine the correct meanings as they are used in the context of the selection.

WORD BANK

a. contradictory (1)	b. profound (3)	c. counterrevolution (9)
d. premarital (11)	e. extramarital (16)	f. conformity (1)
g. conventional (5)	h. conservative (9)	i. stereotype (14)
j. norm (15)		

1. .... describes something that follows tradition
2. .... significant
3. .... average
4. .... outside of marriage
5. .... conflicting; opposite
6. .... generalization
7. .... a revolution that reacts against a previous revolution
8. .... traditional; usual
9. .... before marriage
10. .... actions in accordance with social standards

MyReadingLab

Reading 1 PREVIEW

Discuss the following questions with a partner or small group.

1. Do you think that your generation is more at ease discussing sex than your parents' or grandparents' generation? Why might this be so?
2. Why do you think that attitudes about sex have changed since the last generation, or previous generations?

After you preview the article, write one or two preview questions on the lines below:

MyReadingLab

Reading 1

"Sexual Attitudes in the United States" by John Macionis

The following excerpt is from a sociology textbook by Dr. John Macionis, a professor of sociology at the University of Pennsylvania. He has written 11 books that have been translated into 7 languages and sold internationally. He is a world traveler and is a Prentice Hall Distinguished Scholar. In this selection from *Society: The Basics*, Dr. Macionis examines the sexual attitudes and practices of people living in the United States. As you read, use the four-step reading process and take notes.

What was the basis for sexual attitudes in U.S. history?

1 What do people in the United States think about sex? Our culture's attitudes toward sexuality have always been somewhat contradictory. The early Puritan settlers of New England demanded strict conformity in attitudes and behavior, and they imposed severe punishment for any sexual misconduct, even if it took place in the privacy of the home. Later on, most European immigrants arrived with rigid ideas about "correct" sexuality, typically limiting sex to reproduction within marriage. Some regulation of sexual activity has continued ever since. As late as the 1960s, for example, some states legally prohibited the sale of condoms in stores. Until 2003, when the Supreme Court struck them down, thirteen states had laws banning sexual acts between partners of the same sex. Even today, "fornication" laws, which forbid intercourse by unmarried couples, are still on the books in eight states.

2 When it comes to sexuality, is the United States restrictive or permissive? The answer is both. On one hand, many people in the United

States still view sexual conduct as an important indicator of personal morality. On the other hand, sex has become more and more a part of popular culture carried by the mass media—one recent report concluded that the number of scenes in television shows with sexual content doubled in a mere ten years (Kunkel et al.,2005). Within this complex framework, we turn now to changes in sexual attitudes and behavior that have occurred over the course of the past century.

The Sexual Revolution

Why did attitudes about sexual behavior change in the 1920s?

3 Over the past century, the United States witnessed profound changes in sexual attitudes and practices. The first indications of this change came in the 1920s as millions of people migrated from farms and small towns to rapidly growing cities. There, living apart from their families and meeting new people in the workplace, young men and women enjoyed considerable sexual freedom, one reason that decade became known as the "Roaring Twenties."

4 In the 1930s and 1940s, the Great Depression and World War II slowed the rate of change. But in the postwar period, after 1945, Alfred Kinsey set the stage for what later came to be known as the sexual revolution. In 1948, Kinsey and his colleagues published their first study of sexuality in the United States, and it raised eyebrows everywhere. The national uproar resulted mostly from the fact that scientists were actually studying sex, a topic many people were uneasy talking about even in the privacy of their homes.

5 Kinsey also had some interesting things to say. His two books (Kinsey, Pomeroy, & Martin, 1948; Kinsey et al.,1953) became best-sellers because they revealed that people in the United States, on average, were far less conventional in sexual matters than most had thought. These books encouraged a new openness toward sexuality, which helped set the sexual revolution in motion. In the late 1960s, the sexual revolution truly came of age. Youth culture dominated public life, and expressions such as "sex, drugs, and rock-and-roll" and "if it feels good, do it!" summed up the new, freer attitude toward sex. The baby boom generation, born between 1946 and 1964, became the first cohort in U.S. history to grow up with the idea that sex was part of people's lives, whether they were married or not.

What were the causes of the sexual revolution?

6 New technology also played a part in the sexual revolution. The birth control pill, introduced in 1960, not only prevented pregnancy but also made having sex more convenient. Unlike a condom or a diaphragm, which has to be applied at the time of intercourse, the pill could be taken like a daily vitamin supplement. Now women as well as men could engage in sex without any special preparation.

7 Because women were historically subject to greater sexual regulation than men, the sexual revolution had special significance for them. Society's traditional "double standard" allows (and even encourages) men to be sexually active but expects women to be virgins until marriage and faithful to their husbands afterward. The survey data in Figure 6–1 show the narrowing of the double standard as a result of the sexual revolution. (Laumann et al., 1994: 198). The sexual revolution increased sexual activity overall, and it changed women's behavior even more than men's. Greater openness about sexuality develops as societies become richer and the opportunities for women increase.

Continued...

MyReadingLab

Reading 1

...continued

Figure 6-1 Diversity Sanpshot

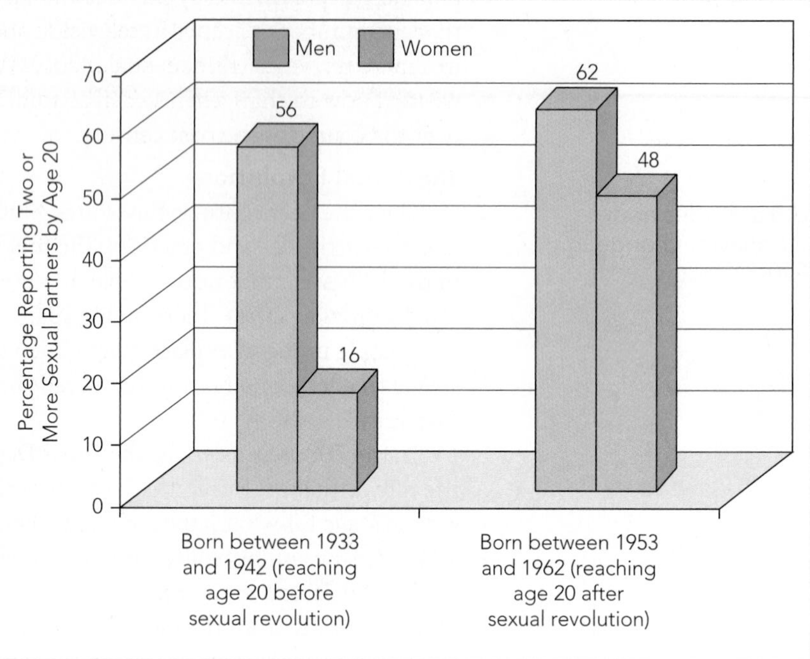

The Sexual Revolution: Closing the Double Standard

A larger share of men than women report having had two or more sexual partners by age twenty. But the sexual revolution greatly reduced this gender difference.

Source: Laumann et al. (1994:198)

Table 6-1 How We View Premarital and Extramarital Sex

Survey Question: "There's been a lot of discussion about the way morals and attitudes about sex are changing in this country. If a man and a woman have sexual relations before marriage, do you think it is always wrong, almost always wrong, wrong only sometimes, or not wrong at all? What about a married person having sexual relations with someone other than the marriage partner?

	Premartial Sex	Extramarital Sex
"Always wrong"	22.9%	80.5%
"Almost always wrong"	6.8	10.7
"Wrong only sometimes"	15.5	6.5
"Not wrong at all"	52.1	1.5
"Don't know"/No answer	2.7	1.8

Source: *General General Social Surveys, 1972–2008:* Cumulative Codebook (Chicago: National Opinion Research Center, 2009), p. 339.

What were the causes of the sexual counterrevolution?

The Sexual Counterrevolution

8 The sexual revolution made sex a topic of everyday discussion and sexual activity more a matter of individual choice. However, by 1980, the climate of sexual freedom that had marked the late 1960s and 1970s was criticized by some people as evidence of our country's moral decline, and the sexual counterrevolution began. Politically speaking, the sexual counterrevolution was a conservative call for a return to "family values" and a change from sexual freedom back toward what critics saw as the sexual responsibility valued by earlier generations. Critics of the sexual revolution objected not just to the idea of "free love" but to trends such as cohabitation (living together without being married) and unmarried couples having children.

9 Looking back, the sexual counterrevolution did not greatly change the idea that people should decide for themselves when and with whom to have a sexual relationship. But whether for moral reasons or concerns about sexually transmitted diseases, more people began choosing to limit their number of sexual partners, or not to have sex at all.

10 Is the sexual revolution over? It is true that people are making more careful decisions about sexuality. But the ongoing sexual revolution is evident in the fact that there is now greater acceptance of premarital sex as well as increasing tolerance for various sexual orientations.

Premarital Sex

11 In light of the sexual revolution and the sexual counterrevolution, how much has sexual behavior in the United States really changed? One interesting trend involves premarital sex—sexual intercourse before marriage—among young people. Consider first what U.S. adults say about premarital intercourse. Table 6–1 shows that 30 percent characterize sexual relations before marriage as "always wrong" or "almost always wrong." Another 16 percent consider premarital sex "wrong only sometimes," and about 52 percent say premarital sex is "not wrong at all." Public opinion is far more accepting of premarital sex today than was the case a generation ago, but our society clearly remains divided on this issue (NORC, 2009).

12 Now let's look at what young people *do*. For women, there has been marked change over time. The Kinsey studies reported that for people born in the early 1900s, about 50 percent of men but just 6 percent of women had premarital sexual intercourse before age nineteen. Studies of baby boomers, born after World War II, show a slight increase in premarital sex among men but a large increase—to about one-third—among women. The most recent studies show that by the time they are seniors in high school, slightly more than half of young men and women have had premarital sexual intercourse. In addition, sexual experience among high school students who are sexually active is limited—only 15 percent of students report four or more sexual partners. These statistics have remained much the same for the past twenty years (Laumann et al., 1994: 323–24, Centers for Disease Control and Prevention, 2008; Yabroff, 2008).

13 A common belief is that an even larger share of young people engage in oral sex. This choice reflects the fact that this practice avoids the risk of pregnancy; in addition, many young people see oral sex as something less than "going all the way." Recent research suggests that the share of young people who have had oral sex is greater than the share having had

Continued...

MyReadingLab

Reading 1

...continued

intercourse, but only by about 10 percent. Therefore, mass-media claims of an "oral sex epidemic" among young people in the United States are almost certainly exaggerated. Finally, a significant minority of young people choose abstinence (not having sexual intercourse). Many also choose not to have oral sex, which, like intercourse, can transmit disease. Even so, research confirms the fact that premarital sex is widely accepted among young people today.

Sex between Adults

What did Kinsey's research prove about sexual activity in the U.S.?

14 Judging from the mass media, people in the United States are very active sexually. But do popular images reflect reality? The Laumann study (1994), the largest study of sexuality since Kinsey's ground-breaking research, found that frequency of sexual activity varies widely in the U.S. population. One-third of adults report having sex with a partner a few times a year or not at all, another one-third have sex once or several times a month, and the remaining one-third have sex with a partner two or more times a week. In short, no single stereotype accurately describes sexual activity in the United States. Despite the widespread image of "swinging singles" promoted on television shows, it is married people who have sex with partners the most. In addition, married people report the highest level of satisfaction—both physical and emotional—with their partners (Laumann et al., 1994).

Extramarital Sex

15 What about married people having sex outside of marriage? This practice, commonly called "adultery" (sociologists prefer the more neutral term extramarital sex), is widely condemned in the United States. Table 6–1 shows that more than 90 percent of U.S. adults consider a married person's having sex with someone other than the marital partner to be "always wrong" or "almost always wrong." The norm of **sexual fidelity** within marriage has been and remains a strong element of U.S. culture. But actual behavior falls short of the cultural ideal. The Laumann study reports that about 25 percent of married men and 10 percent of married women have had at least one extramarital sexual experience. Stating this the other way around, it means that 75 percent of men and 90 percent of women have remained sexually faithful to their partners (Laumann et al.,1994:214; T.W.Smith,2006; NORC, 2009:339).

sexual fidelity: keeping sexual behavior only between two partners who are married or committed to a long-term relationship.

1,580 words divided by .... minutes = ... words per minute

MyReadingLab

Reading 1
REVIEW

A good review strategy to use after reading is to summarize what you just read in your own words. Take a few minutes to think about the author's most important point and any key ideas that helped to support or explain it.

Write a two- or three-sentence summary on the lines below.

....

....

....

....

....

MyReadingLab

Reading 1
COMPREHENSION QUESTIONS

The following questions will help you recall the main idea and details of "Sexual Attitudes in the United States." Read any parts of the article that you need to find the correct answers.

MAIN IDEAS

1. The central point of the reading selection is

a. People in the United States differ in their attitudes about sex according to age groups.

b. The Sexual Revolution began after Kinsey published the findings of his study in 1948 on the sexual behavior of Americans.

c. People in the United States have different attitudes about premarital and extramarital sex.

d. People in the United States have diverse attitudes about sex that have changed over the past century.

2. What is the implied main idea of paragraph 15?

a. What about married people having sex outside of marriage?

b. This practice, commonly called "adultery" (sociologists prefer the more neutral term extramarital sex), is widely condemned in the United States.

c. Extramarital sex is widely condemned by adults in the U.S., and sexual fidelity remains a strong element of U.S. culture.

d. Many people are faithful to their marriage partners.

SUPPORTING DETAILS

3. According to the passage, the sexual counterrevolution occurred because

a. people were concerned about moral decline and sexually transmitted diseases (STDs).

b. people opposed the practice of young teens getting pregnant.

c. birth control was readily available and convenient.

d. the sexual behavior of women was changing more rapidly than the sexual behavior of men.

MyReadingLab

Reading 1

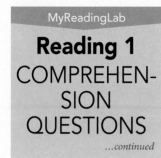

COMPREHENSION QUESTIONS

...continued

4. The two most common patterns of organization found in this passage are

a. time order
b. space order
c. compare and contrast
d. process

5. What is the relationship within the following sentence from paragraph 9? But whether for moral reasons or concerns about sexually transmitted diseases, more people began choosing to limit their number of sexual partners, or not to have sex at all.

a. compare and contrast
b. time order
c. statement and clarification
d. cause and effect

DRAWING CONCLUSIONS

6. According to Figure 6-1, which of the following is true?

a. The percentage of women who had two or more sexual partners by age 20 nearly tripled between one generation and the next one.
b. A larger share of women than men reported having two or more sexual partners by age twenty.
c. The sexual revolution caused a huge change in sexual attitudes.
d. Women are no longer afraid of having sex because of new developments in birth control.

7. According to Table 6-1, which of the following is false?

a. Most people in the survey agree that extramarital sex is "always wrong."
b. The percent of people who believe that premarital sex is "not wrong at all" is almost half of those surveyed.
c. The percent of people who believe that extramarital sex is "not wrong at all" is about the same as the percent of people who think it is "almost always wrong."
d. In general, the people surveyed have a higher approval of premarital sex than extramarital sex.

CRITICAL THINKING

8. Identify the following sentence from paragraph 10 as fact or opinion: But the ongoing sexual revolution is evident in the fact that there is now greater acceptance of premarital sex as well as increasing tolerance for various sexual orientations.

a. fact
b. opinion

9. What is the author's purpose and tone in this selection?

a. The author's purpose is to present one side of the argument that sexual attitudes in the U.S. are more permissive than in most countries and the tone is persuasive.
b. The author's purpose is to inform readers about sexual attitudes in the U.S. and the tone is objective.
c. The author's purpose is to persuade readers that Americans, and particularly women, are too open-minded about sex and the tone is critical.
d. The author's purpose is to explain how sexual attitudes in the U.S. have changed since the 1930s and the tone is nostalgic.

10. How would you evaluate the reliability of the information in this selection?
    a. The selection is factual, the source is cited, the author's name is given, the author is knowledgeable about the topic, and it has a recent copyright date, so it is reliable.
    b. The selection is factual with some opinions, the sources are cited, the author's name is given, but the source is unreliable.
    c. There is not enough information given about the source of the selection or the author, and the date of the publication, so it is not reliable.
    d. The selection has a reliable publisher and author, but not enough information about where the data came from, so it is somewhat reliable.

Reading 1 NOTE-TAKING REVIEW

Complete the notes for paragraphs 4-6 by filling in the missing information below.

QUESTION/CUE	NOTES
What slowed changes in sexual freedom during the 1930s–1940s?	*p. 335 par. 4* ....
....	Alfred Kinsey published the first study of sexuality in the U.S. in 1948, contributing to the sexual revolution. *(par. 5)*
What did his book reveal?	Kinsey's book revealed people in U. S. were ....
What happened in the1960s–1970s?	1960s–1970s: Youth culture dominated: freer attitude about " .... ". Born between 1946–1964, the .... grew up with the idea that sex was part of people's lives. (par. 6)
What new medical drug contributed to sexual revolution?	New medical drug—part of sexual revolution: the .... introduced in 1960—made sex convenient.
KEY TERMS	A revolution that resulted in more open and liberal attitudes toward sex.
....	An opposite reaction to the sexual revolution involving more traditional and conservative attitudes about sex.

Reading 1
VOCABULARY PRACTICE: GUESS THE PHRASE

contradictory (adj.)
profound (adj.)
counterrevolution (n.)
premarital (adj.)
extramarital (adj.)
conformity (n.)
conventional (adj.)
conservative (adj.)
stereotype (n.)
norm (n.)

Directions:

1. Form 2 teams of 2–4 people. One team (team A) will play against another (team B).

2. Write the numbers 1–20 on separate pieces of paper. Shuffle the number cards and put them in a pile face down on the table between both teams.

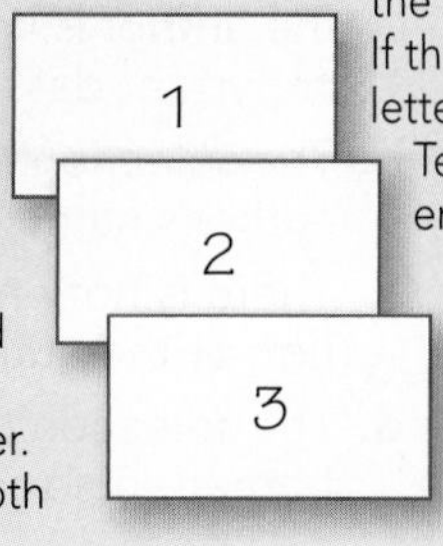

3. Each team will think of a word or short phrase and draw a blank for each letter on a piece of paper. Put the papers face up so that both teams can see them.

4. Decide which team will go first. Team A will draw the top number card and read the matching sentence from the sentences below for that number to Team B.

5. Team B will have 10 seconds to give the word from the word bank that completes the sentence correctly. They may look at the Word Bank, but they will only be allowed one answer. **Each word will be used twice.**

6. If the answer is correct, Team B receives one point and they will guess one letter for the word or phrase on Team A's puzzle. If they guess a correct letter, write the letter into the blanks wherever it occurs. Team B has10 seconds to guess the entire word or phrase, and only one guess is allowed. Guessing the puzzle correctly wins the team 5 points.

7. If the guess is incorrect or none given, the next sentence number is drawn by Team B and they will read the sentence with the matching number to Team A. Follow the same procedure as steps 4–6. Continue playing until all the sentences have been read or until a word or phrase puzzle has been guessed correctly.

The team with the highest number of points wins!

Example

S T U D Y   B U D D Y

1. The study that compared teenagers in 1950 to 2010 showed a .... increase in the percentage of those who engaged in sex before age 18.
2. The early Puritan settlers of New England demanded strict .... in attitudes and behavior.
3. Because of our diverse attitudes, no single .... accurately describes sexual activity in the United States.
4. The report on Mark's research had .... information, with some figures proving it successful and others proving it unsuccessful.
5. Dr. Herman's research has made a .... impact on our understanding of sexual attitudes on college campuses in the U.S.
6. In some societies, it is the .... for parents to choose marriage partners for their children.
7. He proposed to his fiancée in the .... way, by kneeling on one knee and asking for her hand in marriage.
8. An example of a .... is saying that all young adults between the ages of 18 and 24 have the same standards for sexual behavior.
9. Our .... to the standards for sexual behavior is dependent upon factors such as our culture, religious beliefs, and social expectations.
10. The .... of sexual fidelity within marriage has been and remains a strong element of U.S. culture.
11. Some people approve of premarital sex and others do not, so the results of our research are ....
12. Attitudes about sexual behavior in the 1960s changed radically from the more .... views that were held in the past.
13. The numbers of adults engaging in .... sex has increased in comparison with adults in previous generations who waited until they were married.
14. After the sexual revolution of the 1960s, there was a .... in the 1980s that emphasized family values and more conservative views on sex.
15. Mrs. Ford's divorce was filed on the grounds that her husband was having an .... affair.
16. We celebrate Thanksgiving in a .... way by roasting turkey and having a large crowd of people come for dinner.
17. There has never been a .... in technology that caused people to revert back to not using technology.
18. Changing attitudes about having sex before marriage has resulted in more .... sex and unwanted pregnancies.
19. Maya's grandparents have very .... views about premarital sex.
20. Despite differences in sexual attitudes, most people living in the U.S. condemn .... sex as a breach of the marriage contract or vow.

MyReadingLab

Reading 1 QUESTIONS FOR WRITING AND DISCUSSION

Review any parts of the article you need to answer the following questions.

1. Do you agree that sexual behavior is still an indicator of a person's morality? Why or why not?

2. What are some of the intangible, or non-physical, ways that people are attracted to each other?

3. Why do you think that most people living in the U.S. still condemn extramarital sex, but have more liberal views about premarital sex?

4. Do you think that sexual attitudes of people in the U.S. have become too open-minded or not? Why or why not?

5. In many other countries, it is not uncommon to see nudity on regular television programs, or in public beaches and parks. Why do you think laws regarding sexual behavior and nudity are more strict in the U.S.?

MyReadingLab

Reading 2 VOCABULARY PREVIEW

"Saving Children in Cambodia"

by Tibor Krausz

Match the words in the Word Bank by writing the letter of the word next to the matching definition. The paragraph numbers in parentheses indicate the location of each word in the reading selection, "Saving Children in Cambodia." Read the words in the paragraphs to determine the correct meanings as they are used in the context of the selection.

WORD BANK

a. epiphany (1)	b shantytown (1)	c. mogul (2)
d. validation(2)	e. affable (6)	f. humanitarian (9)
g. implemented (13)	h. prolonged (13)	i. genocide (14)
j. fetid (15)	k. derelict (15)	l. sheaf (18)
m. trafficked (20)		

1. .... mass murder of an ethnic or religious group
2. .... a village of makeshift shelters
3. .... in ruins
4. .... friendly
5. .... proof
6. .... a revelation; insight
7. .... a stack
8. .... an important person
9. .... put into action
10. .... stinking
11. .... made longer in time
12. .... sold for sexual purposes
13. .... someone who improves the welfare of others

MyReadingLab

Reading 2 PREVIEW

Discuss the following questions with a partner or small group.

1. What do poor neighborhoods in your area look like? Describe what you have seen.
2. Describe your idea of what it means to be poor in the U.S.

After you preview the article, write one or two preview questions on the lines below:

MyReadingLab

Reading 2

"Saving Children in Cambodia"

by Tibor Krausz

Scott Neeson sold his mansion, his Porsche, and his yacht and set off for Cambodia to provide food, shelter, and education to destitute children.

Cambodia: a country in Southeast Asia

refuse (REF-use): garbage

1 Scott Neeson's final epiphany came one day in June 2004. The high-powered Hollywood executive stood, ankle deep in trash, at the sprawling landfill of Stung Meanchey, a poor shantytown in Cambodia's capital. In a haze of toxic fumes and burning waste, swarms of Phnom Penh's most destitute were rooting through **refuse**, jostling for scraps of recyclables in newly dumped loads of rubbish. They earned 4,000 riel ($1) a day—if they were lucky. Many of the garbage sorters were young children. Covered in filthy rags, they were scruffy, sickly, and sad.

2 Clasped to Mr. Neeson's ear was his cellphone. Calling the movie mogul from a US airport, a Hollywood superstar's agent was complaining bitterly about inadequate in-flight entertainment on a private jet that Sony Pictures Entertainment, where Neeson was head of overseas theatrical releases, had provided for his client. Neeson overheard the actor griping in the background. "*My life wasn't meant to be this difficult*. Those were his exact words," Neeson says. "I was standing there in that humid, stinking garbage dump with children sick with typhoid, and this guy was refusing to get on a Gulfstream IV (jet) because he couldn't find a specific item onboard," he recalls. "If I ever wanted validation I was doing the right thing, this was it."

Continued...

MyReadingLab

Reading 2

...continued

3 Doing the right thing meant turning his back on a successful career in the movie business, with his $1 million salary. Instead, he would dedicate himself full time to a new mission: to save hundreds of the poorest children in one of the world's poorest countries.

4 Much to everyone's surprise, within months the Australian native, who as president of 20th Century Fox International had overseen the global success of block-busters like "Titanic," "Braveheart," and "Die Another Day," quit Hollywood. He sold his mansion in Los Angeles and held a garage sale for "all the useless stuff I owned." He sold off his Porsche and yacht, too.

5 His sole focus would now be his charity, the Cambodian Children's Fund, which he had set up the previous year after coming face to face, while on vacation in Cambodia, with children living at the garbage dump.

6 "The perks in Hollywood were good – limos, private jets, gorgeous girlfriends, going to the Academy Awards," says Neeson, an affable man with careworn features and a toothy smile. "But it's not about what lifestyle I'd enjoy more when I can make life better for hundreds of children."

Why did Neeson decide to leave his successful career in Hollywood behind?

7 He sits at his desk barefoot, Cambodian-style, in white canvas pants and a T-shirt. At times he even sounds like a Buddhist monk. "You've got to take the ego out of it," he says. "One person's self-indulgence versus the needs of hundreds of children, that's the moral equation."

8 On the walls of his office, next to movie posters signed by Hollywood stars, are before-and-after pictures of Cambodian children. Each pair tells a Cinderella story: A little ragamuffin, standing or squatting in rubbish, transforms in a later shot into a beaming, healthy child in a crisp school uniform.

9 Neeson has more than 1,300 sets of such pictures; that's how many children his charity looks after. Every one of the children, the Australian humanitarian stresses, he knows by sight, and most of them by name. "You go through a certain journey with them," he says.

10 Houy and Heang were among the first who started that journey with him in 2004. Abandoned by their parents, the two sisters, now 17 and 18, lived at the dump in a makeshift tent. "We felt sick and had no shoes. Our feet hurt," Houy recalls in the fluent English she's learned. "We'd never seen a foreigner," Heang adds. "He asked us, 'Do you want to study?'" Today the sisters are about to graduate from high school. They want to go on to college.

11 Neeson maintains four residential homes around town for more than 500 other deprived children and is building another. He operates after-school programs and vocational training centers. He's built day cares and nurseries.

What has Neeson done to help the children of Cambodia?

12 His charity provides some 500 children with three meals a day and runs a bakery where disadvantaged youths learn marketable skills while making nutrient-rich pastry for the poorest kids. It pays for well over 1,000 children's schooling and organizes sightseeing trips and sports days for them.

13 "I drive the staff crazy," says Neeson, who employs more than 300 locals, many of them former scavengers. "If I come up with a plan, I want to see it implemented within 48 hours. If I see a need, I want to do something about it. You don't want to see suffering prolonged." He sees plenty of both need and suffering.

14 After decades of genocide and civil war, millions of Cambodians live in

abject poverty. Many children are chronically malnourished, and many never even finish primary school.

15 On a late afternoon, as garbage pickers begin to return to their squalid dwellings of plastic sheets, tarpaulins, and plywood, Neeson sets out on his daily "Pied Piper routine." Navigating a muddy path, pocked with fetid puddles and strewn with trash, which winds among clusters of derelict shacks and mounds of garbage, he picks his way around a squatters' community. Everywhere he goes, children dash up to him with cries of "Papa! Papa!" They leap into his arms, pull at his shirt, cling to his arms, and wrap themselves around his legs.

16 "Hey, champ!" he greets a boy who clambers up on him. "He needs a dentist so badly," he notes, referring to the boy's rotten teeth. His charity offers free health care and dental services to the children and their parents.

17 In 2007 Neeson won the Harvard School of Public Health's Q Prize, an award created by music legend Quincy Jones. In June he was named "a hero of philanthropy" by *Forbes Magazine*. ("Well, I finally made it into Forbes," he quips, "But no 'World's Richest' list for me.")

18 When Neeson spots certain kids, he hands them their portraits from a sheaf of newly printed photographs he carries around. "I want them to have mementoes of themselves when they grow up and leave all this behind," he explains. They give him their latest drawings in return.

19 He stops at a windowless cinder-block shanty inhabited by a mother and her three teenage daughters. The bare walls are adorned with Neeson's portraits of the girls in school beside their framed Best Student awards. "I'm so proud of my children," says Um Somalin, a garment factory worker who earns $2 a day. "Mr. Scott has done wonders for them."

20 Neeson rescued one girl from being trafficked, another from domestic servitude, and the mother from a rubber plantation, after he had come across the youngest girl living alone at the dump. "We always bring the family back together," he says. "We help everyone so no one slips through the cracks."

21 The need is great: Life here can be unforgiving. "This girl has an abusive father. This one here fell into a fire when she was 6. That guy got shot. That one there lost an arm in an accident," Neeson says, reeling off details. Then, flashlight in hand, he doubles back down another path – and steps into what seems like a different world. Behind a high-security fence, children sit in neat rows in brightly painted classrooms, learning English and math in evening classes. Others play on computers in an air-conditioned room. Until recently, the site where Neeson's new school now stands was a garbage dump. "When I started working for him, I was surprised how much he does for the children," says Chek Sarath, one of his helpers. "He places their well-being above his own." Neeson stops by young children who have their eyes glued to a Disney cartoon playing from a DVD.

22 "I miss a lot about Hollywood," Neeson muses. "I miss Sundays playing paddle tennis on the beach with friends and taking the boat out to the islands. Sundays here, I'm down at the garbage dump. But I'm really happy."

1,335 words divided by .... minutes = ... words per minute

To see photos, videos, and learn more about the Cambodian Children's Fund, go to www.cambodianchildrensfund.org

MyReadingLab

Reading 2 REVIEW

A good review strategy to use after reading is to summarize what you just read in your own words. Take a few minutes to think about the author's most important point and any key ideas that helped to support or explain it.

Write a two- or three-sentence summary on the lines below.

MyReadingLab

Reading 2 COMPREHENSION QUESTIONS

The following questions will help you recall the main idea and details of "Saving Cambodia's Children." Read any parts of the article that you need to find the correct answers.

MAIN IDEAS

1. What is the central point of the entire selection?

a. Scott Neeson is a philanthropist who works to improve the lives of others.

b. Scott Neeson founded an organization to help care for the poorest children and their families in Cambodia.

c. It is important to care for other people who need our help.

d. The Cambodian Children's Fund provides a free education for all the children who want one.

2. What is the implied main idea of paragraph 1?

a. Scott Neeson learned about the destitute children of Cambodia in 2004 at the sprawling landfill of Stung Meanchey, a poor shantytown in Cambodia's capital.

b. Scott Neeson had an epiphany in June 2004.

c. Many of the garbage sorters were young children who were covered in filthy rags, and they earned about $1 a day finding recyclables.

d. Scott Neeson was appalled by the destitute children digging through the dump in Cambodia.

SUPPORTING DETAILS

3. According to the article, the reason why Neeson was assured that he was doing the right thing by helping the children was

a. his friends back in Hollywood told him he was doing the right thing.

b. he was tired of working as a movie mogul.

c. that an actor was griping and refusing to get on a jet because he couldn't find a specific in-flight entertainment item he wanted.

d. he wanted the publicity and hoped to win an award.

4. What does the author mean by saying, "Neeson sets out on his daily 'Pied Piper' routine" in paragraph 15?

- **a.** Neeson plays a flute for the people.
- **b.** Neeson tries to play the part of the Pied Piper for the children.
- **c.** Neeson goes out to try to persuade the families to let their children come to his school and daycare facilities.
- **d.** Neeson criticizes the parents for not taking better care of their children.

DRAWING CONCLUSIONS

5. What does Neeson mean in paragraph 7 when he says, "You've got to take the ego out of it...One person's self-indulgence versus the needs of hundreds of children, that's the moral equation."

- **a.** It's better to serve hundreds of children than to save just one.
- **b.** People have too much ego and need to think more about others.
- **c.** A moral equation is about serving hundreds of other people.
- **d.** It is morally ethical to serve the needs of hundreds of children instead of the ego of one person.

PATTERNS OF ORGANIZATION

6. In paragraph 21, the author uses which of the following patterns of organization?

- **a.** process
- **b.** time order
- **c.** generalization and example
- **d.** cause and effect

CRITICAL THINKING

7. Identify the following sentence from paragraph 14: Many children are chronically malnourished, and many never even finish primary school.

- **a.** fact
- **b.** opinion

8. The author's purpose and tone for this selection are:

- **a.** The purpose is to inform and the tone is indignant.
- **b.** The purpose is to persuade and the tone is concerned.
- **c.** The purpose is to entertain and the tone is cynical.
- **d.** The purpose is to inform and the tone is serious.

8. In this selection, the author is

- **a.** biased against the people of Cambodia.
- **b.** biased against Hollywood.
- **c.** biased in favor of Scott Neeson.
- **d.** unbiased.

STUDY SKILLS

9. Which of the following should *not* be included in notes taken from this article?

- **a.** In June 2004, Scott Neeson found children rooting through dumps for recyclables for about $1 a day in Cambodia and decided to help them.
- **b.** An actor was griping and refusing to get on a jet because he couldn't find a specific in-flight entertainment item he wanted.
- **c.** Neeson decided to sell all of his possessions in Hollywood and leave his job as a movie mogul to move to Cambodia and help the poorest families there.
- **d.** Neeson maintains four residential children's homes, after-school programs,vocational training centers, day cares and nurseries, and a bakery where disadvantaged youths learn marketable skills.

Continued...

MyReadingLab

Reading 2 COMPREHENSION QUESTIONS

...continued

10. If you visit the Web site for the Cambodian Children's Fund, you would look for all of the following *except*:

a. factual data that is provable as true or false.
b. bias or persuasive language.
c. products or services offered for sale on this Web site.
d. whether the Web site is listed on major search engines such as Google or Bing.

Reading 2 VOCABULARY PRACTICE: SPEED QUIZ

This activity is played by two teams of 2–4 people on each team. The object of the game is to correctly define the largest number of words in 60 seconds.

Directions:

1. Copy the words and corresponding definitions of each of the words in the word bank found at the beginning of this reading selection onto pieces of paper or index cards. (Each person can write a few to make the task go faster.)

2. Shuffle the papers face down and deal out six to each team. One will be left over.

3. On each team, one person will be a clue giver and another will be the time keeper and score keeper. Decide which team will go first.

4. When everyone is ready, the first team's (Team A's) clue-giver will read off the word on the first card to the other team. The time keeper/score keeper will begin keeping time. Team B has one minute to give the definitions to Team A for each of the 6 words the clue-giver reads. If Team B gets stuck on one word, say "Pass" and quickly go to the next word. They can go back to it later if time allows.

5. Team B gets one point for each definition they correctly give. If they miss a word or give an incorrect definition, no points are given. Only one answer is allowed.

6. When one minute has passed, the time keeper says, "Stop" and the points are totaled.

7. Team B then takes the role of giving clues and chooses a time keeper/score keeper. Team A will have one minute to give the definitions to the 6 words read by the clue-giver on Team B.

8. In the event of a tie, one person from each team will play against each other for the final point. The remaining word will be read to both players and the first correct response wins.

The team with the most points is the winner.

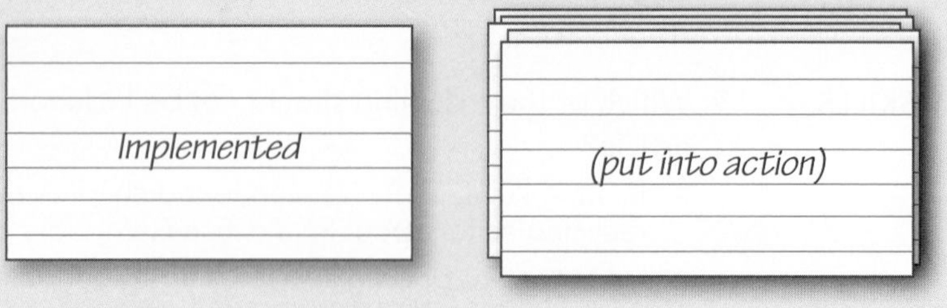

MyReadingLab

Reading 2 QUESTIONS FOR WRITING AND DISCUSSION

1. Many other tourists have also seen the same poverty that Scott Neeson saw when he first visited the dump in Cambodia, yet he was the only one who chose to try to solve the problem. Why do you think some people decide to do nothing while others see a problem and try to solve it?

2. What were the reasons that caused the poverty in Cambodia, and how did the people become so poor that they had to scavenge in dumps to survive?

3. Neeson gives each child a photo of how he or she first looked before becoming a part of his charity. Why do you think he does this?

4. Neeson sold all of his expensive possessions in Hollywood that he had acquired (the Porsche, the yacht, etc.) and used the money to start his charity. Although he misses some of these things, he says he is happy. What does this tell you about happiness? Why do you think he's happy?

5. Do you believe that people have a responsibility to help the poor or do you believe that each person is responsible only to himself or herself? Why or why not?

MyReadingLab

VIEWPOINT FOR CRITICAL THINKING

DEATH PENALTY

Read the letters below to the editor about the death penalty and answer the following questions.

Dear Editor:

Recently a man was convicted of murder in our state and issued the death penalty by the judge. He had been convicted of numerous crimes in the past and had served over 20 years in prison before committing murder. However, I oppose the death penalty for several reasons. First, it is immoral to kill another human being under any circumstances. We are supposed to be a civilized society and many other nations have already outlawed the death penalty. It is simply morally wrong to deny a human being the opportunity to live out his or her life and perhaps someday seek forgiveness. Secondly, in the past, innocent people have been put to death for crimes they did not commit. Since 1976 over 100 prisoners on death row have been exonerated of their crimes for various reasons. But the death penalty is irreversible and permanent. Third, the laws regarding the death penalty are inconsistent. Some states allow it under certain circumstances and other states don't allow it at all. To be fair, the death penalty should be enforced in all states or none. And finally, the death penalty does not discourage criminal behavior. In the states that have the death penalty, the crime rate is equal or higher than in states that do not have the death penalty. It is not an effective deterrent to preventing crime.

Signed,

Life not Death

Dear Editor:

The death penalty is the one final justice we have for cruel and appalling crimes such as the rape and murder of a child. Some crimes are just too horrific to allow the perpetrator to spend his entire life in a relatively safe environment with little or no suffering. Think of the hundreds of innocent people (including children) who have been killed at the hands of terrorists and mass murderers. Letting them sit in prison for life is no punishment at all considering the exceedingly humane treatment of prisoners in today's American prisons. And who is paying for all those prisoners serving life sentences? The American taxpayers. I do not want my hard-earned tax dollars to support someone who deserves death. Most prisoners who have been given the death penalty committed premeditated murder, which means they chose to kill. They are also people who have been in trouble with the law before and continue to commit violent crimes because they can't or won't stop. The method of execution today causes no physical suffering, so it is not inhumane. Judges have the final say in sentencing and most of them will only order the death penalty if they feel it is fully warranted. I don't care if the death penalty is not a deterrent to crime. For horrific crimes, it is the only justice we can and should deliver.

Signed,

Lethal Justice

1. What is the author's argument or claim in the first letter about the death penalty?

2. What is the author's argument or claim in the second letter about the death penalty?

3. With which side of the issue do you agree? Explain why.

4. Do you think there are certain circumstances under which the death penalty should be invoked? Describe the circumstances.

5. Both of these letters contain bias. What words or ideas in these letters tell you that the authors are biased?

MyReadingLab

REAL-LIFE READING

APPLYING FOR CHILDREN'S MEDICAL INSURANCE

Many states now offer free or low-cost health insurance for children. To apply you must read the application instructions to determine if your child qualifies for enrollment. Read the sample below of a typical eligibility statement and application instructions to answer the questions that follow.

CHIPP is our state's Children's Health Insurance Plan Program available to families at little or no cost.

Eligibility

To be eligible for CHIPP, your child must

- be between ages 1 -18 (Babies 0-12 months are covered in our HIP program)
- be a legal resident or legal visitor with documentation of status
- not be enrolled in any other health insurance program
- have a Social Security Number (to obtain an application for an SSN, call the Social Security Administration office or go online to apply)

Once you complete the application, your payment status will be determined. The cost of CHIPP is based on a sliding scale according to your last year's income tax statement. Costs for monthly premiums are $0 - $20 per month depending upon your financial status.

Application Instructions

1. Fill in the information about you and your child including your SSNs. Your personal information and SSN will not be shared with any other agency including Immigration Services. All information will be kept confidential.
2. Include your employer's information including address and phone numbers.
3. Answer the questions for each child who lives with you, including any yet unborn by filling in the birth date as "unborn". After the baby is born, contact our state health insurance department to apply for the Healthy Infant Program (HIP) insurance through this Web site or by calling the state health insurance department.
4. If your child is a non-citizen, write the date of the child's entry into the U.S. and the child' USCIS number. If you are a non-citizen, also attach a copy of the following documents to your application that show your current residency status:
    - Form I-551 (Green Card, Permanent Resident or Resident Alien Card)
    - Form I-94 Arrival/ Departure Record
    - Form I-571 Travel Authorization
    - Notice of DHS receipt of Form I-589 if Cuban or Haitian
    - Form I-6888 or Form I-766 Work Authorization Card

- Passport or Laissez-Passer including the bearer's name and photo, stamped by the Department of Homeland Security (DHS) showing immigration status or visa
- Other documentation of status such as a letter from USCIS, DHS, immigration judge or Board of Immigration Appeals judge
- Letter of eligibility from the Office of Refugee Resettlement
- Proof of residency (valid driver's license, rent or mortgage statement, tax receipts)

1. If your child is covered under your employer's health insurance plan, you are eligible to also get a health plan from CHIPP.

   a. True b. False

2. How do you insure your child if he or she is 11 months old?

3. How much does CHIPP cost and how is this determined?

4. Should you be concerned about including your own and your child's social security numbers on the application? Why or why not?

5. If you or your child is Haitian or Cuban, what must you remember to include with your application?

MyReadingLab

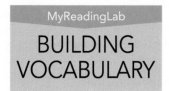

BUILDING VOCABULARY

Knowing the meanings to many word parts will help you determine the meanings of unfamiliar words. Make a list of English words using the word parts in the table below, and give their meanings. If you are unsure about a word, consult a dictionary. Then use the words to complete the sentences below. (* presented in previous lists)

PREFIXES	ROOTS	SUFFIXES
ad-: *toward*	-voc, vok: *to call*	-ate: *to act upon*
re-*: *again*	-vis, vis: *to see*	-tion, -sion: *action; state of**
intro-, intra-: *within*	-spect: *to look; see*	-er, -or: *one who, one that**

WORDS

Use one of the words in your word list above in a sentence that reveals its meaning with a context clue. Read the sentence to a classmate and ask him or her to define the word.

MyReadingLab

CHAPTER PRACTICE 1

(Source of information: Macionis, John *Society the Basics*, 11e. 2011. pp. 356-357.)

THE CAUSES OF WAR

Nations have been waging war against each other ever since the beginning of civilization. Wars have been fought to determine the ownership of natural resources, wealth, and land, or as retribution for an injustice. Overall, though, wars begin for five basic reasons. First, nations war against each other because of perceived threats. If a government's actions indicate that they are a threat against another government, the threatened nation may respond aggressively. A second reason is a social problem such as the prospect of a poor economy or unemployment. One nation may see another nation as the cause of the particular social problem that they face. A third cause of war is political objectives. A government may try to overthrow another to change its political structure, as Communist North Vietnam did in the Vietnam War. War also starts due to moral objectives, such as liberating a nation from an oppressive leader, or suppressing an aggressive or hostile group whose moral standards are different. Finally, war is often the result of a lack of an alternative to mounting tensions between nations. When two or more governments disagree on a number of issues, the tensions may build up until one government commits an act of aggression and the other retaliates.

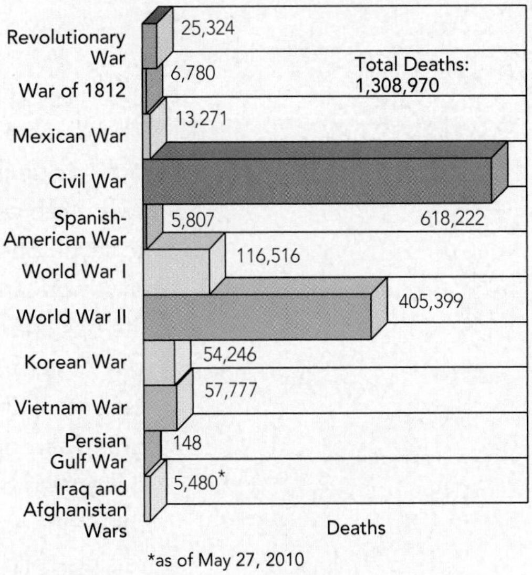

Deaths of Americans in Eleven U.S. Wars

Almost half of all U.S. deaths in war occurred during the Civil War (1861–65).

Sources: Compiled from various sources by Maris A. Vinovskis (1989) and the author.

1. What is the main idea of this passage?
   - a. War is often waged between nations.
   - b. When two or more nations disagree on moral issues, war often ensues.
   - c. The causes of war can be explained by five basic reasons.
   - d. Nations war against each other because of perceived threats or to change another government's political structure.

Continued...

MyReadingLab

CHAPTER PRACTICE 1

...continued

2. According to the table, Deaths of Americans in Eleven U.S. Wars, which of the following statements is true?
   a. The War of 1812 had as many deaths as the Iraq War.
   b. There were about four times more Americans killed in World War II than in World War I.
   c. More Americans died in the Korean War than the Vietnam War.
   d. The Persian Gulf War was the shortest war of all those listed on the table.

3-5 Complete the missing notes for the outline below.

The causes of war can be explained by five basic reasons.

- perceived threats
- (3.) ....
  - poor economy
  - (4.) ....
- political objectives
- moral objectives
- (5.) ....

MyReadingLab

CHAPTER PRACTICE 2

CHANGING FAMILIES

The divorce rate in the United States has declined since the 1980s, but it is unlikely to revert to the level of the early part of the twentieth century when divorce was not as socially acceptable as today. Nonetheless, marriage and family are still an important part of American culture, but are more diverse than in the past. Family life has changed to include a wider variety of situations, including gay or lesbian couples with children, unmarried cohabitating parents with children, one-parent families, and families with grandparents or other relatives all living together. Men have also become more involved in the upbringing of their children than they tended to be in previous generations. There are more men raising children as stay-at-home dads, and more are taking active roles in caring for children. Another trend in families is having both parents work outside of the home in careers or multiple jobs to support the family's economic needs.

1. What is the main idea of this passage?
   a. The trends in marriage and family life in American culture are different than they were in the past.
   b. The divorce rate is decreasing but the number of single mothers is on the rise.
   c. There is less diversity in the structure of families than in the past.
   d. Men are taking a more active role in raising children than in the past.

2. According to the passage the divorce rate has

a. remained about the same as in the past.

b. has increased significantly in the current generation.

c. become less socially acceptable than it was in the early twentieth century.

d. declined since the 1980s.

3-5 Complete the missing notes for the outline below

Changing American Families

- Divorce rate declined since (3) ....
- Family life has changed to include a wider variety of situations.
- (4) ....
- Unmarried cohabitating parents with children
- (5) ....
- Families with grandparents or other relatives all living together

MyReadingLab

CHAPTER PRACTICE 3

A century ago, the campuses of colleges and universities across the United States might as well have hung out a sign that read "Men Only," as almost all of the students and faculty were male. There were a small number of women's colleges, but many more schools—including some of the most prestigious U.S. universities, including Yale, Harvard, and Princeton—barred women outright.

Since then, women have won greater social equality and by 1980, the number of women enrolled at U.S. colleges finally matched the number of men. In a surprising trend, however, the share of women on campus has continued to increase: In 2008, men accounted for only 43 percent of all U.S. undergraduates.

What accounts for the shifting gender balance on U.S. campuses? One theory is that young men are drawn away from college by the lure of jobs, especially in high technology. This pattern is sometimes termed the "Bill Gates syndrome" after the Microsoft founder, who dropped out of college and soon became the world's richest person. In addition, analysts point to an anti-intellectual male culture. Young women are drawn to learning and seek to do well in school, but young men attach

Continued...

MyReadingLab

CHAPTER PRACTICE 3

...continued

less importance to studying. Rightly or wrongly, more men seem to think they can get a good job without investing years of their lives and a considerable amount of money in getting a college degree. This gender gap is evident in all racial and ethnic categories and at all class levels. Among African Americans on campus, only 36 percent are men. The lower the income level, the greater the gender gap in college attendance.

1. What is the central point of this passage?
   - **a.** More women are attending college today than ever before.
   - **b.** There are several theories about the cause of the current gender gap on college campuses.
   - **c.** More men are seeking jobs after high school instead of going to college.
   - **d.** Low-income African American males are less likely to go to college than middle or upper income white males.

2-5 Complete the missing notes for the Cornell Notes below.

QUESTION/CUE	NOTES
Women on college campuses 100 yrs ago	Almost all students & faculty were male.
By 1980	(2) Men & women enrolled were ....
By 2008	Only 43% of undergrads were men.
Theories on causes of gender gap	• (3) Men believe they can ....
Gender gap categories	Gender gap is evident in all racial and ethnic categories at all class levels. (4) African Americans: .... males. The lower the income level, the (5) ....

CHAPTER REVIEW: CORNELL NOTES

Complete the Cornell Notes below for all the learning objectives in this chapter.

QUESTION/CUE	NOTES
How do you take good notes?	Note-taking (p. ....) Step 1: .... Step 2: .... Step 3: .... Step 4: ....
What are Cornell Notes?	Cornell Notes: ....
How do you do them?	Divide paper into .... During lecture, ... Later, ...
What is a formal outline?	Formal outlines ....
What is an informal outline?	Informal outline use ....
When should you begin to study for tests?	Test-taking (p. ....) Studying begins the first day of class by ....
What should you use to study with?	Use .... Pay special attention to learning ....

CHAPTER REVIEW: CORNELL NOTES

...continued

QUESTION/CUE	NOTES
How should you prepare for taking a test?	1. Rest: ____________ 2. Food: ____________ ____________ 3. Setting: ____________
How should you evaluate Web sites?	Evaluating Web Sites (p. ______) 1. Look at the URL to ____________ ____________ 2. Look for dates to determine ____________ ____________ 3. Remember to ____________ ____________ 4. Check the Web site's appearance (professional?) 5. Look for a ____________ ____________

MyReadingLab

READING LAB ASSIGNMENTS

1. Login to **MyReadingLab** and in the menu click on **Study Skills**. In the **Learning Path** you can choose what skills you'd like to review or learn new study skills. Review by reading the brief overviews and models. Watch the short animations and then complete the practices and tests.

2. Click on **Reading Level** and choose two stories to read and answer the questions to the best of your ability. Your Lexile level will increase as your reading comprehension improves.

ON THE WEB

You can learn more about study skills on the Web by doing an Internet search on the term *study skills*. Several Web sites and videos are available on this topic which may enhance your understanding, such as Study Guides and Strategies.

MyReadingLab

MONITOR YOUR LEARNING

In this chapter you learned about using context clues and word part clues to determine the meanings of unfamiliar words. Write a paragraph telling what you learned about these skills, how you learned them, and how you can use them to improve your learning and reading comprehension. When you have finished writing, read your paragraph as if you were reading someone else's paragraph for the first time. Check for missing words, spelling, punctuation, and sentence structure.

Contents

PATTERNS AND TRANSITIONS CHART

PATTERN	CHARACTERISTICS	TRANSITIONS
Definition	Explains the meaning of a word or phrase.	is, refers to, can be defined as, means, consists of, involves, is a term that, is called, is known as, entails, corresponds to, is literally
Classification	Divides a topic into parts based on shared characteristics.	classified as, comprises, is composed of, several varieties of, different stages of, different groups, types, kinds
Time Order (Chronological Order)	Describes events in the order they occurred. Transitions describe WHEN something happened.	first, second, later, before, next, as soon as, after, then, finally, meanwhile, following, last, during, in, on, when, until
Process	Describes the order in which things are done or how things work. Transitions describe WHEN something happens	first, second, next, then, following, after that, last, finally
Addition (Simple list)	Indicates that additional information will follow.	furthermore, additionally, also, besides, further, in addition, moreover, again, first, second, next, finally
Spatial Order	Describes physical location or position in space. Transitions describe WHERE things are.	above, below, besides, next to, in front of, behind, inside, outside, opposite, within, nearby, adjacent to, beyond, close by
Cause-Effect	Describes how one or more things cause or are related to another.	*Causes:* because, because of, for, since, stems from, one cause is, one reason is, leads to, causes, creates, yields, produces, due to, breeds, for this reason. *Effect:* consequently, results in, one result, is, therefore, thus, as a result, hence

Continued...

PATTERN	CHARACTERISTICS	TRANSITIONS
Comparison-Contrast	Discusses similarities and/or differences among ideas, theories, concepts, objects, or persons.	*Similarities:* both, also, similarly, like, likewise, too, as well as, resembles, correspondingly, in the same way, to compare, in comparison *Differences:* unlike, differs from, in contrast, on the other hand, instead, despite, nevertheless, however, in spite of, whereas, as opposed to
Statement and Clarification	Indicates that information explaining an idea or concept will follow.	in fact, in other words, clearly, evidently, obviously, of course
Generalization and Example	Provides examples that clarify a broad statement.	for example, for instance, that is, to illustrate, e.g., i.e., such as
Summary	Indicates that a condensed review of an idea or piece of writing is to follow.	in summary, in conclusion, in brief, to summarize, to sum up, in short, on the whole
Order of Importance	Shows details from most important to least important or *vice versa*	most important, least, first, second, primarily, secondarily

Additional Patterns of Organization

Besides the patterns of organization taught in Chapter 5, here are additional patterns you may wish to know:

Summary Pattern

A summary pattern is most often found at the end of a chapter or an article where the author summarizes the most important points that were discussed. Transitions for the summary pattern are:

to summarize   in summary   as we have seen
as we have discussed   to sum up

Example:

As we have seen, the causes of poverty are numerous and varied. Wars, natural disasters, economic disasters, and environmental problems such as drought can cause poverty on a regional, national, or a continental scale.

Order of Importance Pattern

The order of importance pattern lists details according to their level of importance. The most important details may come first with those of lesser importance following. Or, the details may begin with the least important one and continue with the most important detail last. The order of importance has several transitions which may help you identify the pattern:

less	least	lower (lowest)	most	higher (highest)
more	primary	secondary	level	importance
large (larger, largest)		small (smaller, smallest)		

Example:

In the United States, the **highest** law enforcement authority occurs at the federal level. The Federal Bureau of Investigation enforces criminal laws of the United States as well as foreign threats to national security. At the state **level,** agencies such as State Troopers and other state law enforcement agencies enforce laws within the jurisdiction of the state. Regional law enforcement agencies such as county sheriffs or city police enforce laws within a **smaller** jurisdiction, such as a county or town.

ADDITIONAL READINGS FOR COMBINED SKILLS PRACTICES

The following reading selections will help you apply all of the skills you have learned in this text. You may use them for review, self-testing, or as practice for final exams.

Reading 1

Defeating Procrastination (Psychology)

1 Have you often thought that you could get better grades if only you had more time? Do you often find yourself studying for an exam or completing a term paper at the last minute? If so, it makes sense for you to learn how to overcome the greatest time waster of all—procrastination. Research indicates that academic procrastination arises partly out of a lack of confidence in one's ability to meet expectations (Wolters, 2003). Once procrastination has become established as a behavior pattern, it often persists for years (Lee, Kelly, & Edwards, 2006). Nevertheless, anyone can overcome procrastination, and gain self-confidence in the process, by using behavior modification techniques. So, to keep procrastination from interfering with your studying, systematically apply the following suggestions:

2 • Identify the environmental cues that habitually interfere with your studying. Television, computer or video games, and even food can be powerful distracters that consume hours of valuable study time. However, these distracters can be useful positive reinforcers to enjoy after you've finished studying.

3 • Schedule your study time and reinforce yourself for adhering to your schedule. Once you've scheduled it, be just as faithful to your schedule as you would be to a work schedule set by an employer. And be sure to schedule something you enjoy immediately following the study time.

4 • Get started. This is the most difficult part. Give yourself an extra reward for starting on time and, perhaps, a penalty for starting late.

5 • Use visualization. Much procrastination results from the failure to consider its negative consequences. Visualizing the consequences of not

Continued...

studying, such as trying to get through an exam you haven't adequately prepared for, can be an effective tool for combating procrastination.

6 • Beware of jumping to another task when you reach a difficult part of an assignment. This procrastination tactic gives you the feeling that you are busy and accomplishing something, but it is nevertheless an avoidance mechanism.

7 • Beware of preparation overkill. Procrastinators may actually spend hours preparing for a task rather than working on the task itself. For example, they may gather enough library materials to write a book rather than a five-page term paper. This enables them to postpone writing the paper.

8 • Keep a record of the reasons you give yourself for postponing studying or completing important assignments. If a favorite **rationalization** is, "I'll wait until I'm in the mood to do this," count the number of times in a week you are seized with the desire to study. The mood to study typically arrives after you begin, not before.

9 • Don't procrastinate! Begin now! Apply the steps outlined here to gain more control over your behavior and win the battle against procrastination.

(Samuel E. Wood, Ellen Green Wood, Denise Boyd. *The World of Psychology*, 7th ed. Pearson, 2011. p. 171.)

477 words divided by .... minutes = ... words per minute

QUESTIONS

1. What is the meaning of the bold word in this sentence from paragraph 8? If a favorite rationalization is, "I'll wait until I'm in the mood to do this," count the number of times in a week you are seized with the desire to study.

a. situation

b. logical thought

c. explanation for behavior

d. avoidance

2. What is the central point of this selection?

a. Have you often thought that you could get better grades if only you had more time?

b. Nevertheless, anyone can overcome procrastination, and gain self-confidence in the process, by using behavior modification techniques.

c. Research indicates that academic procrastination arises partly out of a lack of confidence in one's ability to meet expectations.

d. Once procrastination has become established as a behavior pattern, it often persists for years.

3. According to the article, what is one of the causes of procrastination?

a. Television, computer or video games, and even food cause procrastination.

b. Procrastination is caused by not adhering to your study schedule.

c. Jumping to another task when you reach a difficult part of an assignment is a cause of procrastination.

d. Procrastination arises partly out of a lack of confidence in one's ability to meet expectations and failure to consider its negative consequences.

4. What is the overall pattern of organization for this article?

a. generalization and example

b. listing

c. statement and clarification

d. classification

5. What is the relationship shown within the following sentence from paragraph 6? This procrastination tactic gives you the feeling that you are busy and accomplishing something, but it is nevertheless an avoidance mechanism.

a. contrast

b. comparison

c. cause and effect

d. addition

6. According to the information in this article, which of the following conclusions is true?

a. Everyone suffers from procrastination at times.

b. Distractions such as television and video games can cause procrastination.

c. Procrastination is extremely difficult to overcome.

d. Distracters can become tools for rewarding non-procrastinating behavior.

7. Correctly identify the following statement from paragraph 3: Schedule your study time and reinforce yourself for adhering to your schedule.

a. fact

b. opinion

8. What is the author's purpose and tone for this article?

a. The author's purpose is to inform and the tone is objective.

b. The author's purpose is to criticize and the tone is concerned.

c. The author's purpose is to advise and the tone is persuasive.

d. The author's purpose is to instruct and the tone is ironic.

9. Which of the following statements is true about the author?

a. The author is biased against distractions such as video games and television.

b. The author is biased in favor of adequate preparation for studying.

c. The author is biased in favor of earning higher grades in school.

d. The author is unbiased.

10. Fill in the missing detail for the following notes on paragraph 1:

Procrastination:

- wastes time & results partly from lack of confidence in one's ability to meet expectations.
- can become a habit persisting for years.
- Use .... to keep procrastination from interfering with studying.

Reading 2

Angles (Mathematics)

1 Two distinct points A and B determine a line called **line AB.** The portion of the line between A and B, including points A and B themselves, is **line segment AB**, or simply **segment AB**. The portion of line AB that starts at A and continues through B, and on past B, is the **ray AB**. Point A is the endpoint of the ray. See Figure 1.

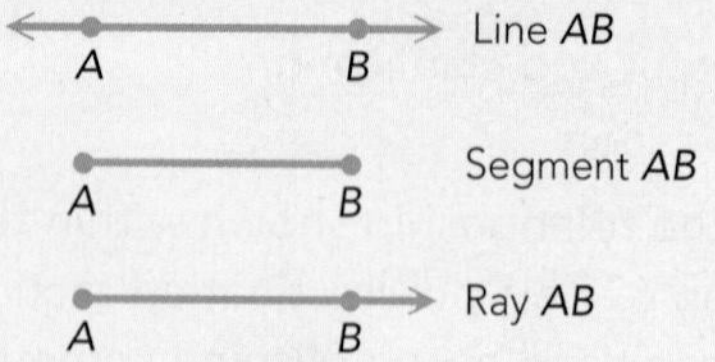

Figure 1

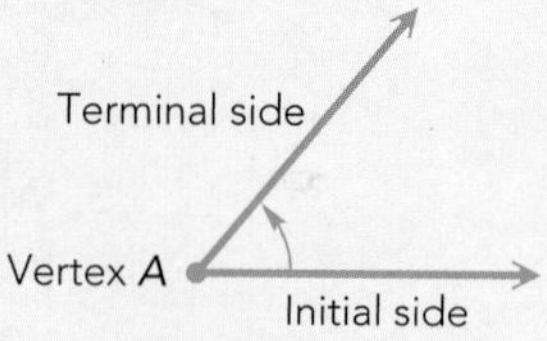

Figure 2

2 In trigonometry, an **angle** consists of two rays in a plane with a common endpoint, or two line segments with a common endpoint. These two rays (or segments) are the **sides** of the angle, and the common endpoint is the **vertex** of the angle. Associated with an angle is its **measure**, generated by a rotation about the vertex. See Figure 2. This measure is determined by rotating a ray starting at one side of the angle, the **initial side**, to the position of the other side, the **terminal** side. ***A counterclockwise rotation generates a positive measure, and a clockwise rotation generates a negative measure***. The rotation can consist of more than one complete revolution.

Figure 3 shows two angles, one **positive** and **one negative.**

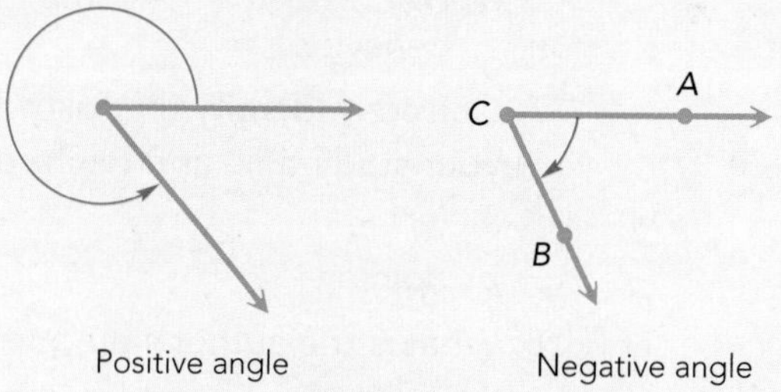

Figure 3

3 An angle can be named by using the name of its vertex. For example, the angle on the right in **Figure 3** can be named angle ***C***. Alternatively, an angle can be named using three letters, with the vertex letter in the middle. Thus, the angle on the right could be named angle ***ACB*** or angle ***BCA***.

Degree Measure

4 The most common unit for measuring angles is the **degree**. Degree measure was developed by the Babylonians 4000 yr ago. To use degree measure, we assign 360 degrees to a complete rotation of a ray. In **Figure 4**, notice that the terminal side of the angle corresponds to its initial side when it makes a complete rotation.

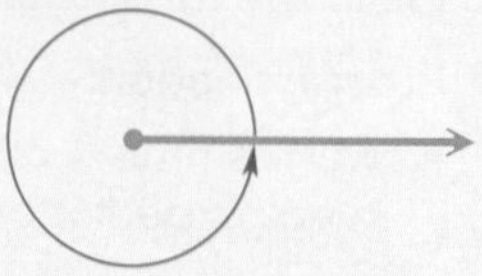

A complete rotation of a ray gives an angle whose measure is 360°. $\frac{1}{360}$ of a complete rotation gives an angle whose measure is 1°.

Figure 4

One degree, written 1°, represents 1/360 of a rotation.

Therefore, 90° represents 90/360 = 1/4 of a complete rotation, and 180° represents 180/360 = 1/2 of a complete rotation.

5 An angle measuring between 0° and 90° is an **acute angle**. An angle measuring exactly 90° is a **right angle**. The symbol ⌉ is often used at the vertex of a right angle to denote the 90° measure. An angle measuring more than 90° but less than 180° is an **obtuse angle**, and an angle of exactly 180° is a **straight angle**.

6 In Figure 5, we use the Greek letter θ (theta)* to name each angle. In addition to θ (theta), other Greek letters such as α (alpha) and β (beta) are often used.

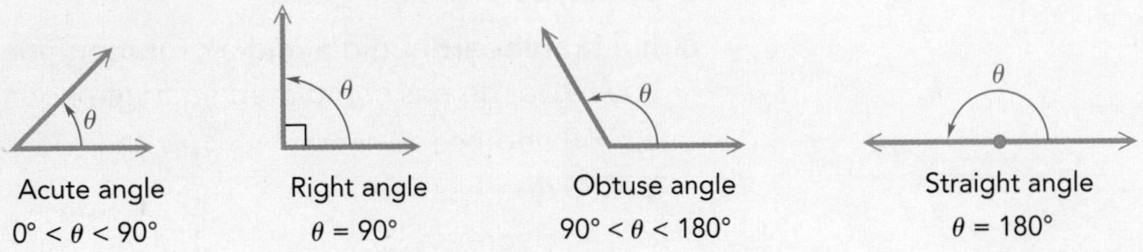

Figure 5

7 If the sum of the measures of two positive angles is 90°, the angles are **complementary** and the angles are **complements** of each other. Two positive angles with measures whose sum is 180° are **supplementary**, and the angles are **supplements**.

(Margaret L. Lial, John Hornsby, David I. Schneider, Callie J. Daniels, *Trigonometry*, 10e. Pearson 2013. pp. 2–3.)

527 words divided by .... minutes = ... words per minute

QUESTIONS

1. What does the word complementary mean in the following sentence? The two angles shown in this figure are complementary angles.

a. angles that complete each other

b. positive angles with measures whose sums are 90°.

c. positive angles with measures whose sums are 180°.

d. an angle measuring more than 90° but less than 180°

2. What is the implied main idea of paragraph 5?

a. There are many types of angles.

b. An angle measuring between 0° and 90° is an acute angle.

c. The symbol ⌉ is often used at the vertex of a right angle to denote the 90° measure.

d. Angles are named according to their measurement in degrees.

3. According to the selection, when a rotating ray has a counterclockwise rotation it generates

a. a negative measure

b. a positive measure

c. an acute angle

d. an obtuse angle

4. **What are the overall patterns for this selection?**
   a. compare and contrast
   b. cause and effect
   c. definition and example
   d. space order

5. **What is the relationship between the following sentences from paragraph 3? Alternatively, an angle can be named using three letters, with the vertex letter in the middle. Thus, the angle on the right could be named angle *ACB* or angle *BCA*.**
   a. cause and effect
   b. addition
   c. classification
   d. compare and contrast

6. **If a skateboarder did a mid-air rotation one and one half times around in a circle, he has completed an angle equal to**
   a. 360 degrees
   b. 180 degrees
   c. 540 degrees
   d. 90 degrees

7. **Correctly identify the following sentence from paragraph 2: A counterclockwise rotation generates a positive measure, and a clockwise rotation generates a negative measure.**
   a. fact
   b. opinion

8. **Identify the author's purpose and tone for this selection.**
   a. The author's purpose is to persuade and the tone is convincing.
   b. The author's purpose is to instruct and the tone is straightforward.
   c. The author's purpose is to entertain and the tone is whimsical.
   d. The author's purpose is to inform and the tone is nostalgic.

9. **For this selection, which of the following statements is true?**
   a. The author is biased in favor of angles.
   b. The author is biased against negative angles.
   c. The author is biased in favor of the Babylonians.
   d. The author is unbiased.

10. **Fill in the missing notes for paragraph 1 of this selection.**

<u>Lines</u>: two distinct points 

Line AB

<u>Segments:</u> Portion of line between two points. 

Segment AB

<u>Ray:</u> The portion of the line ....

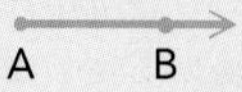

Ray AB

Reading 3

Money for Morality (English)

Money for Morality

1 I recently read a newspaper article about an 8-year-old boy who found an envelope containing more than $600 and returned it to the bank whose name appeared on the envelope. The bank traced the money to its rightful owner and returned it to him. God's in his heaven and all's right with the world. Right? Wrong.

2 As a reward, the man who lost the money gave the boy $3. Not a lot, but a token of his appreciation nonetheless and not mandatory. After all, returning money should not be considered extraordinary. A simple "thank you" is adequate. But some of the teachers at the boy's school felt a reward was not only appropriate, but required. Outraged at the apparent stinginess of the person who lost the cash, these teachers took up a collection for the boy. About a week or so later, they presented the good Samaritan with $150 savings bond, explaining they felt his honesty should be recognized. Evidently the virtues of honesty and kindness have become commodities that, like everything else, have succumbed to inflation. I can't help but wonder what dollar amount these teachers would have deemed a sufficient reward. Certainly they didn't expect the individual who lost the money to give the child $150. Would $25 have been respectable? How about $10? Suppose that lost money had to cover mortgage, utilities and food for the week. In light of that, perhaps $3 was generous. A reward is a gift; any gift should at least be met with the presumption of genuine gratitude on the part of the giver.

3 What does this episode say about our society? It seems the role models our children look up to these days—in this case, teachers—are more confused and misguided about values than their young charges. A young boy, obviously well guided by his parents, finds money that does not belong to him and he returns it. He did the right thing. Yet doing the right thing seems to be insufficient motivation for action in our materialistic world. The legacy of the '80s has left us with the ubiquitous question: what's in it for me? The promise of the golden rule—that someone might do a good turn for you—has become worthless collateral for the social interactions of the mercenary and fast-paced '90s. It is in fact this fast pace that is, in part, a source of the problem. Modern communication has catapulted us into an instant world. Television makes history of events before any of us has even had a chance to absorb them in the first place. An ad for major-league baseball entices viewers with the reassurance that "the memories are waiting"; an event that has yet to occur has already been packaged as the past. With the world racing by us, we have no patience for a rain check on good deeds.

4 Misplaced virtues are rampant through our culture. I don't know how many times my 13-year-old son has told me about classmates who received $10 for each A they receive on their report cards—hinting that I should do the same for him should he ever receive an A (or maybe he was working on $5 for a B). Whenever he approaches me on this subject, I give him the same reply: "Doing well is its own reward. The A just confirms that." In other words, forget it! This is not to say that I would never praise my son for doing well in school. But my praise is not meant to reward or elicit future achievements, but rather to express my genuine delight in the satisfaction

he feels at having done his best. Throwing $10 at that sends out the message that the feeling alone isn't good enough.

Kowtowing to Ice Cream

5 As a society, we seem to be losing a grip on our internal control—the ethical thermostat that guides our actions and feelings toward ourselves, others, and the world around us. Instead, we rely on external "stuff" as a measure of our worth. We pass this message to our children. We offer them money for honesty and good grades. Pizza is given as a reward for reading. In fact, in one national reading program, a pizza party awaits the entire class if each child reads a certain number of books within a four-month period. We call these incentives, telling ourselves that if we can just reel them in and get them hooked, then the built-in rewards will follow. I recently saw a television program where unmarried teenaged mothers were featured as the participants in a parenting program that offers a $10 a week "incentive" if these young women don't get pregnant again. Isn't the daily struggle of being a single teenaged mother enough of a deterrent? No, it isn't, because we as a society won't allow it to be. Nothing is permitted to succeed or fail on its own merits anymore.

6 I remember when I was pregnant with my son I read countless childcare books that offered the same advice: don't bribe your child with ice cream to get him to eat spinach; it makes the spinach look bad. While some may say spinach doesn't need any help looking bad, I submit it's from years of kowtowing to ice cream. Similarly, our moral taste buds have been dulled by an endless onslaught of artificial sweeteners. A steady diet of candy bars and banana splits makes an ordinary apple or orange seem sour. So too does an endless parade of incentives make us incapable of feeling a genuine sense of inner peace (or inner turmoil).

7 The simple virtues of honesty, kindness and integrity suffer from an image problem and are in desperate need of a makeover. One way to do this is by example. If my son sees me feeling happy after I've helped out a friend, then he may do likewise. If my daughter sees me spending a rainy afternoon curled up with a book instead of spending money at the mall, she may get the message that there are some simple pleasures that don't require a purchase. I fear that in our so-called upwardly mobile world we are on a downward spiral toward moral bankruptcy. Like pre-World War II Germany, where the basket holding the money was more valuable than the money itself, we too may render ourselves internally worthless while desperately clinging to a shell of appearances.

(Arguelles, Mary. "Money for Morality," from Long, Elizabeth Cloninger. *Resources for Writers with Readings: Paragraphs and Essays*, 4e. Longman. 2012 pp. 743–745.)

1,076 words divided by .... minutes = ... words per minute

QUESTIONS

1. **What is the meaning of the underlined word in this sentence from paragraph 4? Misplaced virtues are rampant through our culture.**
   - **a.** rare
   - **b.** widespread
   - **c.** worthless
   - **d.** integrity
2. **What is the author's central point for this selection?**
   - **a.** Some people are not generous enough when giving a reward for a good deed.
   - **b.** All good deeds should be rewarded.
   - **c.** Society places too much importance on materialistic things and not enough on good behavior.
   - **d.** We should provide children with good role models of integrity, honesty, and doing the right thing without expecting a reward.
3. **What is the implied main idea of paragraph 6?**
   - **a.** You shouldn't give rewards such as ice cream for eating spinach.
   - **b.** Parents give too many rewards to their kids.
   - **c.** Giving rewards and incentives makes us incapable of feeling a genuine sense of satisfaction for doing the right thing.
   - **d.** Rewards and incentives are sometimes necessary to get people to do what they should do.
4. **According to the article, the teachers at the boy's school raised $150 because**
   - **a.** they felt sorry for the boy.
   - **b.** they felt that a $3 reward was not enough for doing the right and honest thing.
   - **c.** they wanted to show their gratitude to the boy for returning the lost money.
   - **d.** every good deed deserves a big reward.
5. **What is the relationship between the following sentences from paragraph 4: Misplaced virtues are rampant through our culture. I don't know how many times my 13-year-old son has told me about classmates who received $10 for each A they receive on their report cards—hinting that I should do the same for him should he ever receive an A (or maybe he was working on $5 for a B).**
   - **a.** cause and effect
   - **b.** statement and clarification
   - **c.** generalization and example
   - **d.** addition
6. **A conclusion that can be drawn from this article is**
   - **a.** Doing a good deed or achieving a goal should not entitle someone to a reward.
   - **b.** People need incentives to do the right thing.
   - **c.** Kids today get too many rewards for reading books.
   - **d.** Parents are not doing their job teaching children how to be honest.

7. Correctly identify the following statement from paragraph 7: If my daughter sees me spending a rainy afternoon curled up with a book instead of spending money at the mall, she may get the message that there are some simple pleasures that don't require a purchase.

a. fact

b. opinion

8. What are the author's purpose and tone in this selection?

a. The author's purpose is to entertain and the tone is ironic.

b. The author's purpose is to persuade and the tone is concerned.

c. The author's purpose is to explain and the tone is instructive.

d. The author's purpose is to persuade and the tone is light-hearted.

9. In this selection, the author is

a. biased in favor of rewarding good behavior.

b. biased against reading programs in schools.

c. biased against rewarding what is simply doing the right thing.

d. unbiased.

10. With which of the following statements would the author most likely agree?

a. Acquiring money and material rewards has become more important in our society than doing good deeds for others.

b. Any good deed is worth a reward, even a small one like $3.

c. If someone gives you a reward for doing something you should be doing (like getting good grades) then you are better prepared for becoming an adult.

d. Adults get rewarded for things they do every day for their families and employers.

CREDITS

TEXT

CHAPTER 1

Page 7: Figure, The Condition of Education, National Center for Education Statistics, National Center for Education Statistics; page 8: Figure, Bureau of Labor Statistics. 2012; page 20: Kanani, Rahim. "How to Succeed in College: New Advice & Insights" by Rahim Kanani. From Forbes, 9/6/2011. Copyright © 2011 Forbes. All rights reserved. Used by permission and protected by the Copyright Laws of the United States. The printing, copying, redistribution, or retransmission of this Content without express written permission is prohibited; page 27: "Study Methods: Different Strokes for Different Folks," Ciccarelli, Saundra K., White, J. Noland, Psychology, 3rd Ed., © 2012. Reprinted and Electronically reproduced by permission of Pearson Education Inc., Upper Saddle River, New Jersey; page 35: Financial Aid Sources, US Dept of Education, Federal Student Aid, MIranda Bauman.

CHAPTER 2

Page 55: Fritz Heider, Gerrig, Richard J.; Zimbardo, Philip G., Psychology and Life, 19th ed., © 2010. Reprinted and Electronically reproduced by permission of Pearson Education Inc., Upper Saddle River, New Jersey; page 60: How Memory Works, Ciccarelli, Saundra K., White, J. Noland, Psychology, 3rd ed., © 2012. Reprinted and Electronically reproduced by permission of Pearson Education Inc., Upper Saddle River, New Jersey; page 63: Carey, Bjorn. "The Rules of Attraction" by Bjorn Carey from Live Science, February 13, 2006. Copyright © 2006 Tech Media Network. Reproduced by permission of Tech Media Network; page 72: "Liking and Loving: Interpersonal Attraction," Ciccarelli, Saundra K., White, J. Noland, Psychology, 3rd ed., © 2012. Reprinted and Electronically reproduced by permission of Pearson Education Inc., Upper Saddle River, New Jersey; page 81: Understanding Auto Insurance Terms, Hands on Banking, Adults' Resources, Wells Fargo Bank N.A.; page 84: Evolutionary Theory and Gender, Wood, Samuel E., Wood, Ellen Green, Boyd, Denise G., The World of Psychology, 7th ed. Pearson, 2011; page 85: "Note that experiences of..." Gerrig, Richard J.; Zimbardo, Philip G., Psychology and Life, 19th ed., © 2010. Reprinted and Electronically reproduced by permission of Pearson Education Inc., Upper Saddle River, New Jersey; page 86: "These sexual norms are..." Gerrig, Richard J.; Zimbardo, Philip G., Psychology and Life, 19th ed., © 2010. Reprinted and Electronically reproduced by permission of Pearson Education Inc., Upper Saddle River, New Jersey.

CHAPTER 3

Page 95: Overweight and Obesity, Powers, Scott and Stephen Dodd. Total Fitness and Wellness, 3rd ed., Pearson 2009; page 112: "Secrets of the Dead: Doping for Gold: The Dangers of Doping" from PBS (http://www.pbs.org/wnet/secret /features/doping-for-gold/thedangers-of-doping/56/ Copyright (C) 2011. Reproduced by permission of WNET; page 120: "Managing Stress in Your Life," Hopson, Janet, Donnatelle, Rebecca J., Littress, Tanya, Get Fit, Stay Well!, 2nd ed., © 2013, pp. 326–329. Reprinted and Electronically reproduced by permission of Pearson Education Inc., Upper Saddle River, New Jersey.

CHAPTER 4

Page 161: Tobak, Steve. Transcript from CBS NEWS.com of "How to Deal With a Bad Boss" by Steve Tobak (5/14/12). Reprinted by permission of CBS News; page 163: Tobak, Steve. Transcript from CBSNews.com "Seven Signs of a Dysfunctional Boss" by Steve Tobak (4/25/12). Reprinted by permission of CBS News; page 178: Buying a Used Car, Used Car Purchasing Tips, Hands on Banking. Wells Fargo Bank, N.A.

CHAPTER 5

Page 215: "Pyramus and Thisbe," Bullfinch Thomas, Myths of Greece and Rome, Penguin Group (UK), 1979.

CHAPTER 6

Page 250: Practice 1, Withgott, Jay, Brennan, Scott, Essential Environment, 4th ed. Pearson. 2006; page 255: "All the world's a stage," William Shakespeare, As You Like It; page 271: Bergman, Charles. "No-Fly Zone: Denied Their Natural Habits, Millions of Pet Parrots Lead Bleak, Lonely Lives" from The Humane Society of the United States by Charles Bergman. Copyright ©. Reproduced by permission of The Humane Society of the United States. Retrieved from http://www.humanesociety.org/news/magazines/2013/03-04/no-fly-zone-millions-of-pet-parrots-lead-bleak-lonely-lives.html#id=album-181&num=content-3272; page 281: "Quiet Down Below," Quiet Down from Science World, December 10, 2012. Copyright © 2012 by Scholastic Inc. Reprinted by permission of Scholastic Inc.

CHAPTER 7

Page 308: Religion in the United States, Macionis, John. Society: The Basics, 12th ed., Pearson, 2013; page 310: Majority and Minority, Macionis, John, J., Society: The Basics, 12th ed., © 2013, pp. 282–283. Reprinted and Electronically reproduced by permission of Pearson Education, Inc., Upper Saddle River, New Jersey; page 312: Low-Income Countries, Macionis, John, J., Society: The Basics, 12th ed., © 2013, pp. 228–229. Reprinted and Electronically reproduced by permission of Pearson Education, Inc., Upper Saddle River, New Jersey; page 314: Schooling and Economic Development, John. Society: The Basics, 12th ed., Pearson, 2013; page 329 Web Site Questions to Ask, Cowden, Karen and King, Beth, Valencia College; page 334: "Sexual Attitudes in the United States," Macionis, John, J., Society: The Basics, 12th ed., © 2013. Reprinted and Electronically reproduced by permission of Pearson Education, Inc., Upper Saddle River, New Jersey; page 345: "Saving Children in Cambodia," Krausz, Tibor. "Scott Neeson left Hollywood to save children rooting in Cambodia's garbage dumps" from Difference Maker, The Christian Science Monitor, 8/10/2012. Reproduced by permission of Tibor Krausz; page 357: The Causes of War, Macionis, John, J., Society: The Basics, 12th ed., © 2013. Reprinted and Electronically reproduced by permission of Pearson Education, Inc., Upper Saddle River, New Jersey.

APPENDIX

Page 367: "Defeating Procrastination," Wood, Samuel E., Wood, Ellen Green, Boyd, Denise G. The World of Psychology, 7th ed., © 2011. Reprinted and Electronically reproduced by permission of Pearson Education, Inc., Upper Saddle River, New Jersey; page 370: "Angles," Lial, Margaret, Hornsby, John, Schneider, David I., Daniels, Callie. Trigonometry, 10th ed., © 2013, pp. 2–3. Reprinted and Electronically reproduced by permission of Pearson Education, Inc., Upper Saddle River, New Jersey.

PHOTOS

FRONT MATTER

Page iii: Odilon Dimier/PhotoAlto/AGE Fotostock; page iv: Radius Images/Alamy; page v: Hero Images Inc./Alamy; page vi: N J Gargasz/Alamy; page vii: AberCPC/Alamy; page viii: Huntstock, Inc/Alamy; page ix: Jeff Greenberg/PhotoEdit, Inc.

CHAPTER 1

Page 2: Odilon Dimier/PhotoAlto/AGE Fotostock; page 4 (top): Marcio Silva/iStock/Thinkstock; page 4 (bottom): Rafal Olkis/Shutterstock; page 9: Lightpoet/Shutterstock; page 12: Diego Cervo/Shutterstock; page 20: Celia Peterson/arabianEye/Corbis; page 27: Michaeljung/Shutterstock

CHAPTER 2

Page 46: Radius Images/Alamy; page 49: Brownie Harris/Corbis; page 51: ImageSource/AGE Fotostock; pages 54–55: Plush Studios/Bill Re/Blend Images/AGE Fotostock; page 61: Gary Conner/PhotoEdit, Inc.; page 63: DragonImages/iStock/Thinkstock; page 64: Radius Images/Alamy; page 66: M.Sobreira/Alamy; page 70: Conmare GmbH/Alamy; page 72: Jack Hollingsworth/Blend Boost/AGE Fotostock; page 73: John Lund/Sam Diephui/Blend Images/AGE Fotostock; page 79: YanLev/iStock/Thinkstock; page 88: Phil Boorman/cultura/Corbis

CHAPTER 3

Page 90: Hero Images Inc./Alamy; page 92–93: Clive Streeter/Dorling Kindersley, Ltd.; page 94: Debbie Maizels/Dorling Kindersley, Ltd.; page 96: BSIP SA/Alamy; page 98: Dan Race/Fotolia; page 99: INTERFOTO/Alamy; page 103: Hero Images Inc./Alamy; page 112: Sun Media/Splash News/Corbis; page 114: Peter J. Thompson/UPI Photo Service/Newscom; page 120: Chris Rout/Alamy; page 121: Randy Faris/Corbis RF/AGE Fotostock; page 125: Dan Dunkley/Alamy; page 128: Jeffrey Willey/Alamy; page 135: Sandro Di Carlo Darsa/PhotoAlto/Alamy; page 138: Wavebreak Media Ltd./Corbis

CHAPTER 4

Page 140: N J Gargasz/Alamy; page 143: Diana Baldrica/MCT/Newscom; page 145: Moodboard/Alamy; page 155: Kim Steele/Photodisc/Getty Images; page 158: Diffused/AGE Fotostock; page 160: Ricky John Molloy/Cultura Creative (RF)/Alamy; page 161: Wavebreak Media ltd/Alamy; page 169: Wiskerke/Alamy

CHAPTER 5

Page 188: AberCPC/Alamy; page 190: Erich Lessing/PhotoEdit, Inc.; page 193: DEA/A Dagli Orti/De Agostini Editore/AGE Fotostock; page 198: Everett Collection Historical/Alamy; page 202: Alberto Paredes/Alamy; page 209: Everett Collection; page 215: Ivy Close Images/Alamy; page 219: Relativity Media/Everett Collection; page 223: A.Berti/Marka/Alamy; page 227: Universal Pictures/Everett Collection; page 234: Everett Collection Historical/Alamy; page 236: Mike Windle/WireImage/Getty Images; page 240: Wavebreak Media Ltd./Corbis

CHAPTER 6

Page 242: Huntstock, Inc/Alamy; page 245: Thomas Barwick/Digital Vision/Getty Images; page 251: Andre Seale/Robert Harding World Imagery; page 258: Luka Culig/Thinkstock;

page 263: Picturesbyrob/Alamy; page 267: ROM Image Broker/Newscom; page 271: Barcroft Media/Getty Images; page 274: Photoshot Holdings Ltd/Alamy; page 281: Masa Ushioda/Imagequestmarine.com; page 282: Reprinted with permission from Scholastic, Inc.; page 285: Brandon Cole Marine Photography/Alamy; page 290: Huntstock/Thinkstock; page 294: Jim West/Alamy; page 298: Andrew Catta/Alamy

CHAPTER 7

Page 302: Jeff Greenberg/PhotoEdit, Inc; page 304: Wavebreak Media ltd/Alamy; page 309: CulturalEyes-AusSoc/Alamy; page 315: dbimages/Alamy; page 320: Hill Street Studios/Blend Images/Alamy; page 331: Image Source/Alamy; page 334: DCPhoto/Alamy; page 345: Ron Haviv/VII/Corbis; page 359: John James/Alamy; page 362: Phil Boorman/cultura/Corbis

INDEX

A

B

C

D

E

F

W

Z